The Wars inside Chile's Barracks

Critical Human Rights

Series Editors

Steve J. Stern ❦ Scott Straus

Books in the series **Critical Human Rights** emphasize research that opens new ways to think about and understand human rights. The series values in particular empirically grounded and intellectually open research that eschews simplified accounts of human rights events and processes.

Who speaks for soldiers? When a brutal dictatorship gives way to democratic transition, memory wars may erupt. Such was the case in Chile after military rule (1973–90) under Latin America's iconic dictator, General Augusto Pinochet. Human rights advocates and victims remembered the era of atrocity for its moral and civic lesson: never again shall the state rule by violent terror against its own citizens. Military officers and their allies remembered that extreme circumstances justify extreme measures: patriotic soldiers stepped in to save the country from disaster. Lost in these memory wars, however, were most of the soldiers—some 370,000 conscripts, drafted into a machinery of abuse and violation deployed against soldiers as well as civilians. This pioneering account tells how a dictatorship turned low-level soldiers into victims as well as perpetrators, and how the soldiers, neglected by their officers and sidelined by the transition's politics of memory, transformed their experiences into a unique human rights story and demand for recognition.

The Wars inside Chile's Barracks

Remembering Military Service under Pinochet

Leith Passmore

The University of Wisconsin Press

Publication of this book has been made possible, in part, through support from the Anonymous Fund of the College of Letters and Science at the University of Wisconsin–Madison.

The University of Wisconsin Press
728 State Street, Suite 443
Madison, Wisconsin 53706
uwpress.wisc.edu

Gray's Inn House, 127 Clerkenwell Road
London EC1R 5DB, United Kingdom
eurospanbookstore.com

Library of Congress Cataloging-in-Publication Data

Names: Passmore, Leith, 1981- author.
Title: The wars inside Chile's barracks: remembering military service under Pinochet / Leith Passmore.
Other titles: Critical human rights.
Description: Madison, Wisconsin: The University of Wisconsin Press, [2017] | Series: Critical human rights | Includes bibliographical references and index.
Identifiers: LCCN 2017010435 | ISBN 9780299315207 (cloth: alk. paper)
Subjects: LCSH: Draftees—Chile—History—20th century. | Chile—Armed Forces—History—20th century. | Chile—History—1973-1988. | Human rights—Chile—History—20th century.
Classification: LCC F3100 .P375 2017 | DDC 983.06/5—dc23
LC record available at https://lccn.loc.gov/2017010435

ISBN 9780299315245 (pbk.: alk. paper)

Para los valientes

Contents

Illustrations

Maps

Tables and Figures

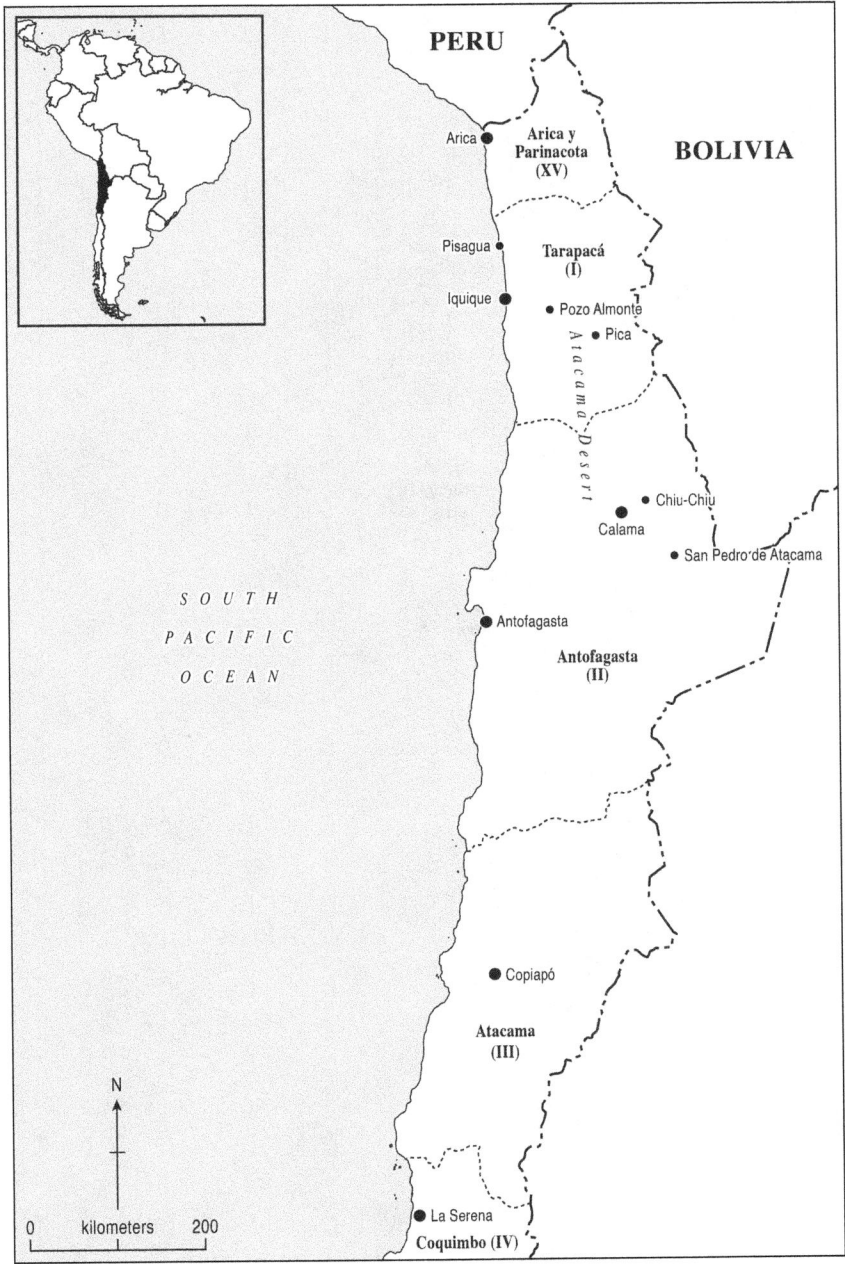

The near and far north of contemporary Chile (Chris Orton of the Cartographic Unit, Durham University)

Central and southern contemporary Chile (Chris Orton of the Cartographic Unit, Durham University)

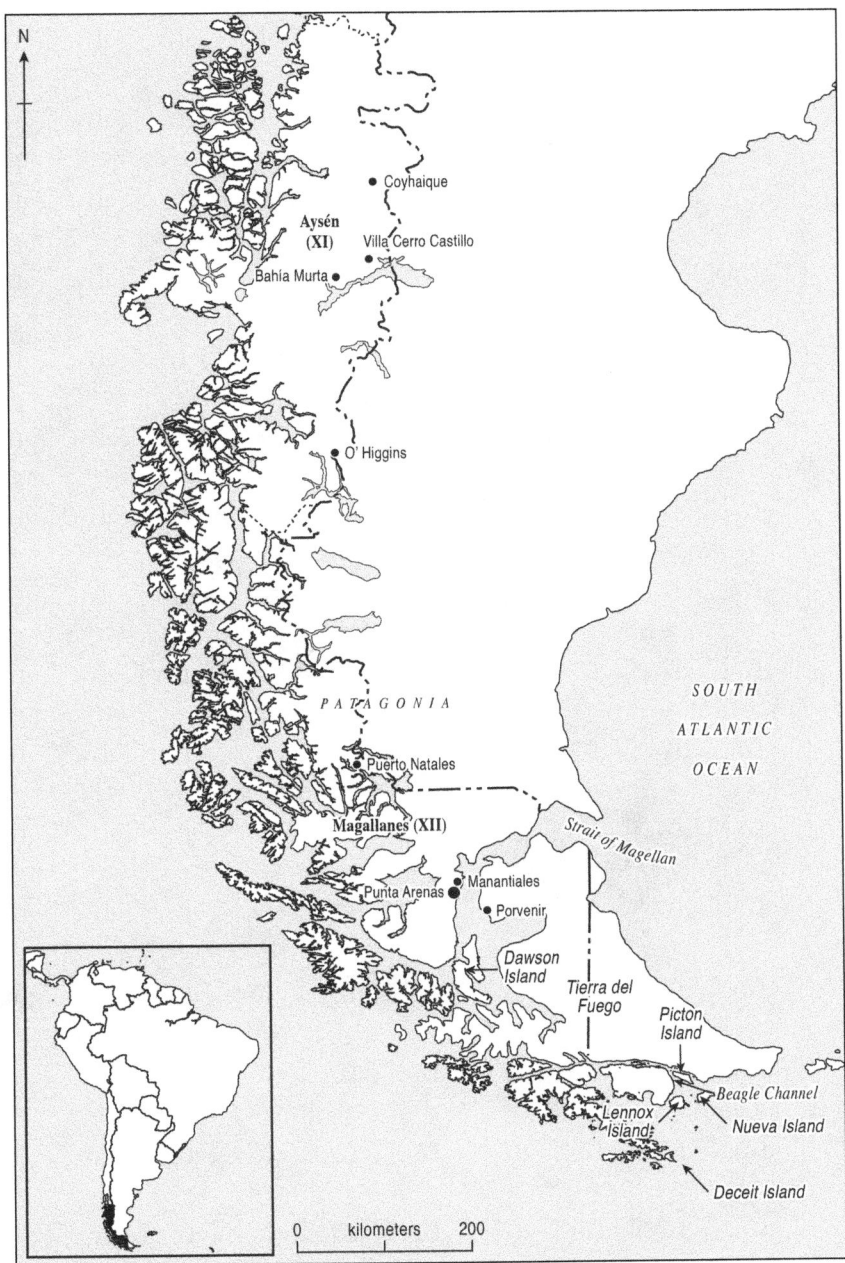

The far south of contemporary Chile (Chris Orton of the Cartographic Unit, Durham University)

Preface

On the morning of September 11, 1973, the Chilean armed forces deposed the elected government. Tanks rolled through the streets and fighter jets bombed the presidential palace, La Moneda, in downtown Santiago. Inside the building, President Salvador Allende delivered a final speech to the Chilean people via radio, before committing suicide. Allende had come to power three years earlier in 1970, with a narrow relative majority of around 36 percent of the vote, and embarked on his "Chilean path to socialism."[1] He nationalized the mining and banking industries, expanded access to education, and dramatically increased spending on social services. He also accelerated the expropriation of agricultural estates that had begun under his predecessor, the Christian Democrat Eduardo Frei, in order to pursue a program of collectivization.[2] Allende's revolutionary project entrenched the polarization of Chilean politics that had emerged and grown deeper in the years before his election.[3] It also sat within a history of oligarchic rule, generational poverty, and underdevelopment stretching back to at least the beginning of the century. By the 1960s, shantytowns populated by the working poor rimmed the capital, and rural workers continued to toil under a feudalistic and exploitative system of land tenure. Support for Allende's transformative political project, therefore, came on the back of decades of frustration and at times violent repression of social movements.[4] However, this long national history also intersected with a broader postwar story.

Allende's election formed part of the revolutionary fervor that spread across Latin America in the wake of the Cuban Revolution. Countries throughout the region embarked on similar programs of modernization, nationalization, and agrarian reform. Both Allende's supporters and his detractors understood his politics to be part of a movement that extended beyond national borders, and as the first democratically elected Marxist leader, he placed Chile and his project at the forefront of the Cold War. The 1973 coup, too, was part of a broader counterrevolutionary wave, with military regimes replacing civilian rule in countries across the continent in the 1960s and 1970s. In the decades following World War II, the doctrine of national security had permeated Latin American militaries and recast their missions in terms of an "internal enemy." Southern cone dictatorships also participated in Operation Condor, a transnational intelligence operation aimed at defeating their common communist enemy and repressing political opposition. Domestically, military regimes sought to fundamentally remake their societies, and in Chile the military junta set about removing the "cancer" of communism.[5]

Political repression under Pinochet was brutal, widespread, and systematic. In the wake of the coup, tens of thousands of people were rounded up and held in hundreds of makeshift detention centers throughout Chile. Detainees were interrogated, and many were subjected to forms of torture that included beatings; rape; mock executions; electrical current applied to their bodies (often the genitals), either via electrodes or using metal frames known as "the grill"; humiliation; or witnessing the torture of loved ones.[6] By the end of 1973, more than one thousand people had been killed or disappeared, with most of the disappeared murdered shortly after their arrest and dumped at sea, buried in the desert, or dropped down disused mine shafts. Family members had no information—or only misinformation—about their loved ones, no confirmation of their fates, no physical remains to bury, and no closure. Thousands of people were forced into exile, where they joined thousands more who had either fled Allende's revolution, left in expectation of the eventual military coup, or escaped the repression in its immediate aftermath. The human rights abuses in Chile drew and retained worldwide attention.[7] Partly in response to this attention, the use of torture became more refined and selective, but it was used throughout the period of military rule to oppress opponents. Beyond instilling fear in the population, the regime set about changing the nation's mentality via a fundamental reorganization of the Chilean economy.[8]

Despite initial improvement in macroeconomic indicators, the socialist restructuring of the economy under Allende had soon produced soaring inflation and deficits, and a falling gross domestic product. The mounting economic problems were compounded by the efforts of local elites to ensure that the administration failed, and interference run by the US Central Intelligence Agency (CIA). The effects of inflation, repeated strikes, fixed prices, and opponents' strategic hoarding of basic goods produced desperate shortages. People waited in long queues to attempt to buy staple goods, or sought flour, sugar, rice, or oil on the burgeoning black market. In the wake of the coup, and drawing on the advice of a group of Chilean economists trained at the University of

Chicago and known as the "Chicago boys," the military junta privatized state assets, restricted union activity, drastically reduced public spending, and removed protections from key industries. Chile quickly fell into crisis and unemployment soared. Joblessness spiked again during a second crisis in the early 1980s on the back of the global oil shock and a burst local debt bubble. Many of the structural and cultural changes made under Pinochet survived the return to democracy, and his supporters point to Chile's "miracle"—a decade-long posttransition economic boom—as justification for the regime's intervention. Further afield, Chile was touted as model for Latin American countries to follow. However, the benefits of rapid growth largely bypassed millions of Chileans, and, while poverty rates fell, the already high level of inequality rose.[9]

The renewed economic crisis in the early 1980s helped solidify protest against military rule.[10] Demonstrations in the streets and the regime's subsequent crackdown on dissent dominated much of 1983 and 1984. In the late 1970s, Pinochet had outlined a vision of a new democracy that was "authoritarian, protected, integrating, technically modern, and with authentic social participation."[11] Shortly after, a new constitution was drafted that banned Marxist political groups, concentrated power in the president, appointed senators, and created the National Security Council that allowed the military to maintain its influence on policy decisions. It also extended Pinochet's term as president for eight years, at which point a plebiscite would be held on the extension of his rule. A vote on the constitution was held on the 1980 anniversary of the coup, amid allegations of electoral fraud and voter intimidation, and Pinochet was sworn in as president in 1981.[12] However, the protests in the following years galvanized opposition, and by the time of the 1988 plebiscite, the regime's familiar appeals to the population's fears of a return to chaos were no longer enough to marshal sufficient support. The "No" vote—to remove Pinochet—received almost 56 percent of the ballots, and Chile returned to democracy in March 1990.[13]

The incoming president, Patricio Aylwin, established the National Truth and Reconciliation Commission in 1990 to investigate, and establish the truth about, violations of human rights during the dictatorship that resulted in death or disappearance. The commission—known as the Rettig Commission after its chairperson Raúl Rettig—delivered its report in February 1991. The Rettig Report revealed the scale and methods of the repression, and it detailed almost three thousand cases of politically motivated death or disappearance.[14] More than a decade later, in 2003, President Ricardo Lagos convened a second truth and reconciliation commission: the National Commission on Political Imprisonment and Torture, known as the Valech Commission, after its chairperson, Sergio Valech. The Valech Report, published in 2004 and revised in 2005, found that nearly thirty thousand people had been imprisoned for political reasons during the regime, most of whom had been tortured. It outlined the methods of torture and, along with the findings of the Rettig Report, codified the pervasiveness of political repression under military rule.[15] Both reports formed the basis for programs of reparations for victims and their relatives.

The truth and reconciliation processes did not lead to accountability. The political landscape in the 1990s was still shaped by the conditions of the negotiated transition that "protected" Chile's democracy as well as Pinochet's continued presence in public life as head of the army.[16] The general stood down as commander-in-chief in early 1998 to take up a seat in the senate. Later that year, the limits of the universal jurisdiction of international law were tested when Pinochet was arrested in London on a Spanish warrant relating to charges of genocide, terrorism, and the torture of Spanish nationals. During the legal battles over his extradition to Spain, and amid concerns for his health, the Chilean government campaigned for Pinochet to be returned home to face a local court. In 2000 he was allowed to return to Chile on medical grounds. At the airport in Santiago, the former dictator was welcomed by representatives of the armed forces and defiantly rose from his wheelchair to walk across the tarmac.[17] However, the legal atmosphere in Chile had shifted. Pinochet's arrest and the attention it drew combined with the persistence of victims' groups and human rights activists to help erode immunity for dictatorship-era crimes. Landmark legal interpretations that were incrementally adopted by the Chilean courts, some of which allowed for the application of international law, began to result in convictions and sentences for officers who had committed crimes during the "dirty" war. For Pinochet, years of legal wrangling over claims he was unfit to stand trial and immune from prosecution resulted in indictments and, eventually, charges of torture, kidnapping, and murder in late 2006.[18] However, the former dictator died in December that same year, without having been convicted of any crimes. The news of his death sparked an outpouring of grief in some parts of Chile, while elsewhere people celebrated in the streets.

The 1973 coup and Pinochet's military regime sit at the center of numerous histories. They dominate political, social, and economic histories in Chile that have roots in the nineteenth century and consequences that echo into the twenty-first. Beyond national borders, the Chilean case is an emblematic moment in transnational histories of postwar revolution and counterrevolution, US foreign policy toward Latin America, clandestine CIA activity in the region, the postwar technology of torture, the global human rights movement, neoliberal economic policy and free-market fundamentalism, social and political transition in postconflict societies, and international law and transitional justice.[19] The hundreds of thousands of young men called up to complete their compulsory military service between 1973 and 1989 found themselves at the forefront of all of these histories and none of them. They were deployed at the front line of Chile's "internal war," and they were at times perpetrators of, witnesses to, or victims of human rights abuses, or all three. They received training based in postwar ideas of counterinsurgency that were imported from abroad and developed locally. They came almost exclusively from sectors of Chilean society that were targeted by the regime's political repression, and that suffered the most and the longest as a result of the economic crises under military rule. A small number of ex-conscripts also later appeared as witnesses as part of the truth and reconciliation processes. Nevertheless, conscripts' own experiences were silenced, and the story of compulsory military service under Pinochet remained absent from the history of the dictatorship and the "struggles" over how to remember it.

Acknowledgments

This book is dedicated to the brave.

During Chile's dictatorship, the military under Augusto Pinochet claimed the idea of bravery for itself. It included the third verse of the national hymn praising Chile's "courageous soldiers" alongside the traditional verse and chorus. Political prisoners in detention camps were forced to sing of their captors' bravery, schoolchildren throughout the country memorized the new version, and defiant regime supporters continued to sing the verse, long after it had been removed from the official hymn following the transition to democracy. The courage I acknowledge here has nothing to do with the self-mythologizing of the Chilean military. It is instead the sum of intimate moments along the length of Chile that made this book possible. Not all, to be sure, but many former recruits had to overcome their fears in order to talk about their military service, a step taken not with me but among their fellow former recruits as part of a growing ex-conscript movement. Moreover, each telling of their story exposed ex-conscripts to a measure of vulnerability, as they risked a hostile or dismissive reception of their most guarded recollections, as well as their own emotional responses to the narration of their experiences. I listened to stories on the edges of group meetings, in corner shops, offices, cafés, public squares, buses, parks, car parks, and a parked car on the side of a rural road in the rain. I was invited into living rooms and I sat at kitchen tables throughout Chile, and I read testimonies of men I never met. My greatest debt of gratitude is to the men whose stories form the basis of this book, particularly those men whose stories resulted from quiet acts of bravery.

Within the loose ex-conscript movement, I am particularly indebted to current or former representatives of ex-conscript organizations: Carlos Palma, Félix Pinares, and René Rivera in Santiago (Agrupación SMO); Fernando

Mellado in Santiago (Agrupación Ex Soldados Conscriptos, and later the Corporación para la Integración de los Derechos Humanos de los Ex Conscriptos del período 1973–1990); Luis Burgos and Daniel Gómez in Temuco (Agrupación de Reservistas de la Defensa Nacional IX Región [Agrupación de Reservistas]); Claudio de la Hoz in Chillán (Reservistas Patrióticos de Chile [REPACH] Chillán); David Wiederhold and Esteban Proboste in Talcahuano (REPACH Talcahuano); Víctor Calderón in Buin (Coordinadora Nacional de Ex Soldados Conscriptos del SMO 1973–1990); Juan Díaz in Nacimiento (Agrupación del Bío Bío de Ex Soldados conscriptos de 1973–1990); Freddy Valdivia and Roberto Flores in Iquique (Agrupación de Ex Conscriptos del período 1973 a 1990); Mario Navarro and Guillermo Raillard in Arica (Agrupación Social de Ex Soldados Conscriptos 1973—Clase 54); Pedro Cáceres and Manuel Ureta in Puente Alto (Agrupación Puente Alto); and Pedro Naigual (Comisión Nacional Víctimas DDHH de ex Soldados Conscriptos 1973–1990). These relationships were often built over extended periods of time and allowed me to establish an extensive network of contacts. I conducted interviews; attended gatherings, events, and protests; and shared lunch, coffee, or *once* in the heart of the capital and across the city in La Pincoya, La Pintana, Puente Alto, and Recoleta, as well as beyond Santiago in San Bernardo, Buin, Valparaíso, Nacimiento, Concepción, Temuco, Talcahuano, Arica, Iquique, Pozo Almonte, and Pica. I value deeply the trust ex-conscript communities throughout Chile placed in me.

The research for this book was funded by a postdoctoral fellowship from the Fondo Nacional de Desarrollo Científico y Tecnológico (Fondecyt project 3120033) and was based in the Department of History of the University of Chile between October 2011 and October 2014. I am grateful to both organizations for trusting me to undertake this work. In particular, I thank the then head of department Celia Cussen for welcoming me and my proposed project to La Chile and for her friendship in the years since. Sergio Grez was not only the supervising academic on the project, but he also shared his time, thoughts, and office space with me, for which I am extremely grateful. Beyond the importance of her own scholarship, Verónica Valdivia was a great source of personal encouragement and—I would later discover—a champion for the project when it needed it. Conversations at different stages of the project with Verónica, Celia, Azun Candina, Cath Collins, Katherine Hite, Elizabeth Lira, Steve Stern, Ximena Tocornal, and Peter Winn, helped shape the way I thought about the materiality and theory of memory. In particular, I must thank Celia and Heidi Tinsman for reading and offering comments on sections of the draft manuscript.

I am extremely grateful to the editors of the series, Steve Stern and Scott Straus, for their interest in my project, and to rest of the team at the University of Wisconsin Press, particularly Gwen Walker, Sarah Kapp, and Sheila McMahon, for their support throughout the review and publication process. Finally, to Clara, Elena, and Tobias go my eternal gratitude and all my heart.

Note on Sources

This book is based on a review of unpublished military statistics; unpublished documents produced by, or on behalf of, ex-conscript groups; legal cases; government and military reports produced in response to ex-conscript demands; hundreds of published ex-conscript testimonies; nearly sixty unpublished written ex-conscript testimonies; two unpublished audiovisual collections of ex-conscript testimonies; published and unpublished ex-conscript memoirs; twenty oral histories I conducted with ex-conscripts in 2012 and 2013; around forty informal conversations with ex-conscripts held between 2012 and 2014; twenty-six interviews with leaders of ex-conscript groups and professionals working with ex-conscript groups conducted between 2011 and 2015; and field notes of twenty ex-conscript events, protests, or meetings I attended between late 2011 and mid-2015.

Nearly all of the published testimonies appear in the collection *Al otro lado de las metralletas*. The lawyer representing the Agrupación de Reservistas in Temuco, Luis Seguel, published hundreds of testimonies provided to the group, covering all cohorts and most regions, under thematic headings. The testimonies appear unedited, with former recruits' names swapped for initials to protect their identities. I read several of the original testimonies that were later included in the collection and can confirm that they appeared unaltered in the book. I also worked with copies of unpublished testimonies gathered by the Agrupación de Reservistas in Temuco (thirty-nine), REPACH Chillán (seven), and the Agrupación de Ex Conscriptos del período 1973 a 1990 in Iquique (thirteen). Whether published or not, testimonies ranged from one to more than ten pages in length, but they averaged between two and four pages. Two groups—REPACH Talcahuano and the Agrupación de Reservistas (Temuco)—also produced collections of short video testimonies. Testimonies revised for this book—published, unpublished, and audiovisual—cover cohorts from 1973 to 1990 and all regions in Chile. They are short and were produced within the context of the movement and for the purpose of pursuing groups' demands or legal cases for recognition and reparations. In contrast to testimonies, memoirs are much longer texts that are not as directly linked to the movement and its goals. Where published testimonies and memoirs are cited in this book, ex-conscripts are identified as they appear in the sources. Where unpublished testimonies are cited, ex-conscripts are identified by a pseudonym. All pseudonyms are denoted by an asterisk.

Oral histories are semistructured life-history interviews that were recorded and lasted between thirty minutes and two hours. I found participants, ranging in the year of their call-up from 1973 to 1983, via my contacts with ex-conscript groups. The plan for the oral histories was that they would run roughly chronologically, covering the participant's youth to the current day. I began by explaining the structure and asking the individual to talk about his childhood. Ex-conscripts willing to talk to me had already told their story within the group context, and they were eager to talk. As a result, oral histories tended to be one-sided encounters, with participants taking the opportunity to tell their stories to someone who wanted to listen. I participated as an active listener, and would follow up on details as we went or return to some points later. Instead of the planned chronological order, oral histories tended to be circular, as participants did laps of their story, filling in gaps each time around. Where oral histories are cited in this book, ex-conscripts are identified by name, where written consent was granted, or by a pseudonym, where requested.

Conversations, for the purposes of this book, refer to unplanned, spontaneous encounters before or after events, on the edges of events or in ex-conscript group offices. These conversations were unstructured and followed the initiative of the ex-conscript in question. At times, that meant that they followed a roughly chronological order, as stories told within the context of the movement often followed a before-and-after structure in order to emphasize the consequences former recruits attributed to their service. I participated as an active listener, and conversations lasted between five and forty-five minutes. If appropriate and consent was granted, conversations were occasionally recorded. Where conversations are cited in this book, I indicate whether I worked from notes or from a recording and notes, and ex-conscripts are identified by a pseudonym.

I also cite interviews with group leaders (twenty-four interviews; twelve individuals), a group administrator (together with a group leader), and a lawyer representing an ex-conscript group. While former recruits representing ex-conscript groups occasionally used examples from their own experiences to make their point, these interviews were focused on group formation, group demands, and group activities. Interviews were not always recorded, and where interviews are cited, I indicate whether I worked from notes or from a recording and notes. I also cite an interview with former draftee Samuel Fuenzalida. Fuenzalida was conscripted in 1973, before being recruited into the intelligence service (the Dirección de Inteligencia Nacional, or DINA) in 1974. In 1975 he fled Chile and provided testimony about the workings of clandestine detention centers from exile. He is not involved with any ex-conscript association. I include our planned and recorded encounter as an interview, to ensure that all oral histories and conversations cited are with ex-conscripts who identify with the ex-conscript movement.

Over nearly four years, I attended ex-conscript meetings, protests, rallies, and celebrations. I recorded my observations in field notes, and where I cite these notes I indicate the location, date, and the nature of the event. Where individual ex-conscripts are mentioned when citing field notes, they are identified by a pseudonym.

Irrespective of how they are identified in this book, ex-conscripts' names, initials, or pseudonyms are followed (in brackets) by the year of their call-up, the year of their discharge, and the location they spent the relevant period or the bulk of their service. If this information is incomplete, this may be because it appears shortly after in the text, but it is usually because the missing pieces of information are not known.

All translations are my own, unless otherwise indicated.

The Wars inside Chile's Barracks

Introduction

War and Memory

emembering his compulsory military service in 2012, Mario Navarro pulled out his reservist identification card and placed it on the kitchen table.[1] He was preparing lunch in his daughter's still-unfinished home in Arica in Chile's far north. As part of a government program to provide low-cost housing, rows of concrete-and-brick shells had recently been constructed on the northern outskirts of the city, stretching toward the nearby border with Peru. On school days, Mario would wait in one of them for his granddaughter to arrive home while his daughter was at work. Nearly four decades earlier, he had been drafted into the army regiment in town. Each year since 1900, a selection of the nation's young men, overwhelmingly from impoverished backgrounds, had been called up to complete their compulsory military service, and between 1973 and 1990 around 370,000 recruits passed through Chile's barracks.[2] Mario was part of the "class of '54," around twenty thousand young men born in 1954 who were conscripted along the length of the country in early 1973. These recruits underwent military training in the relative isolation of the barracks, while on the outside the political crisis that gripped Chile deepened. Mario had been a conscript for around six months when the armed forces seized control of the country on September 11, and he was told he was at war. He received his *cédula* (identification card) when he was discharged in 1975, after his year of service had been extended to two.

Mario and his reservist identification lay bare the ruptures and emergence of ex-conscript memory. On the front of the card is a photo taken just before his discharge, along with his name, rank, specialization, and regiment. The boy in the photo, whose father had told him that military service would make him a man, avoids looking at the camera. He sets up a stark contrast to the nearly sixty-year-old speaking openly about his years of silence, his fears, tremors, health complaints, and period of drug and alcohol abuse, while lining up the herbal remedies that would accompany his meal. A simple set of obligations is printed on the back of the identification, including the requirement to present at the nearest unit in the event of a mobilization. The obligation to reenlist during a conflict underscores Mario's descriptions of his anxiety about being recalled, throughout the 1970s, to defend the northern border against a feared Peruvian attack, and his persistent nightmares about being back in the army. His uneasiness rested in part on his work, which took him around the region, as well as over the Peruvian border, and, in part, on a self-aware sense of patriotism that had filtered tales of Chile's nineteenth-century wars with its neighbors through his experiences in the barracks, the death of his brother in late 1974 at the hands of soldiers enforcing the curfew, and subsequent years living under military rule. Like the memory of military service, the cédula was never lost, but it spent decades hidden. Mario came across the card again, and began carrying it with him, around the time he became involved in the Agrupación Social de Ex Soldados Conscriptos 1973—Clase 54 (Social Group for Ex-conscripts 1973—Class of '54).

In the first decade of the twenty-first century, former recruits who served during Chile's dictatorship began to break decades of silence. Memories of military service under Pinochet appeared from behind a desire to forget; fears of ostracization, reprisal, or prosecution; drug and alcohol abuse; and shame and confusion. Ex-conscripts met throughout the country in gatherings that began locally and informally, functioning initially as support and social networks and soon after as advocacy organizations. From 2006, in particular, groups formalized and called for recognition for former recruits as victims of the regime, reparations for unpaid pension contributions and wages, and damages for the long-term emotional, health, and economic consequences of physical and psychological mistreatment inside the barracks. Associations grew, merged, and began to cooperate within several, often overlapping, regional or national groups and coalitions.[3] Within a decade, nearly 100,000 ex-recruits— around one-quarter of those who completed their military service under Pinochet—had mobilized as part of a loose "movement."[4] Associations differed on strategy: most were represented by one of several national-level coalitions that lobbied the government to pass legislation awarding benefits to former recruits;[5] others, most notably a network of groups headed by the Agrupación SMO (Compulsory Military Service Association) in Santiago, turned to the civil courts for damages;[6] and the Agrupación ex conscriptos 1973–1990 Puente

Alto (Association of Ex-Conscripts 1973–1990 Puente Alto) in Puente Alto (Agrupación Puente Alto) pleaded its case in the criminal justice system.[7] Beyond the diverging strategies, the movement was splintered, too, by the group leaders' personal differences and mutual accusations of profiteering, which saw levels of practical cooperation constantly shifting. Despite these fractures at an organizational level, however, group members had common ways of remembering conscription as a fundamental rupture in their lives. This book historicizes the shared memory narratives of military service under Pinochet that emerged with the twenty-first-century ex-conscript "movement," and it reveals how Pinochet's wars were waged inside Chile's barracks between 1973 and 1990.[8]

Memory

Remembering is understood here as a selective and constructive process that gives meaning to and legitimizes past experience. Memories and their silences are made in the present, and the sense that individuals make of the past is informed by their current circumstances and needs, as well as their hopes and plans for the future. Memories are also inherently social. They are shared frameworks that are embedded within, and communicated via, social networks, collective sets of values, and cultural narratives. These frameworks are made, in part, of circulating pieces of material culture: events, facts, rumors, stories, media reports, texts, speeches, books, films, as well as interpretations of, and responses to, other shared memories. Their formation is facilitated and guided by spokespeople who campaign for the communication of memory, both within and beyond the group. However, shared memories are forged, too, in the more intimate interactions between individuals who identify with the group, and the personal links they quietly make to their own experiences. They both emerge from and inform individuals' day-to-day routines, their working lives, and their relationships with their own bodies. They are therefore neither completely imposed from above or from outside, nor are they the result of a wholly grassroots process.[9]

This book examines the shared memory narratives that bind a population of men who found meaning, legitimacy, solidarity, and companionship in ex-conscript groups in the first decades of the twenty-first century. The memories that unite them are unavoidably shaped by their interaction with, and exclusion from, other shared memories of military rule, as well as the state-led truth and reconciliation processes. Emblematic cases, stories, texts, images, and revelations about crimes committed that echoed through Chilean society also often resonated with former recruits, but usually in unique ways. Within groups, ex-conscript leaders acted as strategists and gatekeepers, playing an important role in determining what information circulated within their communities and how it was interpreted, and in shaping demands made in their members' names. Nevertheless, ex-conscript narratives are more than what is received from society or imposed by group presidents. The efforts of leaders, and the wider context of societal changes, exist in a reciprocal relationship with conversations between members, the process of giving testimony, and the rumors, stories, and ideas that circulated among former recruits. The edges of meetings, events, and protests are where much of the memory work took place. Some members remain cautious about talking beyond the semi-public forum of the group, and others lack the resources, knowledge, or desire to communicate electronically. Important interactions, therefore, are often face-to-face, verbal, and not recorded.[10] In these more intimate contexts, ex-conscripts draw on the experiences of others to corroborate and legitimize their own recollections, and they gravitate toward a mostly unspoken consensus about what is important, what should be remembered, and what should be silenced.

The understanding of memory frameworks as social, constructed, and fluid has underpinned investigations into how political violence and military regimes of the late twentieth century are remembered throughout Latin America. "Memory struggles" across the continent pit competing frameworks against one another in contests to install one truth over another, or others. These frameworks exist in a competitive and antagonistic relationship with each other, are mutually exclusive, and generally include a rejection or rebuttal of other memories.[11] This type of contest is central, too, to Chilean memory of military rule.[12] In his three-volume study of memory in Chile, Steve Stern identifies and tracks the interaction between "emblematic" memories of violent rupture, persecution and awakening, salvation, and memory as a "closed box."[13] The groundwork for an understanding of the coup as the salvation of the *patria* (fatherland) from ruin and civil war was set in the rhetorical buildup to September 11, 1973. After the coup, the military junta—using heavy-handed symbolism and aided by a controlled media—established salvation as the dominant narrative for understanding the armed forces' intervention and its rule. On the margins, however, victims of political repression and their friends and families remembered the coup as a violent personal and national rupture. A related memory of awakening to the human rights crisis solidified slowly and unevenly, as the reality and the scope of the repression emerged from among rumors, and from behind official denials of arrests, torture, murders, and disappearances.[14]

From the end of the 1970s, the dynamic of official dominance over the narrative of the coup and mounting tension with counter-official memory shifted. Responding in part to international pressure over human rights abuses, the military regime called for an end to the "national emergency" declared in the wake of the coup, and sought to legitimize and institutionalize its government. It held a "consultation" vote in January 1978, with ballot papers that featured a Chilean flag above the "Yes" vote in support of the junta, and a box of solid black above the "No" vote. The regime also decreed an amnesty law that granted immunity to anyone who had committed criminal acts during the state of siege between 1973 and 1978. The previous year, in 1977, the National Intelligence Directorate (DINA)—the intelligence service synonymous with torture—had been dissolved and replaced with the National Center of Information (Centro Nacional de Informaciones, or CNI), although it retained much of the same personnel. More quietly, the military began destroying evidence of human rights abuses by moving, burning, or hiding victims' remains. In September 1980, the institutionalization effort was crowned with a national plebiscite that ratified a new constitution, installing a brand of democracy "protected" by advisory roles and appointed representative positions for military figures and political allies, and the repression of political parties. This bundle of initiatives was unified by a desire to forget (*olvidar*). The "war" had been won, and the regime emphasized the need to focus on Chile's future rather than its recent past. It wanted, as Stern terms it, to close the memory box. However, the regime's forgetfulness was countered by activists' insistence on remembering the victims of political repression, as memory emerged as a central strategic variable. From the late 1970s and early 1980s, social and political conflict in Chile evolved as a confrontation between the regime's *olvido* and its opponents' *memoria* (memory).[15]

Discontent erupted in 1983. In the years leading up to it, isolated indications of a growing willingness to confront the regime, despite renewed crackdown on dissent, had paralleled mounting frustration as Chile again slipped into economic crisis. These tendencies came together in the response to the call by the Copper Workers Federation for a national day of protest. On May 11, 1983, the country slowed to a halt as people stayed at home and refrained from carrying out their daily errands. The protest built to a crescendo, and at 8:00 p.m. protesters banged on pots and pans in their own homes. The noise united the *poblaciones* (poor urban neighborhoods) and the middle-class suburbs in an affirmation of broad-based dissatisfaction. Protests followed almost monthly, until the regime declared a state of siege in November the next year. The crackdown produced a second wave of street protest between September 1985 and July 1986 that was smaller and more focused than the first. It also cost around thirty protesters their lives. However, the violent response to the mobilization was unable to return Chile to the pre-1983 memoryscape. New symbols, voices, and acts of defiance expanded the set of cultural referents of counter-official memory, and it sprang the mechanisms of containment put in place by the regime. From the mid-1980s, memory as rupture, persecution, and awakening, which in the 1970s had been largely restricted to the margins, transformed into a "mass experience."[16]

Throughout the 1990s, Chile's memory contest swung between what Alexander Wilde terms periodic "irruptions," or events that forced the memory question into the public consciousness, and a political "conspiracy of consensus"—a widespread preference to forget.[17] The 1991 Rettig Report confirmed the scale and the brutality of the repression and helped entrench memory as rupture and persecution. Its findings withstood scrutiny and were complemented by subsequent revelations in the following years. They also forced an adjustment among the majority of Chileans who were invested in the regime's economic legacy, with many Pinochet supporters shifting from what were now untenable denials of human rights violations to the rationalization of abuses as unfortunate "excesses" or the "modest" cost of salvation. This tendency was coupled with a triumphant narrative of economic modernization. The Rettig Report did not, however, progress the cause of transitional justice. Despite sporadic discoveries regarding human rights abuses and isolated convictions, campaigns for information on the disappeared, and to hold perpetrators of human rights abuses accountable, were repeatedly frustrated. In this context, competing memory frameworks orbited each other, only occasionally colliding. Stern describes this rhythm of posttransition memory as a "rolling impasse" that was sustained by the amnesty laws of 1978; the legislative, political, and judicial protections of Chile's posttransition democracy that had been written into the 1980 constitution; Pinochet's ongoing dominance of public life as head of the army, and his willingness to rattle the institution's sabers to protect his soldiers, his family, and his legacy; and battle weariness after decades of the memory struggle.[18]

The impasse of the "long transition" began to break in 1998. Pinochet stepped down as head of the army and was later arrested in London. The "Pinochet effect"—a renewed focus on international law in light of the former dictator's arrest—as well as increased domestic political pressure from emerging torture victims' groups and generational renewal within the local judiciary combined to begin dismantling immunity. The shifts in Chile's courts were mainly interpretative and worked around the amnesty law, statutes of limitations, and previous obstacles to the application of international law to human rights cases. On its streets, a new extrajudicial push to hold perpetrators to account also emerged, with victims, their supporters, and the children of former political prisoners or the disappeared beginning to "out" torturers and murderers during loud protests (*funas*) at their workplaces or homes.[19] Parallel to the wrangling about Pinochet's potential extradition to Spain, the new and less inhibited atmosphere in Chile produced a formal effort to find common ground between opposing memory camps. The 1999 Dialogue Table brought together military representatives, politicians, human rights lawyers and activists, religious leaders, historians, and a psychologist to establish the fate of the disappeared and examine the causes of the coup. The resulting agreement from June of the following year represented a first building block for a narrative of shared tragedy. It placed the coup not at the beginning of the story but within a context of spiraling violence that stretched back to the 1960s. It also included the first formal acknowledgment from the military of disappearances and other crimes of repression, as the armed forces moved away from the idea of war that had justified the human rights violations in the wake of the coup. The initiative was not universally embraced, and it was subsequently undermined when information provided by the armed forces on the disappeared proved to be unreliable.[20] Nevertheless, over the next decade, a quiet sense that "we are all victims" began to find a foothold.[21]

The openness of the post-1998 "season of memory" allowed the issue of torture to move to the center of the debate. Former political prisoners became increasingly visible, as the societal and personal barriers that had prevented them from speaking publicly about their imprisonment and torture began to crack. The brutal practices of the regime had galvanized elements of the opposition in the 1980s, but in the posttransition decade the issue of torture had been silenced by the victims' own desire to keep their suffering private and overshadowed by the search for truth about and justice for the disappeared. Around the turn of the century, groups of former detainees that had initially mobilized in response to Pinochet's arrest consolidated their presence and pushed for more truth and more justice, as well as reparations. The political landscape had also shifted. After a near miss in the 1999 presidential election, the political right adopted a more conciliatory and proactive stance on the issue of human rights. In this context, President Ricardo Lagos of the governing *concertación* (a coalition of center-left political parties) announced the There Is No Tomorrow without Yesterday initiative in 2003. Thirty years after the coup, the program moved away from the idea of closure, and outlined an approach to memory as ongoing work. It offered a plan regarding reparations, a range of controversial witness incentives intended to expedite the work of establishing the truth, and it included provisions for a second truth and reconciliation commission.[22]

The Valech Commission released its report in 2004, confirming the truth of torture and revealing the brutality, scope, and systematic nature of the regime's violation of human rights. In contrast to the dismissive responses to the Rettig Report by institutions still aligned with the former regime, the Valech Report and its findings were widely acknowledged. Most notably, the commander-in-chief of the army, Juan Emilio Cheyre, accepted the findings, announcing that the institution would assume the responsibility for its part in the "punishable and morally unacceptable acts of the past."[23] Cheyre's statement was partly due to generational renewal in the officer ranks and partly the result of an institutional effort to forge a new role for the army within civil society. It also came on the back of the Riggs Bank scandal and the revelation that Pinochet had a personal fortune hidden in foreign accounts. The general's self-enrichment was irreconcilable with the patriotic mission of the salvation narrative, and the case not only encouraged the army to publicly distance itself from Pinochet's legacy; it also signaled a critical juncture in the level of support among civilian loyalists.

Deep division briefly reemerged on the streets when Pinochet died in 2006. Crowds had kept vigil outside the hospital treating their general, and tens of thousands of grieving people later waited for hours to file past his body in the Military School. Downtown, however, crowds gathered to dance and celebrate. Pinochet's funeral became a flashpoint for an old memory contest, and it produced a burst of combative commemorative and historiographical activity that swung between the immortalization of Pinochet and the memory question, and the idea that his death had finally brought the curtain down on Chile's transition.[24] This irruption came in the first year of Michelle Bachelet's first term as president. Bachelet—a former political detainee and daughter of air force general Alberto Bachelet, who had died while detained and after being tortured—continued the concertación's memory project. She reopened the Valech Commission, with the resulting 2011 report—Valech II—increasing the number of recognized victims, and she expanded state support for the prosecution of crimes of repression. Responding to the persistence of victims' groups, her government also continued and accelerated the state's renewed involvement in the memorialization of the dictatorship's victims that had begun under her predecessor. The most emblematic of the government's commemorative projects was the Museum of Memory and Human Rights. Bachelet had announced the project early in her term, and when she opened it in the final months of her presidency, the completed building revived the idea that the long transition had come to an end.

It was clear by the time the Museum of Memory and Human Rights opened in early 2010 that the conservative candidate, Sebastian Piñera, would win the upcoming run-off election and break the succession of concertación governments that had ruled Chile since the return to democracy. His election as the first right-wing president since the transition also energized the Pinochetista fringe. A vocal minority of loyal supporters had been actively reviving a version of the salvation narrative, in response to the emotional trigger of Pinochet's death in 2006 and the sight of high-profile officers beginning prison sentences at around the same time. Loyalists had returned to memory, insisting that the violence of the years prior to the coup had been forgotten, and with the incarceration of a small number of veterans of the "dirty war," they transformed salvation into a narrative of martyrdom and victimhood that adopted the languages of political imprisonment and human rights.[25] With Piñera's victory, hard-liners expected a sharp reversal in the politics of memory and the release of imprisoned soldiers. However, by 2010, much of the memory question had been settled.[26] Despite several controversial appointments of Pinochet supporters to ambassadorial positions, a renewed focus on fraud in reparations programs, and an understated or tolerant response to high-profile events paying homage to Pinochet or officers in prison, Piñera largely confirmed the fact that the political right had distanced itself from the dictatorship's legacy. With his presidency coming to an end in September 2013, he also closed the Cordillera prison. The purpose-built facility had housed officers convicted of crimes of repression under conditions in stark contrast to Chile's overcrowded prisons, and it had become a symbol of privilege and compromise on the issue of human rights.[27]

Piñera's term also wound down amid a wave of commemorative activity in the lead-up to the fortieth anniversary of the coup. In the days leading up to the 2013 milestone, the outgoing president surprised many from both political perspectives by speaking of the regime's many "passive accomplices" who knew of abuses and did nothing or chose to ignore them.[28] The period of commemoration also paralleled the campaigns to find Piñera's successor. The two main candidates were former president Bachelet and Evelyn Matthei, daughter of another air force general, Fernando Matthei, who was a member of Pinochet's junta from 1978 to 1990. The "generals' daughters" compounded the historical moment of the anniversary and ensured Chile's past accompanied the debate about its future. Bachelet was eventually returned to office with an ambitious reform program that sought to address legacies of military rule. She ran on a platform of free and quality education, committing to a significant restructuring of the sector that had been deregulated under Pinochet, and she promised to draft a new constitution to replace the 1980 charter. She also renewed the government's commitment to human rights and the ongoing work of memory, including a pledge to end impunity by impeding the application of the 1978 amnesty law.[29]

There was no room, however, in Chile's memory struggles for ex-conscript memory.[30] The ambiguous figure of the uniformed recruit—potentially a witness to, participant in, or victim of human rights abuses, or all three—blurred the line between victim and perpetrator and could not be accommodated within any of the grand narratives of the coup and military rule. The truth and reconciliation processes also excluded from consideration the majority of the types of physical and psychological mistreatment alleged by former conscripts.[31] Former recruits often describe themselves as the "ham in the sandwich" to relate their sense of being caught between the two sides of political conflict as conscripts and between the competing narratives of military rule as ex-conscripts. While ex-conscript memory was undoubtedly shaped by its interaction with, and exclusion from, the competing frameworks of the memory contest, it moves to its own rhythm and has its own history. The memories that unite the movement do not imply any particular interpretation of the coup, military rule, or the regime's legacy. They are shared narratives of victimhood without a shared political identity or project, beyond securing recognition and reparations. Instead, service is understood as a series of deep, personal, and intertwined ruptures in the lives of former recruits that do not necessarily operate as a window onto a national story. Ex-conscript memory offers new insights into the memory of military rule, particularly in posttransition Chile, but it also reveals important aspects of the experience of being a conscript during the dictatorship. While the reality of conscription varied between regiments and regions, and across cohorts, military service under military rule was fundamentally defined by the experience of war.

War

In his 2006 testimony, Pablo W.* (1973–74) recalls being woken in Chile's southern ninth region late on September 10, 1973, and flown to the capital, where he and his fellow conscripts performed guard duty around the city in two-week shifts.[32] Like Pablo, recruits throughout Chile found that they were at war on the morning of September 11. In the days prior to the coup, some had been carrying out routine guard duty, and most had been preparing for the annual national festivities a week later. In some regiments, there were murmurs about "something" being afoot, but recruits were mostly caught off guard by movements on the morning of the coup. At times unsure who the enemy was, conscripts were made aware of the stakes and assured by officers that, in accordance with the laws of war, they would be shot for disobeying an order. It was a warning reinforced by shock, fear, rumor, and examples of it being carried out.[33]

The rhetoric of civil war between the extreme left and extreme right had been building throughout the previous decade; however, on the morning of the coup, the armed forces faced only sporadic, disorganized, and poorly armed resistance.[34] The "battle of Santiago" was brief, troops in the countryside faced even less opposition, and the military had control of the country by midday.[35] Despite the fact that the morning of September 11 exposed the Left's role in the discursive buildup to the coup as largely bluster, the junta set about reinforcing the war narrative. It announced that Allende's Popular Unity alliance—aided by thousands of foreign fighters—had been planning to kill the military leadership in the days before the parade on September 19 in order to install a leftist dictatorship. The explosive revelation of what was known as "Plan Z" was followed by staggered "discoveries" of caches of weapons that were intended to prove the existence of Popular Unity's planned "self-coup."[36] While the news of Plan Z was circulated through the country in an effort to shore up the public case for war against an internal enemy, a group of officers toured Chile as part of the Caravan of Death to reinforce discipline inside the barracks. Under General Sergio Arellano Stark, these officers flew in helicopters between the provinces, where the repression had been relatively soft. At each stop, they murdered political prisoners, delivering the message to local soldiers that they were at war, despite widespread civilian compliance and a lack of resistance.[37]

On the day of the coup, recruits were sent out into the streets, where ranks were removed from their uniforms and colored armbands were used to distinguish soldiers from the civilian "enemy."[38] Throughout the day, and in the weeks and months that followed, they enforced the curfew and guarded infrastructure and strategic points such as bridges, fuel stations, highways, and armed forces buildings. They participated in often violent raids on homes and workplaces, looking for the weapons that were to be used to carry out Plan Z. They detained, transported, and guarded prisoners, and shot up buildings. In some cases, they witnessed the abuse or deaths of detainees, and in rarer instances, they were involved in the beating, torture, or murder of civilians.[39] From 1974, the political repression became more focused, the massive detention camps were closed, and the work of dirty war fell largely to the newly created DINA.[40]

In the late 1970s, the "war" ended. On September 12, 1973, the junta had declared a state of siege in Chile, which was interpreted as a state of war and renewed without interruption until 1978. It was lifted as part of the institutionalization of the regime, and reimposed twice during the unrest of the early 1980s, when the feeling of war returned to the streets. Recruits were also mobilized and took part in these confrontations with protesters and patrolled the capital's poblaciones. The narrative of war and chaos—always tied to the idea of salvation—also made a powerful return during the lead-up to the plebiscite, but by the late 1980s it met a widespread weariness with conflict and a yearning for joy. The "No" campaign united behind the catchy slogan "Chile, Joy's Already on the Way" and won with nearly 56 percent of the vote.[41] In posttransition Chile, the discursive pairing of war/salvation continued to offer many a framework for remembering the coup.[42] Inside the barracks under Pinochet, however, the "internal war" was only one element of a broader threat, as counterrevolution and the Cold War became intertwined with the contemporary echoes of Chile's nineteenth-century conflicts with its neighbors.[43]

People from the Araucanía (Chile's ninth region) have no sea legs, explained Hugo M.* (1975–77), remembering the drums designated to hold vomit in the ship's hold on the trip from the forested south to Arica. Having been told in the town of Lautaro that he was at war and to shoot or be shot, he was transported to Chile's far north and the Peruvian border. The trip by sea took five days, with Hugo and his *compañeros* (fellow recruits) squeezed under deck, sleeping in puddles, and making use of the drums.[44] These young men formed part of a mobilization to the north, in anticipation of an invasion by Peruvian forces bent on avenging territorial losses sustained the previous century. Chile fought the War of the Pacific against Peru and Bolivia between 1879 and 1883, over control of the resource-rich Atacama Desert. Under the peace treaties signed after the Chilean victory, Bolivia ceded the province of Antofagasta—and with it, its coastline—to Chile, and Peru gave up the province of Tarapacá. The Peruvian provinces of Tacna and Arica were to be occupied by Chile for a decade, at which point a plebiscite would determine on which side of the border they fell. The vote never took place; instead, a 1929 deal saw Tacna returned to Peru, and Arica retained by Chile.[45]

In the early 1970s, the prospect of renewed conflict grew. Peruvian general Juan Francisco Velasco had come to power in a 1968 military coup, and his left-leaning military regime pursued policies of industry expropriation and nationalization, and agrarian reform. As part of this nationalist program, Velasco also harbored the desire to reconquer lands lost to Chile. Peru steadily grew its military capability, focusing it on its southern border, and whispers of war with Chile circulated throughout 1973. However, General Velasco's personal and ideological affinity with Allende, a leftist president implementing his own regime of nationalization and agrarian reform, helped keep the threat of open war in check. The strike on La Moneda cleared the way for a potential Peruvian assault on the northern city of Arica while Chilean forces were preoccupied with their coup over a thousand miles away in the capital.[46]

The Chilean military had been tracking the talk of war in Lima, watched the buildup on the border, and followed what they saw as General Velasco's heightened rhetoric in the lead-up to the hundred-year anniversary of the War of the Pacific. They observed, too, Peruvian military exercises immediately following the ousting of Allende. In response, Chile fortified the border: the military laid land mines in the desert, dug trenches, positioned antitank defenses along the coast, and sent troops, including thousands of conscripts from southern provinces, north to supplement local recruits. Chile began purchasing arms to close the gap between the two countries' capabilities, and it bolstered the permanent military presence in the northern regions. The Peruvian invasion, however, never eventuated. Ecuador had also boosted its military capabilities, and had its own territorial claims regarding Peru's northern border. More importantly, internal unrest in Peru distracted the regime from war. General Francisco Morales Bermúdez ousted General Velasco in August 1975, installing a regime much more amenable to the Chilean junta. Before moving on Velasco, the plotters assured Santiago that their new regime would put a line under the latent war. Despite having pulled back from the brink of open conflict, tension between the neighboring countries remained and led to an arms race over the coming decade. Concerns about war with Peru peaked again in the late 1970s, when Chile was distracted by the buildup to war on its southern borders. While the immediate danger subsided, Peru remained a potential enemy throughout the 1980s.[47]

At the height of the Peruvian threat in the mid-1970s, Pinochet reached out to the Bolivian military dictator, Hugo Banzer, in an effort to resolve that country's lingering complaints from the War of the Pacific. The Bolivian border with Chile had been set by the 1884 truce signed after the war, and consolidated by a 1904 treaty in which Bolivia gave up claims to the Pacific region in exchange for unrestricted access to Chile's ports. However, the war never really ended for Bolivia, and the now landlocked nation yearned for its coast and its seas. Diplomatic relations between the two countries had been severed for almost a decade, when, in the early 1970s, Bolivia began to again press its claims to the Pacific. Allende and Bolivia's leftist military leader, General Juan José Torres, held talks in 1971, which were abruptly halted when Torres was removed by Banzer in a bloody coup. Banzer instead met Pinochet at the March 1974 inauguration of Brazilian president Ernesto Geisel, where the two resolved to address the persistent border issue. In February 1975, they met again near the Chilean-Bolivian border, symbolizing the improved relations between the two countries.[48]

The negotiations with Bolivia were part of a diplomatic effort to diffuse the threat from Peru.[49] The human rights abuses of Chile's "internal war" had cost it the support of traditional allies, and so it turned to Brazil, Paraguay, and Ecuador—the other right-leaning military governments in the region—to exert indirect pressure on Velasco, and reached out to Bolivia to undermine the possibility of a Bolivian-Peruvian coalition.[50] In late 1975, Chile proposed a plan that would relinquish a narrow strip of land along the Peruvian border. Bolivia rejected the proposal, and in November 1976 Peru entered the negotiations. The 1929 Treaty of Santiago, establishing the Chilean-Peruvian border, stipulated that neither nation could cede land to a third party without the approval of the other, and Peru offered its own solution that involved a corridor linking Bolivia to the coast but also joint, three-way sovereignty over a new coastal zone south of the corridor. Chile rejected the Peruvian plan, but negotiations now involved three nations. Progress slowed and relations deteriorated until Bolivia, pointing to Chilean intransigence, broke diplomatic relations in 1978.[51] Parallel to the diplomatic maneuvering to appease its neighbor, Chile had also mobilized forces to meet the potential Bolivian invasion. Oscar C.* (1974–75, 1976–78) remembers the two days and two nights of vomit and excrement in the hold of a fishing boat that took him and his *compañeros* from Talcahuano to Antofagasta in 1974. After a month in Calama, he was sent to Chiu-Chiu on the edge of Chile, in readiness for the "war with Bolivia that never was." Four years later, and having been called up a second time, Oscar was in Chile's south awaiting war with Argentina.[52]

While the War of the Pacific was being fought to Chile's north, a treaty was signed that established its border in the south. The 1881 agreement settled almost a century of disagreement over the exact border between Chile and Argentina. The interpretation of the treaty, however, was immediately controversial, and the disagreement centered on the Beagle Channel and the Picton, Lennox, and Nueva Islands. The channel served as the border, with all lands to the south belonging to Chile and all to the north to Argentina, but the two countries disagreed on where the channel ran: to the north of the islands, making them Chilean, or to the south, making them Argentine. At stake were not only three small islands, but also resource-rich maritime claims and a strategic advantage in Antarctica. The disagreement led to a series of stalled talks and failed attempts at arbitration throughout the first half of the twentieth century, before the countries agreed to a new arbitration by Great Britain in 1971. In May 1977 the islands were awarded to Chile, but Argentina, emboldened by Chile's increased isolation from the international community and threats on her northern borders, rejected the decision. Parallel to a series of failed diplomatic efforts, Argentina exercised its forces in war games, called up its reservists, and mobilized troops to the border.[53]

Chilean conscripts, too, were sent to the border. Thousands of young men spent months in trenches dug into the hills and within striking distance of Argentine forces, battling hunger, cold, isolation, lice, scabies, and the constant fear of war. They were told to write their last letters home as talks between the regimes failed. With the final deadline set for 11:00 p.m. on December 23, 1978, only the last-minute offer from Pope John Paul II to mediate prevented the outbreak of war.[54] The 1979 Act of Montevideo committed both countries to finding a peaceful solution and scaling back the military buildup in the disputed region to 1977 levels. Tensions and the military presence on the border remained, however, and it was not until 1984, following the fall of the military junta in Argentina and the 1983 election of Raúl Ricardo Alfonsín on a platform that gave priority to resolving the dispute, that a 1980 papal proposal was agreed to by both nations.[55] Chilean-Argentine relations were still highly charged, then, when Argentina invaded the Malvinas/Falkland Islands in 1982. The claim on the British islands was part of the same nationalist push for greater economic and geopolitical presence in the region that had brought Argentina to the brink of war with Chile. It was widely assumed that, if Argentina prevailed in the Malvinas/Falklands, it would swiftly turn its forces on Chile, and the mainland border remained highly militarized during the offshore conflict. Chile maintained official neutrality, but given its interest in a British victory, provided intelligence and quiet logistical support. The swift British victory contributed to the fall of the Argentine military dictatorship.[56]

The front lines of Chile's "internal war," states of siege and emergency, almost wars (*casi-guerras*), pre-wars (*pre-guerras*), wars-that-weren't (*guerras que nunca fueron*), and possible wars (*posibles guerras*), overlapped and crept inside the barracks: "We were at war every day," explained Javier R.* (1981–83) in 2012, for example, while describing his service in Tierra del Fuego.[57] The chapters in this book examine how war was waged inside Chile's regiments under Pinochet as well as how ex-conscripts remember having been at war during their service, and how these shared narratives formed and emerged publicly with the ex-conscript movement of the first decade of the twenty-first century. The first chapter analyzes the contours of ex-conscripts' silence in the decades after their discharge. Silence is understood as a shifting set of mutually reinforcing fears, suspicions, societal barriers, and internalized limits, which restricted what and how much former recruits revealed about their service, the contexts in which they talked, and with whom they shared their experiences. Many ex-conscripts wanted to forget. They framed remembering as a struggle against unwanted thoughts, images, emotional responses, nightmares, or physical reminders, and at times fortified their efforts not to remember with drugs, alcohol, or physical or emotional distance. Ex-conscripts also adhered to a complex and often conflicted "pact of silence" that was anchored most securely in fear. They assumed they were being watched by the intelligence services, and feared reprisal from the military if they talked. At the same time, they felt that they risked being ostracized by society, colleagues, neighbors, and their own families.

Chapter 1 also examines two key concepts that inform ex-conscript silence: responsibility for human rights abuses and the moral imperative to remember. It examines the potential scope of conscript participation in human rights abuses, and how ex-conscript memory frames the notion of conscript responsibility for crimes of repression. Within the context of the broader memory question, the former recruits' silence is often understood by victims' groups, in particular, as complicity. Moreover, the rules of engagement established by the imperative to deliver information about victims of disappearance, murder, and torture had the effect of muffling ex-conscript memory, which was rarely linked to the grand narratives of Chile's memory struggles, and, when it was, did not engage with the contest in a uniform way.

The contours of ex-conscript silence moved with time and in response to the state-led truth and reconciliation processes, Pinochet's fading public influence in the late 1990s, institutional renewal within the armed forces, transitional justice, and increasing accountability. However, the mobilization of ex-conscripts did not result from, or produce, a definitive shift. The decisive moment can instead be seen in a convergence of economic, cultural, familial, and corporeal factors in the first decade of the twenty-first century. Chapter 2 examines that moment. Most ex-conscript groups emerged initially around the issue of unpaid pension payments and wages that former recruits felt they were entitled to (2006–9). Their demands for retroactive payments were soon complemented with calls for health and education benefits and compensation for damages, and after a consolidation and growth phase, different national-level coalitions pursued reparations through the civil courts, criminal courts, and by lobbying the government to pass legislation awarding former recruits benefits (from 2009). The "economics of victimhood" provided a catalyst for ex-conscript mobilization, but the narrow demands were an expression of a broad sense of injustice that was rooted in the moment of their emergence. Amid persistent inequality, wider disenchantment with the transition to democracy, financial scandals involving the Pinochet family, and the reparations awarded to victims, ex-conscript victimhood helped make sense of the ongoing economic precariousness and health issues that confronted many former recruits, as well as years of underemployment and unemployment, and poorly paid and physically demanding work that many came to understand as a consequence of their conscription. This moment was compounded by the contrast between the cyclical poverty many endured in the decades since leaving the barracks, and the hopes and ambitions they had invested in the idea of service as would-be recruits.

The ex-conscript mobilization was also shaped by its interaction with, and exclusion from, the transitional truth and reconciliation processes, and the memory contest more broadly. A growing rights culture and the memory turn at the beginning of the twenty-first century provided former recruits with unifying languages of rights and torture, as well as a model for demands and emblematic points of reference. Ex-conscripts increasingly identified as human rights victims, as what for many had been an isolated and isolating experience was understood within a shared and socially legitimized rights framework. However, posttransition memory debates and state-led reconciliation positioned human rights and victim status as clear-cut political categories, and former recruits not only blurred the sharp lines of the memory contest but also lacked a shared political identity. This "politics of victimhood" meant that the ex-conscripts' collective self-identification as victims could not be accommodated within either of the opposing political narratives of military rule. The human rights paradigm that lay at the heart of Chilean memory at once drove and imposed limits on the ex-conscript mobilization. The movement that emerged in this context was not bound by a coherent or consistent political identity but was fragmented in terms of strategy, and splintered by the group leaders' personal differences. However, the different factions had common demands and, more importantly, former recruits shared common ways of remembering their service as a fundamental rupture in their lives. They found meaning within elements of one, two, or all three of the shared frameworks examined in chapters 3 through 5.[58]

Chapter 3 investigates memory as ruptured patriotism. It traces the nineteenth-century process of aligning ideas of the nation with institutions, traditions, racial mythology, and notions of Chile, which provided a foundation for the twentieth-century military project to define and defend la patria. From the turn of the century, and after the "Prussianization" of the army, officers saw themselves as the moral reserve of the people and the embodiment of the nation and its values, and the introduction of the draft was an important part of the work of guaranteeing the integrity of la patria. Military service would produce citizens and forge the nation by educating the masses, instilling values, and safeguarding against "corrosive" ideologies. This mission, and the role played by conscription, continued through the political instability of the century and adapted to fit the Cold War context of postwar counterinsurgency. It also, however, stood in contrast to the patriotic fervor that drove eager conscripts to the barracks and that was produced and reproduced in commemorative rituals, and consecrated in tales of nineteenth-century wars. This gap between patrias underpins the narrative of disillusionment and the sense of betrayal of ex-conscript memory.

Chapter 3 also examines how conflicting ideas of what it meant to defend la patria organized memory of the "internal war," the "almost-war" with Argentina and the construction of the carretera austral (southern highway), a network of roads connecting the isolated regions of Chile's far south with the rest of the country. It historicizes the staggered emergence of the narrative of patriotic disillusionment, revealing how it incrementally came to frame how many former recruits remember the political repression of the coup and military rule. Moreover, it tracks the equation in military thought of poverty with radicalism, enabling a better understanding of how the front line of the "internal war" shrank inside the barracks. The memory of war within Chile's regiments, and of instructors as the enemy, also shapes descriptions of the potential conflict with Argentina. Ex-conscripts who had waited for war at the border recall a second front line emerging in the trenches between themselves and their superiors. Their testimonies are shaped by both patriotic pride and a sense of abandonment and disillusionment. While recruits were defending the border, others were participating in the construction of the carretera austral, which was the regime's crowning nation-building project and at the heart of its defense strategy. Former recruits who worked on it contrast the regime's narrative of the carretera's enormous benefits with accusations of abuse, mistreatment, deprivation, injury, and death during its construction.

Chapter 4 examines the clash of ideas of what it meant to be and to become a man, which frames many former recruits' memories of their service. Since its inception, conscription had developed as a male rite among those sectors of Chilean society that traditionally fed the ranks of recruits. Parents understood service as an opportunity to instill discipline, military values, a work ethic, and a sense of responsibility in their sons; boys saw service as a test and confirmation of their toughness and virility; and both boys and their parents expected that service would provide training, education, and better employment prospects. In the decades preceding the coup, a nexus emerged between military service, employment, and the masculine responsibilities of being a husband, father, and provider for a nuclear family. However, this civilian masculinity and the boys' vision of their pathway to manhood clashed with military training to produce "hard" men. Being a man inside the barracks meant being resistant to pain, thirst, hunger, and fear, and developing the ability to kill. Former recruits describe being deprived of food, severely and arbitrarily punished, exposed to climatic extremes, forced to witness acts of cruelty against detainees, fellow recruits, or animals, and subjected to torture and brutal methods of interrogation to prepare them for war. The conception of military hardness that emerges from ex-conscript testimony aligns with broader twentieth-century developments in Western military thinking on stress inoculation and desensitization, as well as a context of postwar training techniques and interrogation methods used in dirty war. However, it is also rooted in ideas of endurance and resistance that can be traced back to nineteenth-century wars with Peru and Bolivia, and sits within a longer tradition of violent military discipline and abuse in Chile that echoes, too, in the posttransition decades.

Once they were discharged, the physical, emotional, and psychological scars that resulted from service, or that former recruits attributed to their time in the barracks, undermined their ability and their efforts to live up to societal gender roles. Memory of their conscription is often shaped by failures to live up to the "traditional" responsibilities of forming a family and working to provide for a wife and children. Stories of broken marriages, infertility, domestic violence, unemployment, an inability to pay for their children's education, alcohol abuse, and feelings of uselessness cut through group meetings and individual testimonies. The fear or regret that they have passed on the damage they acquired in the barracks to a new generation is juxtaposed with the expectations of opportunity and social mobility ex-conscripts had once invested in their military service. The ruptured masculinity of ex-conscript memory is also understood within the long arc of Chilean masculine identity and the broader crisis of masculinity that emerged in the gap between the ideals cast in the early twentieth century and the economic realities of life both under military rule and at the turn of the twenty-first century in democratic Chile.

Chapter 5 examines how former recruits remember their military service "in the flesh." It reveals a discourse of "bodily memory" in ex-conscript testimony that frames remembering as a lonely contest between a desire to forget and unwanted and uncontrollable thoughts, emotional reactions, unconscious habits, and physical reminders that plays out within, and against, former recruits' own bodies and minds. Ex-conscripts describe this internal struggle using a language of wounded souls, scarred hearts and minds, and physical reminders. In the group context, the shared will to remember that underpinned the ex-conscript mobilization was also grounded in members' bodies, scars, ailments, aches, and disorders. This "embodied" memory grew in part out of a need for evidence to support conscript victimhood and a medicalization of truth that was unique to former recruits' claims to victim status. At times the personal links that ex-conscripts established between their service and their ailments stretch, or completely breach, the limits of plausibility. However, direct and provable causation was not always the point, as the intersection of aging and aching bodies, underemployment and unemployment, and economic hardship transformed health complaints into an expression of a broader sense of damage and victimization. Sharing their stories at regular meetings, as well as the daily and seasonal cycles of failing health, became commemorative rituals that made and remade the links between the shared narrative of rupture and the recruits' pains, aches, scars, injuries, and diseases. In this sense, their bodies were transformed into sites of memory.

Ex-conscript memory cannot be completely isolated from Chile's memory struggles. Its narratives of victimhood must be understood in the context of their emergence and their interaction with Chile's competing memories of military rule. In addition, there are clear incentives for former recruits to de-politicize how they talk about their service. Nevertheless, ex-conscript memory still demands a unique historical perspective, and the book concludes by pulling together the implications that the preceding chapters have for the historiography of memory in Chile and the region. It reveals the limits of the human rights paradigm and argues for an understanding of shared memory of military rule beyond the "politics of memory" that organize the act of remembering in postdictatorship societies as a contest between political interpretations. The "apolitics of memory" situates conscription, the coup, and military rule also and more firmly within long histories of national identity, patriotism, masculinity, economic precariousness, opportunity, and family life that extend from the nineteenth to the twenty-first centuries. Understanding this other dynamic and its interaction with the memory contest is necessary to tracing the memory and the history of the wars inside Chile's barracks.

1

The Contours of Silence

I t was a love story, I guess you could say," blushed Patricio
Farías, while clarifying in 2013 the need to be guarded
about his experiences.[1] He had been completing his military service in Punta
Arenas when the armed forces took control of the country in 1973. Not sure
what a coup was, and not told who they were at war with, Patricio recalled
being in Chile's far south with ammunition crisscrossing his chest "like a
Mexican," waiting for the Argentines to attack. He later spent several weeks
on Dawson Island in the Strait of Magellan guarding politicians taken prisoner
in the assault on the Moneda and watching the horizon for the lights of the
Russian submarines that his superiors assured him were coming.[2] At the end
of 1973 he was transported to Santiago, where he guarded buildings along the
city's principal avenue, helped enforce the curfew, and patrolled unfamiliar
neighborhoods. There were, he acknowledged, "many bad things" done at
that time, but he insisted that his hands were clean and his conscience clear.
Discharged to the streets of the capital in 1975, with no way of returning home
to the Colchagua Valley, he peddled goods on the city's buses, at one point
trading his watch for wares to sell. He tried to find work, but employers were
suspicious, he explained, and no one wanted to hire an ex-soldier. Later, he
met a girl. They would meet and take walks, until one day she told him that
she was a student leader and had been a political prisoner in San Fernando.
Patricio kept quiet but began to distance himself from her, understanding
that, given his past, the relationship had no future.

In the years that followed, Patricio found stable employment, married,
and formed a family. But he was constantly anxious and afraid. He went
through daily life seeing everyone as his enemy and feeling like they wanted to
attack him. In many ways, democratic Chile was worse. During the truth and
reconciliation processes, he felt abandoned by the Catholic Church as a
murderer, and rejected by politicians as a torturer and a rapist. He was still

wary of talking to his neighbors and colleagues, and he withheld most things from his wife and children. It was something he just had to keep to himself, he reasoned. A friend told Patricio about the Agrupación SMO in 2007, and in the group meetings in downtown Santiago he shared his experiences with other members of the "class of '54." Whether they had served in the north or the south, Patricio found that many ex-conscripts had the same story, and exchanging memories was "like therapy." Outside of the group, however, his anxiety remained. Then in 2011, "something strange" happened. An already slight man, he began losing weight, and he shut himself away from the world, thinking he was going to die. He could not say precisely what it was that afflicted him, speaking of his "illness" in 2013 in unsure and unfinished sentences about mounting stress, others' concern at his gaunt appearance, and physical pain. He was, however, more certain about his recovery, which he linked to the realization that he would never be able to forget the past and his faith. After six months, God, he said, had given him a second chance. He found an inner peace reading the Bible and he gained the weight back. Nearly forty years after the coup, and two years after his illness, Patricio was cheerful, less agitated, and less fearful of the world. He was, however, still pragmatically cautious. "You have to watch who you can talk to about this topic," he explained, "because you cannot do it with just anyone."

Silence is not the opposite of memory. It weaves through Patricio's recollections as a set of mutually reinforcing fears, suspicions, societal barriers, and internalized limits. His love story served to emphasize the potential depth of that silence. He saw the woman again years later, some time after the transition, walking through Constitution Square behind the Moneda. He let her pass by: "You realize that it comes from all sides. They discriminate against us, even in romance. You could not have a girlfriend because you didn't know who the person was that you were dating. Like with that girl, she was nice, but that was the end of the story." Fear, shame, guilt, confusion, and stigma produced a landscape of silence that rose and fell, both through the years and between situations as ex-conscripts moved through their daily lives. This chapter maps the contours of that silence. It examines former conscripts' fears of reprisal from the armed forces, fears of retribution from civilians, fears of rejection by society, and their failed attempts to forget, revealing, too, how these elements of ex-conscript silence shifted over time.

Forgetting

Under military rule, a cultural and political front line was drawn between remembering and forgetting. From the late 1970s and early 1980s, memory became a moral imperative and a cultural reference point in its own right, as activists countered the act of disappearance, government misinformation, and official denials of human rights abuses with an insistence on remembering the victims. At the same time, the junta built its institutionalization of military rule on a strategic forgetfulness. The regime's war had been won, and the military government answered its opponents' "memory against oblivion" by emphasizing the need to look forward and not back. Similarly, those who had benefited from the lopsided economic prosperity ushered in by the regime tended to deny or ignore the scale and brutality of the repression, both under Pinochet and in the posttransition decades. As the "obstinate" memory of human rights violations began to push olvido (forgetting) further to the margins around the turn of the century, regime loyalists, too, turned to memory.[3] As support for the war narrative of the regime was incrementally undone, its adherents increasingly insisted on remembering the violence and chaos of the 1960s, particularly the Popular Unity years and the existential threat posed by global Marxism, which, they argued, had been forgotten. In the memory contest, forgetting and remembering were entwined acts of selection that buttressed opposing narratives.[4] Behind this shifting sociopolitical struggle between memory and olvido, which shaped life under military rule as well as Chile's return to democracy, ex-conscripts internalized a similar, but very personal, contest.

Many former recruits understood remembering as a struggle between their desire to forget and unbidden memories. Despite not wanting to remember, they describe being haunted by the thoughts, sights, and emotions of service. Feelings of shame, guilt, powerlessness, and confusion that were linked to events they had participated in, incidents they had witnessed, or abuse they had suffered at times overwhelmed them. Images of dead compañeros came to mind; the sense of impotence felt when hearing detainees tortured or seeing a fellow recruit brutally punished came over them; or the helplessness, shame, and learned fear of being restrained, humiliated or physically abused during training returned periodically. At times, these "memories" were brought on by identifiable stimuli—a place, a chance encounter, former recruits' own scars—but often the triggers remained unclear. Descriptions of persistent nightmares, constant anxiety, and insomnia also cut through ex-conscript testimony. Many describe taking refuge in drink or drugs, in an attempt to quiet the nightmares and banish unwanted thoughts. Many withdrew from loved ones and society, quarantining their memories behind emotional or physical distance, and they strategically attempted to avoid places, people, or situations that would bring back the memory of service.[5] Ultimately, forgetting failed, but efforts to not remember reinforced ex-conscript silence.[6]

During a conversation in 2012, Diego C.* (1983–85, Tierra del Fuego) explained that he tried not to remember, because he only ended up crying, describing the memory of military service as a "ghost in the night."[7] In his 2010 written testimony, he describes the "torture," the "humiliation," and the punishments of training, the conditions on the southern front line, and the injuries and emotional scars he carries with him. A psychological report kept with his testimony in the Temuco office of the Agrupación de Reservistas Defensa Nacional IX Region (Association of National Defense Reservists, Ninth Region) (Agrupación de Reservistas) notes how, decades after his discharge, news events resembling his experience or reported abuses of power elicit memories and make him anxious. Remembering his service, the report clarified, continued to produce in Diego feelings of anxiety, isolation, helplessness, and sadness. Beyond his desire and ultimately unsuccessful efforts to forget, the psychologist also outlined additional pressures that had maintained Diego's silence. His "vivid memories of his experience in military service" had been "repressed first by the fear produced by threats and later in order to emotionally protect his family."[8] The clinician went on to position his client's descriptions of "experiences, in which soldiers mistreated him in the army" in opposition to his "great sense of loyalty" toward the institution and his recognition of "good people" who had helped him during his service. In his own testimony, however, Diego conflated his fidelity and his fears: "I never notified my superiors [of an injury sustained during training] because in those days, you could not make complaints, because we were under a military government. Furthermore, a complaint of that nature could have affected the treatment I received from my superiors, because for them a good soldier had to be strong. In addition, they always instilled in us a great sense of loyalty to the institution, for that reason it took us as an organization so long to come forward with our complaints. Now, we don't have this fear that we had several years ago, and many compatriots have kept their hardship in their hearts."[9] Diego's silence had been compounded by a sense of loyalty that was difficult to disentangle from his fears.

Fear, Loyalty, and Pacts of Silence

In the years following the transition to democracy, the Chilean military maintained an unbreakable pact of silence. Officers did not participate in the truth and reconciliation process, and the armed forces refused to hand over information on the disappeared. Institutional loyalty, a sense of honor, and the mutual benefit of not talking kept the pact in place.[10] Ex-conscript silence, however, was different. It settled over individuals' participation in political repression, but also and mostly over their own alleged mistreatment at the hands of instructors. The pact that former conscripts adhered to on leaving the barracks—at times an oath, at others a signed document, but often simply an unwritten understanding—was a more complex mix.[11] It was shaped by what remained of recruits' institutional loyalty that predated their service, and at times pride in their perceived role in safeguarding Chile; the indoctrination or degradation of military training; the conflation of talking about their service with treason; an ambivalence that discouraged the betrayal the good memories or personal loyalties to individual superiors; a sense of injustice linked not to the institution but to individual officers or instructors; and a conception of masculine toughness that prevented former recruits from denouncing their own abuse.[12] The threads of this brand of "loyalty" were both permeated with and held together by fear. Representing around five hundred former recruits (1973–90) from the Agrupación Puente Alto, human rights lawyer Hernán Montealegre described it in 2009 as an "ill-conceived loyalty to the armed forces," rooted in the "intense subjugation" inflicted on recruits to "separate their moral, legal and even institutional foundations from the cruel treatment they received and the illegal orders they had to obey," and compounded by the "obvious terror" of narrating their experiences.[13]

Fear on the outside was often an extension of a sense of the insecurity and vulnerability felt inside the barracks. Brutal training methods and arbitrary punishments to instill obedience, as well as persecution for actual or perceived political opinions, sustained constant anxiety. The fear that had underpinned military discipline and loyalty continued to affect ex-conscripts long after returning to civilian life. The armed forces controlled society, and the extent of their reach and influence was often reinforced by specific threats made by superiors to harm recruits' families, to harm recruits, or to "leave them forever silent under the dunes" should they talk about what they experienced or what they witnessed.[14] A.E.G.V. (1973–74, Angol), for example, wrote decades after his service about his desire to erase his memories of participating in the detention of "defenseless people." He considered the majority innocent: *campesinos* (peasants) accused of hoarding food for having several kilos of flour, and others beaten before having their hunting rifles confiscated. Opponents of the regime, he argued, were more rightly targeted. Many were tortured, even pregnant women, and those who tried to escape were shot. At the time of his testimony, he still suffered from nightmares about the "punishments, whippings, tortures and humiliations" that he and his fellow recruits had suffered, and he was wary of revealing his story: "I still fear reprisals from officers, sub-officers, and army personnel for giving this testimony, and I fear losing my job. Many years have passed, but the terrible fear that we felt, that they manipulated us with, marked our lives forever, and it seems the terror is here to stay."[15] Juan de la

Cruz Uribe (Puerto Montt, 1978), too, testified that he had "spent a lot a time afraid": "I never considered denouncing it [mistreatment at the hands of superiors]," he said, "because the army was all-powerful and they would have harmed me. They made me swear an oath of silence."[16] The vigilance described by many former recruits recalls the internalized surveillance identified by Diamela Eltit. In her 1994 novel *The Custody of the Eyes*, Eltit dissects the claustrophobia, atomization, self-control, anxiety, and suspicion of life under Chilean authoritarianism. An atmosphere of mistrust and repression hangs over society but also invades its intimate spaces, shaping the home lives and personal interactions of characters who police their own thoughts and behaviors.[17] In a similar way, ex-conscripts who feared institutional reprisal should they break their silence internalized the control mechanisms of military discipline and intelligence service surveillance.[18] Cracks in this type of loyalty only slowly began to emerge in the years following the end of military rule.

Eduardo F.* (1976–78) identified the transition to democracy as the moment his fear of the armed forces disappeared. "Until the start of democracy," he said, "one could not talk because of the oaths of honor taken inside, where one had to keep everything in the military and die quiet [*piola*] like a good Chilean. And we had the fear that military contacts were everywhere and could have found out."[19] Some former recruits pointed to different moments after 1990, others continued to live with fear, and others still could not pinpoint the time that their fear faded. It is likely that what seem in hindsight to be watershed moments were experienced as messier and less definitive processes. Nevertheless, it is clear that almost all former recruits who described having been afraid ascribed their fear of the institution to Pinochet and "his" intelligence service. "[Before] there was Pinochet" was the simple explanation offered in 2011 by Carlos Palma (1973–75, Iquique), president of the Agrupación SMO, for decades of ex-conscript silence.[20] In 2013 Hernán Montealegre spoke similarly of ex-conscript fear and how it was linked to Pinochet's continued power after the transition, as well as the reach of the intelligence service.[21] Seventeen years earlier, in 1996, former recruit "Cristián" (1973) nearly called off an interview with historian Steve Stern. During the subsequent meeting, Cristián explained to Stern how he had been overcome by fear, and pointed out that Pinochet was still head of the army and the intelligence services were still in operation. He feared the consequences for himself and his family if he talked, and he described democracy in Chile as not yet "full."[22] Throughout the 1990s, Pinochet had embodied military and civilian relations, and the institutional safeguards he had negotiated had shaped the country's "protected democracy." From around the turn of the century, domestic traction on accountability, Pinochet's arrest in London, the cumulative effect of scandals involving the general and his family, political pragmatism on the right, and generational renewal of military leadership produced a significant shift in the Chilean public's perception of the former dictator.[23] Fear of reprisal among former recruits abated slowly and unevenly, but there was a general correlation between the erosion of ex-conscript fear and the general's increasing vulnerability before the courts and fading influence on public life.

Wariness of the military apparatus and intelligence service nevertheless still cut through the mobilization of ex-conscripts during the first decade of the twenty-first century. Soon after the Agrupación SMO formed, the group closed their meetings in downtown Santiago to outsiders and implemented a policy of checking identification cards at the door.[24] Organizers had begun to suspect the group had been infiltrated, and leaders in different parts of Chile harbored similar suspicions. Some members remained cautious about talking, but for leaders the omnipresence of the military and the intelligence services had evolved into a less inhibiting awareness that their activities were being monitored. They felt able to talk, despite being certain that their phone calls were being listened to and their emails read. During a conversation in a café in a Providencia mall, president of the Santiago-based Agrupación Ex Soldados Conscriptos (Ex-Conscript Soldier Association), Fernando Mellado, was convinced that a young man at the next table was using his BlackBerry to record what was being said.[25] In Temuco, another confirmed that "all our phones are bugged, especially the Entel ones," while other representatives present in the office nodded in agreement.[26] Beyond fear of the armed forces as an institution, however, ex-conscript silence also worked on a much more local level.

Political repression was often personal, especially in rural areas. Civilians collaborated with the armed forces, political persecution was used to cloak personal grievances, and victims often knew their tormentors.[27] Silence, too, was intimate, as former prisoners and victims' families at times lived in the same neighborhoods and walked the same streets as those who had inflicted their pain.[28] For conscripts leaving regional barracks, in particular, the reach of the armed forces was far less abstract than the threat of the intelligence service. The Tucapel Regiment in Temuco, for example, is prominently positioned in town on the site of the original fort that established the city as a military base on the southern frontier in the conflict with the indigenous population in the late nineteenth century, nestled between the Cautín River and Plaza Recabarren. The commercial and administrative center of town shifted to the edges of the Plaza de Armas a couple of blocks away, but the barracks and the weight of the town's military history still anchor Temuco. When Omar Arías first entered the regiment in March 1975, greater Temuco was home to around 170,000 people, and his experience straddles the intimacy of repression and the intimacy of ex-conscript fear.[29] Arías had had a verbal alter-cation with a soldier in the house he was renting that ended with punches being thrown. A few days later, a patrol came to Arías's mother's house, where he was lying low. They asked him "where the guns were" and insisted he was a communist over the teenager's denials. He was taken to the regiment, where he was interrogated on several occasions over six days about the whereabouts of "the guns," threatened with death, and had electrical current applied to his abdomen. The following year, he reentered the barracks after being called up to the same regiment to complete his military service.

At the end of 2013, Arías, now a bus driver in Temuco, publicly revealed information about the possible whereabouts of people who had been disap-peared. On several occasions, he told the local press, around forty conscripts carrying small shovels had crawled from the regiment to a part of the training ground on Cautín Island behind the barracks and an area where it was apparent that heavy machinery had been used: "They told us that communist assholes [*huevones*] were buried there." The conscripts' job was to use their tools to make it appear as if the ground had never been disturbed. Arías's public state-ment added weight to rumors about Cautín Island that had long circulated in Temuco. He had previously only told his children and his mother, and his family had been concerned about him going public with the information. They feared he might be linked to those violations and detained. Arías, however, was no longer afraid, he insisted.[30] Nevertheless, shortly after his revelations appeared in the local newspaper, he reported threats he had received to the Policía de Investigaciones (Investigations Police). Someone had called his cell phone twice, saying "that they would be visiting him at his house" after what he had told journalists.[31]

Further north, the criminal case launched by ex-conscripts in the Agru-pación Puente Alto codified confrontations between ex-recruits and their former superiors, as members made allegations against individual members of the armed forces.[32] When group leaders Pedro Cáceres and Manuel Ureta were drafted in 1973, Puente Alto was a village of around 85,000 on the out-skirts of Santiago.[33] Four decades later, it had been met by the capital's urban sprawl and sat on the edge of the metropolis and the southern end of the subway network. Pedro (1973–76) was drafted in Puente Alto and later spent time as a guard in Villa Grimaldi, a DINA compound on the outskirts of Santiago where prisoners were tortured and disappeared. In 2013 he spoke of how he was made to sign a document asserting that he would forget everything he saw and did. His own involvement in the group's case centered on allegations made against the retired colonel and ex-DINA agent Marcelo Moren Brito. "Today Marcelo Moren Brito would be about eighty years old, he's a prisoner in [the] Punta

Peuco [prison]," Pedro said. "I'm not afraid these days." Moren Brito was jailed in 2004 as part of an arc of transitional justice that began in the late 1990s and resulted in a series of high-profile sentences in the first decade of the twenty-first century. Other members among the almost five hundred former recruits involved in the case, however, were making accusations against officers who were not in prison, and some who still lived in Puente Alto.[34]

Pedro and Manuel told their stories and spoke of the group's legal case during a radio interview on the fortieth anniversary of the coup in 2013. The buildup to the four-decade milestone had been tense, and given the annual potential for confrontation on the streets, a car was sent for Pedro and Manuel. On air, Manuel described how, growing up in Puente Alto, he had known many of the detainees who arrived at the regiment. In one instance, he and his compañero took the decision to let prisoners out of the vehicles they arrived in to stretch their legs. As a result, he explained, he was subjected to a mock execution and further interrogation. He participated in raids in nearby poblaciones and later heard, while standing guard outside, the whirring of the same machine that had been used on him as it was used to interrogated prisoners. Talking about the interview several months later, Manuel described how his brother was waiting to embrace him when he was dropped back at his home, after he had heard parts of Manuel's story for the first time on the radio. This moment with his brother provided a bookend to a long and private silence that Manuel had earlier explained with reference to a moment soon after his discharge in 1975. Not long after leaving the barracks, he had attended a family event where a cousin slapped him on the shoulder and asked him, "How many did you kill?" Recounting this incident was the first time during the conversation (in which he also spoke of his experience of the coup and his mistreatment at the hands of his superiors) that Manuel's composure broke. Alongside the "terrible fear" of the army that Manuel felt after his discharge—they knew where he lived, he insisted—a deep sense of societal rejection had also fortified his silence.[35]

Fear, Stigma, and Transitional Justice

In December 1974 Mario Navarro's brother died. His body was found on the streets of Arica without any papers and with fatal head injuries. No investigation was undertaken at the time, but almost forty years later his body was removed from the family niche and an autopsy was performed as part of a belated inquiry. Mario spoke in April 2013 of the investigation and a lawyer who had suggested in court that his brother's death could be related to common criminality. His brother was no criminal, countered Mario, and in Arica at that time, there was no crime. He knew, he insisted, because he had helped enforce the curfew. Mario had been in the barracks for almost two years when "they" killed his brother. His mother never quite believed that he did not know what had happened. Until the day she died, she continued to ask Mario if he knew who had killed his brother. Mario recounted this story after a meeting of the Agrupación SMO he attended in Santiago, when the conversation drifted to the feelings of isolation and discrimination many felt. As the last members to leave loitered in the car park, he spoke of his brother's death and his mother's questions to illustrate the direct or implied accusations that recruits faced when they reentered civilian society and how deep the suspicions ran.[36]

Leaving the barracks, ex-conscripts returned to a society undone by fear. "Chile was and is afraid," wrote journalist Patricia Politzer in 1989. "For some it was the fear of the army; for others, of unemployment; for still others, of poverty, informers, repression, communism, Marxists, chaos, violence or terrorism. Each person had his or her own." Politzer had first diagnosed Chile as a country afraid in 1985. Her book *Fear in Chile* presented interviews with people across political, class, and ideological divides whose stories were united by an underlying anxiety. Fear had emerged as a central political variable in the years before the coup, and it became the defining feature of life under military rule. Social bonds broke under the weight of suspicion and mistrust, and Chileans lived withdrawn and insular "half-lives."[37] It was here that the ex-conscript desire to forget and fear of institutional reprisal met anxiety about what their loved ones, friends, and strangers would say, along with fears of rejection and revenge from civilians.[38]

Many recruits grew up in, and were later discharged to, the poblaciones and regional centers that bore the brunt of the repression. Claudio de la Hoz (1973–75), for example, served in his hometown of Chillán and had welcomed his call-up in April 1973. After the coup, he participated in local raids, including one in nearby Bulnes with *carabineros* (police). They found nothing, but one of the carabineros beat a youngster just "for the fun of it" (*de puro gusto*), until a quarrel broke out between the police and the soldiers. Claudio later patrolled the streets and, he insisted, never mistreated anyone. He and his compañeros detained drunks and people breaking the curfew, taking them to "The Sheraton," which was a fenced area, eight meters by three meters, where they spent the night. Prisoners were tortured, he explained, in a place he never entered. They saw prisoners come in, but they never knew what became of them and whether they left alive or dead. Outside, the repression cut through Claudio's community. His uncle was arrested and tortured, and four friends from his neighborhood were killed. While still a conscript, he was attacked one night with a broken bottle on his way to the barracks by three people accusing him of being a murderer. Later, he said he received death threats. When things changed, "they" said, Claudio would be the first they would kill. He felt condemned by society as a murderer and a criminal.[39] For Patricio Farías, too, the sense of persecution began while still completing his service. On weekend leave, and just like he did when on guard duty, he felt threatened from all sides and feared being shot. That anxiety remained when he was discharged. Returning to an atmosphere of mistrust or isolation, most recruits did not talk about service with their families, wives, neighbors, colleagues, or, later, their children, for fear of their reactions, reprisals, or being denounced.[40] While often an unspoken tension or internalized anxiety, this dynamic was also verbalized as taunts ("Murderer!") and accusations ("How many did you kill?").[41] In late 2013 Hernán Montealegre recognized the silencing effects of this type of stigma. His clients were labeled murderers when they left the barracks, he explained, and this characterization kept them quiet for many years.[42] The insults later followed ex-conscript group activity, too, as familiar accusations peppered the comments' sections on the limited online media coverage of the groups' protests or demands.[43]

Former recruits' descriptions of the pervasive mistrust and discrimination seem difficult to reconcile with accompanying accounts of their enthusiasm to serve.[44] This apparent paradox needs to be understood, however, in the context of the cultural significance of service, the different life stages of prospective recruit and reservist, and the retrospective workings of memory. The societal awakening to the human rights crisis was slow and fitful, fear grew unevenly, taboo smothered talk of politics, and the reinforcement of the official narrative of salvation was, particularly throughout the 1970s, relatively successful. More important than the effects of creeping awareness, however, many boys drafted between 1973 and 1990—perhaps most—wanted to do their service, driven by motivations that typically emerged from a sense of patriotism and economic opportunity far removed from the contemporaneous political repression or human rights abuses. Distinct from the exclusive and politicized patria of the internal struggle, recruits' patriotic fervor was a brand of nationalistic pride built on the commemorative echo of nineteenth-century military victories. Moreover, for boys in the popular sectors, service was often perceived as the sole opportunity to be trained, find work, find better work, or, for the more ambitious, have a stable career as a professional soldier. However, after leaving the barracks, they often found that their experience—or assumptions about their experience—had been incorporated into a broader national story that included them as perpetrators. Remembering this experience within a shared framework of rupture also imposes a strict before-and-after duality on ex-conscript memory that pivots around recruits' time in the barracks. In reality, elements of their private sense of discrimination more likely evolved slowly, unevenly, and parallel to the nation's memory struggle.

The sense of isolation felt by many former recruits deepened with the truth and reconciliation process of the posttransition decade. State-led reconciliation legitimized victims on both sides of the political divide but excluded ex-conscripts.[45] In the text of a 2010 civil suit presented on behalf of a group based in Maipú, lawyer Washington Lizana describes how the "social denial" of the physical and psychological mistreatment of his clients—former recruits who served between 1973 and 1990—had compounded their suffering. This denial, combined with the mistrust that permeated social interactions, wrote Lizana, compelled these men to keep their experiences private. Isolation and marginalization, in turn, bred feelings of guilt and responsibility for the treatment they received, produced self-destructive behaviors, led to low self-esteem, and lay at the heart of the difficult or failed reorganization of their lives. Lizana outlined the effects of fear on families, most notably "the rule of silence, extremely rigid family relations, [and] domestic violence." The lawyer also related the feeling reported by individual ex-conscripts that the pressures on them increased after the transition:

> It is clear, that given the concealment of the reality that has been verified during the democratic period, a sector of our society views those who were forced to complete their military service during the time of the military government with mistrust and suspicion, if not hostility, which has meant a true stigmatization of these Chileans, who, as we have indicated, and just like those who suffered the harshness of the military government due to their political and social convictions, experienced mistreatments, abuse and torture. The lack of awareness of the tragic reality that my clients experienced in their youth ensures that many Chileans unjustly identify them with the perpetrators and oppressors, becoming a true state of discrimination that denied them a reinsertion into their working and social life.[46]

The impasse and irruptions of Chilean memory in the 1990s did not include space for former recruits, and conscript victimhood was compatible with neither of the grand narratives of military rule. This lack of room was later made clear, when ex-conscript claims bounced between the church, the armed forces, and human rights groups without finding an audience, and ex-conscripts were excluded from the process managed by the Valech Commission.[47] The feeling of marginalization noted by Lizana, and the posttransition sense of abandonment and rejection expressed by Patricio, was further reinforced as the layers of immunity that had protected perpetrators of crimes of repression began to erode.

The trajectory of transitional justice began to turn away from impunity at the end of the 1990s, and high-profile officers began serving prison sentences for crimes of repression around the time ex-conscript groups began to emerge. Among former recruits, the gradual dismantling of the social and judicial conditions that had protected the military and entrenched its influence was directly related to the reduction of the fear of institutional reprisal. It also, however, compounded and seemed to institutionalize the stigma and isolation of the conscript experience. Despite some exceptions, ex-conscripts were wary of talking to investigators and afraid of being caught up in human rights cases or prosecuted as accomplices. Fear of prosecution for their role, or assumed role, in crimes against humanity peaked with the revival of the case of Víctor Jara. Jara was a teacher and a much-loved musician, singer, and songwriter, and an iconic artist of the New Song movement, a mix of folklore and social commentary that provided the soundtrack to the revolutionary politics of the 1960s and the Chilean path to socialism of the early 1970s. The day following the coup, he was detained and taken to the improvised prison camp inside the Chile Stadium. Over three days, he was tortured and beaten in the stadium's dressing rooms. On September 16, his disfigured and bullet-ridden corpse was found among five others that had been abandoned on the southern outskirts of Santiago. At the time, rumors of his death and the manner in which he died fueled fears among prisoners, as well as shock at the brutality and reach of the repression.[48] In the decades since, and as one of the regime's most high-profile victims, Jara has become symbolic of the human rights abuses carried out under the dictatorship. The stadium where he was tortured and killed was renamed in his memory in 2003.[49]

In 2008 the four-year investigation into Jara's death was closed, with only retired lieutenant colonel Mario Manríquez, who had been in charge of the detention center inside the stadium, found to bear any responsibility. Shortly after, and as a result of pressure from Jara's family and their lawyer Nelson Caucoto, Judge Juan Eduardo Fuentes reopened his investigation. As part of the appeal to reopen the case, Jara's family had provided new information and called for former conscripts to come forward. It was in this context that José Paredes Márquez (1973) approached investigators.[50] Paredes was subsequently transported to Santiago's high-security prison after he confessed to his part in Jara's death.[51] In May 2009 he walked investigators through the stadium and the details of how Jara was killed. He recalled how he and fellow conscript Francisco Quiroz had been ordered to escort a group of prisoners to a dressing room where Lieutenant Nelson Haase was waiting. He spoke of watching

Sublieutenant Pedro Barrientos play Russian roulette with the singer, firing a bullet into his head, and he described seeing Jara slump to the floor and begin to convulse. Paredes was then, according to his confession, among the conscripts who followed the order to fire at the body.[52] Barrientos and Haase disputed the ex-conscript's version of events, and Quiroz admitted he was with Paredes between September 12 and 15, but insisted neither of them were in the stadium. Paredes soon retracted his confession, saying he had felt pressured to confess during his four-hour interview, and that he had been drunk when detained. He now insisted that on the day Jara died, his section was instead transferred from its base in Tejas Verdes to downtown Santiago.

While Paredes was retracting his confession, efforts were being made to substantiate his original story. The Human Rights Brigade interviewed seventy former conscripts who had been in the stadium on September 15, 1973, and, on the judge's instruction, the Forensic Medical Service (Servicio Médico Legal, or SML) performed an autopsy on Jara's exhumed remains. The SML found that the bullet wounds, including two bullet holes in Jara's skull, were consistent with Paredes's original confession that Jara was shot by the sublieutenant nicknamed El loco (The madman) during a game of Russian roulette, and that the same sublieutenant then ordered conscripts to shoot at the body. However, the forensic evidence also seemed to exonerate the former recruit. It identified the type of weapons used, none of which corresponded to the rifle Paredes successfully identified by its serial number as the one he carried as a conscript. On the strength of this evidence, and after forty-eight days in detention, Paredes was released. He explained that he was able to give detailed descriptions of events and places "from comments made, because everyone was talking about it, that they had killed him in the Chile Stadium, that they had returned to finished him off, and later that they had found him dead."[53]

The sight of Paredes on television in handcuffs sent shockwaves through ex-conscript networks. Attendance at the regular meetings of the Agrupación Puente Alto fell from around five hundred to one hundred immediately after his arrest, estimated Pedro Cáceres in early 2014. Manuel Ureta asked hypothetically if anyone was going to talk about bodies being dropped from helicopters after the Jara case. Of course not, he also answered.[54] At the same time across town, Paola García, who helped with the administration of the Agrupación SMO, fielded phone calls from members who feared being compelled to give evidence as part of the investigation.[55] The case highlighted the potential silencing effect of transitional justice. However, it also had a parallel ripple effect. Ex-conscripts who followed the case closely tended to link their fate very much to that of Paredes, viewing the charges against him as a test case for their own arguments. Despite his eventual release being based on a lack of evidence, many former recruits interpreted it as a vindication of their insistence that they should not be considered responsible for the coup or human rights abuses.[56] A similar dynamic rocked ex-conscript communities six years later with the reopening of the *caso quemados* (case of the burned ones) from the mid-1980s.

Early in the morning on July 2, 1986, in the context of a planned two-day national protest and the preceding years of unrest, a group of young people prepared a barricade using tires that they would later set on fire. Military patrols were also on the streets in anticipation of the protest, and one such patrol intercepted the youths. Most of the protesters escaped, but soldiers detained eighteen-year-old Carmen Gloria Quintana and nineteen-year-old Rodrigo Rojas de Negri. According to the military version of events, a device the youths had been carrying accidentally went off during their arrest, setting the detainees on fire. Rojas and Quintana were found later the same day abandoned on the edge of the city. Rojas died four days later and Quintana survived with terrible scarring to her face and most of her body. The case became emblematic of the lengths the regime would go to in the face of opposition, and it helped establish a visceral and urgent link between atrocities of the preceding decade and the protest scene of the moment. Quintana became an important symbol for those on the street, and the incident also resonated beyond national borders, particularly in the United States, where Rojas had been living in exile with his family. The young photographer had returned to Chile to reconnect with his homeland, and his death cost the regime any remaining support from the Reagan administration.[57] In 1991 the military justice system accepted the official version of events. It deemed no one responsible for Rojas's death or the burning of Quintana but found Lieutenant Pedro Fernández Dittus guilty of negligence for his role in denying the detainees medical treatment. He was sentenced to six hundred days in prison in 1993.

The case was reopened in 2015 on the strength of the 2014 statement given by ex-conscript Fernando Guzmán (1986, Santiago). Guzmán testified that he and around ten other recruits had been on a truck patrolling the streets in the commune of Estación Central on the morning of the protest.[58] When his unit arrived at the scene, the two protesters were already in custody of soldiers under the command of lieutenants Julio Castañer and Fernández, who had arrived in two other vehicles. Castañer, who was dressed as a civilian, ordered a recruit to douse Quintana and Rojas in petrol, before abusing the prisoners and threatening them with a lighter. In line with Quintana's 1987 testimony to Amnesty International, Guzmán testified that Castañer used the lighter to set the protesters alight.[59] Quintana began to run, but conscripts caught her and used blankets to put out the flames, while a sergeant smothered the fire engulfing

Rojas. According to Guzmán, he then heard Castañer suggest to Fernández that it would be better to kill them, but Fernández rejected the idea on the grounds that he was a Catholic. Instead, the lieutenants ensured that Rojas and Quintana were left for dead on the edge of the city.

In his 2014 testimony, and in a 2015 television interview, Guzmán declared that he had lied in his 1986 statement. He explained that two weeks after the incident, he and his fellow recruits were given preprepared statements, which they learned and delivered to military investigators. They also participated in a series of re-creations of the scene designed to bolster the lie that the protesters had accidentally set themselves on fire. After giving their false testimony on Fernández's and Castañer's orders, the recruits were addressed by General Santiago Sinclair, who at the time was second-in-command of the army. According to Guzmán, Sinclair assured the recruits that nothing would happen to them, and they should instead worry about their families. The recruit interpreted the suggestion as a threat. He recalled wanting to confess the lie to Quintana during a reenactment but being unable to get past his fear. He was again threatened toward the end of 1987 after voicing concerns about the case within the regiment. Nearly twenty years after the incident, he insisted that he was still afraid those threats could be made good on. Threats were also coupled with economic incentives, with recruits receiving money and permits. In the days following Guzmán's appearance on television and Castañer's arrest, another ex-conscript came forward. Pedro Franco Rivas (1986, Santiago) had been in the vehicle with Fernández, and gave an account that aligned with Guzmán's testimony. He named Castañer as the person who set Rojas and Quintana alight, detailed how he had received a preprepared statement in the wake of the incident, and described a similar dynamic of incentives and threats to maintain his silence.[60]

The reaction among ex-conscripts to Guzmán's 2015 televised interview recalled the response to Paredes's testimony in the Jara case. On August 5 around one hundred former recruits representing different regions gathered in the Plaza de los Héroes in Santiago. The leadership addressing the crowd expressed their solidarity with Guzmán as well as Verónica de Negri—Rojas's mother—and Quintana, and they welcomed the reception of Guzmán's testimony as a confirmation of their own place in the processes of reconciliation—the coalition had only months earlier changed its name from the Agrupación Nacional de Ex Soldados Conscriptos del Servicio Militar Obligatorio período 1973–1990 (National Association of Ex Conscript Soldiers for the Period 1973–1990) to the Corporación para la Integración de los Derechos Humanos de los Ex Conscriptos del período 1973–1990 (Corporation for the Integration of the Human Rights of Ex-conscripts from the Period 1973–1990).[61] Apart from hope, however, leaders also spoke of having been forgotten and pointed to lingering fears. One speaker noted how, in the wake of Guzmán's interview, ex-conscripts had been called on to break the pact of silence: "What pact of silence?" he asked rhetorically. "We don't have a pact of silence with anyone. We were threatened."[62] Some were still afraid, for others the fear had subsided, or as in Guzmán's case, was still there but no longer overwhelmed the desire to talk. While the sense of openness and possibility was perhaps greater in 2015 than it was in 2009, beneath it there was still deep-rooted fear. As with the Jara case, the quemados case sent concerned, at times panicked, murmurs through private networks, as ex-conscripts feared being involved in the legal proceedings, retribution, or both.[63] Beyond the movement, the ex-conscript as witness also raised questions about responsibility and morality with regard to crimes of repression and ex-conscript silence.

Responsibility and the Morality of Silence

In 2009, and shortly after Paredes's confession, Jara's widow Joan Turner insisted that she harbored no ill feeling toward the "kids": "For those kids—I say kids, because they were only 18—I confess that have no feelings of vengeance towards them. They have lived for 37 years with what they did, or at least one of them has now confessed." She spoke of her intention to find "the people who gave the orders," "those who are morally responsible for all of this."[64] At the same time, and just as he had done when the case was closed in May 2008, Caucoto reiterated his call to former conscripts to come forward with information.[65] He also made it clear that the family was not pursuing them: "We are not interested in going after conscripts, I should be clear: the conscripts are a part of the whole, but the weakest part, the most vulnerable part and we cannot make them responsible." He later added: "I am interested in the bosses who ordered the execution of Víctor Jara."[66] Three years later, as part of a Chilevisión report on a request to the armed forces made by the minister of defense, Andrés Allamand, for the names of all personnel in the stadium at the time of Jara's death, neuropsychiatrist and prominent human rights advocate Paz Rojas spoke of conscripts as having been forced to torture or kill, and to obey orders at times against their own principles. They deserve, she continued, reparations and medical benefits from the army.[67] Carlos Palma (1973, Iquique), president of the Agrupación SMO, kept the clip of Rojas's interview on the computer behind the counter in his Ñuñoa grocery store. He insisted that he had had no involvement with human rights violations but also spoke in broader terms of those who had been implicated as having no choice.[68] The Jara case played an important role in revealing how ex-conscript memory dealt with the issue of ex-conscript responsibility for crimes of repression.

Conscripts under Pinochet did, at times, kill, beat, shoot, shoot at, or detain civilians, and participate in firing squads or the torture of detainees. Most, however, did not. The Rettig Report lists nearly 2,300 victims of death or disappearance, and the Valech Report names approximately 30,000 victims of political imprisonment or torture between 1973 and 1990. The number of dead or disappeared was revised up by nearly 1,000 in 1996, and again by 30 in 2011. Also in 2011, almost 10,000 names were added to the list of victims of political imprisonment or torture. These figures represent a massive and systematic abuse of human rights that directly or indirectly affected a significant part of the Chilean population. Nevertheless, the numbers fall well short of the number of recruits, meaning most draftees were unlikely to be involved in the deaths or torture of detainees. For example, in the most violent period of the dictatorship, between the coup and the end of 1973, the Rettig Report lists 1,261 people as killed or disappeared, while around 20,000 young men were serving as conscripts. The official figures are, however, conservative. They exclude cases that could not meet the Rettig and Valech Commissions' standards of proof and cases of torture that were silenced by the victims' ongoing shame, fear, and desire not to relive the experience. The true numbers are likely higher with credible but unofficial estimates suggesting that up to 4,500 people were killed or disappeared and up to 200,000 were imprisoned or tortured for political reasons. However, the unofficial numbers still fall short of the approximately 370,000 recruits who passed through the barracks. Moreover, acts of political repression were not solely the responsibility of the military. According to the Valech Report, the number of people detained between the coup and the end of 1973, for example, was more than 18,000 and the number of detentions reached 23,000. A little more than 42 percent of these detentions were carried out by the carabineros, and a little under 42 percent were carried out by the branches of the armed forces that drafted conscripts: the army, navy, and air force. From early 1974, the massive detention and torture that characterized the first months of military rule gave way to more targeted programs headed by the DINA (1974–77), and later the CNI (1978–90). From the end of 1973 to March 1990, more than 10,000 arrests, affecting nearly 9,000 people, were carried out predominantly by the carabineros and the intelligence services.[69] During this same period, approximately 350,000 recruits were called up to serve.

Figures on deaths, imprisonment, and torture do not reveal the roles conscripts played in transporting or guarding prisoners, intimidating civilians in their homes or on the street, or raiding poblaciones. They clarify neither the cooperation between services, nor the varied degrees of integration of conscripts into the professional ranks and the intelligence services.[70] Equally, they do not quantify what conscripts witnessed as bystanders, and they cannot capture the motivations of individual recruits involved in human rights violations or recruits' attitudes toward military rule and political repression more generally. Nevertheless, a conservative assumption would suggest that the majority of the recruits called up during the period covered by the ex-conscript movement were neither directly nor indirectly involved in the types of violations of human rights investigated by Chile's truth and reconciliation commissions. Even where conscript participation in crimes of repression did occur, sweeping statements about conscripts as perpetrators or victims are complicated by the range of situations that could lead to participation, the degrees of participation, superiors' use of threats, the abuse of the chain of command, and the scope for the categories of victim and perpetrator to overlap. While it cannot provide a map for the conscript experience under Pinochet, the strict victim/perpetrator binary, and the opposing and totalizing conceptions of responsibility it underpins, is essential to understanding ex-conscript narratives and ex-conscript silence.

Turner's characterization of recruits as kids resonated with ex-conscripts, who, in the context of the movement, had typically expressed their sense of powerlessness by emphasizing how young they had been when conscripted. They rejected the idea of conscript responsibility, pointing out that they had been younger than twenty-one years of age and legally minors at the time of their service.[71] For many young men who left school and began their working lives in their early teens, and for whom becoming a man was linked to sex, work, marriage, starting a family, and often the rite of military service itself, the age of majority had meant very little. Decades later, however, it was a way to codify their lack of power and their argument that they could not be considered responsible for crimes of repression. The starkness of stigma had made the question of complicity central to ex-conscript memory, as former recruits' collective approach to responsibility evolved in part as a response to their perceptions of societal attitudes. Within the movement, rehabilitating those who had participated in abuses of human rights served as a preemptive move to counter what they saw as the assumption of guilt regarding conscripts under military rule. Given the assumption of complicity, absolving those former recruits who had been involved in human rights abuses was a necessary step toward rehabilitating the entire population of ex-conscripts. The Jara case also added a legal framework to that idea. Hernán Montealegre, who had headed the legal case of the Agrupación Puente Alto since 2007, also represented Paredes after taking on the case pro bono. Paredes was not a member of the

Puente Alto group or any other, but many mobilized ex-recruits rallied around him as a broader defense of their own cause. In 2009, and while denying that his client was in the stadium when Jara died, Montealegre made a general statement about conscript responsibility: "From a legal perspective, any conscript who acts, whether shooting a person or committing a crime, is absolved of any criminal responsibility. The only person with any criminal responsibility is the superior who gave the order."[72] This line publicly echoed the position he took when representing the nearly five hundred former recruits involved in the case, "more than fifteen" of whom—according to an estimate by group president Pedro Cáceres—had obeyed orders to shoot.[73] In the text of the case, Montealegre cited the concept of duress and Article 31 of the Rome Statute of the International Criminal Court, which outlines the grounds for excluding criminal responsibility:

> d) The conduct which is alleged to constitute a crime within the jurisdiction of the Court has been caused by *duress* resulting from a threat of imminent death or of continuing or imminent serious bodily harm against that person or another person, and the person acts *necessarily* and reasonably to avoid this threat, provided that the person *does not intend* to cause a greater harm than the one sought to be avoided. Such a threat may either be:
> (i) made by other persons; or
> (ii) *constituted by other circumstances beyond that person's control.*[74]

He also cited the principle of due obedience.

Due obedience is covered in Article 214 of the Chilean Military Code of Justice and stipulates that the responsibility for a crime committed under orders lies with the party giving the order.[75] The legal limits of this defense were tested at around the time the Jara case first reemerged. In early 2008 General Gonzalo Santelices was forced to resign after a newspaper reported his 2002 witness statement, in which Santelices acknowledged having participated in the Caravan of Death. Late at night on October 18, 1973, the twenty-year-old Santelices and another soldier had driven fourteen prisoners from Antofagasta into the desert, where they were brutally murdered by officers. The two young men then loaded the corpses back onto the trucks and delivered them to the morgue in Antofagasta.[76] The investigating judge in 2002, Juan Guzmán, did not charge Santelices, as he had been a freshly graduated sublieutenant. "If he had not obeyed this order," explained Guzmán, "it is most likely that they would have killed him."[77] In 2008, however, the Caravan of Death case was headed by Minister Víctor Montiglio, who did not share Guzmán's reasoning and laid charges against Santelices. The general resigned, saying that he did not want to involve the armed forces in a judicial case and pointing out that, at the time, it had been unthinkable to disobey an order from a superior without risking being shot. The logic of due obedience rejected by Montiglio when he laid charges, and alluded to by Santelices when he resigned, also became the line of the former general's legal defense. The defense was rejected. The Supreme Court had, in fact, not applied Article 214 to any person charged with crimes of repression since 2007.[78] Among the public rejections of Santelices's defense of due obedience there was nonetheless a recognition of the difficulty in not following an order.[79] The Amnesty International director in Chile, Sergio Laurenti, for example, reiterated that "due obedience was not admissible as a defense." He acknowledged the difficulty in not following an order but also pointed out that Santelices had stayed in the army and kept quiet all these years.[80] Santelices's silence, and the associated benefit to the progress of his military career, underscored the ethical dimension of memory and testimony.[81] Ex-conscript memory was confronted with a similar moral code.

Both former recruits and representatives of victims' groups eliminated any gray area in their understanding of conscript complicity.[82] On the one hand, the ex-conscript narrative included participation in crimes of repression within the broader sense of victimhood by pointing to the recruits' youth, arguing that they were following orders, and emphasizing the existential threat associated with not following orders. On the other hand, representatives of victims' groups tended to conflate members of ex-conscript groups with perpetrators of human rights violations. In particular, victims' representatives dismissed the idea of ex-conscript victimhood by pointing to former recruits' silence regarding the fate of the disappeared. Most prominently, Lorena Pizarro, president of the Agrupación de Familiares de Detenidos-Desaparecidos (Association of Relatives of the Detained and Disappeared) (AFDD), evoked a morality of memory, suggesting that former recruits' silence disqualified them as victims. In 2014, for example, she conceded that "they were conscripts, we cannot deny that their lives were in danger," before adding, "They never cooperated with the judiciary, never provided information. Then they re-appear, declaring themselves as victims, saying they had to obey orders, asking for indemnity, and in some kind of schizophrenia of state terrorism, they transform themselves from victimizers into victims."[83] She insisted they could have come forward since the transition but had chosen not to do so.[84] The same reasoning can be seen, for example, in public responses to media reports on ex-conscript demands. In July 2014 the Chamber of Deputies approved the latest in a series of nonbinding resolutions (*proyectos de acuerdo*) stretching back to 2007. Resolution 967 requested that President Bachelet award pensions, reparations, and health benefits to ex-conscripts (1973–90), and the first online comment on an article reporting the passage of the resolution came from Reinaldo Segundo Gomez Sanhueza, who remarked, "Mrs. Bachelet, It's the least we deserve." Franklin Solar was the first to respond, asking: "Really???? and when are you going to hand over the details you have on: the killed, the tortured, the disappeared, women who were raped and disappeared, because according to you 'maricones' [faggots], you only received orders from your superiors. Have you provided any names of these 'brave officers'??????"[85] This logic equated silence with complicity and included former recruits reflexively and uncomplicatedly within the military pact of silence. It also positioned information on the disappeared as the prerequisite to participation in public commemorations, debates, or other ways of advancing the cause of truth, justice, or reconciliation.

The reopening of the Jara and quemados cases are concrete examples of ex-conscripts providing important testimony; however, how much useful information about the fate of the disappeared was to be found among the population of former recruits was open to conjecture. Pedro Cáceres, who had put a figure on the level of participation in human rights violations among his group's complainants, doubted how much light those fifteen members out of five hundred giving testimony in the group's case could shed on the murdered and disappeared. He gave the hypothetical example of a conscript who was ordered from his bed and made to participate blindfolded in a firing squad; this man would have little information to offer on the victim's identity or whereabouts, he argued.[86] Conversely, the president of a Santiago-based group, Fernando Mellado, made increasingly bombastic claims about the combined knowledge held by his members. In 2011, when attempting to secure an audience for his demands, he framed the group's capacity to reveal information as both an insurance policy and a bargaining chip, and he claimed that details were not revealed due to a lack of protection for his members.[87] Mellado ratcheted up his statements in 2014, assuring journalists that he could most likely resolve all of the remaining cases of the disappeared.[88] In terms of ex-conscript silence, however, more important than what former recruits knew or did not know were the rules of engagement established as a result of the moral imperative to remember the disappeared and the tortured, and the role of the ex-conscript as a witness to human rights violations.

A gathering of ex-conscripts in August 2015 in the wake of Guzmán's public statement was a mix of established groups with long-standing demands, energized by the conviction that the recent quemados case signaled that transitional justice was now open to ex-conscripts and the movement's claims.[89] The gathering also took place in the context of the Bachelet administration's increased focus on human rights and transitional justice and coincided with renewed and strident calls from victims' groups to abolish the 1978 amnesty law and open the embargoed files from the truth and reconciliation processes. However, ex-conscript witnesses did not feature in this debate as the narrators of their own stories or the experience of military service. Instead, ex-conscript testimony in high-profile cases moved within the logic of the memory contest and did not challenge the morality that drove it. The obligation to remember installed revelations about human rights violations committed against detainees as the point of entry, and it stymied from the outset narratives of ex-conscript victimhood. This gateway was impenetrable to the majority of former recruits whose experiences and testimonies could reveal little to nothing of crimes of repression. The prerequisite to provide information also had little to do with ex-conscripts' own stories, which were most often narratives of personal rupture and included allegations of abuse and mistreatment suffered by the recruits. Their sense of victimhood was rarely linked to a larger memory question, and when such connections were made, they were not made in any consistent manner. Moreover, many within the movement lacked the moral imperative to publicly remember, much less remember publicly in a manner consistent with the ethics of the twenty-first-century memory struggle. Beyond the con-tested issue of the level of conscript responsibility, therefore, the morality of memory that had been so important in driving the human rights movement and, in turn, revealing much of the truth about human rights violations under Pinochet also contributed to the silencing of the ex-conscripts' stories, by de-manding that they be told through the prism of the fate of established victims. This effect compounded other pressures, all of which cut through ex-conscript group activity.

Silence in Groups

The formation of ex-conscript groups from 2006 provided a space where former recruits could share stories among people they felt were able to understand.[90] In 2012 the group REPACH (Reservistas Patrióticos de Chile [Patriotic Reservists of Chile]) Talcahuano celebrated its sixth anniver-sary with a cultural event held in a gymnasium to accommodate the hundreds of people, where the leaders reported back to the group members and their families on the progress that had been made with respect to their demands. Later, a smaller group of guests and regional and national representatives went out to dinner at a local karaoke restaurant. After the food had been served and collective renditions of Chilean standards had been sung, the mood turned solemn. A microphone was passed around the room and, one by one, former recruits told their stories. One of the men talked about his experiences for the first time that night. He spoke deliberately, tearfully, and with his hands clasped in front of him, and he thanked God for the opportunity to share his experience, something he had never thought would be possible.[91] For many, the group context is a source of great camaraderie built on a shared experience, and the only place to talk about that experience. However, the closed doors of group events, meetings, and offices did not completely realign the contours of silence. The same pressures and limits shaped interactions within the movement.

Meetings of the Agrupación SMO (1973) in downtown Santiago were closed to the public and were called every couple of months to update members on the progress of their civil suits. In 2013, progress was slow. The group was appealing the rejection of one of their cases and, given the pace of the judicial process, there was often little to report. What began as questions, comments, or doubts about the group's case often ended up as narrations or re-narrations of what the members present had been through as conscripts.[92] Nods of recognition and interjections of agreement continued the group work of building and maintaining a shared narrative. However, some were still wary of talking, particularly when the meetings were recorded, which they sometimes were, especially when the group's lawyer attended.[93] Less constrained exchanges instead occurred after the conclusion of the meetings, when the camera was turned off, and as members milled about in smaller groups. The least inhibited conversations took place between members who later lingered in the car park outside in even smaller groups. It was predominantly on the edges of these events and gatherings that former recruits spoke most freely about their experiences. It was also where lore was built: descriptions of military weapons being used to stage photos of seized caches of weapons circulated within these peripheral networks; the name of The Prince, the infamously sadistic guard at the Chile Stadium, was shared here before it was publicly known; and various, and sometimes contradictory, accounts of the death of Víctor Jara were embellished in this informal setting, prior to the reemergence of the case.[94]

Ex-conscript lore, and stories that were shared during and on the edges of meetings, rarely made it to paper as part of testimony. President of the Agrupación SMO, Carlos Palma, explained that the group had formed out of a sense of solidarity, and when it shifted toward advocacy and required members to write their memories down, many simply left.[95] Among those who stayed and those who subsequently joined, there remained a tendency to balk at providing written or recorded statements.[96] Many of the testimonies the group did collect included few details, and they were, according to the group's own administration, "not very interesting."[97] They describe the scarcity of food, sleep deprivation during twenty-four-hour guard duty, and how cold it was on the streets of Santiago. During a 2013 conversation in the office of a downtown auto workshop where she worked, group administrator Paola described as "strange" (*los insólitos*) a selection of members who compared their cold, hunger, and extended guard duty with the suffering of the disappeared. Her husband, a mechanic in the workshop, took a break to make himself a coffee and spoke of having been a twenty-year-old conscript in 1973 but wanting nothing to do with the agrupación. Service, for him, had been an enjoyable experience, he explained. Yes, noted Paola, but he did not see any corpses. The insólitos notwithstanding, she also noted what she interpreted as internalized limits that produced the pared-down testimonies many provided. She mentioned a member who began to shake at the thought of talking, and others who seemed to her to hold back.[98] Patricio, a member of the group, explained during an interview how he had left out of his testimony details of his political party membership before entering the barracks. As a teenager, he had been a member of a socialist party: "more than socialist, you could say," he said as he smiled, unwilling to name the party. He explained both his involvement with politics and volunteering for service in the agricultural south as economic decisions; party membership was useful to find work—"[finding work] was the only purpose, I was very naïve in that sense"—and, as a conscript, the army would provide for him for a year. Looking back, he was in part thankful that he had been in the barracks, because had he not been a conscript he could be have been "on the other side": "I would have been detained, because of my background. [. . .] On the one hand, perhaps [military service] was good for me, otherwise I would have been exiled, or disappeared. My story is a little complicated, and [. . .] I haven't told it to anyone else, not even in the agrupación. I didn't say anything. I included only the most basic things, I did not include everything."[99] The first thing he did on returning to civilian life was tear up his membership card.

Details of recruits' experiences were concealed, too, behind the collective voice of the movement. While the safety of the group narrative allowed many to engage with the demands, privately legitimize their own experiences, and publicly or semi-publicly speak about their time in the barracks, it also, at times, obscured as much as it revealed. Héctor L.* (1973), for example, sank into his chair and kept his body language closed when talking about his service. His descriptions were short and short on detail. He later switched to discussing service in the context of the entire cohort, leaning forward to describe the abuse of conscripts in the barracks and common sleep complaints. Héctor was clearly more comfortable talking about the shared experience. It enabled him to open up, but it also buried his story among common themes and shared reference points.[100] Recruits' experiences could also be hidden behind euphemism and omission. One leader of a local group spoke furtively in 2013 of cleaning up a member's testimony. An ex-conscript (1973) had come to him and detailed how he had been forced to beat detainees and shoot at civilians. The group president advised the new member to write instead of his involvement in "transporting" prisoners and "enforcing the curfew." Otherwise, he reasoned, his fellow ex-conscript would be classified as a perpetrator.[101] This type of self-censorship was usually less overt and less considered, resulting instead from an unspoken consensus about what could and could not be talked about.

The group context also often lacked the moral imperative to participate in the truth-making processes of the transition. In 2013 the founding and then former president of the Agrupación SMO, René Rivera (1973), spoke of what he understood to be the reasons behind the ex-conscripts maintaining their silence: fear and ignorance, but also a lack of commitment or sense of responsibility, as well as a dismissal of the political processes.[102] By the time he made his comments, René had scaled back his involvement with the group, but the dynamic he described was on display at a meeting in October 2013. At the meeting, articles about the negotiations of lobby groups and the interest surrounding the recent anniversary of the coup sparked a discussion about whether members should speak out publicly. A press conference was mooted and a plea for people to make public statements was made. It prompted an exchange about the longer-term approach the group had taken between group leaders and several members from the floor. One former recruit linked his claims about his own suffering closely with his loyalty to the group's aims and strategy, indirectly questioning the experiences of another member who had doubts about the path the group had taken. The insinuation hung in the room as the conversation spiraled between the two individual members in the audience and the leaders seated at the front, until the ex-conscript in question felt compelled to address it. He described arriving with other conscripts at a location in 1974 to be confronted with a number of bodies, one of which was the naked corpse of Miguel Enríquez. His job was to load the bodies onto a truck. He described the difficulty of lifting a body so destroyed by bullets, gesticulating to emphasize the formlessness of the corpse. It was something he had never told his wife and children, and something he would not talk about outside the group. He did not see the point; everyone already knows, he insisted, and he would prefer not to tell stories just because people want to hear gory details.

The personal and societal pressures, limits, and strategies that defined the edges of private memory also operated within the ex-conscript movement. Shared memory was shaped by the silences generated by wanting to forget, intimate and abstract fears of the armed forces, personal and generalized fears of marginalization from society, and a moral obligation to first address a memory question unrelated to the experience and sense of victimhood of many former recruits. The emergence of a shared conscript narrative of victimhood did not produce, or result from, a seismic shift in ex-conscript silence. Instead, the ongoing process of adjustment met a decisive cultural moment in the first decade of the twenty-first century, and both can be seen in a 2008 letter from the Agrupación Social de Ex Soldados Conscriptos 1973—Clase 54 in Arica to President Bachelet. In the letter, the group leadership sketched the contours of its approximately 150 members' silence. It described quietly suffering "the ghosts of the past" and gave as examples of this struggle a case of catatonic schizophrenia attributed to the humiliating treatment the former recruit received at the hands of his superiors, various cases of continuing alcohol and drug abuse, attempted suicide inside the barracks, and suicide after being discharged. The letter also addressed both the abstract and intimate fear of institutional retaliation for talking: "The most important [reason for not addressing the issue earlier] was fear of possible reprisals at the hands of Armed Forces' personnel (Intelligence Service), via the systems that still prevailed in our country, (many members were born in Arica or settled in the city, and they regularly recognize, and are recognized by, personnel from the institution who, until a few years ago, were still in the military[)]." Furthermore, the group leaders wrote, there was a lack of political support and a lack of room for them within the state-led truth and reconciliation process. The "reparations laws created by the democratic governments regarding detainees who were disappeared, shot, or tortured and those who lost their jobs [for political reasons, the *exonerados*]," they noted, "did not take into account the general experiences of humiliating treatment, which even included torture, in many cases, suffered by conscripts in the period."[103]

According to the letter, local former recruits had met in June 2008 with the intention of forming a group. They saw reason for hope in the passing of Resolution 287 in 2007. The resolution was a nonbinding petition to the president of the republic, approved by the lower house of Congress, to establish benefits for ex-conscripts who had served in 1973, compensating them for the consequences that service had had for their pensions and the opportunities lost as the result of their conscription, and for their frustrated hopes for employment that recruits had harbored when entering the barracks. It took as a model for reparations the benefits awarded to the exonerados and victims of torture, political imprisonment, or exile, and it made the case for processing ex-conscript demands within the existing institutional framework for reconciliation. From Arica, former recruits reiterated the unmet expectations they had had that they would gain employment or study after being discharged.[104] The shifting contours of silence had converged with state-led memory policy, revelations of the truth of human rights abuses, reparations programs, members' failing and aging bodies, histories of employment difficulty, and a renewed cycle of frustrated social mobility to give shape and voice to ex-conscript victimhood. Elements of this ex-conscript narrative, as well as a language in which to articulate it, only solidified at the beginning of the twenty-first century. The memory of military service must therefore be understood in the moment that the movement emerged.

2

A Movement

In May 2012, in his living room in the población of La Pincoya on the northern periphery of Santiago, Daniel Pizarro (1973–75, Los Andes and Santiago) recounted an incident from September 1973.[1] The week before the coup, he and his fellow recruits had been guarding gas stations around the city and escorting fuel trucks, riding on top with their rifles.[2] On the morning of September 11, they were told that the armed forces had taken La Moneda, and that anyone not wearing the correct color armband—white in the morning, pink (*salmón*) in the afternoon—was a communist and a dead man. In the weeks that followed, they guarded bridges around the capital in shifts that lasted forty-eight to seventy-two hours. One day, on one of the bridges, a carabinero vehicle carrying ten or twelve extremists pulled up in front of Daniel and his fellow recruits. "'Extremists,' that's what they called them," he explained, "but they were Chilean citizens." A captain ordered the conscripts to shoot, but there was one recruit who knew about the constitution and the law, recalled Daniel, and he refused on behalf of the group. The captain assured them that he was the law that day, that they were at war, and that he could kill them for disobeying orders. He could shoot, agreed the same conscript, but he would have to kill them all. The captain turned and shot the "extremists" with a burst of machine-gun fire, almost cutting one of them in half. They all died, some only after pleading to be killed given their horrific wounds. The conscripts stayed with the bodies until the next morning.

That day weighed heavily on Daniel. He described it as "engraved" on his psyche and something that he had to "keep for life and with a lot of pain, on the inside." It was remembered in his daily life, he explained, as the "fatal question" posed by friends or even his own children: "How many did you kill?" "It's like you take on a weight," he said, and while "as a young man, you don't see it that way, these days you do see it that way, because, what's more, in inverted commas, these days I am a Christian and I know that God gives and takes life. [. . .] It's like a weight that we have, and that weight got heavier when [. . .] Pinochet got sick and they discovered that he had three ingots of gold." Pinochet's gold—a reference to the 2004 Riggs bank scandal involving the general, his family, and millions of dollars in secret bank accounts—ran through most of what Daniel remembered. His memory played off the now cynically remembered idea of being told that he was a hero who had liberated the country against the present contradiction between his own continued economic struggle and the Pinochet family fortune. After leaving the barracks, he was chased out of his first job with the Transandine Railway after nine months and began working informally at fruit and vegetable markets (*ferias libres*). In 2012 he still worked transporting and selling fruit and had a total of five months of pension contributions made over his working life. Daniel recalled his time in the barracks through the prism of workplace discrimination, poverty, his difficulty raising and providing for his family, decades living in the población with the fear of retribution, and "the discrimination of [the question] 'how many did you kill?'" "I have had a lot of problems," he explained, "because I was a soldier of '73. I have nothing for my life, for my future old age. My future is lost, lost, for having done my service in 1973." Service was a "stain" on his life that was brought into sudden and disillusioned relief by the Riggs case and Pinochet's secret monies: "Those three ingots of gold, psychologically it killed me, it killed me [. . .] it mocked the young men who one day joined up to serve la patria." Daniel's personal disenchantment was part of a broader societal moment that helped spark the emergence of the ex-conscript movement. This chapter examines the convergence of economic, political, cultural, judicial, and corporeal factors in the first decade of the twenty-first century that produced that moment and shaped the movement.

The Economics of Victimhood

In December 2013 ex-conscripts met in a local hall in Buin, twenty miles south of Santiago. Outside the hall, Jovino S.* spoke of being recalled to the barracks on September 17, 1973, having already completed his service between 1971 and 1972. Those reservists with specializations were called back after the coup, he explained. His main task was guard duty in nearby San Bernardo during the curfew. In the initial phase of the repression, the infantry regiment in San Bernardo was a site where prisoners from the surrounding area were detained, tortured, and executed. Without being specific, Jovino acknowledged his awareness of the risks to civilians who were arrested at the time. On the streets, he and his compañeros detained people who were breaking the curfew for their own protection, he said. Instead of handing them over to their superiors, they locked them in their guardhouse until morning, and then let them go. Only God, he insisted, can kill people. When he was discharged, he returned to Buin and told people he had been working out of town. He could not say that he had been a conscript. Jovino had no lingering physical damage from his service and insisted that he had mostly good memories of his time as a conscript. He had instead joined the group, he said, to campaign for his "economic rights" to wages and a pension.[3]

"Economic rights" were central to the formation of ex-conscript groups throughout Chile. In 2006 army intelligence investigated the "rumor" circulating through Chile about compensation for ex-conscripts or the retroactive payment of pension contributions to former recruits. The resulting report identified a number of ex-conscript groups, detailed their activities, and, in some cases, included descriptions or quotations from inside meetings. It also identified the size of the groups' membership base and their common demands that their pension payments be made, that their savings accounts be returned to them, that deductions made from their pay be returned, that they receive a social pension (*pensión de gracia*), and that they be awarded compensation for damages and losses.[4] The issue of pension payments had provided a catalyst for ex-conscript groups to form throughout the country.[5] Organizations formed first at a very local level, often building on existing social networks within small towns and rural communities.[6] Informal meetings, where ex-recruits would share stories over a drink or around a *parrilla* (barbeque), solidified into formal advocacy groups, which were driven by individual group leaders and grew quickly.[7] The 2006 intelligence report, for example, was requested after a sudden surge in the number of requests made by ex-conscripts to the General Archive of the Army for their certificates of service. Certificates indicate when and where former recruits served and their rank on discharge. They are generally provided by the archive for background checks and bureaucratic purposes, but ex-conscript groups throughout Chile also made them a requirement of membership. In December 2013 the head army archivist spoke of a "boom" in applications around 2005 that had overwhelmed his small team. He pointed to boxes containing an estimated five thousand requests made by ex-conscript groups that sat in the corner waiting to be processed. The archive did not have internal statistics for before 2005 (staff began tracking applications precisely because of the "boom") or beyond September 2009, and the searchable database of certificates issued was only implemented in early 2011. Nevertheless, a review of the available figures reveals a total of around ninety thousand requests for certificates made between 2005 and the end of 2013, with a peak in annual totals in 2008. While not an exact barometer of ex-conscript mobilization, the numbers of requests for certificates do suggest that within a decade, around one-quarter of the approximately 370,000 conscripts who served under Pinochet had mobilized, and that at least half of that number had done so by 2009.[8]

The first years after the "boom" (2005–9) represent a consolidation phase. Proactive group leaders sought audiences with, and allies among, politicians,[9] army representatives,[10] church leaders,[11] the press,[12] and human rights lawyers.[13] They held meetings,[14] made calls for members,[15] created blogs,[16] organized marches and demonstrations,[17] and set up offices to process new members, collect dues, gather documentation, and disseminate information.[18] They traveled the country, holding public meetings[19] and establishing regional and national alliances with other groups, and they developed their demands and their strategies to meet those demands.[20] The effort to bring groups together was partly an organic process, and partly a direct response to the suggestion from government representatives that they could only deal with national-level organizations.[21] The Temuco office of the Agrupación de Reservistas de la Defensa Nacional (Agrupación de Reservistas), which was led by Germán Padilla and Luis Burgos, emerged as the headquarters of one national group. By late 2008 this agrupación headed a coalition of groups based in Lautaro, Galvarino, Curacautín, Villarrica, Victoria, Loncoche, Lonquimay, Futrono, Bulnes, Santiago, Puerto Montt, Ancud, Quellón, Queilén, Puerto Natales, Punta Arenas, and Castro.[22] At the same time, another national level coalition emerged led by Ricardo Inzunza (Talchuano), Juan Diáz (Nacimiento), Víctor Calderón (Buin), Pedro Cáceres (Puente Alto), and Fernando Mellado (Santiago).[23] These five representatives already led groups that had resulted from more local-level cooperation.[24] By late 2008 this coalition represented forty groups in locations across Chile under the banner of the Coordinadora Nacional de Ex Soldados Conscriptos del SMO 1973–1990 (*coordinadora*) (National Coordinating Group of Ex-conscripts 1973–1990).[25] Other organizations that operated at a national level also formed, such as AGEXSCO Chile (Asociación Gremial de ex Conscriptos [Ex-conscript Union]) led by Máximo Núñez; CENAEXSO (Centro Nacional de Ex Soldados Conscriptos [National Ex-conscript Center]) led by Juan Suárez; the Agrupación Ex Conscriptos de Maipú (Ex-conscript Association of Maipú) led by Rubén Cornejo; and the Agrupación V Región Centro Norte Sur (Association of the Fifth Region, Center North South) led by José Castillo.[26] During the consolidation phase, these overlapping national networks were superimposed over scattered local groups. Whereas geography had primarily driven the pattern of the emergence of ex-conscript groups, national groups and coalitions coalesced instead around strategies and individual leaders.

National associations formed a lobby group that petitioned the government to pass legislation that would award ex-conscripts benefits in line with their demands. However, the lobby was splintered by strategic and personal differences, ensuring that, while they pursued the same goals using similar arguments, coalitions campaigned largely parallel to each other. As a result of lobbying efforts, sympathetic members of congress worked on the nonbinding Resolution 287, which was approved by the lower house of Congress in 2007. The resolution petitioned President Bachelet to establish benefits for ex-conscripts who had served in 1973. It aimed at compensating former recruits for the impact that service had on their pensions and their work opportunities in the decades since their conscription.[27] Two years later, Resolution 842 extended the demands made in Resolution 287 to include cohorts up to 1978 but also those who were forced to extend their service at any time between 1973 and 1990. It also reflected the expanding base of ex-conscript demands, including claims of conscript deaths and long-term physical and psychological damage alongside the nonpayment of wages and social security contributions, and the interruption of former recruits' studies. The document demanded compensation for "social security rights" (*derechos previsionales*); recognition of time served in the armed forces when calculating pensions; the retroactive payment of benefits, such as the "location allowance" (paid to recruits sent more than 100 km from home); as well as retroactive pensions for wounds, injuries, and partial or total incapacitation due to physical or psychological damage suffered during service; incorporation into the PRAIS health system (the Program of Reparation and Comprehensive Health Care [Programa de Reparación y Atención Integral de Salud]); and pensions for mothers, children, and spouses of conscripts who died during service.[28]

As nonbinding agreements, congressional resolutions did little to advance the cause of receiving benefits, but Resolution 287 and the specific issues of work and pensions did resonate with former recruits. It was, for example, a major catalyst behind the formation of the Agrupación Social de Ex Soldados Conscriptos 1973—Clase 54 in Arica. However, the group led by Mario Navarro in Chile's north did not join the ex-conscript lobby, aligning itself instead with the Agrupación SMO based in Santiago.[29] While the splintered lobby represented the vast majority of former recruits who sought recognition and benefits, the agrupaciones in Arica and Santiago were part of a network of organizations that limited their representation to ex-conscripts who had been recruited in 1973 and pursued reparations through the civil courts.[30] They found an ally in high-profile lawyer Hugo Gutiérrez, known for his participation in human rights cases, including the Caravan of Death case. With Gutierrez's support, groups representing members of the "class of '54" prepared three separate suits for moral damage, alleging physical and psychological mistreatment inside the barracks, and long-term psychological and employment consequences of their service.[31] At the same time, the Agrupación Ex Conscriptos de Maipú paralleled its involvement in the lobby with its own civil suit for damages. The case represented former recruits from all classes that served under Pinochet, and claimed damage for unpaid pension contributions as well as physical and psychological mistreatment.[32]

During the consolidation phase, the Agrupación Puente Alto (1973–90) also chose a different strategy. After its initial involvement with the coordinadora, the group engaged prominent human rights lawyer Hernán Montealegre in 2007, and prepared a criminal case citing human rights violations inside the barracks, including the torture of conscripts and the forced participation in the abuse of prisoners and fellow conscripts.[33] In 2008, while the case was taking shape and the group was still involved in the lobby coalition, representatives recognized that their organization had formed with the principle objective of seeking compensation for the years spent in service without receiving their pensions, as well as the long-term impact of mistreatment inside the barracks.[34] At around the same time, the group's blog confirmed its original platform in its online profile: "That the government take responsibility for the damage to our pensions, equal rights as the politically exonerated, reparations for physical and psychological damage."[35] As with the majority of groups, the Agrupación Puente Alto's set of demands and allegations quickly expanded, but the initial spark was the issue of former recruits' pensions.

With regard to the "rumor" about pension payments, the 2006 intelligence report noted that during a meeting of reservists in the rural commune of Los Sauces in the ninth region in August 2006, those present were told that "via a 'decree the army had recognized the pensions missing since 1973, and that they would be held in the Ministry of Finance.'" Anyone interested in pursuing his claim had to pay the group 15,000 pesos (approximately US$30) for the paperwork. It went on to cite the rejection in May 2006 of conscript claims to economic rights by the minister of national defense, Vivianne Blanlot, on the basis that they fell outside the statute of limitations. The report concluded that former recruits subsequently drawn to ex-conscript groups would be "victims of fraud and scams." Similar allegations of opportunism and money-grubbing, as well as direct and indirect accusations of lying, were leveled at ex-conscripts by victims' groups, politicians, and former members of the armed forces.[36] Accusations were loudest, however, among ex-conscripts, who traded charges of profiteering, lying, and "macho exaggeration" between groups in attempts to discredit leaders and their strategies, as well as within groups when trying to install their own suffering at the top the hierarchy by casting doubt on claims made by others.[37] However, while the sharply drawn distinction between genuine suffering and economic opportunism, and the dismissive argument that former recruits were cynically and simply after money, perhaps capture the edge of the mobilization, they fundamentally mischaracterize the economics of victimhood at its heart. Demands for pensions, payments, and benefits became an expression of a broad sense of injustice rooted in the convergence of economic precariousness, health issues, and the benefits paid to official victims of the regime.

Throughout the 1990s, and on the basis of recommendations made in the Rettig Report, different categories of victims of the military regime were awarded reparations, including monthly pensions, priority access to the public health care system, and for the children of the disappeared and the murdered, educational benefits. The Valech Commission later made recommendations for reparations to victims identified in its report, and subsequent legislation from 2004 awarded pensions and health care and educational benefits to former political prisoners and victims of torture. Benefits awarded to others routinely punctuated testimonies by ex-conscripts and conversations with group members. They also provided a model for the goals and the sets of demands that groups developed, with many former recruits feeling they were now next in line.[38] This sense of entitlement was at times underscored by cynicism with respect to victims' suffering: rumors of "fake political prisoners" circulated, and some ex-conscripts insisted on comparisons between the days of political imprisonment suffered by political prisoners and the years of "imprisonment" that they had endured as draftees. Others dismissed the reconciliation process as rewarding those with political interests—from both sides—who had caused the crisis, while the young men who had been caught in the middle received nothing, and still others argued that the exiled had been lucky to escape the suffering.[39] The most commonly referenced category of victim, however, were "the exonerated" (los exonerados).[40]

In the mid-1990s, people who had lost their jobs for political reasons under military rule—los exonerados—were awarded benefits. In 1998 a second law expanded the scope of the benefits to include members of congress, the judiciary, and the armed forces, producing a landside of new applications from the military and the Pinochetista right. Controversially, many were awarded pensions.[41] The process was again reopened to applications between June 2003 and June 2004, shortly prior to the ex-conscript mobilization. The resonance of los exonerados among ex-conscripts rested on former recruits' tendency to view their employment trajectories and their economic circumstances in terms of their service. They understood their working lives to have been limited by discrimination, emotional and psychological issues, physical damage, the struggle to re-adjust to civilian life, and a lack of opportunity and education that could be traced back to their time as a conscript.[42] This sense of economic rupture was underscored by the hopes for a better future many recruits had attached to the idea of military service before entering the barracks. Pedro Cáceres in Puente Alto, for example, insisted that he could have been a professional, but for the three years he spent as a recruit, including two as a guard in Villa Grimaldi. Similarly, there were no professionals in the group he represented: "We are all taxi drivers, shopkeepers, market workers, etcetera, etcetera."[43] A 2010 report by a social worker on sixty ex-conscripts in Osorno found that most (83 percent) had not finished secondary school. Of those, just under half (48 percent) put their abandonment of school down to their familial situation (low income and a high number of children) and the need to work, as well as the long distances they needed to travel to schools in rural areas. The other half put it down to military service itself: they felt too old by the time they left the barracks, or they blamed shame, a lack of opportunities, a change in familial fortunes while they were serving that ruled out going to school, or the psychological effects of conscription. As a result, the report continued, reproducing the ex-conscript narrative of damage, many former recruits were unemployed, and those who were employed tended to work independently and informally in jobs that were often poorly paid, seasonal, and physically demanding with long hours, such as agricultural workers, drivers, factory workers, cleaners, gardeners, or construction workers.[44] Few could expect a livable pension.

Before 1980, Chile's pay-as-you-go system provided pensions on the basis of the number of years an individual paid into the scheme. This model was replaced under military rule with a privatized investment account model that calculated pensions based on pesos invested rather than years of contributions.[45] In the early twenty-first century the majority of ex-conscripts, like a significant sector of working Chileans, did not qualify for a pension, or received only the minimum payment, which was not enough to live on, typically falling to between one-third and one-half of retirees' wages. At around the time ex-conscript groups were forming, President Bachelet proposed reforms to the investment account model, as well as universal minimum pensions. The reforms failed, however, to capture the self-employed or workers in the informal sector—groups that included many mobilized former conscripts.[46] The eldest cohorts of ex-conscripts were coming to the end of their working lives, and they believed, or hoped, that their service would boost their pension entitlement. Many recalled being told that amounts deducted from their pay were social security payments made on their behalf. Others insisted that their time as a conscript was not recognized under the old system.[47] Ex-conscripts' concerns about their financial present and future were further compounded by the fact that their bodies were beginning to fail them.

The emergence of ex-conscript groups coincided with, and was in part prompted by, worsening injuries, aches, pains, and emotional scars, or emerging disorders and ailments that former recruits attributed to their time in the barracks. Alonso G.* (1973–75, Angol) testified to an accident during his service that had, decades later, affected his ability to work. "Because of this accident," he wrote, "I am limited. I cannot strain myself. What's more, I work independently and I have to do my pension myself." His aspirations had been undermined, he argued, and he wanted his sacrifice recognized: "and for this recognition to be health [benefits] and a social pension."[48] "Health benefits" refer to access to PRAIS, the program set up in 1991 as part of the reconciliation process to deliver free and preferential treatment via the public health system to former political prisoners, relatives of detainees who were disappeared or killed, the exonerados, those returned from exile and their families, and torture victims.[49] Given the presumed impact of service on former recruits' bodies, and therefore their working lives, the ex-conscript demand for access to PRAIS was also related to the issue of employment. Medical expenses were at the heart, for example, of the 2007 testimony by Leonardo S.* (1973–75, Traiguén). He described his ongoing inability to sleep, and being haunted by constant intrusive memories of participating in political violence and witnessing torture. He also wrote of seeking treatment for, and incurring the costs of, old injuries sustained in the barracks including a broken jaw and torn tendons in his right leg. The lingering effects of his service were made worse, he clarified, because at the time he provided his statement he found himself without work and having to support a family.[50]

The prospect of education benefits—that were transferable to a child, spouse, or mother of a child—not only tapped into the perceived toll that military service had taken on the former recruits' own lives but also resonated with the beginning of a new cycle of opportunity. By the end of the first decade of the twenty-first century, education had overtaken military service as the path to social mobility, but many former recruits were struggling, or felt they had failed, to educate their children. The tertiary sector had been deregulated in the 1980s, producing enormous growth but also fees that outstripped the ability of many to pay. In 2009, at around the time of the peak of ex-conscript mobilization, for example, there were sixty-one universities in Santiago, and Chilean families dedicated around a third of household income per capita— one of the highest rates in the world—to tertiary education.[51] In 2006 hundreds of thousands of high school students had taken to the streets with specific demands about the cost of buses and tertiary education entrance exams, which developed into sweeping calls for universal and quality education in the first months of Bachelet's first term (2006–10).[52] In 2011, however, the university student movement calling for free and quality university education over-shadowed any focus on secondary education. Regular, massive, and persistent protests succeeded in shaping Bachelet's campaign for a second term in 2013, as well as her administration's agenda for office (2014–18).

The convergence of pensions, health, work, opportunity, and memory can be seen in the testimony of Manuel T.* (Valdivia), who was eighteen years old when called up in 1972. He left the barracks in June 1973, only to be recalled following the coup and discharged in 1976. He spoke in 2012 of constant guard duty, with no sleep and no food, and of his fear of being punished or killed for not following orders. He and his compañeros had been sent out onto the streets, where they beat civilians and sprayed bullets for fear of being shot. Sometimes, he said, he was blindfolded by his superiors. Manuel could not be sure if he had killed anyone, even family members, but he emphasized his youth, his ignorance, and his fear, to mitigate any sense of responsibility. He was unable to forget but kept his memories "on the inside" for decades. He did not want to burden his family with what he "carried in his mind," but his silence was also a way of guarding against their reaction to things he was forced to do. He described beginning to talk about his service as part of what he saw as the wider "recognition" in the final years of the first decade of the twenty-first century of what had happened in Chile. Hopefully, he said, the president would also recognize his experiences. He felt the state owed him and other ex-conscripts "for what they did to our lives." He spoke specifically of his missing pension payments and lack of wages, explaining that the army recognized only one year—1973—of the four he spent in the barracks, which compromised his ability to retire. Those four years also cost him the chance to study, work, and provide for his family. After his discharge, his mind "was mixed up" and he was unable to continue his education. Decades after his service, Manuel's employment history, his current struggle to provide for his family, and his hopes for retirement converged with his failing health: "Now the illnesses are coming." He ascribed his missing teeth, bad back, and psychological issues as a nearly sixty-year-old man to the hours he spent standing while on guard duty, the lack of food, the poor hygiene of the barracks, and the things he was forced to do and witness as a conscript. His back pain, in particular, he said, made it difficult to work, and all he wanted was for his pension contributions to be paid.[53]

The ex-conscript nexus of ailing health, underemployment and unemployment, and economic precariousness tightened in the context of massive income inequality and broader disillusionment in the first decade of the twenty-first century. From the end of the 1990s, disenchantment with the failed promise of the transition emerged as economic growth slowed, unemployment rose, and large sectors of society saw little or no benefit from the booming posttransition decade. The triumphalism of the political right about Chile's macroeconomic successes masked a growing sense that most Chileans had been excluded from the country's rapid growth. While national income had grown and poverty rates had fallen, Chile's income inequality remained among the worst in the world: the richest 10 percent held triple the wealth of the next richest 10 percent, while two-fifths of the population lived in poverty, or precariously close to it. In 1990 President Aylwin had spoken of a "social debt" accrued under military rule, which was to be paid back under the concertación. A decade later, however, that debt remained, and a sense of abandonment and bitterness grew in the gap between proclamations of economic success and the everyday reality of unstable and irregular work, exploitative employment practices, and spiraling personal debt.[54] In this context, the threads of ex-conscript memory, disillusionment, cynicism, poverty, failing health, as well as their senses of victimization and entitlement, were definitively knotted together by the Riggs Bank scandal.

Allegations of corruption against the Pinochet family punctuated the memory struggles of the 1990s. Revelations about checks totaling around three million dollars that were paid by the army to Pinochet's son emerged in the twilight of military rule. The resulting 1990 investigation into the "Pinocheques" threatened the narrative of salvation and the image of the general as a selfless patriot, and in response Pinochet called his troops to the barracks, placing them on alert. The government effectively shelved the investigation. New revelations about deals involving the army and the general's son caused the case to be reopened in 1993. In May black berets (*boinas negras*) appeared in downtown Santiago, guarding the armed forces' buildings across from the Moneda. The "*boinazo*" succeeded in forcing the investigation into the Pinochets to once again be reined in. It was not until the Riggs Bank scandal that the scale of Pinochet's self-enrichment became clear. In 2004, and amid attempts to charge the former dictator for his role in human rights violations and his strategic claims of dementia to avoid indictment, it came to light that Pinochet had millions of dollars in secret accounts with the Riggs Bank. The discovery led to a senate inquiry and criminal charges for fraud and tax evasion. By the time charges were laid, estimates of the size of his fortune had risen to anywhere between 27 and 100 million. This personal financial gain was too much for many supporters, and the scandal marked a tipping point in loyalists' support. Coupled with mounting human rights charges, the armed forces' search for a socially sanctioned role in civil society, and generational renewal among the officer ranks, the scandal proved a key motivation for the army to publicly step away from the legacy of the dictatorship.[55]

For ex-conscripts like Daniel Pizarro, the scandal brought their economic situation into sharp relief and gave a broader context to a personal and specific sense of economic betrayal. It tapped into Daniel's frustrated ambitions, his family's financial hardship, and a sense of economic injustice, and it bound his memory of service to a longer cycle of economic struggle. Amid the housing crisis of the decades prior to the coup, Daniel, his parents, and his siblings had been living with other families in cramped and crowded homes (*allegados*) in Santiago. In the late 1960s, they participated in the land invasions (*tomas*) that gave rise to the población of La Pincoya on the edge of the capital. In 2012 Daniel and his wife still lived in the same población, where they now shared a home with their children and their grandchildren. Here in La Pincoya, the faded promise of the 1960s tomas met twenty-first-century disenchantment with democratic Chile and Daniel's sense of injustice regarding his service. The Pinochet family's fortune resonated with victims of political torture in the población in a similar manner. Clara Han notes that the Valech Commission and its subsequent report informed how former political prisoners in La Pincoya experienced economic precariousness. The prospect of official recognition of their experiences and of reparations created a link between their suffering under the regime and their battles with debt, unemployment, and their own disillusion with the promise of democracy. The Riggs case reinforced that link. Han relates the story of Héctor, a torture victim, and his wife, Ruby, who in the years before the Riggs scandal broke lived in Ruby's mother's home, along with her two sisters and brother, and their partners and children. In early 2004 they moved into a small home of their own, only one street away. Not wanting to relive or publicize his torture, Héctor had stayed away from the Valech process, but the 2005 settlement reached by the Allbriton family behind the Riggs Bank provided 8 million dollars to be divided among Pinochet's victims, including "non-official" victims like Héctor. Ruby stressed Héctor's right to reparations and connected this right directly to the family's current economic struggle.[56]

For many ex-conscripts, the Riggs case also validated a specific sense of betrayal. Former recruits from all years describe their monthly payments being reduced to very little or nothing by deductions for services they received, as well as some they did not, such as films they never saw, a non-existent hairdresser, and a laundry service for clothes they washed themselves.[57] In 2013 the army confirmed that "wages were used to maintain conscripts during their stay, and the use of services provided by the army, such as food, the use of sports fields, etc., was deducted from pay slips. The balance was enough to allow recruits to travel around and eat on their free days." It also indicated that conscripts had signed for their monthly payments at the time, but that records had been burned after ten years.[58] In ex-conscript testimony, these deductions were often set against descriptions of hunger, scarce and poor food, cold climatic conditions, and inadequate, ill-fitting, or damaged clothing. Specifically, former recruits remember being told that money was being put aside for them in savings accounts held for them for when they left the barracks. At the end of their service, however, they received nothing.[59] "It is no less than twenty-five years since leaving the barracks," writes D.J.M.F. (1980–82, Coyhaique), "and I am still waiting for that money to be returned to me and with interest incurred over the years, it should be a fortune."[60] In 2012 Carlos Palma (1973, Iquique) recalled having amounts for clothes, laundry service, as well as contributions to social security and a savings account discounted from what he received. He was happy about it at the time, he said, but there was no account waiting for him, and no record of his pension contributions when he was discharged. Where was that money now, he asked rhetorically.[61] For many, the Riggs scandal seemed to identify whose "unscrupulous pockets" the money had ended up in.[62] The secret fortune regularly came up, for example, as former recruits in Nacimiento shared empanadas after a regional meeting in 2012.[63] In late 2011, and in front of a meeting in the municipal stadium in San Bernardo, Fernando Mellado (1973, Santiago) went further, drawing a direct link between the pesos "stolen" from conscripts and the dollars in the Riggs Bank. The hidden money should pay for reparations, he told gathered ex-conscripts; after all, it was rightfully theirs anyway.[64]

The economics of ex-conscript victimhood are a complex and fluid mix of dashed hopes, unmet expectations, cyclical poverty, lack of opportunity, familial responsibility, years of unstable unemployment, a sense of entitlement and betrayal, aging bodies, and health concerns, within the context of transitional efforts to repay victims of the dictatorship and broader disillusionment with the economic promise of a democratic Chile. They helped produce the conditions for the emergence of ex-conscript groups and the narrative of victimhood that bound it; however, the mobilization of ex-conscripts was also shaped by their interaction with, as well as their exclusion from, the transitional truth and reconciliation processes.

Human Rights and the Politics of Victimhood

On the morning of January 29, 2014, Pedro Naigual headed a small group of ex-conscripts gathered in Constitution Square behind La

Moneda. He spoke of his group in Osorno that formed eight years earlier around the issue of missing pensions. He had also been involved in the coordinadora in 2008, but on this day, he was representing a coalition of groups from Osorno, Chillán, Lebu, Talca, Puerto Montt, and Puerto Octay that had come together in August of 2012 as the National Commission for the Human Rights of Ex-conscripts 1973–1990 (Ex-conscript Commission).[65] The Ex-conscript Commission had produced an almost four-hundred-page report detailing the alleged physical and psychological mistreatment of conscripts, and delivered the document to the government. On this day in early 2014, a handful of former recruits gathered to quietly protest the lack of response. Both the coalition and its report were fashioned as an unofficial extension of the truth and reconciliation process, supplementing the reports produced by the Rettig and Valech Commissions.[66] In the late morning, police politely requested that the ex-conscripts take their banner from the center to the side of the square, in order to accommodate a much larger housing protest. After the drums and the whistles of that protest had dissipated, the square filled with boy scouts, and the former recruits retreated further to the side.[67] The Ex-conscript Commission and its report are indicative of how the human rights movement and, in particular, the work of the Valech Commission provided former recruits with a language of victimhood, a national context for personal suffering, and a model for pursuing recognition and damages. The sidelined protest is also a microcosmic example, however, of the lack of space in the public sphere for ex-conscript claims to victim status and the former recruits' complicated engagement with human rights.

While ex-conscript groups initially rallied around the issue of pension payments, the conditions for the emergence of a collective sense of victimhood and the evolution of ex-conscript demands were rooted in the language of rights. In Chile, a rights consciousness emerged in response to abuses carried out under military rule, but it grew, in particular, in the posttransition decade, and extended beyond the regime's legacy to broader social issues.[68] It also helped lay the groundwork for the mobilization of ex-conscripts in the first decade of the twenty-first century. In the late 1990s professionals with the Corporation for the Promotion and Defense of the Rights of the People (CODEPU), Rosella Baronti and Álvaro Toro, indirectly made this argument by extrapolating their experience with conscripts who served in the posttransition decade and who denounced abuse. In addition to a "learned submissiveness" and the "immense fear" that they assumed had prevented the denunciation of the mistreatment of conscripts who served under Pinochet, Baronti and Toro understood allegations made by posttransition recruits as the result of a growing culture of rights.[69] At the time they were writing, the debate about rights

A Movement

violations in Chile focused on the issue of dictatorship-era torture and would eventually give rise to Chile's second truth and reconciliation commission.

Ex-conscript groups formed in the years following the work done by the Valech Commission and the release of its 2004 report. Former political prisoner advocacy had, from the turn of the century, both driven and resulted from a new focus on political torture and its consequences. Victims had gathered primarily to collect evidence in the context of the cases brought against Pinochet in 1998, and their efforts soon shifted to campaigning for truth and justice and demanding damages. In making a case for his ex-conscript clients, human rights lawyer Hernán Montealegre described the late emergence of ex-conscript complaints as part of this same evolution of the memory struggle. It was necessary, he argued, that the reconciliation process focus first on the disappeared, the tortured, and the politically detained. It would have been impossible for ex-conscript groups to claim victim status before political detainees and torture victims had done so.[70] Beyond the perception among former recruits that they were next in line, a rights culture and the memory turn at the beginning of the twenty-first century provided former recruits with a unifying language of rights and torture. They offered a common and socially legitimized framework within which to talk about aspects of their service.[71] Importantly, too, they allowed many former recruits, decades after being discharged, to interpret their experiences within a broader narrative, in terms of a collective voice, and within a rights framework. Ex-conscripts like Andrés V.* (1975–77, Temuco) had instead primarily understood their conscription within a narrow, often very personal, perspective. In 2012 Andrés spoke of the physical abuse of training and his emotional, psychological, and drinking problems in the decades since. He had led a withdrawn life, and lived with his parents until they died. For Andrés, his recollections were not a window onto a larger national history or examples of institutionalized abuse. They were instead limited to the context of the unit and the orders of his "crazy" instructors. He had "never had a problem with Pinochet," he explained: "He never beat me."[72] By around 2005, the cumulative effect of an awareness of rights, a language of torture, and the work of the Valech Commission had provided the basis for a unifying ex-conscript sense of victimhood, as well as models for making demands.

By the end of the consolidation phase of the ex-conscript mobilization (2005–9), the majority of the former recruits who would join up had done so, and much of the internal negotiations over expanding sets demands and legal tactics had been settled. In the years that followed, ex-conscript associations entered a second phase, during which they more formally pursued their different strategies. In 2009 the association in Puente Alto launched its criminal case: 438 ex-conscripts made direct allegations of abuse against more than 400 of their former superiors.[73] Lawyer Hernán Montealegre argued that the former recruits he represented were victims of human rights violations in two senses. First, they suffered direct abuse, such as seeing fellow recruits shot for disobedience; physical abuse that left some disfigured; the torture technique known as the "submarine"; the application of electrical current to their bodies; being forced to eat excrement; being tied up for days; mock executions; witnessing prisoners shot and being made to move their bodies. Second, recruits were forced to participate to varying degrees in the violations of others' rights.[74] The case passed through the criminal courts before being heard in the military justice system, as the group slowly collected statements. In early 2015 it passed from the military prosecutor to the general legal adviser of the army, who was to issue a ruling on whether to close the case or continue and question the accused.[75]

In mid-2015 Montealegre raised the prospect of commencing civil cases once the military justice process has been exhausted.[76] In 2009 and 2010 the network spearheaded by the Agrupación SMO had already launched three civil cases for damages, arguing that recruits who had served in 1973 had suffered violations of their human and fundamental rights as the result of inhumane treatment, including physical and psychological torture at the hands of their superiors; the obligation to witness or participate in crimes against humanity against their conscience; and the lingering consequences of psychological problems and societal stigma.[77] The cases spent the following years slowly working their way through legal processes. The rejection of the first of the three suits because it fell outside the statute of limitations was upheld by the court of appeal in 2013, while the remaining two languished in the civil court system.[78] The group's long-term plan, after exhausting local options, was to take the case to the Inter-American Court of Human Rights. Also in 2010, the Agrupación de ex Conscriptos 73–90 de Maipú launched its own civil cases for damages, citing unpaid pension contributions and service beyond the mandated period, as well as psychological damage from forced participation in raids and patrols, witnessing executions and torture of others, and the physical abuse, inhumane punishment, and physical and psychological mistreatment of recruits inside the barracks.[79] The cases did not advance far and have been inactive since 2012 and 2013, as the Maipú group focused instead on lobbying the government.[80]

The lobby also shifted in 2009. One important moment was a letter from the then–subsecretary of the interior, Patricio Rosende, in which he classified ex-conscripts as victims of human rights abuses: "This subsecretariat joins previous administrations of this ministry that have recognized the status of victims of human rights of those who completed their military service during the years of the dictatorship."[81] The Human Rights Program of the Ministry of the Interior was created to contribute to the establishment of the truth regarding human rights abuses under Pinochet, promote respect for human rights, provide legal and social assistance to the families of victims, and oversee the implementation of reparations programs. Parallel to the emergence of conscript groups, there had been a discussion within the program about military personnel as victims. The letter reflected the vague conviction within the program at the time that military personnel who were forced to commit crimes under the threat of death in the first years of military rule could also be potentially considered victims. It was, however, a symbolic gesture, the beginning of a discussion. There remained an enormous gap between the recognition offered in the letter and reparations.[82] Nevertheless, many former recruits, particularly the leadership of the coordinadora to whom the letter was addressed, interpreted the letter as a definitive confirmation of their status as human rights victims.

Rosende's letter came as Bachelet's first term as president (2006–10) was winding down, and the second important moment came during the campaign to elect her successor. While on the campaign trail, Rodrigo Hinzpeter committed Sebastián Piñera's future administration to examining ex-conscript claims, and providing a response guided by the need to ensure "the appropriate recognition, dignity, valuation and reparation to this determined group of compatriots who, in very difficult conditions, did their duty to their country."[83] The commitment energized ex-conscript groups, and former recruits interpreted Hinzpeter's words as a firm commitment to deliver reparations in return for their vote. Following Piñera's election in 2010, the administration invited the five largest national lobby organizations—the Agrupación de Reservistas, CENAEXSO, the Coordinadora Nacional de Ex Conscriptos, the Asociación Nacional de Ex-Conscriptos (National Association for Ex-Conscripts), and the Agrupación V Región Centro Norte Sur[84]—to participate in a working group with representatives from the Ministries of Defense, the Interior (including the ministry's human rights program), Work and Social Security, and Finance. The working group imposed a unity that had previously not existed between the different coalitions,[85] and in 2011 they produced a joint document outlining their demands and their preferred framework for reparations for the "violations of the [recruits'] human rights." In addition to claims for unpaid wages, missing pensions, compensation for extended service, unpaid location allowance, health and education benefits, and damages, the demands also included pensions for wounds or disabilities from service, a lump sum payment and pension for the families of recruits who died during service, compensation for work on the carretera austral, compensation for guarding a nuclear facility, a lump sum housing benefit, damages for recruits who were married or single fathers when recruited, and damages for recruits who were not fit for service when drafted.[86] In January 2012 the subsecretaries of the interior, the armed forces, and finance, and representatives of the Ministry of Work and Social Security committed to producing a report regarding the groups' demands, and subsequent meetings were dedicated to receiving information.[87]

While the language and institutions of human rights provided the basis for a collective sense of victimhood and a model for advocacy, they also imposed limits. Ex-conscript leaders became aware of these limits as soon as they began to mobilize and their demands were passed between the armed forces, the government, and the Church. Some had expected to find allies in victims' groups but instead discovered an unwillingness to recognize "murderers" as victims.[88] Ex-conscripts were explicitly excluded, too, from the state-led processes. Beyond the human rights appeal to universal ideals that are above politics, the Rettig and Valech Reports avoided partisanship by legitimizing victims and suffering on "both sides."[89] At the same time, however, they also reflected a strict political dichotomy that defined Chile's memory struggles by confirming victim status and human rights as political categories. One hundred and two former conscripts testified before the Valech Commission, for example, but given the commission's mandate, it determined that "it was not possible to declare as victims persons who denounced imprisonment or torture while completing their compulsory military service, as it was not possible to clearly determine the political motivations for the events described."[90] The politics of victimhood—defining victim status in terms of the political conflict—meant neither the truth and reconciliation process, nor the memory contest more broadly, could accommodate ex-conscript claims to victims status. In her work on the Rettig Report, Elizabeth Lira noted a tendency among the families of the disappeared and murdered to underplay political affiliations. It was as if, she writes, "recognizing the reality of the conflict reactivated political polarization, ideological differences and hatred, and hindered memorialization."[91] Ex-conscripts, too, tended to underplay any political dimension of their stories, not to avoid reactivating ideological conflicts from decades earlier but to prevent engaging the contemporaneous politics of memory.

The central ambivalence of human rights as both an impetus for ex-conscript mobilization and a barrier to inclusion in the memory contest can be seen in the resonance of emblematic cases. One of the most significant to emerge from the truth and reconciliation process was that of conscript Michel Nash, whose disappearance in 1973 provided former recruits with a socially confirmed point of reference. As a member of the Communist Youth, Nash asked to be excused from participating in raids on homes in the wake of the coup. On September 29 he was shot in Chile's far north, while "trying to escape," and his body was never found.[92] At the same time, Carlos Droguett

(1973) was serving in Santiago. In 2013 Carlos produced a photocopied image of Nash, and a short text detailing his fate, during a conversation after a group meeting.[93] He used the pamphlet to contextualize his own suffering, fears, and sense of vulnerability. During a subsequent oral history in his home in La Pintana, he spoke of his health issues and the depression that he traced back to his service, and said he had only learned of Nash's death many years after leaving the barracks. He also went on to speak of conscript deaths in his own regiment, but he chose the case of an official victim from thousands of miles away to make sense of his experiences.[94] While the fate of Nash resonated with many former recruits as confirmation of their worst fears, it also turned on political purity that removed it from the general conscript experience. Nash's story was embraced by victims' groups, but most former conscripts did not take a principled stand against the regime's actions, or even hold firm political positions.[95] This difference can be seen in the public echo of Nash's fate, not as a reference point for the experience of military service during the regime but as the centerpiece for the conscientious objector movement of the 1990s.[96] A more widely accessible reference point for the ex-conscript narrative of suffering was the Antuco tragedy from the following decade.

In May 2005 five companies of recruits from Los Ángeles set out to march across the side of the Antuco volcano in southern Chile. Despite concerns about approaching bad weather, the order was given to proceed with the exercise, and a group of recruits found themselves caught in freezing conditions. Over the following weeks, the bodies of forty-four conscripts and one sergeant were recovered.[97] "The same thing happened to us," confirmed two former conscripts in the minutes prior to a 2012 meeting of former conscripts in Nacimiento.[98] Former recruits identified with the cold, the "crazy" orders, and the deaths, and the Antuco tragedy was able to tap into the widespread grief that poured out as the bodies were found, without activating the memory contest and the rigid assumptions about victimhood that otherwise forced conscripts into the gray zone between narratives of military rule. It became more useful, for example, than the Nash case. The editor of a 2007 collection of testimonies contextualized for his readers a vastly exaggerated estimate of six thousand conscript deaths under military rule as equivalent to "134 Antuco tragedies."[99] Similarly, a nine-minute video used by the Agrupación de Reservistas in Temuco in its meetings with politicians splices footage of its members describing the lingering damage from military service, members showing their physical scars, or mothers of dead conscripts talking into the camera, with media coverage of the aftermath of the Antuco tragedy. The television footage shows a grieving father speaking of his rage and his feelings of helplessness, and a distraught mother asking: "Why did you kill them?" The words superimposed on these images read: "Not only in Antuco did conscripts die doing their duty."[100] A similar shift away from the human rights framework can be seen in the lobby, which had initially sought inclusion in the processes and institutions of the state-led reconciliation processes.[101] Resolution 606 (2012), for example, included "human rights" in the title, but called in the body of the text for the "recognition of those conscripts [who served between 1973 and 1990] as victims of illegal and arbitrary acts of the state of Chile via the actions of the armed forces."[102] Resolution 965 (2013) reinforced the language of "illegal and arbitrary acts" but also went further, arguing for the establishment of new processes to identify victims, and proposing guidelines for reparations and the investigation of cases of death or suicide.[103]

More fundamental than the strategic depoliticization of the ex-conscript narrative, however, was the fact that ex-conscript stories did not connect with the grand and competing narratives of military rule in any consistent manner. Most former recruits insist that, as boys in the countryside or the poblaciones, political engagement was both secondary to subsistence and buried by fear and taboo. Some had been politically engaged prior to being called up, while others dismissed political activity as youngsters as nothing more than boyish fun. Still others had internalized the military regime's historical perspective while boys or been politicized—in support of the regime or in opposition to the dictatorship—by their service. Many became politically aware after leaving the barracks through very local and concrete issues, and often the ex-conscript movement itself represented former recruits' first instance of political engagement. More still profess indifference, insisting that politics was, and remains, "dirty." As individuals, therefore, ex-conscripts' twenty-first-century interpretations of the coup and military rule varied significantly, and were informed by their family history, childhood, time in the barracks, experience of military rule as civilians, employment history, pathway to political awareness, and, importantly, the same memory contest that cut through the rest of Chilean society.[104] The collective ex-conscript movement that emerged from around 2005 could therefore not be based on a shared political identity. It was based, instead, on a common sense of personal victimhood, where the personal was not necessarily, and often not at all, a window onto a larger political or national narrative.

With Piñera's term as president coming to an end in late 2013, the artificial strategic unity of the political lobby strained under the weight of unmet demands. Groups and their political supporters sought to compel his administration to provide the response they felt had been promised.[105] In October, Hinzpeter, now minister of defense, and Andrés Chadwick, minister of the interior and public security, pledged a response within ninety days. Ex-conscript lobbying also paralleled the 2013 presidential election campaign that pitted Bachelet against Matthei, as well as a rare level of commemorative activity in the buildup to the fortieth anniversary of the coup that included unprecedented and short-lived interest in the conscript perspective of the coup.[106] The annual commemorative season tends to end, however, with the celebration of Chile's independence on September 18. Despite the unusual level of activity, 2013 was no different, and the memory question was quickly put to rest. On November 11, two months after the anniversary of the coup, ex-conscripts began a three-day march from Rancagua to Santiago's Plaza de los Héroes to pressure the government to make good on its ninety-day pledge. When they arrived in Santiago on the morning of November 13, the plaza was full of people and armored police vehicles were stationed along the its edge. However, the crowds had gathered in support of a national council worker strike that had paralyzed municipal services for weeks.[107] The ex-conscript march suffered from poor organization, but like the sidelined protest of the Ex-conscript Commission, the lack of space in the plaza is also indicative of the lack of traction that ex-conscripts were able to achieve. The government report prepared by the ministry of the interior and public safety was delivered in December, and apart from some minor technical concessions, it dismissed the ex-conscript lobby's demands and rejected its legal arguments.[108]

In wake of the 2013 election, the movement persisted. The lobby reassembled, with some old alliances dissolving as some new ones forming, while civil and criminal cases continued their slow progress through the courts.[109] A decade after groups had begun to emerge, the economics and politics of victimhood gave rise and shape to a loose movement of ex-conscripts who had served under Pinochet. It was "loose" because it was splintered by personal and strategic differences. It was nevertheless a "movement," because ex-conscript organizations made similar demands for benefits and recognition, and, more fundamentally, because ex-conscripts had a common way of remembering their service. The movement's collection of demands and legal arguments are the narrow outward expression of a common sense of victimhood.[110] They certainly reflect and inform ex-conscript recollections, but they are also shaped by groups' resources and strategies, their perceived chances of success, leaders' individual styles—legalistic, procedural, or sensationalist; antagonistic or conciliatory—when publicly representing their cases, and the expertise of their professional allies. At its heart, however, and across any organizational or strategic divisions, the movement is united by its members' shared memory narratives of their service. Former recruits understand military service as a fundamental point of rupture in their lives, a fulcrum around which their life stories revolve: their conscription left them physically or psychologically damaged, undermined their masculinity, or challenged their national identity. The following chapters examine these narratives of ex-conscript memory, the moment of their emergence in twenty-first-century Chile, and what they reveal about how Chile's wars were waged inside the barracks between 1973 and 1990.

3

Defending *la Patria*

little more than four decades after Félix Pinares (1973–76, Iquique) was drafted, the discord between ideas about what la patria was and what it meant to defend it that framed his memory of military service played out publicly on breakfast television. September 11 reignites debate every year in Chile, but the fortieth anniversary of the coup in 2013 produced a wave of interest and commemorative activity more intense than usual. In the lead-up to the milestone, and for the first time, former conscripts who had experienced the coup were sought out for their recollections by radio, print media, and television outlets, with one such interview conducted on the morning television show *Mañaneros*.[1] The program's panel spoke in the studio with Hermógenes Pérez de Arce, an outspoken defender of the Pinochet regime and officers serving prison sentences for human rights violations. Félix and fellow ex-conscript Carlos Palma (1973–75, Iquique) participated via a live feed from a park near Carlos's almacén in Ñuñoa and around the corner from the National Stadium. At one point, Félix insisted that he had never been interested in politics and did not have any political allegiance. He had sworn an oath to the flag and to his patria, but it would never have occurred to him to shoot a defenseless Chilean.[2]

Several months earlier, in his living room in the Santiago comuna of Recoleta, Félix had spoken more broadly about his sense of patria.[3] His family—his parents and ten siblings—was from Coronel on the country's coalmining coast, where his father had held an important position in a mine. They hit hard times, however, after remorse and a subsequent investigation into a fatal on-site accident drove Félix's father to drink. Félix was about ten years old at the time of the accident, and shortly after he abandoned school to start earning money. In 1968 he left for Santiago to join his older brothers and find work in the city, and three years later they sent for the rest of the family. In 1973 he was drafted into the army and sent by train to Iquique.

On the morning of September 11, Félix and his compañeros were informed by a superior that "from this day forward, from the lowliest soldier to the commandant of the regiment, we are the government. And that [. . .] should fill us with pride. We are the government and we have to save the country." Félix's thoughts at that moment, he recalled, turned to his family in Recoleta, where, he later found out, his father and brother had been arrested. In Iquique, he witnessed the "unnecessary" violence of the raids on local homes and saw how some—few, he said, but some—of his fellow conscripts agreed with what was happening. He guarded political prisoners who arrived at the regiment and could hear when they had electrical current applied to their testicles via field telephones wired for torture. The prisoners, however, were not dangerous people, he insisted, and the "war" was not his war. To illustrate the contradiction he had lived as a conscript, Félix returned to the oath of allegiance to the flag. Recruits swear loyalty to the flag and la patria, pledging their lives, should it be asked of them, after their basic training is complete. For Félix, the "atrocities" of political repression rendered the oath "the biggest lie there is." La patria, he explained, is "the land that God gave us to live as brothers." He would not hesitate to defend it, "even giving my life if it were necessary, as the oath says, any time Chile's sovereignty or my family . . . were in serious danger." His voice spiked at the mention of his family, and a pause afterward let that emphasis sink in. At one point, he had refused orders to aim his weapon at a prisoner, telling his lieutenant: "I swore to the flag for something else."

In August 2013, in front of the television cameras, Félix restated his conception of la patria as an extended national family within sovereign borders. He reiterated, too, his readiness to defend those borders against foreign invasion. Asked by one of the show's hosts whether he had participated in armed confrontations with "terrorists or subversives in inverted commas," Félix related the story of a compañero who had died by his side. He was not killed by extremists, the former recruit clarified. Instead, he had been shot by the regiment's own soldiers during a simulated attack designed to prepare them for assaults on the barracks. Pérez de Arce, who throughout the interview had represented the war narrative of the Pinochetista right, reflexively dismissed Félix's story as the leftist version of history, because he felt Félix was "concealing the fact that [at the time] he was facing an armed enemy." "I did have armed enemies," countered Félix before listing them: "my lieutenant, my captain, my major, my commandant. These were the armed enemies I faced. I never, never had a civilian point a gun at me."[4] The dissonance between patrias exposed in this brief exchange on Chilean morning television in 2013 is representative of a broader rupture in conscript memory. Many former recruits from all classes under Pinochet recall their at times "euphoric" enthusiasm at being called up to do their national duty, and others eagerly volunteered to serve and defend la patria.[5] However, the experience of military service is often understood as a betrayal of the patriotism recruits carried with them into the barracks. This chapter examines the clash of patrias in ex-conscript memory, and reveals how Pinochet's "internal" and "almost" wars in defense of la patria were waged inside the barracks.

The Army, the Nation

By the end of the nineteenth century, almost one hundred years of compounded military heroism had merged with an older warrior mythology to provide a foundation for Chilean national identity and patriotism. The anticolonial push of the first decades of the nineteenth century was driven by revolutionary fervor that had made its way from France, via North America, to Latin America. Patriotic songs proclaimed hatred of the Spanish as well as Pan-American solidarity, and throughout Chile a variety of concentric notions of la patria coexisted, gathering around the family, the village, the region, the country, and the continent. Independence (1810–23) was therefore not the final expression of a restless, preimagined national identity. Instead, it initiated a long and uneven process of aligning ideas of la patria with geographical borders, and clarifying conceptions of Chile and the nation that incorporated political institutions, cultural traditions, ideas about the Chilean race, and a glorious, sovereign past. Chilean elites guiding the nascent independence movement set the foundations of a unique national identity, borrowing heavily from the symbolism of the French revolution, and reviving a pre-Hispanic, indigenous warrior heritage. Epic sixteenth-century poetry had established the Mapuche reputation as fierce fighters, and the indomitable indigenous people, undefeated by the Spanish, lent independent Chile a heroic history.[6]

Chile soon went to war again, driven by the need to protect its newly won independence against an expansionist northern neighbor, as well as what remained of fading Pan-American solidarity. The decisive battle of the War of the Confederation (1836–39), between the Confederation of Peru and Bolivia and Chilean, Peruvian, and Argentine forces, was fought at Yungay on January 20, 1839. The victory drew a euphoric response back in Chile, inspired new songs about a new victory over tyranny, and reawakened the myth of the warrior race. The Battle of Yungay became an important symbol of heroism and military might, and the anniversary was celebrated as a national festival. By 1860 the annual celebration had fallen out of favor, and the army was kept busy with skirmishes with the Mapuche population on the southern frontier.

The heroes of Yungay were revived decades later, however, during the War of the Pacific.[7]

The war effort between 1879 and 1883 racialized la patria by embodying the warrior myth in the figure of the *roto chileno*. The term *roto* had long been used to refer to Chile's peasant class; however, during the War of the Pacific the roto was installed as the hero of la patria and the embodiment of a homogeneous national race. The monument to the roto chileno erected in 1888 in Santiago's Plaza Yungay depicts him as a poor young man holding a rifle, with his trousers rolled up and a bushel of wheat resting by his bare feet. At the beginning of the twentieth century, Nicolás Palacios traced the roots of the "Chilean race," arguing that the roto represented the perfect blend of two warrior peoples: Spanish *conquistadores* and the indomitable Mapuche.[8] The turning point in the war was a sea battle off the coast of Iquique on May 21, 1879. During the Battle of Iquique, the Chilean vessel the *Esmeralda* was taking fire from the beach and from the sea when she was rammed by the *Huáscar*. Chilean captain Arturo Prat boarded the Peruvian ship and fought valiantly before being killed. The *Esmeralda* was rammed again and sank. The tale of Prat's heroism helped mobilize Chileans behind the war effort, and this lost battle is still celebrated as the most significant moment of the conflict.

The War of the Pacific helped consolidate the processes of aligning la patria with the nation and a population with shared traditions and a common culture and history, but it also laid bare military deficiencies.[9] Victory owed as much to luck and the state of the Peruvian and Bolivian forces as Chilean bravery, martial prowess, or perceived racial superiority. Officers had no real military training, and in addition to volunteers inspired by a sense of adventure or economic opportunity, troops had been forcibly rounded up from among the poor, drifters, drunks, and criminals. The push to reform the antiquated force gained momentum soon after the war ended, and in 1885 the government assigned the task of training its officers to the Prussian captain Emil Körner. The reformed army complemented the legacy of uninterrupted military victory and the idea of the Chilean people as a military race with a transcendental love of la patria and a self-identification with the nation. The underlying concept went beyond a love of the land, customs, and traditions; it was a spiritual and metaphysical sense of la patria, expressed in metaphors of collective souls, origins, and destiny. Officers shared a distaste for politics and politicians, and they saw themselves and the institution as the true embodiment of the nation, its moral reserve, and defenders of its values. In 1913, Colonel Ernesto Medina described the military's "most noble mission" as "assuring the internal and external safety and integrity of society, and [. . .] contributing to the moral and economic progress of the country."[10] This twentieth-century military mission to build and defend la patria was a geographic, spiritual, moral, educational, economic, and industrial project, and compulsory military service was central to it.[11]

The annual draft was introduced in 1900, initially as nine months of service for all men between twenty and forty-five years of age. Most immediately, conscription would meet the need for a trained contingent capable of defending national borders given the threat at the time of war with Argentina. Both this potential conflict and the conscription legislation it helped ease in emerged as points of protest for new social movements. Burgeoning anarchist, socialist, communist, internationalist, and pacifist movements rejected the militaristic patriotism that underpinned the reformed army, as well as the talk of war with Chile's neighbor. Protest against the draft became a fundamental issue for libertarians, and anarchists called for a boycott of the barracks, while socialists demanded the armed forces be dismantled entirely. The idea that military service degraded recruits and transformed them into killers who could be used against their countrymen was confirmed for opponents of the draft by the armed forces' role in the deaths of striking port workers in Valparaíso (1903), protesters during Santiago's meat riot (1905), and striking nitrate workers in the Santa Maria School Massacre in Iquique (1907). The army, in turn, dismissed anarchism, socialism, pacifism, and antimilitarism as treasonous ideas that were foreign to Chile and that threatened la patria and its glorious history. It countered the characterization of conscription as a "school of crime" with the idea of the barracks as the "school of the people." Military service was part of the military's claim to legitimacy in the face of opposition, but also part of a mission to forge the nation in its own image and overcome the deep divisions that cut through Chilean society in the early decades of the century.[12]

In his 1920 classic of Chilean military literature *Vigilia de armas* (*Vigil of Arms*), Tobías Barros dismissed the idea of the "roto, patriot by nature, soldier by lineage and instinct" as a "farce" and the stuff of novellas.[13] Supporters of the draft celebrated military service as a way to civilize, discipline, educate, and instill morals in the Chilean people; cure societal vices; and encourage hygienic habits, along with values such as thriftiness, punctuality, and work ethic. It would build the nation by making citizens of *paisanos* (a pejorative term for civilians), and the patriotism cultivated in recruits would in turn combat ideas of social change and act as an antidote to the "socialist ideas" that had "contaminated" workers in the cities and the countryside.[14] In addition, having rich and poor men serve together would be a "democratizing" and "homogenizing" force that would erode societal differences and contribute to national harmony. By the time Barros was writing, however, service as an exercise in "democracy" was recognized as a failure.[15] Few eligible men registered, fewer presented at the barracks, and the laws could not be effectively enforced. Draftees in these early years were predominantly young men who could not avoid conscription. Societal attitudes toward the draft shifted throughout the following decades, and by the time of the 1973 coup, service had become a source of pride and an attractive economic option among Chile's poor. Nevertheless, annual cohorts continued to represent only a small percentage of the male population, drawn almost exclusively from among the most impoverished sectors of society, as young men of means evaded service.[16] In 2013, for example, Félix recalled being struck by the segregation of surnames when he entered the barracks. "The same names are repeated a lot [among the professional soldiers]. Names that, for us, are a little odd. [These names] were not in the [conscript] ranks. I never saw an . . . Irarrázaval [among the conscripts], or anyone with the names of people who live in the other Chile up that way," he said, waving his hand eastward from Recoleta toward the *cordillera* (Andes mountain range). "There were [only] Gonzálezes, Pérezes."[17]

The military also saw itself as the driver of economic progress and the improvement in the living conditions of the masses as a way to safeguard la patria.[18] Poverty, officers reasoned, produced cracks in national and social unity where corrosive ideas could gain a foothold. Moreover, the lesson the Chilean army took from World War I was the correlation between military power, infrastructure, economic development and self-reliance, and modernization. "Total war" required not just a standing reserve of trained men but also entire industries that could be mobilized in defense of the nation.[19] Also in the wake of World War I, Chile fell into economic and political crisis, as European markets for exports disappeared and dramatic increases in unemployment fed social unrest, threatening the social order built on the niter mines and maintained by military force. With no political consensus on how to tackle the crisis, officers trained under Körner, and less bound to the oligarchy, intervened and pressured President Arturo Alessandri to resign. Two short-lived military juntas in 1924 and 1925 were followed by an administration led by Alessandri, who returned to Chile to complete his term. Carlos Ibáñez del Campo, one of the military power brokers behind the coups and later a minister under Alessandri, entrenched his political influence and in 1927 won a largely uncontested presidential election. As president, Ibáñez spent heavily on public works, promoted industry, and oversaw economic growth built largely on foreign capital. His administration laid the foundations for the welfare state, introduced social security, and broadened, while maintaining control over, political participation. A focus on development was coupled with the forceful repression of political opponents to maintain "unity" and reduce the Marxist threat. The Great Depression brought an end to the Ibáñez government, as the country was crippled by foreign debt, withering export markets, massive unemployment, and mounting unrest. Ibáñez went into exile in 1931, and after a period of political volatility, which included a number of failed or short-lived military interventions, stability was restored in 1932, when Alessandri again returned to office, and the armed forces withdrew from politics.[20]

The military mission survived the return to the barracks, and conscription was central to its new pared-down role in public life. The armed forces continued to protect the nation's borders and the idea of la patria by educating recruits and instilling in them patriotic values. Education had been a focus of service since its inception, when illiteracy rates reached more than 70 percent, and in the first decades of the draft an increasing number of conscripts left the barracks literate. From the late 1930s, in particular, the state expanded public education, but the still limited coverage failed to include Chile's peasant class. The reach of the military was far greater, and the barracks remained the only place for many young men to gain a basic education.[21] From 1953, military service also included training in a variety of trades. Ibáñez, who had returned from exile and won the presidential election the previous year, introduced the Military Work Service (Servicio Militar del Trabajo or SMT), which was renamed the Military Work Corps (Cuerpo Militar del Trabajo or CMT) in 1960. The SMT and the CMT strengthened the nation-building aspect of the military project by completing agricultural, emergency, and public works projects, as well as constructing roads, bridges, airfields, and canals in isolated parts of the country.[22]

In the second half of the century, the Chilean military project served as the foundation for the Cold War doctrine of national security. Western counterinsurgency complemented both the existing anticommunism and distaste for politics and politicians among Chilean officers, as well as established "developist" and repressive tendencies in local military thought.[23] National security had begun to influence military thinking in the region in the previous decades, but throughout the 1960s it fundamentally reframed the armed forces' mission for the postwar context. As the Left mobilized and social movements throughout the continent adopted Marxist language, Latin American officers trained in the US-run School of the Americas, and focused on defeating the internal and insurgent enemy within their borders. This repressive strain was nevertheless still paralleled by an emphasis on the need for development and modernization. From the 1960s, the US-led Alliance for Progress had pushed social and economic development in the region, including land reform. The policy advocated social reform as a means to reduce poverty, integrate marginalized groups, and, as a result, undermine the communist threat.[24]

The deepening polarization of Chilean politics from the 1960s, Allende's 1970 election, and the mounting social conflict under the Popular Unity government cemented in military thinking both the emphasis on repression and neutralizing the Left, and the need for progress and modernization.[25] In the decades prior to the coup, military service remained central to the armed forces' defense of la patria. In response to mounting tension and widening ideological division, the military began to question the doctrine of "professionalism" that had maintained decades of subordination to civilian rule, and it strengthened the draft. Recruits would be imparted with patriotic values and schooled in military history and traditions. Once discharged, they would act as ambassadors for this brand of patriotism and help slow the spread of revolutionary ideas. In 1970, and echoing decades of military thought, an army major argued that the military's "manifest" function was to be the armed protector of the state, and its "latent" duty was to protect Chile's "glories and traditions, providing cohesion and national integration."[26] Under Pinochet, political repression was widespread and brutal. However, the junta also retained a social mission. The regime set about dismantling unions, political parties, and collective action, but it also kept a focus on development as a way to "change Chileans' mentality" and "defeat Marxism in the Chilean consciousness." The regime's efforts to address socioeconomic problems rested on the widespread assumption at the time that underdevelopment bred Marxism and extremism.[27] In this sense, the junta continued the twentieth-century project to build and defend the nation that politicized la patria, partially decoupled it from geographic borders, rested on a self-identification with the nation, leaned heavily on the analogous citizen-building mission of military service, and evolved tangentially to, and largely isolated from, recruits' ideas of la patria.

Uniforms, Parades, and Toy Soldiers

Claudio de la Hoz (1973–75, Chillán) could not initially put his finger on why he had always wanted to do his military service. "I don't know," he said, as he instinctively straightened in his chair and tugged on the lapels of his imaginary uniform: "It was a passion that I had to sign up to do my military service." He went on to clarify that his father had always dreamed of seeing his son in uniform.[28] The patriotic passion that fueled Chilean boys' enthusiasm for service, or compelled them to volunteer, tended to be rooted in a love of tasseled uniforms, military parades, and tales of old wars. It was an expression of la patria locked in a commemorative cycle that continually looped back to the glories of the nineteenth century. The military's twentieth-century mission to define and defend the nation evolved in the relative isolation of Chile's barracks, while the most vital connection Chileans had with their military was a calendar of commemorative rituals.[29] With hindsight, ex-conscripts described the barracks prior to their service as a mystery and what they discovered when drafted as a different world, a separate world, a different country, or an island where time worked differently.[30] From the beginning of the twentieth century, a gap emerged and widened between the patria of the military's nation-building project and the "timeless" patria of myth, ritual, and monuments.[31]

In 1920 Barros dismissed the vast majority of recruits that entered the barracks as uncivilized, unhygienic, and unpatriotic, and the idea of the roto chileno as a literary invention, but he also conceded that a minority of those called up possessed the appropriate national spirit. This minority of rotos patriotas that filled Chile's regiments in times of danger had, he wrote, "endured the suggestion of martial music and the attraction of the national flag accompanied by hundreds of naked blades during September."[32] In his novella published in 1951, and based on his own service in Valparaíso at around the time Barros was writing, Gonzalo Drago similarly writes of the "contagious spectacle" of the military parade. Drago's conscript narrator describes a training march through a village where the men come out to see them, the women wave their handkerchiefs, and barefooted boys run alongside the recruits in admiration. Bands play and flags fly during the national celebrations, and he suspects that many of the boys and men in the crowd would willingly exchange places with the conscripts in their helmets, uniforms, and new boots. At another point, a different recruit, a little bewildered, declared that he had not entered the barracks to learn how to kill: "What would my mother say if I told her that I was learning to kill men? She would think I was crazy. She has always thought, I'm sure, that soldiers are there to parade in the reviews and the national festivities."[33]

"Contagious spectacles" became increasingly important as living memory faded. Annual commemorations of independence, the War of the Confederation and the War of the Pacific maintained a united national identity. The boys that would form the "class of '54" grew up on the outer edge of living memory of the final glory of the previous century. Guillermo Raillard (1973–75, Arica) remembered attending church as a young boy with his mother in downtown Santiago. There used to be an old woman along Avenida Independencia in a long, dirty, blue skirt and a dirty, white blouse, and barely one and a half meters tall. The woman was pointed out to Guillermo as having been a Sargento Candelaria in the war.[34] Mario Navarro (1973–75, Arica) remembered a veteran from the War of the Pacific who used to live around the corner from his childhood home in Arica. The elderly man used to wear his medals and march in the parades alongside the other veterans. When the veterans of the "War of '79" passed by, everyone stood to applaud them. "It was a tradition," recalled Mario.[35] These traditions, rituals, and related commemorative sites and practices maintained the narrative of nineteenth-century glory for the majority of those who entered the barracks between 1973 and 1990.

Ricardo Flores (1973) was seven years old when he joined the pre-military brigade in Iquique. Every branch of the armed forces had one, he explained, and seven or eight was about the normal age for boys to start. They wore replica uniforms and their hair short, like real soldiers, and were taught how to parade, rehearsing on the weekends for the important commemorations, most importantly the May 21 anniversary of the Battle of Iquique and the fiestas patrias (the September 18 celebration of Independence and the September 19 Day of the Glories of the Army). The brigades were founded in the mid-twentieth century, and they inculcated boys with values associated with the War of the Pacific: bravery, gallantry, virility, discipline, and manliness.[36] As boys, they admired soldiers immensely for the values they embodied and the respect they commanded, explained Ricardo, and while many eventually changed their mind, every boy in Iquique grew up wanting to be a soldier. There were, after all, only three pathways in the annexed territories of the militarized north: mining, fishing, and the military. Next to Ricardo, Freddy Valdivia (1973, Iquique) agreed, explaining that for Christmas boys wanted either toy soldiers or a drum to practice for the parades.[37] While Freddy and Ricardo were participating in the brigades in Iquique, young people in Chile's agricultural south took part in a broad-ranging 1967 survey. Almost a decade since the Cuban revolution, young people in the rural south predominantly looked beyond contemporaneous figures, or recent history, to the nineteenth century for their idols, including Bernardo O'Higgins, Arturo Prat, and Diego Portales.[38]

Under military rule, the junta positioned its mission above politics and moored it firmly in the nineteenth century. It equated the 1973 coup with the fight for independence, and emphasized the return of the nation to the values of the autocratic nationalism shaped by Portales. The Portalian years between the 1830 and the 1891 civil wars were a period of relative stability and economic growth that oversaw the expansion of Chile's national territories, with military victories in the north and the "pacification" of the indigenous population in the south. An important mechanism for linking the regime with the heroism of the previous century was the annual season of memory in September when official commemorations reflected the regime's narrative. The anniversary of the coup celebrated national salvation and unity and led into the fiestas patrias a week later. Huge crowds gathered on September 19 for the military parades that brought Chileans together across class divides. School children, too, paraded. War bands based in schools replaced the pre-military brigades, and students in uniform marched on August 20—O'Higgins' birthday—and May 21.[39] This patria of parading and old wars continued to attract boys to the barracks under the dictatorship.[40] In his memoir, former recruit Nelson Castillo (1978–79, Iquique) recalled the slow train trip north. Seeing the plains outside of Antofagasta and heading toward Iquique, his thoughts turned to familiar war stories and he felt part of a tradition of bravery and glory.[41] In 2012 Enrique P.* (1982–84, Tierra del Fuego) explained that he had had a positive impression of the army before entering the barracks by insisting that he had always liked the uniform.[42] J.H.B. served at the same time as Enrique and also in Tierra del Fuego, and he, too, framed his patriotism in terms of the commemorative rituals: "Since I was a boy," he wrote, "I wanted to serve la patria and do my military service, I admired those in uniform and I liked very much attending the parades. With service I wanted to receive an education with equity and values, and strengthen my love for country."[43] As the ex-conscript movement emerged and grew, Chile's commemorative calendar was still organized around the anniversaries of battles and military victories. September 11 was no longer a holiday, and while the date continued to revive debate about military rule, the violent clashes between the carabineros and protesters that characterized the anniversary in the 1990s and early years of the twenty-first century had begun to wane. The fiestas patrias and the military parades were still a largely unifying experience. Goose-stepping soldiers wearing traditional helmets and gold-buttoned uniforms appeared on billboards in the Santiago metro system promoting the yearly intake for the military school, and war bands and regular parading continued to form an important part of life, particularly in the north. This pattern of commemoration that dominated the twentieth century and has continued into the twenty-first underpinned the sense of patria that many former recruits felt was betrayed by service under Pinochet.

In October 1977 J.D.S.M.N. reported for service in Lautaro in the southern ninth region, and thirty years later his memories of his conscription were organized disenchantment. "Throughout my 'service to la patria,'" he wrote, "I learned a new concept and a new patria."[44] This clash of patrias structured many ex-conscripts' shared memory of disillusionment, as former recruits contrasted their dreams of joining up as boys, their hopes for their time in the barracks, and their patriotic sense of duty with their dashed expectations, the abuse they suffered, their experience of political repression, and their lingering fears.[45] Félix explained this rupture by pointing out the absence of photos of himself in uniform in his house. His living space was decorated with collections of mementos and knickknacks, but no images of himself as a conscript. Previously, he said, people had proudly displayed photos of relatives in uniform, but his would not be hung. More than providing an overarching structure to ex-conscript memory, the gap between the patria of uniforms, parades, and toy soldiers and the patriotism of the twentieth-century military mission shaped former recruits' experiences and memories of Pinochet's wars inside the barracks.[46]

The Front Line of the "Internal War"

The coup clearly and instantly established the front line of the "internal war." Recruits throughout the country were informed that the armed forces had seized control of Chile, and that anyone who did not agree with the action should take a step forward. Decades later, ex-conscripts recalled being held in formation by a mixture of confusion, uncertainty, concern for the safety of their families if they broke ranks, and the assumption that they would be immediately shot if they dissented.[47] It was made clear that civilians were the enemy and that the edge of the patria that underpinned the junta's war extended only to the outer edges of Chile's regiments.[48] The same logic was instilled in recruits from subsequent classes, who testified to being obliged to make enemies of anyone not in uniform and everyone beyond the walls of the barracks. The standard for this type of loyalty was a willingness to kill family members. L.D.T.L.R. (1986–87) wrote two decades after his service that "after the third month when we had already submitted, the brainwashing started. They made us believe that every person who thought differently to the regime or was on the political left was an enemy of la patria and had to be killed, even if they were our parents or siblings."[49] "The brainwashing was so strong in those 18 months," wrote Isidoro G.* (1987, Punta Arenas), "that at one point I thought that I could kill my own family, because they always spoke of an adversary, and that everyone outside of the regimental base was a potential enemy."[50] Being prepared to kill one's parents was still the measure of patriotic zeal in Peldehue in the early 1990s. In a 1992 statement, Jorge Antonio Concha Meza (1991–92) testified to constant beatings, electrical current applied to his neck, being forced to eat off the floor, forced standing, and threats of death should he talk about his training. During one exercise, he was taken "prisoner of war," beaten, pressed for the names of his instructors, and asked whether he would kill his parents. On replying that he would not, the beating intensified.[51] Where la patria was, for many, an extension of family, military training pitted the two against one another.

Defending *la Patria*

The Valech Report referred to what former recruits often describe as "brainwashing" as "indoctrination." It noted the hostility fostered toward civilians in the barracks but argued that the brutality of the repression was also enthusiastically taken up by carabineros in isolated towns and by conscripts who were "only superficially exposed to the work of indoctrination." Some, it continued, followed orders fearing the price of disobedience, while others "enjoyed the new work."[52] In 2013 an ex-conscript (1973) spoke of both fear and enjoyment. During a group meeting he described his involvement in the Tancazo, a failed coup attempt in June 1973. He and his compañeros were told they were being taken to Peldehue, but they ended up in front of the Moneda. The sixteen-year-old next to him wet his pants. After the meeting, he conceded that in the weeks after the coup there were conscripts who did things "on their own initiative" (*por su cuenta*). "On their own initiative," he repeated for emphasis. They enjoyed the power, he explained, and "did foolish things" (*hacían weá*). He remembered one conscript talking with pride and excitement about how he had seen an old woman in the street, taken aim at her, and watched her fall.[53] In the 2010 documentary *El soldado que no fue*, an ex-conscript spoke of never knowing if he or the recruit next to him was responsible for shooting someone. Asked how he felt firing in front of the Moneda, he spoke of a similar adolescent sense of power within a permissive context. "The truth?" he asked, "or should I lie?" The truth was, he said, that he had been a criminal as a young man, and with a gun in his hands he "felt proud, strong, excited": "If they sent me to kill, I killed. If they sent me to attack, I attacked." He paused to consider how to best explain his feelings. "It was exciting" (*tenía ánimo*), he said and he reenacted how he had sprayed downtown buildings with bullets "just for the fun of it" (*por pura weá, no más*).[54] An internalization of the military narrative also ran through this mix of fear and empowerment. The clash of patrias that shaped the memory of service within the twenty-first-century ex-conscript movement emerged fitfully and at different moments for individual former recruits, as their perspective on the coup and the regime was shaped not only by their experience of service but also by the subsequent decades of life under military rule and the transition to democracy.

Paola helped with the administration of the Agrupación SMO, which represents former recruits drafted in 1973. Over coffee in the office of the mechanics' workshop where she worked in 2013, she described her own awakening to the truth about human rights abuses in the late 1980s. Born in 1971, Paola grew up under military rule, and watching television, she explained, she thought Chile was "the best." She pinpointed her awareness of another reality to the 1987 visit to Chile by Pope John Paul II, which came in the wake of years of protest and in the buildup to the 1988 plebiscite. Despite the Vatican's preference for non-provocation and the regime's advertising campaign that presented a united and peaceful nation, the pope's appearances produced moments that broke free of their choreography. Televised conversations with *pobladores* (people from the poblaciones) turned to discussions of political repression, chants about human rights resounded around the National Stadium, and violent clashes at Parque O'Higgins cut through the state censorship. They laid bare, however briefly, Chile's memory struggles.[55] For Paola, it was the moment she realized there was another Chile, one shaped by violence and repression. She told this story to illustrate her experience of awakening and, by analogy, the experiences of a segment of the agrupación's members. Many, she said, had left the barracks proud and thinking of themselves as heroes of la patria. Revelations about human rights violations over the years had altered that self-perception.[56] Across town, human rights lawyer Hernán Montealegre, who represented ex-conscripts (1973–90) in Puente Alto, also spoke of staggered realizations that the "internal war" had not been real. For some, especially those without firsthand experience of the repression, it came years after service. For others, it had been immediate.[57]

Félix described most prisoners as having been arrested just for thinking differently, while others had no idea why they had been detained. To make his point, he spoke of the night he had fallen asleep while guarding Freddy Taberna, a well-known socialist in Iquique who had reported voluntarily to the Telecommunications Regiment on September 16. Like most ex-recruits, Félix reported being deprived of sleep in the weeks following the coup, when they were sent from one twelve-hour shift directly to the next, and then the next. They were, he recalled, "zombies." On this night, he fell asleep. Taberna reached across and woke Félix, warning him not to sleep on duty. His superiors could punish him, he warned, or even court-martial and execute him. "'Point your gun at me,' he said. 'Do your job well,'" recalled Félix. "If he were so dangerous, why did he do that?" he asked rhetorically.[58] Taberna was transferred to Pisagua, where he was sentenced to death by the second war council on October 29 and executed the following day.[59]

Pedro Cáceres (1973–76, Puente Alto and Villa Grimaldi) and Manuel Ureta (1973, Puente Alto) both encountered relatives or friends among the detainees during their service. In addition to these moments of instant recognition, they also described a fuller process of realization about the extent of the dictatorship's abuses that stretched over decades.[60] They mentioned the 1978 discovery in Lonquén of the remains of fifteen victims who had gone missing in late 1973. The find rocked Chile, providing the first hard evidence of the practice of forced disappearance. Pedro and Manuel noted, in particular, the impact of the book about the case by Máximo Pacheco, the first edition of which was banned in 1980, before a second edition was printed in 1983.[61] They recalled secretly watching the 1982 film *Missing*—banned under Pinochet—which dramatized the search for the American journalist Charles Horman, who was murdered in the week following the coup. They also spoke of Patricia Verdugo's 1985 book *Los zarpazos del puma*—also originally banned—and its explosive account of the Caravan of Death and the brutality of the invented war.[62] The conversation during which they reconstructed important moments of realization for the ex-conscript population took place in early 2014, and Pedro explained that he had also learned new things about the coup from the recent documentary series, *Chile: The Forbidden Images* (2013). The sum total of these personal processes and individual moments is a shared narrative within the ex-conscript movement that recruits were used as part of an invented war, which, instead of saving la patria, turned a nation and a people against itself.

Ismael Catalan entered the barracks in 1972 and completed his service in early 1973. He explained in 2014 to television journalists that it had a positive influence on him, teaching him to be responsible and instilling a deep love for la patria. To emphasize the point, he recited the oath to the flag on camera. The day after the coup he was recalled as a reservist, but it was not the same. The punishments meted out to conscripts were much worse, he said, and he was forced to witness and participate in the torture of detainees, including being involved in applying electrical current to various parts of prisoners' bodies. He implored viewers to not put everyone in the same bag: "All of the officers, all of the corporals, all of them were allied to a patria, but I never signed up in order to do those things, never."[63] Similarly, Sergio Munizaga (1973–75, Iquique) spoke in 2012 of the sense of lawlessness within the military in the wake of the coup. He recalled that he and his compañeros got to know a young local woman who lived next to where they were posted. One day, a superior officer saw the young woman greet the soldiers and accused her of mocking them. She was taken away and raped. The rapist returned, telling Sergio to do what he wanted with her, to which Sergio countered: "I'm here to do my military service, to learn. [. . .] I came to defend la patria, if at some point we have to defend la patria, not to do the bad things you're doing."[64] The same sense of patriotic betrayal underpins other former recruits' descriptions of civilians—including, at times, civilians they detained—not as the enemy but as compatriots, Chilean brothers, or simply also Chileans.[65] Martín P.* (1984–86), for example, served when "war" returned to the streets in the mid-1980s. In his 2011 testimony, he wrote of the punishments of training, clarifying that "no one told me that was how to serve la patria." He and his fellow recruits were later kitted out for war and sent out on the street during the new state of emergency: "But war with whom?" he asked. He went on to note the fear in the street as people began to tremble at the sight of them. "I used to think about defending my patria," he wrote, "but against a foreign enemy, not my own people."[66]

The different elements of the ex-conscript memory of the front line between themselves and civilians can be seen in a conversation in the documentary *El soldado que no fue*. Gathered in a garage, former recruits from the "class of '54" spoke of a sense of adolescent adventure, of "brainwashing," and they shared experiences in terms of the clash between exclusive and inclusive concepts of patria. One ex-recruit described how his instructors had "changed his life, changed his mentality." Amid the constant pressure and the isolation of the barracks, he said, "they convince you," and he left his service as a Pinochetista. He framed his recollections of a raid on a radio station in terms of a collision of the sight of crying staff members, his own confusion, and his "movie mentality." A second ex-conscript also spoke of how they had "played" soldiers during raids, taking their cues from what they knew from television and movies. He reiterated, too, how instructors had insisted that civilians—"our own compatriot brothers"—were our enemy. A third former recruit similarly described how he had "repressed" people he had had no reason to repress because they were "human beings just like me." All of them also spoke of the danger inside the barracks that recruits faced. A fourth ex-conscript recalled how he had volunteered for military service and seen things in the desert that he could not talk about as threats made against his family still hung over him. He remembered, too, his own punishment and the danger of holding political opinions on the inside. Despite the coup ostensibly establishing the edge of the barracks as the front line, Chile's "internal war" inevitably shrank inside its regiments, as recruits were drawn from those sectors of society that bore the brunt of the political repression and that were most threatening to the armed forces.[67]

In the decade leading up to the coup, leftist groups identified the military with the bourgeoisie and called for the armed forces to be dissolved. Some announced their intention to infiltrate the military, including the conscript ranks, or boasted that they had already done so.[68] The groups' calls for defiance within the lower ranks was echoed in the music of the New Song Movement (Nueva Canción) that identified ordinary soldiers with the people (*pueblo*) and officers as the enemy.[69] Potential and rhetorical attacks on the armed forces fed into military concerns about subversion and infiltration, and they paralleled both an internal power struggle between constitutionalists and *golpistas* (officers who supported the idea of military intervention) and the growing unrest and rhetoric of "civil war" outside the barracks.[70] Beyond leftist plans to infiltrate the military, military fears of subversion, and the subsequent purging of the professional ranks under military rule, ex-conscript memory reveals an institutional suspicion of recruits, rooted in longer-term military thinking that equated the poor with the Marxist threat. Postwar counterinsurgency and social conflict in the 1960s and early 1970s underscored the importance of conscription in military thought as a tool to safeguard la patria by educating recruits and disseminating patriotic values. However, it also and increasingly meant that conscripts themselves were seen as potential threats to the nation as they were drafted from among the "internal enemy."

In the mid-1970s, reservist lieutenant "Pérez" spoke—using a pseudonym—of the simple formula that equated the poor with radical and leftist politics: "The first enemy is the enemy inside the country: the civilian, and above all the civilian who is poorly dressed, the roto. Because the roto is a Marxist, and the Marxist is against the unity of the state, of the whole nation. So this is enemy number one. [. . .] The external enemy is everything that is outside the national territory. In the Chilean army, all the courses are oriented toward instructing the troops that the external enemy is Argentina, Peru, Bolivia."[71] At around the same time, "ex-soldier" "Ramírez" described the attitude toward recruits he encountered inside the barracks in the years leading up to the coup: "Of the conscripts, they used to say that they joined the army because they had nothing to eat on the outside. Being inside for a year assured them that they would eat. There was a tremendous contempt for the conscripts, due to their proletarian origins. [. . .] The enemy is the civilian, anyone from the poor classes, workers."[72] The assumption that the rural masses and the urban poor were frustrated and revolutionary had shaped Chilean military attitudes toward conscription, education, and economic development since the beginning of the century. It had also underpinned postwar counterinsurgency and US foreign policy, as well as the theory among revolutionaries that the guerilla actions of the vanguard could harness simmering mass discontent and spark a popular uprising. By the time of the coup in Chile, however, the link between poverty and extremism was already being questioned. A decade after the Cuban Revolution, the spread of radical ideas through the slums, shantytowns, and countryside of Latin America had not occurred. In Chile, pobladores were far from a homogenous group in terms of their politicization, politics, willingness to protest or make demands, perspective on opportunity, conception of the future, or their ideas of agency. The heterogeneity of the working poor was often overlooked in the political parties' efforts to mobilize them, and even hidden behind the blanket term *pobladores*. Across the spectrum, however, concerns in the poblaciones tended to be concrete: housing, food, and employment. Pragmatism, not ideology, drove a lot of political activity, which then faded as demands became more abstract. Protestors under military rule, too, were often aspirational and sought not revolution, but inclusion and integration.[73] Tina Rosenberg relates exchanges with residents in La Pincoya, a población known for political activism under Allende, but where by 1988 fear, the realities of economic hardship, and the populist social policies of the regime had dulled the locals' militancy. As political party volunteers toured the población to muster support for the upcoming plebiscite, one local woman insisted that she did not "mix in politics," before asking if it were true that she could be arrested for registering to vote. A young man with no job and no home reflected widespread resignation: "Getting rid of Pinochet won't change anything," he said, "they're all the same." Others signed up to the National Advance Party campaigning in favor of Pinochet, and promising to help locals access housing assistance in return for votes. Irene Pérez signed up, saying about the plebiscite: "We're not against or in favor. We just want a better house."[74] Rosenberg also cites a 1985 survey in which Chileans ranked the country's problems; highest on the list were economic problems, followed by a lack of work.[75] Despite the complexity of the situation, ex-conscript memory reveals the persistence in the barracks of the simple equation of poor with radical.

Lore among the "class of '54" suggests that the "class of '55" was much smaller, because the military was wary of recruiting "terrorists" from among popular sectors. The armed forces preferred instead to recall reservists and extend the service of serving conscripts from one to two years.[76] Military figures show a reduction of around one-third in the annual cohorts between 1973 and 1974, bucking the trend of gradual yearly increases for most of the previous decade. The extension of service to two years under military rule effectively reset the cohort sizes, and the annual intake did not approach 1973 levels until the late 1970s. Whether or not this shift reflects military concerns about who the draft would bring into the barracks, the lore about the "class of '55" is indicative of a sense of animosity toward conscripts that was felt by recruits throughout the regime. R.A.S.V., who volunteered in the early 1980s out of love of patria, wrote that the "military command was 'Pinochetified,' the army was politicized with the class struggle and the doctrine of national security. Because they were civilians and in the vast majority came from the popular classes (because the rich never did military service), conscripts were viewed as potential traitors to the patria, to this concept of patria that no one clarified for us."[77] César Rivas Vergara (1984–86, Manantiales), who had signed up in the mid-1980s as way of avoiding the street violence on the southern edge of the capital, recalled how he and his fellow recruits were welcomed at the barracks with insults, such as "communists," "thieves," "faggots" (*maricones*), and "criminals" (*patos malos*), and told "that judgment day had arrived for all the protests and disorder [they] were responsible for in Santiago."[78] Within this general context of suspicion and mistrust toward draftees, targeted political persecution cut through the conscript ranks.

Recruits recall the danger of being labeled a communist, enemy, or traitor, and the feeling that they were at risk of punishment, torture, or death. Reasons for being targeted varied, including lapses in discipline, disobeying an order, disagreeing with the regime, suspected political activity, an actual history of political engagement, or even Russian or "leftist" sounding names.[79] Recruits were not immune to the effort to purge the military ranks of opponents and were at times interrogated about their political beliefs or those of family members.[80] It was René Martínez's familial connection, for example, that cost him his life. The twenty-year-old reservist was recalled to the San Bernardo barracks on September 22, 1973, and is listed among the disappeared. His father, Juan, was detained in December 1973, prompting the family's attempt to contact René. His family was initially told that René was unavailable, but they later found out that he had, in fact, already been executed and his remains buried in Patio 29 of the General Cemetery of Santiago. He had been accused of participating in the organization of a counter-coup, with suspicions resting on the fact that Juan had been a socialist leader.[81] Decades after their service, most former recruits insisted they had had no idea about politics, while those who were members of political parties or youth groups tended to explain their involvement in terms of economic strategy or boyish fun.[82] Whatever their motivation, they kept their political pasts and opinions quiet in the barracks. L.R.V.R. (1973), for example, had been an active Popular Unity sympathizer as a young man, and he wrote of being told on September 11 that "la patria [was] at war." "The point is," he wrote, "that they did not tell us who we were at war with." It soon became clear that there was no war, he wrote, and that the repression was targeting the people they were supposed to be protecting, and he began to fear being detained. His fears only grew after witnessing the mock execution of several compañeros for attempted desertion.[83] A similar narrative of fear, disillusionment, and bitterness also echoes through descriptions of alleged political persecution inside the barracks during the immediate posttransition years.

The plebiscite and transition to democracy in Chile coincided with revolutions throughout Eastern Europe, the fall of the Berlin Wall, the beginning of the dissolution of the Soviet Union, and the reunification of Germany. Nevertheless, the Chilean army only officially moved on from the Cold War paradigm in the early twenty-first century.[84] Deserters and conscripts who had served in the early 1990s and subsequently approached CODEPU denouncing mistreatment and seeking legal, psychological, or medical assistance testified to the danger of being labeled an enemy.[85] They described mistreatment and torture that resulted from accusations of familial political activity, their own alleged political beliefs or plans to launch attacks from within the barracks, or having the name Lenin.[86] Psychologists who worked with the young men identified political motivations for alleged abuse between 1990 and 1992. In subsequent years, they observed no particular motivation for harsh treatment, other than undermining conscripts' free will. They also write that in some cases the recruits had admired the military and had wanted to do their military service, and that most struggled to reconcile the idea that the instructors mistreating them were not the enemy but "defenders of la patria," "guarantors of the nation," "brave," and "committed to the country."[87]

In addition to the suspicion and persecution of recruits, the front line inside the barracks manifested as the existential threat of training exercises in which recruits played the part of the civilian enemy. In 2012 Raúl Acuña (1976–78) recalled such an exercise in 1976, in which recruits were woken to defend against a civilian attack. Twenty-four conscripts were ordered to report with live ammunition and instructed to put the first bullet in the body and the second in the air. He later recognized one of the civilian attackers as a fellow recruit, and not understanding what was going on, he secured his rifle and headed off with another compañero to guard the infirmary against the "extremists." His compañero was later struck by an attacker with a rifle butt, and as he fell his own rifle went off, hitting the "extremist" in the neck and killing him almost immediately. He died in Raúl's arms, soaking his uniform in blood. Not until that point did it become clear to Raúl that the alleged attack had been a simulation.[88] Realism and the use of live ammunition in conscript training exercises is widely reported, and N.R.M.P. (Punta Arenas) wrote that "the danger of taking a bullet and losing your life was always there in the combat exercises and war simulations, and every now and then conscripts used to die."[89] For J.D.U.G. (1980), the training led him to consider his instructors to be the "true enemies."[90]

The memory of a front line within the barracks clashed publicly with other narratives in March 2014 at the inauguration of a monument to Pedro Prado in Iquique. Prado was the name of the conscript who Félix Pinares insisted on television in 2013 had been shot at his side by the regiment's own soldiers.[91] What is not disputed is that Prado died on October 1, 1973. According to the official version of events given at the time by the military authorities, Prado was killed by political prisoners Jorge Marín and William Millar, who had been detained in late September. During an attempt to escape, the prisoners took refuge in the cemetery that abutted the Telecommunications Regiment in Iquique, where they allegedly killed Prado. The following year, on the anniversary of the coup, Avenida 11 Oriente, which traverses nearly the entire city, was renamed Soldado Pedro Prado Ortiz. Decades later, the Rettig Commission found the official version implausible, citing the unlikelihood the prisoners could have escaped. The commission's report instead included the updated explanation that Prado had been shot by unknown, politically motivated civilians while patrolling the cemetery, and it lists Marín and Millar among the disappeared.[92]

By 2007 the story behind the street name Pedro Prado had largely faded in Iquique, but the decision to again rename the street to honor Salvador Allende upset many retired soldiers. Retired subofficer Guido Díaz had completed his military service with Prado, and led the push by ex-officers to honor the fallen conscript. They first proposed reverting the street name from Avenida Salvador Allende Gossens to Soldado Pedro Prado Ortiz for the section that runs past the cemetery and the site of former regiment. In the end, however, they settled for attaching the recruit's name to the small square in front of the cemetery. Díaz also personally provided half the funds to erect a monument to the conscript in the square: a statue of a uniformed soldier standing on a plinth with his rifle in front of him. When asked whether the monument was to a victim of "terrorism" or "human rights violations," Díaz insisted that the controversy did not interest him. He was motivated, instead, by having served with Prado. Nevertheless, he remained convinced of the revised official version of events, with the bullets that had killed Prado coming from unknown civilians. Moreover, the conceptualization of the memorial framed Prado as an emblematic martyr of leftist, civilian aggression in the midst of the "internal war." The monument's plaque read: "To the Soldier Pedro Rolando Prado Ortiz, who fell in the line of duty on 1 October 1973. The citizens of Iquique and the Telecommunications Regiment No. 6 Tarapacá, in recognition of your courage and your valuable sacrifice."[93] As the statue and the plaque were unveiled, narratives literally competed to be heard.[94]

Héctor Marín, brother of Jorge Marín and president of a group representing relatives of murdered or disappeared prisoners in Iquique and Pisagua, used a megaphone to speak over the top of the ceremony. He led a funa that sought to make the wider point that the monument did not reflect the truth of the incident, and specifically to defend Jorge's reputation. After the ceremony, the protesters placed a poster over the plaque that read: "Pedro Prado: Victim of the dictatorship." A larger banner held in front of the monument read: "Honor and glory! Pedro Prado and Michel Nash: Victims of the dictatorship." The pairing of Prado with Nash was part of an effort to link the monument to human rights cases. The debate over the street name and the monument coincided with renewed investigations into the "Nash and others" case about executions and disappearances in the region in the weeks after the coup. This process also led to new accusations and pieces of information about Marín and Millar, filling out scenarios in which the prisoners were brutally tortured and later killed. Army representatives attended the commemoration but made no statements to the press. Héctor Marín, however, told local journalists that the "army should tell the truth about the death of the soldier Pedro Prado."[95] He had earlier spoken directly to Prado's mother, saying, "My brother did not kill your son. Soldiers killed him."[96]

Prado's mother Violeta and his sister Gilda had traveled from Santiago to attend the ceremony. Violeta spoke of her sorrow and her joy on the day. She was happy and grateful that her son's life was being remembered, "because they don't do this anywhere."[97] The family was proud that Pedro had gone from the Santiago comuna of Quinta Normal to Iquique to do his military service. He had wanted to do it, she said, and to do it far from home so his family would not see him in uniform. She recalled her son as a young man who liked cars, mechanics, and boxing. If the family had known what was to come, they would have convinced him to stay in Santiago. Their effort to attend the unveiling was not a tribute to a "valuable sacrifice" but an expression of a family's grief. The friction during the event left Violeta overwhelmed and sobbing, and she was unable to take part in the ribbon-cutting as planned.

Félix had not been able to speak during the ceremony/funa, but he later addressed the remaining *funadores* (protesters): "Pedro Prado was not killed by a civilian, everything came from inside the Telecommunications Regiment. For me, it's surprising that they blame his death on two detainees, when the detainees were tightly guarded."[98] The army's 1990 presentation to the Rettig Commission lists Prado's death among those resulting from political conflict: "Shot by a sniper while patrolling the población of Baquedano."[99] It also documents the names of thirty-three further conscripts who lost their lives "in the line of duty" during the dictatorship: twenty-one in 1973, six in 1974, and six more between 1975 and 1986. The total is more than the seventeen conscripts listed in the Rettig Report;[100] however, neither set of figures is representative of conscript deaths.[101] The Rettig Report focused on politically motivated acts—by armed forces personnel or civilians—that resulted in death or disappearance, excluding many of the types of fatalities later reported by ex-conscripts. The cases presented by the army in 1990 were part of a belligerent insistence on the war narrative that used newspaper reports about caches of weapons and lists of military victims to document the other side of the "war." While the army presentation does not offer a reliable number, it does align with conscript morality rates (see chapter 5) in as much as it suggests that the greater threat to conscript safety was not beyond the barracks' walls but inside

Chile's regiments. Of the thirty-four dead conscripts, eight (including Prado) reportedly fell to "terrorist aggression." A further nineteen conscripts were "accidentally shot"—one by an unknown shooter, sixteen by a fellow conscript, and two reportedly accidentally shot themselves—and the remaining seven deaths were the result of other, mainly traffic, accidents.[102]

The ceremony to honor Pedro Prado became a flashpoint for competing memories of military rule as expressed through the recruit's story: one family's grief at the loss of a son and brother, another family's defense of their sibling's reputation, the ongoing search for the truth regarding the disappeared, the armed forces' war narrative, alleged military misinformation, and victims groups' protest activities. Prado is also a focused example of a broader sense of bitterness and patriotic betrayal among ex-conscripts, as well as the narrative of the front line of the "internal war" receding inside the barracks. Similarly conflicted notions of la patria also frame ex-conscript memory of Chile's "almost wars" and its internal frontier.

The Internal Frontier and "Almost-War"

In 2012 Miguel Saavedra (1977–79, San Bernardo) published his memoir *My War* about his military service on the front line of the almost-war with Argentina. The book resulted from the regular meetings of a group of former conscripts in San Bernardo who had remained in contact after leaving the barracks. Saavedra writes of his pride at having been a member of the armed forces, as well as the youthful enthusiasm of his fellow recruits to wear the uniform. He also includes images of a card as an example of the mail soldiers in the far south received from the public. On one side, a hand-drawn image of Our Lady of Mount Carmel—patron saint of the Chilean army—sits underneath the greeting "TO A BRAVE SOLDIER!" On the reverse, the hand-written text reads:

> . . . courageous soldiers who of Chile have been the
> backbone, etc. . . .
> Only God knows how much we owe you, brave soldier.
> We admire you, we respect you, and we love you, brave
> soldier.
> Came back soon and happy, we are waiting for you,
> husband, son, brother, brave soldier.
> Merry Christmas,
> . . . By our sons they will also be known.
> ¡VIVA CHILE!
>
> Dec. 1978.

They had thought of themselves as heroes of the entire nation, Saavedra writes, and that pride still remained. However, while his recollections of his service during the Beagle Channel conflict are shaped by an unshakable patriotic pride, they also include a countercurrent of bitterness, disillusionment, and abandonment. He writes of the unit's affection for particular officers and "acts of solidarity and nobility" on the part of some instructors but also of the physical mistreatment and psychological anguish of both training and life in the trenches. Moreover, the reception that awaited recruits on their discharge was not as welcoming as the 1978 Christmas card had promised, and decades later many were not happy.[103]

Saavedra's company swore the oath to the flag on July 9, one month after being mobilized to the south. The ceremony takes place annually on the anniversary of the Battle of La Concepción, when in 1882 heavily outnumbered Chilean troops were wiped out by Peruvian forces. Almost a century later, the commemoration seemed prescient, as young recruits once again faced dying at the hands of a much more numerous enemy. Conscripts on the southern border were assured that the Argentines had a significant advantage and they were made to write their final letters home because, as F.D.G.B. (Punta Arenas) clarified, "the war was coming and we could not know if we would return dead, alive, wounded, crippled, etc."[104] Nevertheless, from the moment they took the oath, Saavedra and his fellow recruits transformed into "true soldiers of our beloved patria," and they were prepared to give their lives.[105] The relentless anticipation of war, however, took its toll, and former recruits recall the slow emergence of a second front line that did not separate them from the Argentines but cut through the Chilean trenches.

Descriptions of the months spent waiting on the border are dominated by cold and hunger.[106] Like many former recruits who were stationed on the border, Saavedra writes of clothing that was inadequate for the climate and the lack of food. To supplement their diet—at one point "two large loaves of bread that had to last us seven days"—they stole lambs and hunted birds. With time, he also felt an increasing empathy for what he imagined young Argentines were going through, and his bitterness was directed at "irresponsible" politicians and diplomats. He goes on to describe how the aggression shown toward conscripts in Patagonia and framed as "discipline" sowed discontent and undermined morale: "to the point that we no longer thought of the war with our neighbors, as those we wanted to kill were our own superiors."[107] H.H.P.P. (1978–80, Lautaro) also recalled his service via the parallel war that played out in the trenches. It was, he writes, painful and humiliating, and his instructors seemed to enjoy the conscripts' suffering. He was later sent to the border, where he and his fellow recruits "spent several months in position in the trenches on alert and hidden in caves without food and fighting against hunger, the cold, the fear of dying, nervous breakdown, psychological collapse, and having to tolerate abusive punishments. These were the true enemies that we had to face."[108] G.E.V.R. (1977–79, Lonquimay) similarly wrote of the cold, hunger, and fear on the border and the physical punishments that drove some to desert: "We [were] confused, we [did] not know who was really the enemy, the Argentines or our instructors and superiors who constantly 'attack[ed]' us with blows."[109] With the emergence of this other front line, ex-conscripts recall their patriotic fervor as being incrementally matched, or in some cases overwhelmed, by a different type of readiness for war.

H.M.N.C. (1978–79, Punta Arenas) wrote of the three months of basic training being reduced to fifteen days, given the urgency of the impending war. His preparation included exercises where shots were fired over conscripts' heads, and simulations in which dogs were killed and their blood smeared on recruits who were beaten and stripped. His sense of vulnerability during the simulated war of training was later matched by his fear of actual war: "it is necessary to point out that the uncertainty, the threat of war, and the situation of constant anxiety of facing, day and night, the unexpected moment of crossing from life to death is something really horrible. [. . .] We were all in a bad way psychologically, under the extreme pressure of the specter of the war that was coming, that was on its way." One of his compañeros shot himself, "putting an end to the anguished nightmare and terror that were hounding us all."[110] Decades after their service, former recruits describe this compounding fear of death, their mounting rage and frustration at the mistreatment they received, and their emotional and psychological exhaustion as having fueled a desire for the battle to begin.[111] A.D.C.F. (1978, Temuco), who had entered the barracks with hopes of a military career, later recalled the mistreatment and constant fear, the tension of waiting for war, and the "smell of [impending] death" that undercut his aspirations. "In those moments [waiting for the war]," he wrote, "the only thing we wanted was that there would be war, that it started once and for all, to kill or be killed and end the distressing situation. [. . .] There were only two options: kill or die for la patria!"[112] L.A.J.F. (Punta Arenas), too, wrote of the brutality of the training, as well as the physical and mental exhaustion of his five months in the trenches: "our hairs were constantly 'on end' because the war could come at any moment with its message of death. / Besides the cold and our hunger, we only thought of war [. . .]. We were there, barely 18 years old to defend la patria. And where was our patria to protect us from the abuse, strikes, hunger, and the cold that we were subjected to?"[113] L.A.J.F.'s sense of abandonment is also representative of the narrative that came to shape ex-conscript memory of the almost-war and the return to civilian life.

In his memoir, Saavedra writes of how being hit had fed the unit's desire for the war to start, so they could displace anger and take revenge by killing as many Argentines as possible, even if it cost them their lives. Conflict with Argentina was avoided at the last minute, and on their arrival in Punta Arenas, the soldiers in Saavedra's unit were feted. Locals lined the streets, waving handkerchiefs and giving "V for Victory" signs at the passing column of trucks. This reception soon gave way to a "bitter taste" after the low-key and dismissive manner in which they were discharged from the army. The end of the buildup to war was, he writes, on one level a disappointment. After such a long wait, he felt it had all been for nothing. Moreover, the "war psychosis" left "marks [. . .] on our young minds. We felt like veterans of war without having fired a shot at the enemy." Over the coming decades, physical and psychological consequences of service and what Saavedra terms neglect of ex-conscripts in San Bernardo after their discharge began to emerge. The memories of recruits like Saavedra are organized by the tension between steadfast patriotism and the bitterness that grew in the trenches and was confirmed on discharge, and subsequently by life as a civilian. "We still feel proud," he wrote in 2012, "about how we responded to an entire nation, without going into what happened, we remember that at the same time, Chile was experiencing an internal situation that none of us had asked for. We were coming out of an adolescence, in which politics did not interest us. All the more reason why we did not understand foreign relations or the border problem. All we knew was that, due to the year of our birth, we had been the lucky ones."[114] These "mixed feelings" were also captured, for example, in one of the banners displayed during meetings in 2007 and 2008: "WE DID OUR DUTY TO LA PATRIA. WE WANT LA PATRIA TO DO ITS DUTY TO US."[115]

Parallel to the buildup of troops on the border, conscripts had at the same time also been defending la patria with a shovel instead of a rifle.[116] In early 1982 the *El Mercurio* newspaper reported a tense confrontation in the Beagle Channel between two Chilean torpedo boats and an Argentine vessel anchored off Deceit Island weeks before Argentine forces invaded the Falkland Islands.[117] This spike in neighborly tensions shared the front page with news about Pinochet's attendance at a ceremony to open a stretch of the Carretera Longitudinal Austral (CLA), referred to more commonly as the carretera austral, between Chaitén and Coyhaique. "This is how patria is made, this is how a nation is built," said the minister for public works, Brigadier General Patricio Torres, while extolling the benefits of the carretera. Pinochet also officially inaugurated Villa Santa Lucia, the first small town (*villorrio*) established as a result of the CLA.[118] As part of the same tour, the general told the locals in Tierra del Fuego that they were exercising Chilean rights over the southern regions.[119] The news that week brought together two strategies for defending the nation: the military defense of the border and the construction of a network of roads.

A portrait of Pinochet hangs in the marble hallways of the Military School for officers in Las Condes, Santiago. The caption next to the painting highlights his entrance into the school in 1933 and his graduation in 1936 as a sublieutenant, his rise to commander in chief of the army in August 1973, and his "assumption" of "the role of President of the Republic and Commander in Chief of the Chilean army" between 1973 and 1990. The centerpiece of this short synopsis of Pinochet's career, however, is the CLA: "during his government, many works benefiting the Chilean nation were realized, among the highlights is the construction of the Carretera Longitudinal Austral that linked thousands of compatriots by land and opened up a territory full of previously unknown mineral, forest, and tourist riches."[120] The construction of the CLA was central to the general's personal vision and his legacy.[121] It was also part of a longer military geopolitical tradition. Under Pinochet's rule, the army revisited earlier military attempts to push back the "internal frontier" and connect the extreme south to the rest of the country. In geopolitical terms, the internal frontier is the territory within the nation's borders, but beyond its influence or control.[122] The heartland of the country is its cultural and administrative focal point, and beyond that lies the hinterland, which provides resources for development, a territorial buffer for greater security, and a site of future expansion. Conquering the internal frontier means aligning the edges of the hinterland with the edges of the nation. For the armed forces, a network of roads that provided access to Chile's southern regions, which had previously been cut off by extreme weather conditions as well as the challenging, frozen geography of the far south, represented the country's greatest geopolitical challenge of the twentieth century.[123]

The edges of Chilean sovereignty were set in the late nineteenth century. The War of the Pacific (1879–83) set the northern borders, and Chilean troops then pushed south of the Bío Bío River, which had long demarcated Mapuche territory. The border with Argentina was set in by a treaty in 1881, and Chile annexed Easter Island in 1888. The growth phase in the geopolitical life cycle of the Chilean state then gave way to consolidation. The "Chilenization" in the north sought to put down cultural roots and to establish Chilean traditions in the formerly Bolivian and Peruvian regions. Similarly, in the first half of the twentieth century, Chilean governments continued efforts that began in the mid-nineteenth century to colonize the far south and solidify the Chilean presence.[124] They also made repeated and largely frustrated attempts to better integrate the far south, which was only accessible via precarious sea routes or over land via neighboring Argentina. The project was driven in large part by the concern that southern settlements could be more easily assimilated—both economically and culturally—into Argentina.[125] From 1976, the military regime renewed and redoubled its effort to build roads connecting the most southern regions with the heartland.

In a 2013 press interview, former general, former head of the CMT (the Military Work Corps) (1990–94), and former minster for public works (1989) Hernán Abad spoke of his time working on the CLA. He described people in Chaitén seeing automobiles for the first time, thanks to the army presence in the region. The military also brought live television and twenty-four-hour electric light to Santa Lucia, Chaitén, and Futaleufú. Importantly, continued Abad, the CLA also delivered national rituals and celebrations: "These people had never had an 18 of September [celebration]," he said, describing a photo of the first fiestas patrias parade in Alto Palena. "They did not feel Chilean. They dressed like *gauchos* [Argentine cowboys] and did not identify with national symbols." Abad also went on to frame the CLA as a Cold War mission, arguing that if it had not been built, the Soviets would have taken the Strait of Magellan.[126] While he couched the project in terms of the contemporaneous hemispheric conflict, the regime's effort to drive the internal frontier further south was also part of a longer history of colonization, as well as the same geopolitical tradition and concept of national defense that lay at the heart of the potential conflict on the border in the late 1970s and early 1980s.

According to army figures, from 1976 until 1981, work on the carretera was primarily carried out by men in the Minimum Employment Program (Programa de Empleo Mínimo, or PEM) managed by the municipalities of Puerto Montt and Chaitén.[127] Given the economic crisis and rising unemployment in the mid-1970s, the military regime implemented the emergency work program in 1974, and by 1976 it employed 200,000 men. By 1983, when Chile was hit with a second crisis, the PEM employed more than half a million men, and an additional emergency program, the Occupational Program for Heads of Families (Programa Ocupacional para Jefes de Hogar, or POJH), was introduced. Work as part of the PEM and the POJH was transitory and unstable, and workers were very poorly paid, receiving around a third of the already reduced minimum wage.[128] By the time the POJH was introduced, the involvement of workers in the programs on the CLA was winding down. From midway through 1982, the PEM workforce was almost entirely replaced by conscripts under the command of the CMT in Puerto Montt and Coyhaique. Army figures list 12,116 PEM and POJH workers as participating in CMT projects between 1976 and 1990, the majority of them (11,341) prior to 1983. During the same period, 7,378 conscripts—6,647 of them after 1983—worked on CMT projects. While the CLA was the largest and most important of the CMT projects, these numbers are not restricted to work on the carretera. It is also unclear whether all conscripts who worked on the road did so officially as part of the CMT. Similarly, the numbers do not capture the employees of private companies contracted to work on the CLA.[129] Nevertheless, it is clear that between 1976 and 1990 thousands of men built hundreds of kilometers of roads through Chile's harshest terrain, stretching from Puerto Montt to Cochrane.[130] Work continued after the transition, and by 1996 the CLA had been extended further south, connecting Puerto Montt with Puerto Yungay. The section between Puerto Yungay and Puerto Natales was still under construction in 2017.

The project was ambitious. The geographic isolation, impenetrable landscape, and extreme weather had previously stymied attempts to connect the far south, and the challenges facing this most recent attempt were equally formidable. Between Coyhaique and the border of the tenth region, for example, more than one million cubic meters of rock and nearly two million cubic meters of earth were removed; 1,077 meters of minor bridges and 465 meters of major bridges were built; and 277,000 kilograms of explosives were used.[131] Despite the difficulties, the costs were kept comparatively low. A 1988 document prepared by the National Planning Office emphasized the low cost of the construction. It reported that completing the CLA down to Puerto Yungay would require the removal of three million cubic meters of rock and five and a half million cubic meters of earth, and that more than sixty long bridges and more than five hundred short bridges had already been constructed, with an average of fifteen hundred people working on the project. The cost of US$198 million represented, the report continued, one-third of the cost of the construction of lines one and two of the Santiago metro, which began in the late 1960s and was completed in the late 1970s.[132] However, what appears in government documents as efficient use of resources is often remembered by ex-conscripts as deprivation and exploitation.

Ex-conscript recollections of the conditions on the CLA are dominated by descriptions of the cold, their hunger, and clothing unsuitable for the climate.[133] The work itself was labor intensive, as many parts along the route were accessible only by sea and off-limits to heavy machinery. The days were long and former recruits testify to physical abuse, daily quotas, and punishments if quotas were not met.[134] Francisco L.* (1983, Angol) wrote in 2008 of having to complete three trips a day carrying eight wooden planks the seven kilometers from Río Sucio to Lago Blanco. If he or his fellow conscripts did not complete the three trips before dark—due to exhaustion, the rain, the cold, or the weight of the waterlogged lumber, he clarified—they were punished: hit while doing army crawls, psychologically and verbally abused, or deprived of food or sleep.[135] José Pedreros (Angol) also entered the barracks in 1983 and spent six months on the CLA. He arrived in Chaitén and, along with three hundred others, was given rubber boots, blue jeans, a blue shirt, and oilskins, before being put to work. The recruits worked Monday to Sunday, and were given leave once a month to go to Chaitén. He mentioned frequent accidents, as well as daily targets: "There was a certain number of kilometers that had to be done by each section, and when we didn't finish it, they punished us with double the hours, or they left us in the rain for three hours with all our gear on."[136] The work was also dangerous. Former recruits describe safety standards as low, safety training—particularly with explosives—as nonexistent, and accidents as regular.[137] At times, too, accidents were fatal.

B.D.P.T. (1984) was sent to Chaitén to work on the CLA, and in his testimony describes an accident in Contao, where an inexperienced conscript driver rolled his tractor in the rain and snow and was crushed underneath it.[138] Former recruits' accounts of frequent accidents and numerous deaths echo locals' descriptions of the highway being paved with the bodies of the dead, but it is difficult to quantify the conscript lives lost on the CLA.[139] Without offering supporting evidence, Resolution 851 (2009) refers to thirty-five recruits who died in explosions and many others who had returned home injured.[140] Figures provided by army engineers in 2014 list a total of forty-five deaths in acts of service in the CMT while working on the CLA between 1969 and 2011. This number includes twenty conscripts. Of the eighteen deaths between 1974 and 1989, seven were conscripts.[141] However, more important to the ex-conscript narrative than military statistics is how the sense of danger, along with the injuries, the cold and hunger, the punishments and the working conditions, established a stark contrast to the grandeur of the military's project.

The regime celebrated the benefits of the CLA to the nation: greater resources, tourism, fisheries, and hydropower. A group of twenty-one ex-conscripts who, decades later, put their names to a written account of their work on the carretera contrasted the announcement of the grand project to unite all of Chile, the epic scale of the undertaking, and the extraordinary benefits with their experience on site: "To escape such a depressing and deplorable situation [the physical and psychological abuse, and constant fear that characterized service], many conscripts voluntarily accepted a transfer to the area near Chaitén to participate in the construction of the [. . .] carretera, without really knowing what they were going to or what awaited them. Others were not even asked, they were simply sent there [. . .]. They went expecting a change for the better, because nothing could be worse than what they were living through in the so-called military instruction."[142] It was, however, worse, they wrote. They worked twelve hours a day, without appropriate clothing or protection. They worked in the mud, wind, cold, and rain, with scarce food and "strict methods of punishment characterized by cruelty and indifference, as if they weren't human beings." The punishments were more brutal, they insisted, for anyone who tried to escape. The recruits supplemented their diet by collecting shellfish and eating worms, they used explosives without training, and "the cold was so intense that many young conscripts urinated in their pants in the middle of the day." The road was, they insisted, "a silent witness to the blood, sweat, and tears spilled by so many sad, lonely, afraid young men with no contact with their families."[143] Like others who worked on the road, they referred to the CLA as a "concentration camp."[144] Other former recruits indicated their disillusionment by sarcastically referring to the "glorious" national project of the carretera, their exploitation as cheap labor or "slaves," or both.[145]

N.G.S.T. (1982) went from Lautaro to the area between Puerto Cárdenas and Villa Santa Lucía to work on the CLA:

> We were never treated like soldiers of la patria, but simply as slaves; in addition to the light clothing, they gave us a construction worker's helmet in the place of a military helmet; instead of a rifle they gave us shovels and pickaxes. For a bed just a thin mat, two blankets and two sheets, that were dirty and smelly from the previous group. There were no toilets or showers, just a type of pool or large pit constructed by a bulldozer full of muddy water, a mix of mud and melted snow, in which we were forced to bathe. But the truth is that we got out dirtier than when we got in, and with hypothermia due to the low temperature.[146]

In his testimony, Iván C.* (1983–84, Valdivia) also articulates the discord between work on the CLA and his idea of patriotic service. He describes beginning his military service "excited to start a new stage in my life and to live up to my civil responsibilities as a Chilean soldier." He was later sent to Coyhaique to work on the CLA between Bahía Murta and Cerro Castillo. According to the military historian Ignacio Bascuñan, the CMT had advanced the road in that area thirty-one kilometers between April 1982 and 1983. The workers battled rain and temperatures in winter that reached fifteen degrees Celsius below zero, freezing the fuel and lubricants in the machinery. Recruits also struggled against the landscape, with more than fifty-four thousand kilograms of explosives brought in by barge over that period.[147] Iván arrived shortly after, and later recalled his experiences through a sense of betrayed patriotism. He wrote of working with pickaxes and power saws, the poor food, having to heat the pipes to access water, bathing in freezing water, and being beaten as punishment: "I was a true slave. I was not a servant of the patria."[148]

From a military perspective, and in addition to constructing roads, the CLA was also intended to continue the tradition of forging productive citizens out of recruits. Parallel to completing public works, the original objective of the SMT was to provide military instruction to conscripts completing their service, "delivering to the country efficient reservists as engineer-soldiers and citizens conscious of their duties and rights."[149] The CMT retained these twin missions. It was described in 1966 in an army periodical as performing work in the public interest to further the country's economic and social interests, as well as, "after the period of conscription, returning citizens who, along with having learned how to defend their *patria*, have contributed to the strengthening of the economy and, what's more, to varying degrees, have learned a trade that prepares them for their careers in civilian life. [. . .] The instruction that the contingent that works for the C.M.T. receives, provides private industry with personnel highly qualified in driving a variety of heavy machinery and other vehicles, and other titles such as squad leader, explosives, etc."[150] Similarly, and with specific reference to the construction of the CLA near Chiloé, civil engineer and later a politician representing the Aysén region, Antonio Horvath, wrote in 1981 that "although the wages are low, personnel receive lodging, food, and tools, and they have the chance to learn a profession on the ground, and to the extent that they do so efficiently, they will be hired by firms in the private sector."[151] However, ex-conscript memory undermines the training aspect of the construction project. Former recruits instead express bitterness at not being paid, being treated poorly or abused, or being used as cheap or forced labor. Moreover, far from improving their employment prospects, they complain of leaving the barracks just as unqualified as when they entered and of carrying injuries that limited their ability to find a job. However, this mismatch between ex-conscript recollections and the training role envisioned for conscript labor sits outside the narrative of patriot disillusionment and instead informs the memory framework of ruptured masculinity.

The gulf that emerged between the twentieth-century military project and the patria of commemoration, myth, uniforms, and parades came to frame twenty-first-century ex-conscript memory of Chile's wars under the dictatorship. It shaped how the "internal war" and the "almost-war" with Argentina were waged, and how the front lines of those conflicts crept inside the barracks and trenches. It also underpinned a deep sense of disappointment and disillusionment with military service, and informed how former recruits remembered Pinochet's wars and the geopolitical struggle to push back the internal frontier. Nevertheless, these discrepancies between ideas of what la patria was and what it meant to serve and defend it did not mean that the army's nation-building project was wholly ignored or rejected by those parts of Chilean society from which recruits were typically drawn. Throughout the first half of the twentieth century, the mission to defend la patria by educating, training, disciplining, and moralizing the masses resonated with boys' families and was internalized by many young men entering the barracks. However, recruits did not primarily understand their engagement with the armed forces in terms of a collective project to build a nation and forge citizens. Instead, they understood the strong cultural links between military service and education, employment and productivity to be a personal and familial rite that would make them men.

4

Making Men

ecades after his service, Andrés V.* (1975–77) remembered walking to the regimental barracks in Temuco, southern Chile, in 1975 with his carabinero father's voice in his head: "That's how men are made; they'll teach you to be a man."[1] He recalled reluctantly obeying his father and inwardly providing his own rationalization that service would at least help him find a job: "I said [to myself], fine, doing my military service [means] I'll have more opportunities, in a variety of things, in work, a lot of things." Andrés's thoughts on the way to enlisting reveal ideas about conscription entrenched in Chilean society. Since its inception, military service had, among working-class and poor Chileans, developed into a male rite of passage in terms of social and familial responsibility, discipline, education, employment, and physical toughness. The army, it was understood, made men. Once inside the barracks, however, many recruits under Pinochet remember being confronted with very different ideas of what it meant to become and to be a man. This chapter examines the conflict between popular, civilian manhood and military masculinity, and how this rupture serves as a framework for ex-conscript memory. It reveals how the training inside regiments throughout Chile was designed to produce "hard men" who were ready for war, resistant to pain, hunger, and thirst, were able to kill, and how this process rested, in part, on undermining important elements of civilian masculine identity. Moreover, on leaving the barracks, the physical scars, psychological damage, and lost opportunities attributed to service undercut the ability of many to live up to societal gender roles. For many ex-recruits, the memory of their service is shaped by this discord between manliness inside the barracks, civilian ideas of manhood, and societal and individual expectations about making men of boys.

Boys

"We were just boys," wrote C.D.C.A. (1982, Punta Arenas).[2] An insistence on youth runs through conscript testimony, with former recruits routinely recalling themselves during their service as boys, just boys, youngsters, barely eighteen, adolescents, beardless youths, and minors under the law.[3] Decades prior to C.D.C.A.'s 2007 testimony, and only shortly before he entered the barracks in the southern ninth region, the Vicaría Pastoral Juvenil (Pastoral Youth Vicariate) produced a working document arguing that males in rural Chile were, in fact, never boys for very long: "If for young working-class people in urban settings, the period of 'being young' is usually very short, in the case of the countryside, it practically does not exist."[4] Despite the apparent contradiction, both C.D.C.A.'s testimony and the Vicaría's report describe the same thing: a world defined by poverty, subsistence, little and poor education, work, and familial responsibility. The Vicaría assessors saw a childhood cut short, while former conscripts recall a boyhood far removed from the political polarization that split Chilean society. The conflation of youth and political naïveté in the ex-conscript narrative is, in part, a defensive mechanism to underscore recruits' lack of power and responsibility, and highlight the chasm between the world of boys before their call-up and the politicized world of men they encountered during their service. However, it also reflects a common lived experience, in which daily life squeezed out room for ideology and politics. Despite the emblematic role played by sections of Chile's youth in the agrarian reform of the 1960s, Allende's path to socialism and, particularly, in the anti-regime protests under Pinochet, the daily lives and future hopes of significant segments of young people never connected to geopolitical struggles, hemispheric conflict, or critiques of Chilean society.[5] Would-be recruits were aware of the expressions of political conflict around them: goods shortages and land seizures, repression in the wake of the coup, and the protests and crackdowns of the 1980s. Their attention, however, was instead focused locally on immediate needs and personal trajectories. The same pressures that shaped the apolitical experience of boyhood had, over the course of decades, also forged many of the individual and societal expectations of military service that recruits carried with them into the barracks.

In Temuco in 2012, Daniel Gómez (1978–80, Punta Arenas) emphasized that recruits "were very young, we didn't know anything about politics, many of us were from the countryside, without any political knowledge."[6] He later conceded, as an aside, that those conscripts who had been politically active would probably not mention it.[7] And there are good reasons not to mention it. The shared ex-conscript narrative avoids the political largely because no consensus exists among former recruits. Underplaying or denying the political also avoids activating Chile's memory struggle, which excludes the possibility of conscript victimhood.[8] The narrative of apolitical boyhood is, in part, the result of this process of strategic or instinctive omission, but it also resonates with the dominant themes of family, lack of schooling, and work in the lives of many young males. Daniel's description of life in Chile's rural south in the mid to late 1970s echoes the findings of a sociological study conducted in the late 1960s. The survey found that young men in the countryside—between eighteen and twenty-four years of age—talked predominately about work, sports, and sex. Politics barely rated. The researchers found entrenched political apathy or resignation, and a nonantagonistic view of society. A majority said they felt indifferent to both the upper and lower classes, and approximately half felt neutral toward the middle class. The response rate to the question regarding the middle class was low, however, reflecting the fact that most did not conceive of a middle class. When asked to stratify society, 60 percent of campesinos broke it down, without animosity, into rich and poor.[9] Politics was a waste of time, ugly, dirty, or simply not something for young people. "Young people never participated in anything, not in the countryside, nothing, it was only the old guys (*viejos*)," recalled Luis Cortés (1973, Iquique), speaking about growing up in Illapel in the fourth region. "I remember that my dad was liberal, I worked in a house and the gentleman was a committed communist. He had [the place] full of propaganda, he was a fanatic for sure, but I said, what's the attraction in being like that?"[10] The dominant frame of reference for rural youth was, instead, the family unit and their role within it.

The nuclear family with a male head solidified around the turn of the century as the principal economic unit of Chilean industrialization. Subsistence within this context was a collaborative effort, with boys playing a significant role. A study from the first decades of the twentieth century estimated that the contribution of children and mothers to household income hovered at around one-third, with the largest contribution made by the eldest son.[11] The rhythm of daily life had changed little by the late 1960s, with campesino boys in the agricultural south amid Eduardo Frei's agrarian reform abandoning school at an early age to start contributing to the family's subsistence. Seventy-eight percent of them began working by the time they were fifteen years old, 58 percent of them before finishing their primary education, and roughly a third of young men earned more than half of the household income.[12] Frei's reform process targeted male heads of families as the subject of reform, without significantly shifting family dynamics. Efforts to mobilize young people via youth groups affiliated with political parties tended instead to remind young men and

Making Men

women of their obligations within the family unit. At any rate, youth groups suffered from poor attendance, with young people more likely to be active in sporting clubs or religious groups,[13] and tending to avoid or abandon the political organizations of their parents.[14]

The survey of southern youth was conducted two months after the death of Ernesto "Che" Guevara, and participants were asked what his death meant to them. Twenty-three percent of young working-class males, and almost 60 percent of rural youth, were unaware of the news. One young campesina tried to cover her ignorance of who Che was, saying she had been very young when it happened.[15] After the election of Allende three years later, radical youth culture inspired by the romanticism of the Cuban Revolution and the figure of Che flowed from urban centers into the countryside with greater urgency.[16] Agrarian reform also expanded under the Popular Unity government. The speed of expropriations accelerated and the scope widened. Allende was also less willing than Frei had been to reign in expectations, or to prevent unauthorized land occupations. As tensions mounted between landowners and workers, youthful radicalism moved into the countryside, with young activists and agitators— particularly university students—seeking to mobilize the rural youth. There remained, however, a significant gap between these students and the young men who abandoned school for work.[17]

Boys who would later enter the barracks as recruits were not insulated from political division under Allende. Ex-conscripts remember the escalating violence, the gridlock, the truck strikes, the land invasions, and their mothers standing in the long lines to buy flour or sugar at highly inflated prices. Fernando Gálvez (1973–75, Calama) had to leave the *fundo* (agricultural estate) Santa Cecilia in Pirque, where he was working as a teenager, when it was occupied in 1972. He remembers the conflict in the early 1970s that was caused, in his interpretation, by people not wanting to work. When the fundo was taken over, Fernando went to Santiago and the población of Roosevelt, where he worked fitting out trucks. Political activity had become a normal part of life in the city, and sometimes, he recalled, demonstrations brought the streets to a standstill.[18] While Fernando was avoiding protests to get to work, Guillermo Navarrete (1974, Arica) was in the thick of it. In 1973 Guillermo was completing his fourth year of secondary education at a technical school, which he remembers as being highly politicized: "It was surely the school that had the most strikes in Santiago, [. . .] because it was full of people [. . .] from suburbs [. . .] that had a lot of politics, lots of communists, socialists, [such as] José María Caro, San Gregorio, and the suburb of Alessandri." However, Guillermo did not, he continued, get involved in politics: "I did take part in the strikes, because I went along to have fun with my classmates [. . .] we used to go downtown more to create a ruckus, and to stop cars, but it wasn't political, no, no, it was more just being boys, having fun."[19] Daniel Pizarro (1973–75, Los Andes and Santiago) likewise stayed away from politics. "No, no, no, I was never involved in politics," he recalled four decades after being drafted. "I was in the Communist Youth for a while, but that was more because there were some pretty girls," he smiled. Daniel had begun working at age seven. At the time, he, his sister, his mother, and his alcoholic father were living with friends and family (*allegados*) in the poblaciones of Santiago. In the years before entering the barracks, his father was still drinking, and Daniel worked to feed his sister and his mother. He also reentered school, and at seventeen he had completed his second year of secondary school. For Daniel, daily life in the lead-up to his military service and the coup was structured around football and girls, work and his family responsibilities.[20]

The economic crises, factory closures, reduced real wages, and high unemployment that resulted from the junta's economic policies only intensified the pressure on families in the popular sectors. The economy plunged into recession in the years following the coup, and working-class and poor Chileans had not yet recovered when the crisis of the early 1980s hit. Children were expected to help out: girls worked in the home, and boys were sent out to work at a young age.[21] Sociologist José Weinstein put that age at around twelve years in Santiago in the mid-1980s, and it was at about that age that Luis Zapata (1981–83, Punta Arenas) abandoned school.[22] Luis grew up with eight siblings in the Santiago barrio of La Victoria, a focal point of protest against the military regime. His communist father died when Luis was very young, and his much younger and illiterate mother struggled to make ends meet. He left school after his fifth year of primary education to earn money for pants and shoes, and to help the family. When he was called up to do his military service, he could not read or write, and he had "no idea about politics." Decades later, Luis still had no idea about politics, which he put down to fear and his own ignorance.[23] His early working life was in line with the expectation among parents in Santiago's poblaciones that male children should take care of themselves and at least pay their way. It was an expectation that was also internalized by boys who worked to avoid being a burden on the family.[24]

The report by the Vicaría Pastoral Juvenil in the late 1970s highlighted similar dynamics in the countryside.[25] It noted the impact of worsening poverty due to the "paralyzation" and reversal of agrarian reform on young people in Chile's rural coastal region. Young men, the report continues, feel they have to work at a young age to avoid being a burden on the family, or because family disintegration or an alcoholic father have forced them prematurely into positions of responsibility.[26] This more pressing need, along with the poor quality of rural schools and the fact that parents rarely valued education, contributed to few completing their primary education or going on to secondary school. In terms of their political consciousness, the report describes how young people felt they belonged to their social class but lacked a clear vision of society as a whole. They did not venture beyond their village or region and often had difficulty forming an opinion about their social, political, and economic situation, either as individuals or as a class. In the 1980s, toward the end of the military rule, sociologists tracked the increased education of rural youth compared to previous generations, and the accelerating urbanization of their musical tastes and fashion choices. They also noted the "traditional" context these shifts took place in; boys, in particular, began waged seasonal work from a young age or undertook agricultural work on the family plot.[27] Throughout the decade, they commonly combined school with work before abandoning school completely, particularly during economic crises. The family remained the unit of production and consumption, and the contribution made to it by young men stood in constant tension with the monetary and opportunity cost of boys' education.[28] Diego C.* (1983–85, Tierra del Fuego) was fifteen when he stopped going to school in the ninth region around 1980. After eight years of primary education, the family needed him to contribute to the household more than it wanted him to go to school.[29] They worked, he explained, to survive, and it was not only education that was pushed aside but politics too. Anyway, he recalled in 2012, growing up in the late 1970s, you were not allowed to have a political opinion.[30]

The military regime set about destroying the institutions of political culture.[31] Leftist political parties were banned and others were recessed, unions were outlawed, and political engagement dissolved in an atmosphere of fear and mistrust. A significant sector of the population growing up in this context had little political awareness. Speaking about the Santiago commune of Maipú a decade after the coup, for example, agronomist Ximena Quezada described a complete memory loss of the past due to a breakdown in communication between the generations. Young people had no idea, she said, of what had happened before 1973, no idea about agrarian reform or any Chilean tradition of democracy, and no idea what a union was. Instead, they had a vague sense that organization was bad.[32] Censorship, too, stymied politicization. The opening up of the Chilean economy in the mid-1970s flooded Chile with cheap televisions: according to a 1978 survey, while only half of Chile's poorest homes had a sink in the kitchen, 84 percent had a television set, and between 1979 and 1983 the number of sets in Chile doubled.[33] What they broadcast was a mix of tightly controlled news bulletins, local and Brazilian telenovelas, football, cartoons, and military marches.[34] At school, the new curriculum silenced politics, and was instead reorganized around the themes of order, security, and family, as well as Chile's traditions and national symbols.[35]

The depoliticization of Chilean society opened up a deep fissure in the country's youth between a politicized minority and the "non-political," "non-university," "non-organized" majority.[36] In the southwestern población of José María Caro, psychologist Domingo Asún broke this majority down further into engaged but conformist youths with little capacity for social critique; youths who abandoned the educational system and were erratically or underemployed while trying to maintain a nuclear family; and youths living in extreme poverty, who ultimately failed to assume adult responsibilities.[37] In 1988 the young pobladores were the most difficult demographic to mobilize to vote in the plebiscite on Pinochet's rule, and they spoke of a distinction between the "inside" and the "outside." For them, politics belonged to the "outside," the city beyond the poblaciones, and the result of the vote, they felt, would not affect their lives on the "inside."[38] On the inside, work and finding work remained for many the principal parameters of their lives. It was on the inside, too, that ideas of boyhood and manhood overlapped with attitudes toward military service.

Boyhood implied certain markers of masculinity and pathways to manhood. Drinking and shows of strength were important statements of manliness for young men among their peers. Heterosexual and premarital sexual activity confirmed their sexuality, and initiated them into the *machista* social order as men: strong, autonomous, emotionally controlled actors with social, economic, and sexual privilege over women but also a deep respect for their mothers and a sense of duty to protect female family members. Becoming a father, in turn, confirmed a man's virility, with the number of children serving as shorthand for manliness. The most definitive of the staggered thresholds to manhood, however, was work. Becoming a man meant assuming, or being in the position to assume, economic responsibility for others as the head of a nuclear family.[39] It was in these pathways out of boyhood that civilian masculinity overlapped with military service. For the sectors of Chilean society that filled the conscript ranks, the same pressures of poverty and family that shaped the experience of boyhood and ideas of manhood had also, since the first decades of the century, forged their expectations of military service as a way to become a man. Boys expected to be toughened; parents awaited responsible, disciplined, and brave young men; and both boys and their parents linked military service with training, employment, and a chance for social mobility.[40]

While service, at its best, represented a chance to make a life and to get ahead, at its most basic, it provided a reprieve from poverty and relief for families by assuring recruits food and shelter. Álvaro B.* (1976–78) had grown up without parents on the streets around Valdivia, and he saw the army as the chance for some stability, even comfort. "I didn't sleep in a bed until the army," he explained.[41] At the time Álvaro was living rough, Eduardo F.* (1976–78, Iquique) had postponed his service. Drafted in 1973, he thought a year in the barracks would be a year wasted, and he deferred his service in the hope of attending university. Two years later, he was still not studying and only able to find sporadic and unstable employment. Increasingly desperate, he presented at the barracks in 1976 in order, he said, to stop being a burden on his family.[42] That same year, Alberto C.* (1976) volunteered. He had left home at fourteen years of age to work but returned to live with his parents in Temuco when he went back to school. After realizing his father's policeman's wage was not enough to support himself and his ten siblings, he left for the barracks to sign up.[43]

For Luis Cortés, too, service offered an immediate solution to poverty. He was working and attending school in the fourth region when he was called up in April 1973. He recalled wanting to do his service, "to leave the village there, because the people of the village were very poor. It was very difficult for us; imagine, eighteen siblings . . . and my father was the only one working, and to maintain all of us. So, there were a lot of poor people, very poor, and to leave the village we opted [for service]." However, Luis's memory of his motivations also points to the transformative attraction of service: "My first thought was of [becoming a man], becoming responsible, something like that, because when I was in the countryside . . . I was seventeen, eighteen years old, and I didn't obey my father much. There was no money; if you wanted to buy something, you didn't have the money to buy it, so I said to myself, I have to leave this place so I can be a different person."[44] Patricio V.* (1973–76, Arica) was doing his fourth year of middle school in La Serena, also in Chile's fourth region, when he was called up. He entered the barracks "interested in having a secure future and providing support to my family, which comprised seven siblings, and in which only my mother, who was a domestic servant, worked; we were a very poor family and often we did not have the necessary food, so I wanted to belong to the Chilean Armed Forces."[45] A year after Patricio was drafted, Juan S.* (1974–76, 1978, Temuco) volunteered. Raised by his single mother, he had begun working at fifteen to contribute to the household. He signed up "with the idea and desire to be part of the army, with hopes of a better quality of life for me and my family."[46] Military service represented the only real option for social mobility, and the benefits of service for later employment and the chance of a stable career in the armed forces continued to attract young men to military service throughout the 1980s.

Under military rule, and in line with a broader twentieth-century trend, young people stayed in school longer than their parents' generation.[47] Education was increasingly seen as the way out of poverty, and expectations rose along with the average number of years spent in school. However, given the weak economy, in which the poorest were hardest hit, more education did not readily translate into greater opportunity. Men struggled to find work, and young men found it nearly impossible. Young pobladores and campesinos realized quickly that a university education was out of their reach, that finishing secondary school was not an advantage for them in the labor market, and that they were destined for poorly paid work, underemployment, or unemployment.[48] Heightened expectations quickly turned to cynicism.[49] In the early 1980s psychologist Domingo Asún spoke of attitudes of young men toward employment workshops in José María Caro. The boys were aware that the workshops were preparing them for subemployment at best but would make it easier to remain in the armed forces after they finished their military service, which for many, Asún noted, was an attractive option.[50] A few years later, in the late 1980s and amid high general and higher youth unemployment, half of all young people living in Santiago's poblaciones did not agree with the assertion that finishing a fourth year of secondary education would help them find work. Instead, they looked to military service as a better way into the labor market.[51] At the same time in the countryside, boys—including those who had abandoned the school system—thought military service would teach them a trade that they could then use to make themselves economically independent. Leaving the barracks, reservists found that service did not, in fact, help them find work, but this reality did not undermine the economic attractiveness of service among prospective recruits.[52]

In his 2011 memoir, former recruit César Rivas Vergara (1984–86, Manantiales) writes of seeing military service as the only way out of his neighborhood in southern Santiago. He remembers eavesdropping in 1975 on the conversation of a group of ex-recruits who had served during the coup and were sharing stories of shootouts. Some of the tales were funny, some were sad, but they sounded like an adventure to ten-year-old César and made him want to join the army. In 1983, when he and two classmates approached the local naval barracks to sign up, this sense of adventure had been reinforced by a growing desire to get out of the neighborhood. The three friends were warned by recruits guarding the gate not to enter, but César only turned back after seeing an officer hit a recruit inside the walls. He returned home and completed his secondary education. The following year he enrolled for the draft and eagerly went to check the list of draftees when it was posted at the Lo Ovalle metro station. He was stuck, he writes, in a job barely better than the poorly paid and unpredictable positions in the emergency work programs the military government had implemented in the face of rising unemployment. The streets were also increasingly violent, given the protests in March 1984. His friends participated in the protests and the looting, but César saw no future for himself where he was. His way of escaping economic crisis and social unrest was to join the army.[53]

Debate about the role and existence of military service ignited periodically throughout the 1990s.[54] A movement emerged during transition protesting the draft, advocating the right to conscientious objection, and defending the rights of recruits. Politicians drafted proposals to create exceptions to the draft, reduce the length of service, or abolish it altogether. At each point, spikes in the public debate were accompanied by reports of mistreatment within the barracks and of conscript deaths. Behind the rolling controversy, however, the young men most likely to enter the barracks continued to view military service as their best or only pathway out of poverty. Psychologists working with recruits and deserters in the early 1990s noted the perception among young men that service offered not only shelter, food, and stability but also the chance at an education and training that would help them find future work. They also highlighted the expectations of families in the popular sectors that service would "make men" by "disciplining," "educating," and "straightening out" their boys.[55] In the 1990s, for example, friends of Pedro Soto Tapia, who disappeared while a conscript and whose remains were later found in a cave, were not surprised at his decision to sign up: "It's tough and you have to put up with jerks ordering you around and hitting you. But if you get through it, you can have a military career. Something more secure than being a seasonal worker around here."[56] The Soto Tapia case captured public attention in 1997, the same year the double draft was implemented, which called first for volunteers to sign up for service, before filling what remained of the annual quota with conscripts. The following year, too, cases of deaths and desertion made headlines, while the percentage of volunteers rose from 39 percent to 42 percent, the majority coming from poor households.[57]

In April 2012 former conscript Rodrigo G.* (1973) dropped into the Temuco office of the Agrupación de Reservistas to pay his dues. While there, he spoke of his experiences and lifted his pant leg to show where he had lost a section of flesh in the barracks. During the conversation, he also proudly produced from the inside pocket of his jacket a photo of his youngest son in uniform. The annual cohort had recently entered the Tucapel Regiment half a dozen blocks away from the office, and photos of the recruits were being sold that morning in the square opposite.[58] Rodrigo's son had volunteered for military service at a time when the traditional mix of motivations had reached a potential tipping point. In March 2012 the subsecretary for the armed forces, Alfonso Vargas, projected that volunteers would not fill the annual quota.[59] In 2006, the year after the Antuco tragedy, the mechanisms for encouraging volunteers had been strengthened, and since 2007 the military's annual quotas had been filled by those willing to sign up. Vargas's projection, therefore, raised the prospect of compulsory military service. A number of reasons were presented for the shortfall: a reduced pool of eighteen-year-old males, the strikes during the student movement of 2011 that interrupted the regular recruitment, and a shift in educational prospects that meant more young men aspired to further study. Perhaps most significant, however, was that the economic benefit conscripts enjoyed was simply not competitive. "What they receive," the subsecretary said at the time, "is CLP46,900 a month and today, if I take this youngster to the countryside, in three days, four days, he will earn that picking fruit."[60] Vargas explained in a television interview on Canal 13 that previously many families had welcomed the conscription of their sons as an economic relief and an assurance that they would be fed, clothed, and sheltered, but in 2012 things had changed: "Today they can be a tremendous support, they can study."[61] In 1992 leading military figures had opposed the idea of abolishing military service by reaffirming the almost century-old arguments that it prepared conscripts to be citizens, that it promoted national unity, and that it instilled in recruits a set of national values.[62] When selling service to prospective recruits, however, campaigns appealed not to patriotism or nation-building but to potential volunteers' own futures. Public campaigns to promote military service since the inception of the double draft had focused on personal opportunity; the 1998 slogan on radio, in print, and on television was "Military Service: Your Opportunity to Grow."[63]

The conscript quota for 2012 was eventually filled with volunteers. Nevertheless, the moment of doubt revealed the consistent set of historical drivers behind the attitudes toward military service that bound conscription with employment, family, and masculinity. Throughout the twentieth century, boyhood in those sectors of Chilean society that filled the conscript ranks was shaped by little and poor education, family pressure to work, and a desire not to be a financial burden. Immediate concerns were not political but familial, and daily life was defined by poverty and work, not ideology. This profile remained relatively consistent and independent of the fluctuating trajectory of political struggle and ideological division of the twentieth century. Moreover, these parameters also framed attitudes toward, and expectations of, military service that recruits carried with them into the barracks. For poor and working-class boys, military service cut across familial and societal thresholds to manhood. Parents sent their boys off and awaited educated and responsible young men capable of managing the demands of adulthood, while conscripts entered expecting to leave strong, tested, bearing the prestige of the institution, and with training and education that would help them carve out a better future for themselves and their families. Inside the barracks, however, these expectations and recruits' ideas of what it meant to be and become a man were undone by the military project to make hard men.

Hard Men

Recalling the training for what was assumed to be imminent war with Argentina, Vicente A.* (1977–78) insisted in 2012 that "a soldier doesn't get cold, get hungry, doesn't get anything. A soldier doesn't feel pain, doesn't feel anything."[64] Being a man in the barracks meant being hard, both in body and mind. It demanded recruits be resistant to pain, climatic extremes, and hunger and thirst, and, above all, that they were ready for war and able to kill. Making men hard meant conditioning draftees via a series of mutually reinforcing, and often overlapping, processes of desensitization. It implied deadening the body to physical suffering, severe weather conditions, and its own instincts, as well as instilling blind obedience, numbing recruits to compassion, and making them indifferent to the pain of others. These processes were part of basic training, survival training, resistance training, simulated warfare, and ritualized punishments.

Basic training lasted for the first three months and is characterized in ex-conscript testimony by physical brutality and psychological degradation, often administered in a place called the "valley of tears." Barracks throughout Chile had a "valley"; it may have been a frozen island in Patagonia or a designated area of the northern desert plains, but the reported exercises were relatively consistent across different regiments.[65] Former recruits describe a pattern of exercises and punishments designed to toughen the body and teach them to resist the blows. Cristóbal L.* (1982–84) spoke of beatings he and his compañeros received, which, he said, drove several to suicide: "I remember the commander, the lieutenant [. . .], he gave the order, the order that soldiers have to be hard." He recalled this order thirty years later as a slight, quietly spoken man who was neatly dressed with a broad smile and an impeccable part in his white hair. When talking about his military service, his body language shifted, his eyes fell, and he became small in his chair: "I didn't feel pain; we were accustomed to the blows that came. [. . .] You know, we didn't feel because we were used to it, we got used to it, this rhythm, but deep inside, deep inside, in those years."[66] Exercises that involved being struck with fists, poles, and blunt objects, being kicked, exposed to tear gas, and trampled, crawling over the spines of the *calafate* plant—"'to harden the skin,' they told us"[67]—and endless army crawls echo throughout former conscript testimony as defining features of basic training.

Arbitrary punishment was also intended to harden recruits' minds. "The repeated strikes and 'beatings' were designed," writes F.E.L.D. (1986, Arica), "to make our personalities disappear, our superiors and the officers told us that it was all to transform us into true 'dogs of combat or dogs of war.'"[68] Physical brutality was complemented by humiliation, sexual humiliation, sleep deprivation, insults, threats, and mock executions, which served to instill in young men the verticality of command and unquestioning obedience.[69] The principles of basic training were in line with a broader twentieth-century trend. Physical punishment, humiliation, and isolation from personal support networks were the main tools used in Western militaries to erode recruits' self-worth and disrupt civilian attitudes and morals. They reorganized recruits' thinking and behavior to be in line with military codes and values, replaced a sense of individuality with loyalty to the group, and produced in young men unthinking discipline and automated behaviors.[70] "A few days after entering," wrote Juan Azocar (1976, Puerto Montt), "they took us to a sector removed from the regiment, where they subjected us to multiple beatings, tear gas, low-flying bullets and diverse physical and psychological mistreatments designed to remove lo 'paisano' from us; we had to have a new form of education to, according to them, make us more manly and more patriotic."[71] Making men required first the unmaking of boys and their civilian identities.

Pride is among the conflicted feelings that M.S.M.P. (1978) has when remembering his service. He survived the brutal treatment in the valley of tears that left his body punished, worn and aged before its time, and left many of his compañeros broken or nervous wrecks. The army, he thinks, owes him something, but he is also proud of having been able to come through the brutal treatment and of having been prepared to give his life for the patria if necessary.[72] Persistent patriotism is common in ex-conscript testimony, but pride at coming through the brutalization of military service is less common. Most had expected, and many had welcomed, a grueling physical test as a confirmation of their manliness. Eugenio T.* (1977–79) explained that life in rural Chile was already tough, and "instructive" beatings were appropriate. "But such aggression?" he asked.[73] Being broken or humiliated by military "hardness" left many with a deep, and often ongoing, sense of confusion, shame, powerlessness, or anger.[74] Failing to live up to the standards of hardness also set the limits of military masculinity.

Gendered insults and punishments equated falling short of military hardness with femininity and homosexuality. M.A.G. (1973) testified to the desperation of three of his fellow recruits and their self-inflicted gunshot wounds. Feigning injury or illness, exaggerating the severity of injury or illness, suicide, and—as in this case—self-mutilation are reported as having been regular attempts to escape punishment and training.[75] Worse than the injuries, continued M.A.G., was that those who drove the three to self-harm with "their demonic and perverse acts of punishment" did not register the seriousness of the situation, asking only: "Why didn't you simply put a bullet through your balls, maricón [faggot]?"[76] As failed man-soldiers, the three had no use for their testicles. Gendered punishments included shaving the conscript's head and dressing him in a "baby-doll," a white nightdress "like women use."[77] Being dressed in white was a shaming device used to indicate the individual being punished was "less than the others,"[78] and it was often used in combination with corporeal punishments: beatings, whippings, exposure to climatic extremes, or stress positions, such as guard duty overnight with a backpack full of rocks. Former conscripts also remember being beaten with *la nena* (the little girl) or *la flaca* (the skinny girl, a female term of endearment)—described as a plank, a length of broomstick, or a stick.[79] W.R.J.M. (1986, Puerto Montt) recalls being hit with *la flaca*, which he describes as a steel rod. It was used, he writes, in combination with electricity applied to his teeth and testicles, and he was forced to "sing over and over 'my corporal rapes my mother and my sister while I hold them down.'"[80] The feminized punishment and the physical attack on his genitals were combined with undermining his civilian masculinity, including his sense of respect and honor as a son and a brother, and his masculine role as the protector of female family members. Recruits' civilian identities as males were anchored not only by familial relationships but also by *machista* heterosexuality, which was undercut by insults—*maricón, pelao culiao*—and sexual humiliation.[81] Forced nudity and attacks on the testicles are reported as a routine part of both training and punishment. L.A.H.C. (1980, Coyhaique), for example, remembers being tied up in the valley of tears, put into drums of snow, and beaten in the testicles. He also recalls the shame of having to display his genitals. "Before going to bed," he writes, "they made us strip and we had to parade around in nothing at all, showing our intimate parts and our 'bits' to everyone present."[82] In Punta Arenas, the humiliation and the physical and psychological degradation began almost immediately on entering the barracks, writes M.E.D.D. (1979, Punta Arenas): "According to the lieutenants and instructors, they were preparing us for the war that was coming and we had to be hard."[83]

Hardness also meant resistance to one's own bodily instincts, as well as extreme weather conditions. "The cold combats the cold!" L.A.M.E. recalls being told while being covered with snow after being pulled from the Strait of

Magellan during a training exercise.[84] Raúl Acuña (1976) remembers the naked training exercises in which he and his compañeros wore nothing but a rifle in the snow of Punta Arenas: "so that the skin would resist the cold, [the instructor] would say."[85] In the northern regions, memories of service are dominated instead by heat, thirst, and hunger. Sergio Munizaga (1973–75, Iquique) described training in Pica in the northern pampa, during which conscripts were punished by being hit and forced to stand still, sometimes all day, in the desert sun in full gear, helmet, and their backpack: "According to them, one had to become a man, because the Chilean soldier had to be like that, had to suffer . . . sometimes they didn't give us water so we'd resist. If there were a war, one had to resist. They always spoke of the war with Bolivia and Peru."[86] The ideal of physical resistance was rooted, in part, in the exploits of nineteenth-century heroes, with the mythology of the indomitable Chilean race that solidified during the War of the Pacific framing efforts to make recruits resilient almost a hundred years later. "They didn't give you water, they took it off you," said Samuel Fuenzalida (1973–74) in 2012, recalling his training in Calama: "They told you the Chilean army, the brave soldiers, did not drink water . . . When they came to fight at Topáter [during the Battle of Calama in 1879], they came from Antofagasta without water, without anything, and they fought and won." Brave soldiers, he remembered, did not drink water: "So we didn't drink water."[87]

Conquering hunger, thirst, and the climate were goals of Chilean military training from the beginning of the century. A defender of the draft wrote in 1920 that "from the first day that the conscript arrives at the barracks, the exercise of his will begins, resisting the rough physical exercises, obeying without talking back, defeating hunger, thirst and the harshness of the weather, enduring the fatigue of long marches and watches until reaching the goal of submission: the supreme sacrifice of one's life if necessary in the line of duty."[88] However, these ideas of resistance were also compounded by contemporaneous anti-guerilla survival training.[89] Former conscripts testify to eating rotten meat, cat meat, dog meat, and drinking urine during survival training on *campaña* (field training). "We were that hungry, we didn't care that it was dog," writes J.C.G.V. (1973) of eating dead dog and drinking his urine in the northern desert.[90] The Rettig Report understands "survival training" in the context of the military's adoption of guerrilla methods. The logic of postwar counterinsurgency and irregular warfare had made the norms and rules of war obsolete, and the new enemy was immoral and indiscriminate; it killed prisoners and employed torture. To confront guerrilla tactics, anti-guerrilla forces had to adopt the same methods. Survival training developed these methods and included exercises that the report describes as "degrading to one's own dignity."

Making Men

In testimonies that echo the report's description, former recruits describe training that broke down moral and ethical limits.[91] Survival exercises were justified with the refrain "a soldier steals, kills, and covers his tracks."[92] Desperate recruits turned to stealing from local farmers, begging in the street, and killing sheep, birds, pets, "guanacos and anything with four feet."[93] The behavior and the attitude were an affront to the military prestige, values, and morality that many recruits had expected. "There is no military honor," insists J.C.P.A. (1985–87, Temuco), "in [eating off the ground like animals] at all, and they taught us to steal, lie, and cover up."[94] Survival exercises were also routinely combined with "prisoner exercises."

There were two types of torture, recalled Daniel Gómez (1978–80, Punta Arenas) matter-of-factly: political persecution and training; and those conscripts deemed politically suspicious by instructors suffered both. The point of the training, he continued, was to "harden the mind and the heart."[95] The hardening of conscripts' minds and hearts took place in the "prisoner camp" (*campo* or *cancha de prisionero*), where recruits were taken during simulations after being captured and detained as the enemy. Ex-conscripts testify to being subjected to punishments during "prisoner exercises" that included being beaten, submerged in cold water for long periods of time, starvation, the forced ingestion of horse, dog, or human excrement, the "guitar" (a hard object scraped down exposed ribs), asphyxiation (exposure to tear gas, or having their head submerged in water, excrement, or urine), sexual humiliation, and the application of electrical current to various parts of the body, including the testicles.[96] The 2012 report produced by the Ex-conscript Commission includes sketches accompanied in each case by the ex-recruits' passport photos and short, handwritten descriptions of "CP" (*campo de prisionero*) exercises. One image, titled "football goal [*arco*] of torture" and detailing alleged exercises from 1979–81, includes a naked figure hung by the wrists from an arco, being kicked by one uniformed figure while his ankles are held by another. A second illustrates testimony from a recruit who served in Coyhaique (1979) and shows four simple figures: the first bound to a pole; the second with his arms bound to a pole in a kneeling crucifix position; the third with his hands bound behind his back and suspended upside-down by his ankles; and the fourth, seemingly nude, with his hands tied behind his back, and in the "tripod" position. A third sketch depicts training in Osorno (1980–82) and shows three uniformed figures around a fourth figure in a hole and two lines running from the figure in the hole to one of the uniformed men kneeling over a box. The description reads: "torture, during a (p.c.) or prisoner camp the soldier was tied to a pole, and in a hole, with water and mud, blindfolded, where they then applied electric current to the soldier using a radio."[97]

The goal of prisoner training was to instill in recruits a resistance to the treatment they would inevitably receive at the hands of the enemy. During exercises, "prisoners" were pressed for the names of their superiors or interrogated about their unit.[98] In 1979, and after basic training in Temuco, E.V.V.R. and his compañeros were sent east to the Argentine border region to relieve troops in Lonquimay. "They made us eat food with dirt and worms," he wrote three decades later, "and later they took us to the 'prisoner field' totally nude in the Andes at 5 degrees [Celsius] below zero. They made us pass through a tunnel full of *michay* thorns, after they made us put our head in a drum ¾ full of water, holding us by the feet, according to them to make us men, more soldierly, and so that we would not give away any secrets or positions to the enemy, be the enemy Peruvian, Bolivian, Argentine, communist, or terrorist."[99] In his memoir, Miguel A. Saavedra (1977–79) describes impromptu sessions further north in San Bernardo, during which conscripts were pulled one by one into a small room and interrogated. Instructors used physical blows and bolts of electricity applied via magnets to extract from recruits information about the unit and its personnel. After the interrogation, conscripts were sent to the showers marked with either a star indicating their loyalty or a cross to show that they were traitors. This type of exercise was incorporated, too, into "prisoner camp" training in San Bernardo.[100]

In his commentary on Saavedra's description of training, which was published with the memoir, military engineer Adolfo Alvarado writes that Saavedra and his compañeros endured "the rigors of training full of improvisations and doctrines poorly interpreted by their superiors."[101] Alvarado blames instructors' lack of clear orders for the abuses testified to by Saavedra and his fellow recruits, along with their isolation from a command structure that was spread too thinly to cover Chile's four fronts. The armed forces did feel stretched and under siege, and there was potential for slack in the chain of command.[102] Instructors were also at times illiterate, or second-year conscripts handing out the sorts of treatments they had previously endured.[103] However, while space for "improvisation" did exist, it is also clear that a doctrine of resistance was deeply embedded in the local military mythology as well as ideas of counterinsurgency that were exported to Latin America in the postwar decades.

The methods and theories of Chile's dirty war were to a significant degree the cumulative result of US torture research. While a tradition of political torture and prisoner abuse—including specific methods used under military rule—predated notions of counterinsurgency in Chile, it was Cold War antisubversive warfare that, under Pinochet, honed local practices into the massive and systematic application of torture.[104] In the aftermath of World War II, fears grew of the communist ability to control minds. Extraordinary confessions extracted by communist interrogators led observers to assume that they were the result of Soviet mind control or Chinese brainwashing. In response, the CIA first began investigating hypnosis and hallucinogens, before shifting its attention to behavioral psychology in the 1950s. This new approach aligned with US military training that drew, in particular, on the reported experiences of American POWs in Korea and focused on the effects of isolation, self-inflicted pain, stress positions, humiliation, and sleep deprivation. The techniques that emerged from CIA research, US military training, the feedback loop with French counterinsurgency in Vietnam and Algeria, and the US experience in Vietnam were eventually codified and exported to Latin America.[105] The technologies of repression evolved further during the campaigns of political persecution, assassination, and torture throughout the continent in the 1960s, 1970s, and 1980s, and ideas on torture were also shared between regimes.[106] Antisubversive torture was, however, initially and always about resistance. The CIA was motivated by the desire to safeguard US personnel and US information against communist "brain warfare" and enemy interrogation techniques. Similarly, the US military focus on psychological degradation emerged as Survival, Evasion, Resistance, Escape (SERE) training, designed to prepare soldiers—volunteer Special Forces, not draftees—for captivity. The theory behind resistance training was "stress inoculation": that exposing participants to the torture techniques they would face if captured by an enemy that did not respect the Geneva Conventions would make them able to resist interrogation and not reveal sensitive information. Cadets were forced to live off the land for a number of days before being taken "prisoner" and subjected to stress positions, the application of electric current, sleep deprivation, forced standing, and isolation.[107]

Torture and resistance went hand in hand. They were the two sides of the same Cold War fears, and both—as Daniel noted—shaped the wars in Chile's barracks. An unnamed Chilean "navy man" cited by Wolfgang Heinz confirmed that the "ill-treatment of soldiers was to [enable them to] resist interrogation. The enemy will not respect [the] Geneva [conventions]." Similarly, Chilean "General C" stressed that a "soldier must not be a prisoner, he must escape. He receives training to resist interrogation. He must get accustomed to harden up. Many times there can be a tendency to exaggerate. There is no code for this situation, but these cases are isolated and many were separated from the service. The interrogation is very tough."[108] "General C's" comments were made with respect to his experience with commando training, not conscription.[109] Survival and resistance exercises imported from the United States had been part of Special Forces' training in Chile since at least the years before the coup, where "concentration camp classes" included beatings, the ingestion of excrement, humiliation, sexual humiliation, and the application of electricity.[110] Ex-recruit testimony suggests that, under Pinochet, elements of this specialist training, as well as an institutionalized "tendency to exaggerate" or "improvise," shaped the instruction of conscripts. The use of such techniques, while uneven and not universal, seems to have been widespread in Chile, throughout the country and the years of military rule. Guatemala's Historical Clarification Commission described a process whereby Cold War torture, resistance, and "prisoner" exercises moved from specialist forces to the regular forces, as from 1980 graduates of commando courses were stationed throughout the country's regiments, where they acted as a "multiplier" of brutal training techniques.[111] A similar multiplication is likely to have occurred in Chile, as graduates of training courses set up in the decade prior to the coup moved through the ranks and within an institutional atmosphere that enabled, even condoned, brutality.

The instructive benefit of torture and abuse went beyond teaching men to resist pain. The same methods were used to discipline men and teach them to inflict pain.[112] Claudio de la Hoz (1973–75) recalled witnessing a scene similar to resistance training during his service. "They took a soldier," he remembered, "they blindfolded him as if he were an Argentine soldier and they beat him, they tortured him, saying 'this, this is what is going to happen to the Argentines,' but they were torturing a compañero of ours and we couldn't do anything." Unlike resistance training, however, the target of this particular exercise was not the blindfolded "Argentine prisoner," but the recruits watching. After all, concluded Claudio, they "prepared us for war, they were teaching us to kill."[113] Teaching men to kill meant overcoming the fear of battle and an aversion to mistreating other people via simulations of war and exercises to desensitize recruits to the sights, sounds, and emotions of war and the pain of others.

During simulations, recruits were often surprised in the middle of the night and taken from their beds to guard the unit against a mock attack. The element of surprise, tear gas, and live ammunition were used to create the type of fear that would be experienced in real combat situations. N.R.M.P. (Punta Arenas) for example, testified to the sense of mortal danger he felt during simulations, a fear that was occasionally underscored by conscript deaths during training.[114] Such exercises also re-created the numerical disadvantage Chilean soldiers would have to overcome during war. The Argentine army had eighty thousand conscripts, while the Chilean army had only eight to ten thousand, explained Daniel Gómez: "They prepared [one of] us to fight against eight or ten [of them], like in the case of war." The beatings were designed to "harden" them to be able to take what the Argentines would do to them. It broke many, he continued, but they were being trained to defeat three countries, and they had to "kill the enemy, no matter what."[115]

Recruits were exposed to the fear, blood, and death of war, most readily by killing dogs. "Once, the sublieutenants [. . .] and all the corporals brought in a dog and began quartering it in front of us without first killing it," remembers Felipe Q.* (1975–77, Calama). "After I was discharged, I could not get those images out of my head, the dog was moaning as if it were a human being. Afterwards, they gave us blood and parts of the dogs to eat raw."[116] Eating dog meat and drinking dog blood were part of "survival" exercises, but these practices were also central to ritualistic killings in front of recruits.[117] M.E.M.C. (1982–84) remembered such a spectacle in Punta Arenas, where his instructors "sacrificed" a dog in front of the entire company, then hung the carcass and ordered one of his compañeros to slice open the animal's abdomen from top to bottom. One by one, the conscripts were made to drink the warm blood. Having refused to take part, M.E.M.C. testified that he was beaten to the ground, where two corporals forced his mouth open and poured the blood down his throat.[118] M.J.S.S. (1979–81, Punta Arenas) remembers five dogs staked out in the valley of tears, their stomachs slit open by machete, revealing their entrails: "[The instructors] made us pass by one by one, putting our heads into the empty abdomen of the animal, covering ourselves with its blood and excrement while telling us that these dogs were our enemies."[119] At that time in southern Chile, where H.M.N.C. (1978–79) was taking part in nocturnal training in the valley of tears, the predominant enemy was Argentina. Recruits were attacked from all sides in the darkness, without being able to see the blows coming. Conscripts taken prisoner were stripped naked while bullets flew overhead. "Not just pistols; rifles, and machine guns 'roared with their rounds of death,'" testified H.M.N.C., "we also heard chilling barks and howls of dogs that were sacrificed with knives or bullets, as if it was nothing, it didn't matter if the poor animals suffered, they were Argentines and their blood, Argentine blood. / I saw many compañeros naked, like prisoners, bathed in blood from head to foot, with the blood of these poor animals that accompanied us in the night with their howls of pain, agony, and death. We had to smell blood everywhere. They were preparing us to kill the Argentine enemy!"[120] The point of forcing recruits' heads inside dog carcasses, and, in his case, retrieving an apple from among the entrails with his mouth, clarified Raúl Acuña (1976), was to "instill courage [to kill], because we didn't have it. . . . It was German training, totally Hitler, that style of training, just killing, pure killing, that was the training we had."[121] Raúl's comparison to Nazi Germany is perhaps understandable. The pointed helmets worn by the Chilean army during parades, rigorous discipline, and transcendental love of the patria were clear legacies of the "Prussianization" of the institution at the end of the previous century. As a cultural reference, too, the brutality of Nazism proved useful for some former recruits when describing the mistreatment they suffered.[122] However, the Chilean army had long opened up to other international influences, Prussia was not Nazi Germany, nor was there a straight line between the army reforms and Chilean fascism. Moreover, the training described in conscript testimony sits within contemporaneous Western military trends toward realism and desensitization.

From the early twentieth century, significant concerns were raised about the number of soldiers who did not kill, or even fire their weapon, during modern warfare. Military thinkers drew on contemporaneous psychological theories to advocate for greater exposure to warlike stimuli, in order to ensure that soldiers were accustomed to the "din" of battle, to make "instincts" and "habits" of their reactions to the sights and sounds of war, and to overcome the paralyzing fear of combat and their reluctance to kill. By World War II, Allied armies had already begun to implement thinking on realism during "battle inoculation," using, for example, humanized targets and live ammunition during exercises. By the time of the war in Vietnam, the logic of desensitization and psychological conditioning was entrenched in Western military training.[123] Extreme versions went further than using real bullets to produce in soldiers realistic fear. During British hate training in the 1940s, for example, trainees were also covered in sheep's blood during bayonet exercises and, during trips to slaughterhouses, they rubbed blood on the faces, experienced how it felt to plunge their knives into actual flesh, and were confronted with images of the destruction of war.[124]

Similar to the path taken by the logic of torture/resistance, desensitization in Latin America evolved from a Western tradition of inoculation that was tempered in the heat of Vietnam, exported by the United States to Cold War allies, augmented by local practice, and shared between the special forces of the continent's repressive regimes.[125] Like torture/resistance, too, military psychology was directed both internally and externally. Psychological warfare—the attempt to weaponize mass psychology and use it to rally support or demoralize the enemy—was the other side of realism in training. The theory was a significant thread of Chilean military thought in the decades prior to the coup, and the *White Book*, which was released by the junta in late 1973 to retrospectively document the existence of Plan Z as well as justify the coup and the regime's narrative of war, stands as an example of its practical implementation.[126] Parallel to psychological warfare, Chilean officers in the first half of the twentieth century were aware of the trends in military psychology that elsewhere laid the foundation for the brutalization of basic training and "battle inoculation."[127] In the 1960s and 1970s, while not advocating the types of abuses testified to by ex-conscripts under Pinochet, army handbooks for combat training pointed to a need for realism, including the use of live ammunition, to "familiarize soldiers to the atmosphere of violence and inclemency that would be the norm in war."[128] Later, the report of the Guatemalan Historical Clarification Commission noted the influence of Chilean commando courses—as well as US, Peruvian, and Colombian training—on the instruction of the Guatemalan Special Forces.[129] The report details methods based on survival and torture, during which trainees killed dogs, ate their flesh, and drank their blood. In reasoning that echoes Raúl's comments about his military service in southern Chile, the ritual was designed to be proof of "courage" (*valor*).[130] These bloody rites also made their way into the instruction of normal soldiers. "In the training centers for regular forces' recruits, the instruction was savage," a Guatemalan soldier told the commission: "They made me eat raw dog flesh and drink its blood [. . .] they sent four soldiers out to the street to find a dog [. . .] an officer killed it and began handing everyone a piece . . . we were all forced to eat it [. . .] and at the end they gave us human excrement to eat."[131] A report by the archbishopric of Guatemala describes such exercises in desensitization as the first step in training men to commit crimes of repression and to take life.[132] In Chile, former recruits recall a similar logic of desensitization.

R.J.M.M. (1977–79, Temuco) was also made to put his head inside a dead dog. "Afterwards," he writes, "and covered in blood, they passed the heart around and we had to eat part of the still-warm vital organ."[133] In this instance, he had killed the animal himself. Similarly, in Valdivia, D.I.M.B. (1980–82) was passed a machete (*corvo*) to kill a dog hanging from a tree. He hesitated: "the corporal struck me in the chest with the butt of his rifle and grabbing the machete, stuck it into the live animal and pulled it down from top to bottom saying: That's how it's done, conscript! He then made me put my head in the guts and wash myself with blood."[134] The killing of dogs represented the high point of the desensitization to death and culminated in an act of slaughter. Descriptions of such desensitization are not limited to the dictatorship. In his 1951 fictionalized account of his own military service in Valparaíso in the 1920s, Gonzalo Drago wrote of three conscripts being assigned the "pleasant task," as the instructor in the novella calls it, of using a rock to beat the heads of three mangy dogs until they were dead.[135] The logic behind the treatment of animals is also reflected in threats like the one made to Franco G.* (1988, Valdivia) by his sergeant: "On repeated occasions he aimed his caliber 38 revolver at me, threatening me with words such as: 'If I kill you, it would be like killing a dog.'"[136]

In moments reminiscent of ritualized animal cruelty, recruits describe punishments in which they or their fellow recruits were strung up and whipped. Staged punishments served a number of purposes at once: they disciplined the individual being punished; they served as a warning to rest of the group, guarding against subordination; and exposed recruits to suffering, often making them complicit. A.A.P.G. (1972–73, 1973, Temuco) wrote of conscripts being tied to the "moaning post" (*palo de lamentos*) in the regimental courtyard and whipped by their fellow recruits. The rest of the group was made to watch and count out the lashes in chorus, before untying their compañeros and dragging them to their rooms.[137] G.A.S.C. (Temuco) remembers a recalled reservist who did not immediately comply with an order, and was punished with fifty lashes in front of the battalion. "They ordered my best friend to give the lashes," he writes, "and as the commandant of the regiment thought that he was whipping too softly, he ordered that they apply the same quota of fifty lashes to him, to his, of course, naked torso. So, the next day, my friend was tied to a post in the main courtyard and he received the punishment of fifty lashes with a wet whip passed through sand to make the whole thing crueler. In addition, they dressed him in white and paraded him through the regiment for two weeks to humiliate him even more."[138] In 2014 Luis Álvarez (1987–89) testified to having been raped by a compañero toward the end of the dictatorship, as part of a training exercise. Álvarez's allegations formed part of the criminal case pursued by the ex-conscript group in Puente Alto, and he recounted the incident for television cameras. In 1989 Álvarez and his fellow recruits were woken with tear gas and shouting, and along with several others, he was stripped and ordered into the tripod position: feet and forehead on the ground, hands behind the back, legs straight. He alleged on camera that sublieutenant Marcel Prada González then ordered a conscript named Quintero to rape him. After the recruit protested, Prada González put a pistol to his temple. After again refusing, the sublieutenant cocked the weapon, fired over the recruit's head, and repeated his threat to kill him. The young man complied with the order. The reason given for the assault, said Álvarez, was that the naked recruits had been at that moment assigned the role of Argentine soldiers as part of a simulation and were violated for being "traitors." Álvarez and his rapist are part of the same ex-conscript group, and they tell the same story. Sometimes, Álvarez said, the two men cry together.[139]

The same underlying assumption that witnessing or participating in the mistreatment of others would desensitize recruits runs through accounts of political repression.[140] "After the military coup," writes Angelo J.* (1973), "we were treated worse, because we were witness to more severe punishments for soldiers; they were tied to a post and their naked torso was whipped until blood ran down their backs." He and his compañeros were also "forced to look at the remains of the bodies shot in the ammunition depots or firing ranges," and beat detainees who had their hands tied, "to get them to say what our superiors wanted to hear, and if we refused to beat the detainees, they punished us."[141] For Carlos R.* (1973), the layered functions of mistreatment—punishment, warning, hardening—came together in an incident from the days following the coup. He was witness to the execution of fellow conscripts, who were interrogated and later shot in the head. "After they were executed, their clothes, rings, watches, and shoes were taken, and the coup de grâce was a blow with a rock, which broke the skull," recalled Carlos for TV cameras nearly four decades later, his face pixilated to protect his identity: "I could tell it broke from the noise it produced. And with that they had made us good men and good soldiers. We were resistant to anything."[142]

Exposure to the stresses of battle and capture, however, did not necessarily build resistance to pain, or erode the aversion to inflicting pain. Elsewhere desensitization had been found to undermine soldiers' self-respect and was rejected as psychologically counterproductive; realism had been rejected as having the potential to produce real "shellshock"; and resistance training had left soldiers broken and unwilling to abuse prisoners.[143] In Chile, too, ex-conscripts reported deep and ongoing feelings of fear, guilt, shame, and impotence. D.A.G.V. (1983–85, Punta Arenas), for example, described his participation in the punishment of a fellow conscript who had "rebelled" against his corporal as the "saddest experience" he could remember. He had been part of a group sent to "drown" the rebel in a reservoir, a "crazy order that left several of us traumatized, seeing our compañero crying and screaming in desperation, begging for his life when he was able to pull his head above the water." The punishment stopped with the conscript barely breathing.[144] Osvaldo F.* (1977–78), too, was labeled a rebel and traitor for not complying with an order to beat a fellow conscript, and he received the beating he had refused to administer. At the back of an ex-conscript gathering in Paseo Bulnes in downtown Santiago in October 2012, he went silent midsentence, and tears welled in his eyes at the memory of his suicide attempt. The feeling of helplessness still plagues him. "I feel powerless," he explained after a pause.[145]

A shift in institutional practice and thinking did not coincide with the end of military rule. After the transition, the army only gradually stepped away from the Cold War vision that had both produced and justified the type of practices testified to by ex-conscripts under Pinochet, and similar abuses appear in cases from the early 1990s.[146] CODEPU psychologists who worked with conscripts and deserters called up in the early posttransition years wrote of "normal training," which included isolation from those ties that had until then constituted the recruits' world, initiation via a series of rituals, a strict hierarchy, the loss of individuality, obedience without thinking, and a regime of physical punishments. The young men who approached the corporation seeking legal, medical, and psychological assistance described exercises similar to those testified to around a decade later by conscripts who had served under military rule, including strikes with fists and feet, beatings, being hung, asphyxia, threats of death or disappearance, incarceration, application of electrical current, humiliation in front of their compañeros, and in some cases, sexual abuse, attacks with tear gas, simulations of war, beatings, mock executions, sensory deprivation, withholding of food, exposure to climatic extremes, as well as being forced to slit the throats of, and disembowel, animals that they had cared for. The goal of these exercises, write the psychologists, was to establish a resistance to physical pain, and numb the body to hunger, thirst, and tiredness, to the point of eliminating them altogether.[147] They assert, without explanation, that they were able to verify that such practices were similar to those used during the dictatorship. They also claim that abuses of this kind had occurred in military units throughout Chilean history, but intensified with the armed forces' adoption of the doctrine of national security.[148] Given her experience with posttransition recruits, psychologist Rosella Baronti spoke of the logic of military service being to produce tough subjects, capable of killing, who were desensitized to human suffering. The instruction was tough, she continued, they killed dogs, were mistreated, were made to face suffering, and subjected to the cold (in the south), hunger, and pain in order to prepare them for being taken prisoner during a war.[149] In his testimony to CODEPU, Rigoberto Antonio Mallias Diaz (1996) explained that the "torture and cruel, inhumane and degrading treatment" recruits suffered was "common practice designed to, according to them, make us men."[150]

The project under Pinochet to create hard men of boys brought the front lines of Chile's wars inside the barracks. Ex-conscript memory reveals a guiding principle of resistance, which was a mix of twentieth-century military thinking on realism, postwar fears of guerilla warfare, and a Cold War logic of torture/resistance resting on a Chilean tradition of brutal penal practice, military discipline, and torture, as well as the nineteenth-century mythology of the indomitable Chilean race. An unsophisticated and exaggerated application of theory and the armed forces' siege mentality produced a brutal regime of physical and psychological abuse that eroded the distinctions between punishment and training, between torture and instruction, and between preparing for war and waging it. The masculinity of the barracks clashed with conscripts' expectations of service, and systematically undid their civilian identities as males, and their civilian ideas of becoming a man. For many, conscription also undermined their ability to be men when they left the barracks.

Broken Men

Thirty years after his military service, Luis Zapata (1981–83) worked seven days a week, selling mittens and scarves outside Santiago's Central Station. He took a break to talk about his time in the barracks in the privacy of his small storage space among the shops and arcade games of the station complex, leaving his wife to run the stall.[151] Luis's first marriage had failed, he explained, because of the effects of his service. Standing between boxes of wares, he spoke softly of his interrogation at the hands of the intelligence service while a conscript, the death threats, sleeping with rats, the beatings, and the application of electrical current to his fingers during questioning about photos of people he did not recognize from his old neighborhood of La Victoria. His questioning was interrupted by the buildup of forces on the Argentine border. The almost-war "saved me from the torture for a while," he recalled, as he was returned to the ranks, told to write a last letter to his family, and transferred to the front line. He spoke, too, of living with the consequences after his discharge. Sometimes, he conceded, he took his frustrations out on those around him, as he had done with his first wife. Luis's voice finally cracked, however, when talking about the ramifications of his conscription on his children from that marriage. One is healthy, one has a form of leukemia, and another suffers from debilitating epilepsy. He insisted the ailments have no precedent in his family, and he cannot explain them, but he suspects his extended exposure to *piedra alumbre*—potassium nitrate or saltpeter—as a conscript made his children sick: "It may be my fault," he reasoned, with tears in his eyes.

The routine use of piedra alumbre as a food additive to dull recruits' sex drive is an important piece of ex-conscript lore.[152] Group leaders used it as an example when talking about the movement, their members, and their demands, and many individuals remembered their service through the presumed toll piedra alumbre had taken on their bodies and their families. They describe the additive as radioactive and carcinogenic, and they associate it with a variety of ailments, including persistent sexual dysfunction, infertility, birth defects in their children, and even infecting their wives with cervical and uterine cancer.[153] The reality of the use of piedra alumbre in the barracks is difficult to ascertain beyond the anecdotal evidence from former conscripts and political prisoners, and the assertion of improbable, and at times impossible, causal links to the array of health problems attributed to it decades later is more problematic still.[154] However, piedra alumbre is most important as a flexible narrative device that provides a specific hook for a diffuse sense of victimhood, and, as in Luis' case, a painful link between military service and contemporary difficulties. It is a concentrated part of a broader memory narrative of damage and ruptured masculinity: lingering damage done to recruits as young men, damage they fear they have passed on to their loved ones, damage that has meant they have been unable to live up to their masculine responsibilities, damage that left them, in some way, broken men.[155]

The societal norms that reservists faced on leaving the barracks, and the internalized conventions they measured themselves against, defined adult, masculine identity in working-class and poor Chile as the intimately intertwined roles of father, husband, worker, and breadwinner. This masculinity was cast during industrialization and the emergence of the modern welfare state in the first decades of the twentieth century. Industrial efficiency and social progress demanded that the "vices" of turn-of-the-century working-class culture be addressed, including drinking, gambling, prostitution, illegitimate children, and absentee fathers. The social and legal framework of the modern economy tied sex to marriage, and male work to family and familial responsibility, installing the nuclear family with a sole, male breadwinner as the basic unit of the modern workforce. In practice, family life did not catch up to the rhetoric, and very few men were able to provide for their families on their own. Nevertheless, by midcentury forming a nuclear family, work, and providing for a wife and children had solidified as fundamental elements of masculine identity, and the political upheaval of the following decades did not challenge the ideal. The reformist program under Frei in the late 1960s, Allende's revolutionary agenda between 1970 and 1973, and the rhetoric of the military regime all confirmed the central role of the nuclear family and traditional gender roles as its bedrock. The "traditional" model only began being questioned at the beginning of the twenty-first century.[156] At around the same time, many former recruits remembered their conscription as having undermined, and continuing to undermine, their ability to live up to this dominant, twentieth-century masculinity.[157]

After prisoner training exercises in mid-1975, P.O.B.F. (1974–76, Temuco) feared he would be left unable to father children. He and his compañeros were stripped before having their hands bound and electricity passed through their hands, feet, and genitals. "I consider it a miracle that we did not end up infertile," he said.[158] E.O.G.T (1980–83) was not as lucky. Blows to his genitals left his testicles swelled to six times their normal size and landed him in the Coyhaique infirmary for four months. On returning to civilian life, he married with the hope of starting a family. However, after not being able to conceive, he and his wife underwent tests and discovered that "she was fine, could conceive, it was a different story with me because the diagnosis was of 'irreversible sterility' caused by the beatings in the army. Tears of pain, helplessness, profound sadness rolled down my cheeks, not only did they screw up my life, but they prevented the birth of the children I will never have!"[159] Attacks on the testicles are reported by former conscripts to have been one of the staple elements of both training and punishment, and many carry scars or suffer from disease that they attribute to physical abuse of their genitals. The inability to father children, linked by former recruits to mistreatment inside the barracks, cut to the core of what it meant to be a man. After returning home from the barracks, J.E.S.L. (1979–81) married and, like any "well-raised young man with a good image of family life," looked forward to starting a family. Eventually, however, he was diagnosed as infertile, due to poorly healed bruising of his genitals. Recalling the kicks to the testicles during nocturnal exercises, he lamented: "One of the most sacred things a man has, his biological virility, had been affected forever."[160]

Family formation was further undermined by lingering emotional and social problems. Upon leaving the barracks, former recruits often struggled to relate to other people, maintain existing relationships, and enter into new ones. They withdrew from society, and they were short-tempered and prone to breaking down and crying, or lashing out violently for what seemed to others as no reason. J.I.M.J. (1974–76, Temuco and Calama) complained of having his personality transformed in the army. At twenty-one, he married the girl he had left behind when he entered the barracks: "But obviously I could not be the loving and affectionate husband I would have been without the traumatic experiences I went through in the army, and after two years of marriage, we had to separate in the face of our failing marriage."[161] A 2010 report compiled by a social worker in Osorno listed 17 percent of the sixty local members who participated in the study as single and having never married. Statistically, the observation is not significant, but the reasons given for the broken relationships and never marrying are representative of what ex-recruits self-report throughout the country: fear, a sense of failure, difficulty relating to people, and feelings of isolation.[162] "The deep damage done to us in those times marked us for life," insists Alfredo C.* (1983–84, Punta Arenas) in his 2007 testimony: "Unfortunately it has consequences for our families and in our personal lives as fathers. I have had problems living with people, with self-esteem, which resulted in two failed marriages; my own personal case is stained with domestic violence, I could never lead a normal life as a father or a husband."[163] More than just "marking" Alfredo, he describes how he had passed on the "deep damage" to his wives and children.

A sense of burden and contagion runs through ex-conscript memory.[164] Andrés V.* (1975–77), for example, never married. "No, no, no, [when I left the barracks] I was more sick than in love," he smiled wryly more than three decades later, "my life was destroyed." He took to drink "a little," remained single and unable to work, and he lived with his parents until they died. He dismissed the idea of having children: "No, it's better that I didn't have children, because, imagine breeding a sick child [. . .] because I have problems in my head, I have problems in my brain."[165] Fear of, and shame about, passing the damage from the barracks onto children and loved ones emerges at times as a vague feeling of "sickness," like in Andrés's case. More generally, however, the sense of contamination is articulated as physical and emotional abuse, a failure to provide financially, and specific illnesses attributed to recruits' service.

The lore of piedra alumbre and its long-term health effects for former recruits and their families is one way ex-conscripts remember their service through the health complaints of their children and partners. A similar, but narrower, example of conscript lore relates to exposure to nuclear radiation. In 2009 sixty-five former recruits and the parents of two deceased ex-conscripts who guarded medical nuclear facilities in Santiago between December 1988 and September 1989 launched a claim against the state and the Chilean Commission for Nuclear Energy for around US$84 million in damages. The ex-recruits cited health concerns they traced back to their conscription: brain tumors, liver cancer, eye cancer, leukemia, chronic diarrhea, chronic digestive problems, migraines, bone pain, and neurodegenerative diseases. Beyond their own health problems, they were also concerned that the damage had extended to their families. Pedro Araya (1988–89) was not sick, but he believed his younger sister, who had washed his uniforms by hand while he was on leave, was an indirect victim of his service after she was diagnosed with cancer in late 2010. Ex-recruits were also concerned about having passed on the damage to their own children, who displayed similar symptoms to their fathers, or suffered from birth defects. Marco Muñoz (1988–89) was successfully treated for brain cancer soon after his discharge, and at the time of the claim he was healthy and had a healthy daughter. However, he ruled out having any more children, citing his fear of producing unhealthy offspring. The case reemerged in March 2011, in the weeks following the Fukushima reactor meltdown in Japan. Chile was in the midst of an energy crisis exacerbated by a drought affecting the country's hydroelectric plants, and there was high-profile, public opposition to proposed new projects in Patagonia. The Japanese disaster sparked renewed debate about the potential dangers of nuclear power. Congressman Sergio Ojeda suggested that the 2009 case regarding the conscripts had been covered up in the interests of the nuclear industry. The damage done to conscripts in the 1980s should be enough, he argued, to rule out nuclear power for Chile.[166] Around the same time, exposure to nuclear radiation was included in a text produced by a coalition of four representative groups that outlined their preferred framework for reparations. In conversations with group leaders, too, radioactivity had a role disproportionate to the number of members it affected, when explaining how service affected families.[167]

Former recruits' families also suffered direct, physical abuse. "It gets transmitted," said Daniel Gómez (1978–80, Punta Arenas), referring to how the violence of the barracks was passed on in the home.[168] Testimonies describe not a cycle of violence, but a spiral that moved from officers and instructors, through conscripts, eventually reaching beyond the barracks to reservists' homes. "What they suffered during military conscription," explained Claudio de la Hoz (1973), "they later took back to the family."[169] Emotional abuse, authoritarian parenting, and domestic violence, often compounded by the abuse of alcohol, are common themes in general descriptions by group representatives of ex-conscripts as a cohort, as well as important parts of individual stories.[170] On the edge of a gathering outside the Moneda in January 2012, for example, Pedro M.* (1976–78) explained that he had not talked about his experiences with his family. He spoke quietly of the violence of his service—running a gauntlet of people beating him, being dressed in white, having to bind the hands of people subjected to mock executions—before euphemistically referring to his "very unpleasant" treatment of his wife and son once he got out.[171] Similarly, an unnamed former recruit cited by the Ex-conscript Commission witnessed the torture of a friend and fellow recruit: "'In that moment you feel so humiliated because you cannot do anything at all; on the contrary, they make you watch, they enjoy it, they laugh. [. . .] So it really makes you furious, because you feel powerless, seeing how they laugh at the cruel things they do, how they enjoy them . . . and when I drink alcohol, I get violent for that reason . . .' [he broke into tears remembering]."[172] In his testimony, Maximiliano F.* (1983, Temuco) also describes domestic violence as one of the lingering effects of the beatings, the sexual humiliation, being forced to eat excrement, and having electricity applied to his fingers and stomach as a "prisoner." More than twenty years later, he writes, he is still jumpy, he has trouble sleeping, is emotionally temperamental and sometimes violent: "Because of all the tortures I went through, unfortunately I passed it on to my family and what I regret the most is that my children are affected." He goes on to write of his inability to hold down a job, which he ascribes to psychological problems resulting from his service, as part of the damage he had transmitted.[173]

The failure to properly provide for their families provides the counterpoint to the hope and the expectations that many had invested in the idea of military service as boys. A 2012 psychological report on 123 ex-conscripts in Osorno articulated this discord. At the time of their call-up, the report outlined, many were attending school or working to maintain their siblings. They envisaged continuing their schooling inside the barracks, a possible career in the army, or the chance to have a career on the outside. The report reproduces the conscript narrative, describing these ambitions as "false hopes" that "generated a high level of frustration." They returned home damaged, with no studies or training, and with no way to support their families.[174] This document was part of the larger Ex-conscript Commission report that described how the "shame" of former recruits who were mistreated was "accentuated" by the contrast between their experiences and the "cultural significance" of military service: "To this day, the belief exists that, as a soldier, a young man will be more manly, more upstanding, better qualified, etc. To say the opposite is embarrassing."[175]

The cycle of frustrated ambitions was completed as the failed promise of military service met the failing promise of education. Recruits received no training in the barracks, and the struggle to readjust to civilian life, economic crisis, and a lack of opportunity meant most did not return to school. Decades later, the compounded cost of a poor education, as well as ongoing emotional problems, lost aspirations and ambition, and persistent and emerging health issues attributed to service meant former recruits felt unable to provide their children with opportunities. Diego C.* (1983–85, Tierra del Fuego) had only a primary education when he was drafted. In his 2010 testimony he recalled a 1983 recruitment pitch in a gymnasium in Loncoche. During the talk, soldiers explained where recruits would be sent and the opportunities they would have to study, and they assured the young men that they would have pension payments made on their behalf. Diego received no education, and instead he remembers the extreme cold and the physical demands of service that "did not affect [him] at the time, but several years passed, my body began to feel the effects as consequences of those incidents." These effects, he continued, forced him to abandon the only type of work he had ever known in the ninth region's labor-intensive forestry industry. Finding new, less physical work was in turn complicated by his lack of secondary education.[176] A generation after Diego was drafted, education had replaced service as the pathway to social mobility, but it was expensive, and many former recruits struggled to meet that expense. Speaking about his conscription two years after giving his written testimony, Diego referred specifically to the wrist he had fractured during his service, which in recent years had been causing him increasing pain, and which brought his story full circle. As a boy, he said, his family's daily struggle to survive had curtailed his schooling, and now, as a man, his daily struggle was to work to pay for his children's education. He explained, with a nod to his wrist, that the effects of his service meant that, decades after leaving the barracks, he could not provide for his children "as he should."[177]

For Miguel M.* (1973), it was not leaving the barracks damaged but entering them in the first place that denied him a chance to live up to his responsibilities. Young men who at the time of their conscription had already assumed the role of provider—usually for mothers and siblings, but at times also their own children—recall their service as a burden. Any benefits of conscription to Miguel and his family, for example, did not outweigh the cost of his absence, as his father had a weak heart and his mother depended instead on her son.[178] As Miguel was entering the barracks, David Wiederhold (1977–79) had already left school to work with his fisherman father. As the only son, David assumed responsibility for his mother and twelve sisters, when, in 1974, soldiers killed his communist father. His ability to live up to that responsibility was taken from him in 1977, when he was drafted at the age of seventeen: "They ruined my life, they ruined my life and the lives of my entire family."[179] At around the same time, Manuel Soto A. (1978–79, San Antonio) was living with his family in an encampment along the train line in Llolleo. As the eldest child, he was working in the local fishing industry to help provide for his seven siblings. Conscription, for Manuel, was not an opportunity: "We fell on hard times. For me, the worst was being uprooted from my family, because I knew that they would be poorer without me at home."[180]

The narrative of a ruined life (*proyecto de vida*) and the denial of the provider role was also codified in group documents. Resolution 606 (2012), for example, insisted that "according to the law of the time, that stipulated that the age of majority was 21 years, those conscripts [1973–88] were all minors under the law, between 18 and 19, and, as such, C.M.S. [Compulsory Military Service] restricted or limited their possibilities in education, trade, profession and/or employment." It also noted that conscripts generally came from "poor families, in which they performed important roles as providers for their nuclear or extended families; in many cases they were married and/or were single fathers." Military service worsened poverty by separating these young men from their families and "preventing them from performing their obligations to feed and protect their families."[181] In a separate document, in which it presented its preferred framework for reparations, the ex-conscript coalition that pushed for Resolution 606 also emphasized the interruption to recruits' education and the implications conscription had for their earning power in subsequent decades. It listed among its demands a monthly pension for former conscripts with physical or psychological damage that affected their capacity to work and education benefits that could be transferred to their children, wives, or mothers of their children. Moreover, the text argued that forcibly recruiting young, single fathers and young, married men and fathers, and forcing them to leave their families without protection or a provider, had prevented some recruits from performing their "sacred duty to protect as enshrined in the rights of the family, in our penal code, and in the International Convention of the Rights of Children."[182]

The undermined masculinity described by ex-conscripts, as well as their anxiety about transmitting their suffering, mirrors obstacles and fears faced by former political prisoners. For example, Clara Han relates the story of Héctor, a former militant and torture victim living in La Pincoya in first decade of the twenty-first century, who did not talk about his experiences with his children, fearing that the narration of his torture would "deform" them. When his first son was born, Héctor's wife followed convention and gave the child his father's name, but Héctor worried that this direct connection would somehow pass "the toxicity" on to little Héctor.[183] Héctor had preferred to keep his experiences to himself, and he did not provide testimony to the Valech Commission. On the basis of the testimonies it did receive, however, the commission's report describes the ways many victims of political repression struggled to live up to gender expectations. Former prisoners suffered from infertility due to injuries to reproductive organs. They speak of changes to their personalities, depression, feelings of isolation, and disturbed social, intimate, and sexual relationships that result in the estrangement of families and the breakdown of marriages. Many rue their lost aspirations, educational opportunities, and jobs, and are shamed by their inability to provide for their families and give their children a better life. Subsequent unemployment and a precarious economic existence under the regime compounded the social and psychological effects of political torture, and produced feelings of failure and guilt. The lost path to social mobility had been particularly difficult for those victims from working-class and rural families, who had had expectations of a gradual, but continual, improvement in their living conditions. For male victims, the irretrievable gap in their proyecto de vida also had emotional, physical, and economic consequences for their partners and children.[184] While the ex-conscript narrative of undermined masculinity in the decades after their service echoes the difficulties faced by political prisoners, it must also be seen in the context of a broader crisis of masculinity in Chile.[185]

On leaving the barracks, young reservists—still poorly educated, still untrained—reentered the labor market, now as men, with different expectations and responsibilities placed on them by both society and by themselves. At the same time, they entered a labor force substantially different from the one that had forged and fostered the strict, gendered division of labor and tied adult, male, working-class identity to work and providing for a family. While the reorganization of the Chilean economy under military rule was ushered in amid rhetoric that affirmed the ideal of the patriarchal, nuclear family, with a male breadwinner and a stay-at-home wife and mother, the consequences of its economic policies effectively undermined it.[186] The junta's program of privatization of state assets, slashing of government spending, and the removal of protectionist tariffs from around key industries plunged the economy into crisis in the mid-1970s; real wages plummeted and unemployment rose sharply, with the official figures hiding the hundreds of thousands of men working in emergency work programs. For those with jobs, restrictions on unions and a permissive labor code eroded job security, entrenched short-term, seasonal work, and sparked a growth in the informal sector. The poorer and hardest hit sectors of Chilean society had not yet recovered when depressed global demand in the wake of the 1979 oil shock and a burst local debt bubble that had inflated in the deregulated financial sector sank the Chilean economy into a new crisis in the early 1980s. Interest rates trebled and unemployment reached levels higher than the peak of the first crisis. In this new economy, many men struggled to provide for their families, and young men found it particularly difficult. Youth unemployment ran much higher than the general rate, informal employment grew, and those able to find work found they were paid less than older workers with a similar level of education. This pattern had an infantilizing effect on a generation of young people who found the transition to adulthood and the assumption of adult responsibility increasingly out of reach. In poor urban areas, households grew larger and more extended, as grown children could not afford to move out. For young men, work and the nuclear family remained fundamental reference points for adult masculinity, even as both became more difficult to attain. Emasculation and infantilization, driven by unemployment, underemployment, irregular, unstable, and informal employment, were compounded further by the entrance of women into the workforce.[187]

The junta's economic changes upset and reset gendered employment patterns. As public and industrial sectors were reorganized, women could often more easily find work as domestic workers than their husbands in the civil service or in factories. In the countryside, too, the export-oriented agricultural, forestry, and fishing industries promoted by the military regime brought with them a dependence on wage labor and seasonal work. Established employment opportunities for men in the rural economy were dismantled and male unemployment as well as insecure, unstable, and temporary work forced women out of the home and into the workforce, where they took jobs in the new fruit-packing and fish-processing plants.[188] Women had always contributed to household income, but often by selling homemade goods, and without challenging the gendered division of labor. However, women entering the workforce, often earning more than their husbands, and potentially supplanting them as the breadwinner of the family became an economic reality that for many men compounded the shame of being unemployed and poorly paid. Pamela Constable and Arturo Valenzuela recount an anecdote from Father

Oscar Jiménez, a priest in Pudahuel on the western edge of Santiago, who offered counsel to a man who had lost his factory job. The humiliation at being supported by his wife was so great that he would not eat. "Work was their whole identity," Father Jiménez explained, "and without it they were nothing."[189]

Within the crisis of masculinity, ex-conscript memory was built on the gap between expectations of service and the experience and consequences of service. In the twentieth century, military service established itself as a rite of passage and an opportunity for recruits to have an education, a career, to improve their prospects. Under Pinochet, however, the process of making "hard" men unmade boys' identities, assumptions, and aspirations. Chile's wars shifted inside the barracks, and the brutality of basic training, the degradation of survival training, the humiliation and helplessness of resistance training, and the powerlessness and trauma of desensitization left many draftees, to varying degrees, broken. Ex-conscripts felt their ability to live up to what it meant to be a man on the outside had been compromised by infertility, unemployment, domestic violence, alcoholism, psychological problems, physical injuries, and a lack of education, which could be traced back to their service. Their time in the barracks and its long-term effects meant they were unable to assume or fulfill their societal roles as husbands, fathers, and breadwinners. As failed patriarchs, many felt they transmitted the damage from the barracks to their wives and children as illness, emotional or physical abuse, or financial hardship. Amid the failed promise of democracy in the 1990s, the shared narrative of memory as a rupture in masculinity made sense of the experience of military service and decades of economic, emotional, and familial struggle.

5

In the Flesh

Hugo M.* (1975–77, Arica) did not want to sit, and he punctuated his words with rhythmic taps of his cane. "Who will believe it?" he asked rhetorically and repeatedly in 2012 in the small Temuco office of the Agrupación de Reservistas. He recalled being a normal, sporty boy growing up in Chile's ninth region, who had no interest in politics and understood little of it when he was drafted in 1975. The barracks had been a mystery before his service, he said, and inside it felt like a different world. In nearby Lautaro, he was told that he was at war, and to shoot first at the body and then into the air. Later, he was sent to the northern border as part of the buildup for the potential conflict with Peru. It is difficult to explain, he said, because there are no witnesses, and no one—not civilians, not family members, not psychologists—can understand, because they were not there, but this is "what we lived in the flesh [*en carne propia*]."[1] Like Hugo, many former conscripts insist that they experienced what they describe in conversations, interviews, and testimonies "in the flesh," as a way of underscoring their recollections and guarding against disbelief.[2] This chapter examines the ways in which military service was remembered "in the flesh." Former recruits' recollections are shaped by a discourse of "bodily memory" that frames remembering as a lonely and often debilitating contest between their desire to forget and unwanted thoughts, emotions, behaviors, and persistent physical reminders. This individual contest played out within their bodies and minds, and it plagued, in particular, their silence. With the emergence of ex-conscript groups, a collective will to remember recast intrusive thoughts, illnesses, and scars as evidence of victimhood. The timing of the ex-conscript movement, the formation of group demands, the testimony process, and the sharing of stories also helped ex-conscripts embody their memory narratives. Former recruits established and maintained links between shared memory and their own bodies, transforming them into sites of memory.

Bodily Memory

Remembering his service, A.E.G.V. (1973–74, Angol) emphasized his desire to forget: "I still have nightmares about what I saw and the punishments, the whippings, tortures and humiliations that we suffered and experienced in the flesh, the details of which I want to erase from my mind and despite this, over the years, I have not been able to do it."[3] A.E.G.V.'s recollections are representative of a discourse in conscript testimonies that understands memory as a contest within recruits' bodies and minds between their efforts not to remember and memories that lay "alive and latent" within them.[4] Bodily memory pits former recruits' efforts to forget against physical reminders of service, unbidden thoughts or images of their time in the barracks, emotional and physiological reactions to certain triggers, lingering fears, shame or guilt, learned behaviors, and permanent shifts in personality.

Ex-conscripts testified to lasting changes in their thinking and behavior that they insist resulted from their service. Some described how in the barracks "they changed my way of thinking" (*me cambiaron el chip*), and how the mentality and emotions of conscription had stayed with them.[5] They detail, too, ingrained fear, attitudes, actions, and reactions that remained long after their discharge. In his testimony, Amaro S.* (1974–75, Calama) wrote of brutal training during which they fought dogs and saw their compañeros strung up and screaming with pain. "Every night," he wrote decades later, "I have enormous problems getting to sleep, even getting up 4 or 5 times in the night, I wake up every hour just as I used to in the regiment, because I had to be ready for any eventuality. My family has suffered my irritability, my bad temper in silence; I am often unsocial, I explode easily at the smallest provocation [and] on leaving the regiment, I was never the same person that I had been, which left me marked forever. What hurts the most and what I regret is that my family had to bear the burden of all the consequences due to the atrocities I experienced."[6] Maximiliano F.* (1983, Temuco), too, described being constantly on alert: "In recent years I have had problems with my children and my wife because I am very nervous and jumpy. I wake up at night at the slightest noise and I get up to see if anyone is in my home. I have objects that I use to defend myself if someone tried to break in and rob my home. I almost never sleep to protect my family. When I am in my home, it's like I'm on guard duty. I check every corner of the house and during the day I work. [. . .] Where I live, they call me 'the soldier.'"[7] In his 2006 testimony, Miguel M.* (1973) wrote of being forced to shoot at people against his will. He was unsure whether he hurt anyone. "Today I think of those people," he wrote, "and I want to believe that they are alright, that I didn't do them any damage and that they are happy despite everything." He saw conscripts "who were called enemies" punished or killed for not shooting, so he pulled the trigger to be able to "see my mother's face again." In addition to fearing his superiors, he describes being constantly on edge when patrolling the streets or on guard duty. On September 14, 1973, he and a friend had been waiting to be transferred, when he heard a shot without being able to identify where it came from. His compañero was hit and died in his arms: "After my discharge, I suffered depression that lasted for some years. I couldn't find peace anywhere. I overreact even to fights between dogs, ambulances or the firecrackers for the [festivities on the] 18th [of September]. To this day, I cannot forget the face of my dying friend." He went on to describe the memory of the incident as "a pain that I carry in my soul." For some time afterward, he had trouble sleeping because the image of his dead friend came to him every time he shut his eyes.[8]

Nightmares and difficulty sleeping in the years or decades after leaving the barracks were common complaints. J.H.Z.C. (1973–75) wrote of never having been able to get over the beatings, the punishments, humiliations, and the pressure that had him "on the edge of collapse" and drove others to take their own lives. He recalled one suicide in particular. While on guard duty one night on the Puente Pedro de Valdivia in Valdivia, his compañero said he was going down to the river to urinate. J.H.Z.C. soon heard a rifle shot and went down to find his fellow conscript on the ground, the rifle still in his hands, his fingers on the trigger, the barrel still smoking, and his head "totally destroyed." "I went nights, weeks, and months," he wrote, "without being able to eliminate that fateful image from my mind."[9] Similarly, Leonardo S.* (1973–75, Traiguén) testified to having to participate in raids and witness torture, and how "permanently remembering these episodes" prevented him from sleeping.[10] After returning from the trenches on the Argentine border, J.A.F.M. (1978, Punta Arenas) felt isolated and mistrustful of everyone, and he had trouble concentrating. "At night," he wrote, "everything that happened during that year and nine months came back to me, I had nightmares of war and I woke everyone in the house."[11] M.A.F.G. (1976, Coyhaique) also had trouble sleeping for a long time after leaving the barracks. He described suffering from "war nightmares," of being scared awake by visions of life on the border and the familiar tension of constantly waiting for the enemy to appear: "We had to be alert and awake 24 hours a day, blinking could mean the difference between life and death."[12]

Memories come to Julio Bahamondes (1973–75) at any time, day or night. In 2014 he reenacted his participation in a firing squad for television cameras. As a conscript, he had been ordered to fire on a detainee. Next to him, his compañero "went crazy," he recalled, walking forward and continuing to fire at the prisoner. The lieutenant present had to administer the coup de grâce to the badly injured man, explained Bahamondes. The ex-conscript had struggled with the memory of that day. "I've had a hard life," he said, and "the bad memories that I experienced during my service, I kept them forever, and I got used to living a double life and showing everyone else that I was alright, but in my mind . . ." He continued, "Sometimes it happens once a month, an epileptic fit, sometimes daily, when I have this type of memory that is the most painful." Bahamondes spoke of the mind as a "hard drive" that records everything. What it recorded, he said, would return to his mind without warning.[13] Andrés V.* (1975–77) also spoke of being unable to forget. Service left him with a "weight" that "marks his thinking." "We were prepared to die," he said, "we were not interested in life, because the treatment they gave us was too much, that is, I think a physical punishment is doing push-ups, but beating a person like dog, I don't understand it and it left me marked. I have things in my mind that don't let me live my life in peace, because there are memories, and I think these are scars, because my mind always makes connections, it makes me think of those days, that time. We can forget little."[14] For Alberto C.* (1976, Temuco), unexpected things made the connection to service in his mind. Like Andrés, Alberto spoke of indelible and involuntary memories. He blamed his service for his two failed marriages, having nothing to offer his two small children, and his nightmares: "In the night, I used to scream, I had nightmares. Things you saw, they would later come to mind." Years after serving, footage of the Iraq war made him want to go and fight in the Middle East, he said, laughing at the idea.[15]

Triggers for memories varied. J.A.M.R. (1974) wrote of shaking with fear at the sight of doctors, soldiers, or police. In 1974 he had been transferred from Temuco to Calama. A fellow conscript in the company was investigated by the Servicio de Inteligencia Militar (Military Intelligence Service), and they discovered that between 1971 and 1973 he had been a political activist. He was subsequently interrogated and pressed for names of other activists in the company. Under torture, the recruit gave up the names of the two nearest at hand, including J.A.M.R. During his own interrogation, J.A.M.R. was knocked unconscious, and when he came to, two uniformed men handcuffed him and applied electricity via his fingers: "They told me that this method didn't fail and that one way or the other I would have to tell the truth." Later, he writes, they applied current to his ears and testicles. He was hospitalized and warned that if he mentioned what had happened, he would be killed. They said they would know where he was, he writes, and how to get to his family: "The psycho-logical damage that they caused is irreparable and still, despite the time that has passed, I tremble with terror when I see doctors, soldiers or carabineros. / I remember everything I experienced. The clear memories of that terror and the torture I suffered permanently return to my memory, without me being able to forget them, as if I was living it now."[16] Television sparked memories for J.C.G.V. (1973, Lautaro). He described being beaten and kicked, and crawling through spiny vegetation during basic training in the ninth region, and later, on campaña in Antofagasta, being forced to drink urine and eat dogs they had just killed. When they were taken out into the streets, he wrote, he and his compañeros were threatened with death if they did not "act against civilians." "I will never be able to erase it from my mind," he wrote, "much less my heart, because the experience has profoundly affected my soul, irrevocably damaging my spirit and my personality." He wrote of being unable to forget, "because every time I see images of soldiers on the television, my mind is affected and inundated with raw memories of the pain and despair I lived through inside the regiment."[17] Enrique P.* (1982–84, Tierra del Fuego) served a decade later and described memories coming suddenly to him when he is alone. Around thirty years after his service, he still had trouble sleeping and would cry at the slightest thing without wanting to. The example he gave was seeing family disputes on television.[18]

For Patricio Farías (1973–75, Punta Arenas), walking through downtown Santiago brought back memories of guard duty outside the Moneda in late 1973 and the corporeal sense of vulnerability. "Every time I pass by there I remember," he said, "I stood there [on guard duty] an entire day. Now it looks like they've put a statue of Eduardo Frei there. I always remember when I pass by, and everything comes, fills my mind. [. . .] I cannot remove all these things, everything I went through, [. . .] the nervous tension that we had [while on guard duty]."[19] For Jorge P.* (1983–85, Temuco), everyday situations and experiences made him remember. In 2012 he spoke of his nightmares, feelings of inferiority, and low self-esteem, as well as resentments and prejudices that he believes were formed in the barracks. He also spoke of how seeing a former instructor on the streets of Temuco evoked thoughts of service. The instructor had been one of the good ones, he noted, but seeing him nonetheless brought a flood of memories of the bad ones. Memories came, too, when he met people with the same surname as his instructors, or when he encountered certain smells.[20]

Omar A.* (1973, Iquique) tried to combat his memories. In 2011 he wrote of the accidental death of a compañero that continued to haunt him. A shot was fired by mistake and his friend fell, his head "destroyed," to Omar's feet, staining his clothes with blood. Later, the group was told that "there were losses in all wars and that it would soon be forgotten." They sought "different forms of forgetting," wrote Omar. He took to drink as his escape, while another compañero and friend of the dead soldier "lost himself in drugs."[21] Further south in Temuco, J.C.C.B. also turned to alcohol. "I still have a very traumatic memory," he wrote decades after his service, "that marked my life forever and that I have still not been able to forget due to the psychological traces and scars that remain. Despite the time that has transpired, I still wake up in the night frightened, and I cannot sleep deeply like a normal person." Weeks after the coup, he had been ordered to lash a fellow conscript. Having not carried out the order, he was stripped, tied to a post in the middle of the regiment's court-yard, and whipped across his back. This incident followed him after his discharge. He began to drink, he explained, "to drown the ghosts of a painful past that won't leave me alone."[22]

In 2012 Mario Navarro (1973–75) compiled impromptu statistics for his hometown of Arica. Fifty locals entered the Rancagua Regiment in February 1973, he remembered, and they were joined by seventy conscripts from the south on the day before the coup. "Of the fifty who entered first," he explained, "by 2012 twelve to fourteen former compañeros had died, and of these at least five died from drugs or alcohol." Mario had almost joined them. He had begun drinking during his service, returning drunk from leave (*franco*). When he left the barracks his legs trembled uncontrollably, and he could not sleep, he re-called, citing the punishments on the inside and the mistrust on the outside. He began to smoke marijuana, and for a short time he used cocaine. The con-sequences of service often revealed themselves slowly in former recruits in the years after leaving the barracks, he explained, and they stayed with them. He spoke of alcoholic ex-conscripts on the streets of Arica, and he detailed cases of former recruits, including several friends, who had taken their own lives years after leaving the barracks.[23]

Like Mario, Patricio V.* (1973–76) served in Arica and began drinking during his service while on franco. Prior to being called up, he had been com-pleting his fourth year of middle school in La Serena, in Chile's fourth region. He entered the barracks keen to take advantage of the opportunity the army represented in order to help his seven siblings and his mother who worked as a domestic servant. However, he grew disillusioned by the political repression, his participation in raids, witnessing the abuse of prisoners, and the death of a fellow conscript. He began to hate everything and everyone, he wrote: "I felt that the world was my enemy and I turned negative, I felt impotent and I took refuge in alcohol." After his discharge, he was taciturn and solitary, and he continued to drink. He also went "far away" and did not return until 1986.[24] For some former recruits, isolation was a way to avoid the people, places, and situations that triggered thoughts of their service. They became withdrawn from their families and from society, or they left their hometowns, the region, or even Chile, in an effort not to remember. Many, however, carried their reminders with them. Ex-conscripts describe their injuries and illnesses as permanent *recuerdos* (memories or reminders) of their service that undermine forgetting.[25] Back pain, joint pain, blindness, hearing loss from blows to the ears, missing teeth, scars, and missing body parts or lingering disabilities from acts of self-mutilation, or attempted suicide, for example, provided a constant link to the memory of the recruits' service. J.D.S.M.N. (Concepción, 1977–79), for example, described the long-term effects of the blows he received. The injury and ongoing treatment meant it had "proven impossible to forget."[26]

The discourse of bodily memory emerged in the written testimonies and verbal recollections as part of the ex-conscript movement in the first decade of the twenty-first century, but it is generally retrospective, referring to years of silence and private torment that can also extend through to the present. It describes a self-contained struggle, or the hidden half of a "double life," where the desire of individuals to forget was confronted by their physical scars, emotional responses, fears and anxieties, nightmares and unbidden thoughts, and their feelings of guilt, shame, and powerlessness in the face of the abuse and mistreatment they witnessed, participated in, or suffered. Ex-recruits' efforts not to remember were often fortified by physical or emotional distance, violence, or alcohol and drugs to "kill" the memories.[27] The contest of bodily memory between remembering and forgetting, as described by ex-conscripts, regularly resembles the symptomology of posttraumatic stress disorder (PTSD)—adaptive emotional responses and conditioned behaviors, hypervigilance, fear-conditioning, anxiety, intrusive thoughts, nightmares, and psychophysiological reactivity to external stimuli or emotional reminders[28]—and many former recruits have been diagnosed with PTSD. Bodily memory, however, is most typically expressed in terms of marked or changed mentalities, of weights and wounds, of permanent damage and of indelible scars on former recruits' minds, souls, and hearts.[29] The language and diagnoses of posttraumatic stress instead played an important role in the parallel embodiment of ex-conscript memory that located a collective will to remember and shared narratives of victimhood in the bodies of former recruits.

Embodied Memory

A video produced by REPACH Talcahuano includes group president David Wiederhold (1977–79) describing his experiences in the barracks and noting that "a number of these effects [*secuelas*] are still felt in my body." He finishes by lifting his shirt and pant leg to reveal his scars. He is followed by a former recruit (1973–75) who nervously speaks of his attempt as a conscript to take his own life in order to escape the punishments of training. This man then takes off his shirt to reveal thick scars that cut across his stomach and curl around his torso and upper arm. Another group member (1978) removes his dentures to show his missing teeth, as well as scars on his hip, arm, and knee, before describing the scar hidden underneath his beard that resulted from the same blow that cost him his teeth. "I entered healthy and left . . . ," he says, trailing off. From off-camera, David finishes the sentence: "in the condition that you've had to endure until today."[30] This shared framework of physical rupture emerged with the ex-conscript mobilization as former recruits organized their shared will to remember around their scars, illnesses, and disorders. The processes of exchanging and documenting their stories and crafting group demands often coincided with group members' failing health and its economic implications, allowing former recruits to memorialize their narrative of victimhood in their bodies.

From the turn of the century, the number of memory sites in Chile has increased dramatically. Early efforts to memorialize victims of the regime reflected the rolling impasse of the 1990s, with the country's memory struggles reproduced in contests for control of emblematic sites and the problematic gestation of high-profile commemorative projects. With the transition to democracy, the Aylwin administration had initiated the construction of the Memorial to the Disappeared in Santiago's General Cemetery, and in 1992 the initiative and persistence of human rights activists secured government support for the expropriation of the Villa Grimaldi detention, torture, and disappearance center, and its conversion into a peace park. However, by the time the wall in the General Cemetery bearing the names of the disappeared or murdered was inaugurated in 1994, the government had backed away from the expressive politics of memory and set the tone for successive concertación governments. Aylwin's successor, Eduardo Frei Ruiz-Tagle, was pointedly absent, for example, at the 1997 opening of the peace park on the Villa Grimaldi site. The following year proved a watershed moment in Chilean memory, and from 1998 an increasing number of grassroots initiatives produced an explosion of commemorative sites. In 2003—in the context of the thirtieth anniversary of the coup—government policy shifted to meet the private demand for commemoration, and over the next decade the state's Human Rights Program partnered with community groups to build thirty-nine memorials.[31] Nevertheless, these projects were significantly outnumbered by hundreds of wholly private sites throughout the country.[32] Memorials along the length of Chile were inaugurated by communities of people that invested their shared will to remember in locations, objects, and physical spaces. They grounded their memory narratives and maintained the connection between place and remembrance via group or personal commemorative rituals.[33] The ex-conscript movement emerged alongside this "new memorialization" of the first decade of the twenty-first century. While interest groups claimed and reclaimed sites of torture, built memorials, constructed parks, and erected plaques to create a new "geography of remembrance," former conscripts were quietly undertaking the memory work that turned their own bodies into sites of memory.[34]

The conscript will to remember came with a significant and internalized burden of proof, and in order to counter the skepticism, former recruits often pointed to their bodies. In April 2012, for example, former air force recruit Germán F.* (1983–85) walked into the office in Temuco for the first time. He was tall, with shoulders that would have been broad had they not hunched forward. He spoke—slowly, with lips quivering—of daily beatings. When he reached the end of his story, he took a step forward and leaned in, asking those in the office to feel the "egg" on his head as confirmation.[35] Within advocacy groups, this individual tendency was formalized and reinforced by the testimony process. The almost five thousand individual files that lined the walls of the office where Germán told his story contained written accounts of military service, prefaced with a cover sheet that provided the date and location of the former recruit's service and the names of three corroborating witnesses, as well as details on the individual's current employment situation, and the current state of his health. On the back, the sheet included categories to check if applicable, including physical, psychological, and economic secuelas. The typed and notarized testimonies regularly alluded to individuals' psychological and medical reports that were also included in the file and catalog scars, symptoms, and treatments, and, often, diagnose PTSD. Remembering service within the movement recast unwelcome physical reminders and psychological damage as important pieces of evidence.[36]

The same pattern emerged throughout Chile, as groups sought out medical professionals to treat their members but also buttress their claims. The document produced by the Ex-conscript Commission, for example, included three reports by different psychologists that had been solicited by the Agrupación de Reservistas Alas Azules in Puerto Montt in 2010, the Agrupación de Reservistas in Osorno in 2012, and the group Reservistas de las Fuerzas Armadas de Puerto Octay (Armed Forces' Reservists of Puerto Octay) in 2012. The reports summarized psychologists' work with local cohorts in the years prior, and the findings largely coincided with the ex-conscript narrative, restating it in clinical terms. They described former recruits as exhibiting symptoms such as poor control of impulses and their emotions, repressed aggression, a low tolerance for frustration and stress, low levels of empathy, poor interpersonal skills and little interest in establishing new relationships, substance abuse, low ambition, memory loss, and difficulty maintaining attention. They traced members' depression, sleep disorders, anxiety disorders, PTSD, alcoholism, and domestic violence back to their service. The commission's report also included a 2009 medical report compiled for the Osorno group that cataloged the enduring physical signs of abuse suffered during service. The most common were chronic pain, particularly chronic back pain, scars from injuries, and hearing loss. Similarly, a 2010 report produced by a social worker in Osorno included an appendix of photos of former recruits revealing their scarred limbs, torsos, faces, and heads and short descriptions of the events that produced them. In the section that introduces the medical and psychological reports, the Ex-conscript Commission is clear about what it considers to be their probative value: "This Commission wishes to establish that the application of torture existed [inside the barracks], and the proof of that are the physical scars and the behavioral and mental disorders of the [conscript] victims." The truth of conscript victimhood was to be found on and deep inside former recruits' bodies, and the Ex-conscript Commission sought it using doctors, psychologists and even "x-rays, electroencephalograms, blood tests [and] magnetic resonance imaging." This type of medicalization of memory and truth that emerged with conscript groups was absent from the reconciliation process that provided the model for the Ex-conscript Commission.[37]

The Rettig Report described as outside its remit the accidental deaths of soldiers, deaths from illnesses attributed by relatives to torture where the commission could not establish torture as the cause, and suicides attributed to political harassment where a direct and immediate connection between harassment and suicide could not be established.[38] The Valech Commission acknowledged the damage of political imprisonment and torture: physical scars, as well as the psychological and emotional effects and the related social and economic repercussions. It rejected, however, the type of uncomplicated "epidemiological nexus" the doctors in Osorno found between military instruction and the diseases and disorders they observed decades later.[39] Specific acts of torture could not, the Valech report read, be reasonably verified by medical examinations carried out years or decades after the incident in question. Causality could not be established for scars and disorders, and many abuses did not leave lasting marks on the body. In addition, the Valech Commission also acknowledged the potential psychological damage that requiring victims of torture to relive their experiences could cause. As a result, and in contrast to the ex-conscript process of collecting testimony, Valech interviewers used checklists that did not highlight the long-term effects of imprisonment and torture. Instead, victim status for the purposes of the Valech Report was established by proving politically motivated imprisonment—itself a human rights violation—and not by proving specific acts of torture via their lingering side effects.[40] From around 2006, however, courts hearing cases relating to dictatorship-era torture began requesting expert medical opinions in an effort to substantiate survivors' claims. Files compiled during the Valech process had been sealed, and any information it had gathered could not be used. The Forensic Medical Service (the Servicio Médico Legal, or SML) instead provided expert testimony after carrying out medical and psychological evaluations, but many survivors felt insulted by having to again "verify" their suffering.[41] Such requests to provide medical proof of abuse were not only of questionable probative value, they often clashed with torture victims' established and already socially legitimized victim status. Unlike in the ex-conscript case, medical "proof" was not integral to the formation or the maintenance of former political prisoners' victimhood.

In a parallel context to the truth and reconciliation process, psychologists from CODEPU diagnosed conscripts and deserters who served in the immediate posttransition years. CODEPU was among the groups that responded to the crisis of human rights abuses in the 1980s; it treated former political prisoners and helped develop the professional practices that would eventually provide the framework for the Rettig and Valech commissions.[42] In the context of its work with recruits and deserters who served in the early 1990s, the organization reported recurring symptoms, such as depression, anxiety, reactive anxiety-depressive state, reactive anxiety, reactive psychosis, panic attacks, and panic attacks with suicidal tendencies.[43] Given their experience with posttransition recruits, Rosella Baronti and Sachiko Alfaro wrote that "in the case of situations of torture or cruel treatment, we can confirm that the aggression was always simultaneously directed towards the physical and the psychological. The blows, forced positions and all the physical damage were accompanied by insults, threats, humiliation. [. . .] These techniques sought to trigger in the young men feelings and perceptions of uselessness, the annulment of the sense of individuality and destructuration. So, the pain, the fear and the confusion took them over, causing a break in their sense of self." They concluded that "the manifestations and psychopathologic symptoms observed [among posttransition conscripts received by CODEPU] do not differ from those described in the cases of torture of political prisoners."[44] While they briefly acknowledged— without substantiating the claim—that such treatments had been used against conscripts during the dictatorship, the alleged abuse of posttransition recruits and CODEPU's engagement on their behalf was framed in terms of the contemporaneous debate about the right to conscientious objection and not as a legacy of the military regime or as a part of national reconciliation. The nexus of body, memory, and medicine was central, nevertheless, to the way conscripts who served under Pinochet remembered their service and confirmed their own sense of victimhood within the ex-conscript movement.

In his 2009 testimony, Rubén A.* (1982–84, Lautaro) was confident about the scientific link between his service as a young man and his failing health decades later. He describes being subjected to "all types of abuses and mistreatments," which had "physical and psychological consequences that stopped [him] from living a normal life." He names the two corporals and two lieutenants who, he writes, took advantage of the conflict between Argentina and Chile to abuse their power. They gagged and beat Rubén to "teach" him "the type of torture that the [Argentine] enemy had to receive if he crossed the border." He also suspects that he was sodomized while unconscious. Years later, he wrote of suffering from joint pain and "uncomfortable, painful, and irreversible" hemorrhoids, which inhibit his ability to work and which he traces back to the "mistreatments and tortures" at temperatures below zero. "Even though I don't have medical records to prove my story," continues Rubén, "I know that science today is advanced and can determine when the injuries were incurred and I am prepared to submit to the medical procedures that the authorities stipulate."[45] Whether or not Rubén's faith in medical science was justified does not diminish the strength of his personal connection between military service and his current health complaints. Many former recruits made similar connections via a personal, often very specific logic that located their past military service in their present ailments. They traced tumors and cysts back to individual blows, attributed headaches and cancers to punishment, and explained epilepsy as the result of a specific beating. One former recruit cited going gray before his brother as evidence of the premature aging brought on by his service.[46] In this context, an important mechanism that established the link for many was the lore of piedra alumbre.

Although they were left out of civil suits, the criminal case, as well as much of the documentation produced by the ex-conscript lobby, anecdotes about piedra alumbre did inform the way conscripts within the groups talked about themselves and their experiences. Stories circulated and were mutually confirmed in a school hall in Nacimiento in the moments before a 2012 regional meeting; the hundred or so ex-conscripts gathered on the concrete stands of the municipal stadium in San Bernardo in 2011 were reminded about their consumption of the substance, its anaphrodisiac qualities and its long-term side effects; and group leaders routinely used it as an example when talking about the movement, their members, and their demands.[47] They described it as radioactive and carcinogenic, and associated it with persistent sexual dysfunction, infertility, premature aging, premature deaths, various cancers, diabetes, heart conditions, high blood pressure, kidney disease, eyesight problems, blackouts, and birth defects in their children.[48] For individuals, too, it formed an important link between their past and present suffering. Born in a small town on the desert plains on northern Chile and drafted to Iquique in 1974, Martín S.* (1974–75) testified in 2012, briefly and at times vaguely, about what he had been through: "During my time serving my patria as a conscript, I was subjected to various acts by my superiors that were not in accordance with my way of thinking, because after all, we are human beings." He was transferred to Fort Baquedano in 1975, and relates that "during this period I received mistreatments while in the army. I was beaten, went hungry, was humiliated, and suffered psychic and psychological mistreatments. [. . .] Furthermore, the food was bad and had piedra lumbre in it, which until today has affected me." His concrete, lived link to his service was his short-sightedness, which he understood as "the consequence that stayed with me from the piedra alumbre that they gave me in the food."[49]

The embodiment of ex-conscript memory must also be understood in the context of the emergence of the movement. An important catalyst for the formation of groups in the first decade of the twenty-first century was the convergence of the recruits' aging bodies and failing health with continued unstable employment and economic frustration. It was at this time that many of the effects attributed to service began to "blossom."[50] In his 2012 memoir that grew out of the meetings of a small group of men in San Bernardo who had served in the late 1970s, Miguel Saavedra wrote that "as decades passed, some started to show signs of psychological damage, a product of their experience, such as: permanent somnolence, alcoholism, extreme aggression, and the most serious, those who do not remember anything, not even their loved ones."[51] Similarly, Carlos Palma spoke of illnesses that emerged decades after service, and in some cases claimed the lives of ex-conscripts, as the result of mistreatment, but also the compound effect of decades of fear and anxiety.[52] Old injuries worsened, and aches, pains, disease, and the effects of aging and lifestyle increasingly impinged on daily life. For the majority of recruits, their deteriorating health was also deeply entangled with their employment situation. They often worked informally, in labor-intensive jobs, or both. Their failing bodies reduced their capacity to earn, and it exacerbated their existing sense of economic insecurity, the difficulty some faced in meeting their familial responsibilities, and the associated strain on marriages.[53] At the same time, the groups' formulation of their demand to access health benefits via PRAIS for ex-conscripts and their families further entrenched the centrality of the current state of recruits' health to their shared narrative of the past. There was a reciprocal relationship between individual former recruits' bodies and shared ex-conscript memory, as failing health provided a trigger for a group narrative, which was in turn projected back onto ex-conscripts' bodies.

The intersection of work, family, failing health, and group demands for health benefits with the emergence of the ex-conscript movement meant that former recruits' ailments could not be disentangled from a broader shared narrative of damage. Just as physical, psychological, and economic secuelas were listed together on the Temuco cover sheet, they were also often insepa-rable in ex-recruits' articulation of their victimhood. Health complaints became an expression of ex-conscripts' sense of economic victimization, their ruined proyectos de vida, their failure to meet their responsibilities, and their sense of entitlement to reparations. As a result, former recruits were also able to follow the pattern of framing their recollections with a catalog of diseases, scars, or disorders, without making an explicit connection to their service. After a meeting in May 2013, for example, Ariel C.* (1973) outlined his disdain for communists and his assessment of the mess the country was in before the coup. He then jumped forward to the Pinocheques scandal of the early 1990s, his missing pensions, and assurances that the concertación, too, was corrupt. He concluded his account with details of his high blood pressure and diabetes.[54] Lucero D.* (1973–74, Baquedano) was also part of the "class of '54" and simi-larly ended his 2011 testimony with a list of complaints. He had witnessed the "abuse" of civilians while on patrol and their "mistreatment" during the curfew. He wrote of his hunger, the cold, and three weeks guarding political prisoners in Pisagua, where he witnessed the "humiliating punishment" of prisoners and participated—on the orders of his superiors, he clarifies—in the beating of civilians. He finished his testimony describing his joint pain and other health concerns: "I am 57 years old, and I feel very tired and I have a lot of physical complaints, such as high blood pressure, diabetes and high choles-terol, and I am very short-sighted."[55] Also in 2011, Joaquin G.* (1973–74, Iquique) described simulated warfare and the mistreatment of conscripts in the barracks, threats made against recruits, and having to listen to the "infer-nal noise" as a guard in Pisagua. "These days," he writes, "I find myself having had an eye operation (I was almost blind), I also have prostate problems, and I was operated on for my peritonitis, which almost killed me. I went eighteen months without my intestines and with a colostomy bag."[56] Like Joaquin's, many testimonies and recollections were weighted toward recruits' ailments and scars, whether an explicit link to conscription was offered or not.[57]

The mutually reinforcing desire for proof, the medicalization of truth, personal links between service and health issues, the intimate relationship between failing health and the emergence of ex-conscript memory, the overlap

of economic, physical, and psychological victimization, and the collective demands for health care produced an inclusive and shared framework of rupture.
Former recruits located a collective victimhood in, for example, their scars
from attempted suicides or physical abuses, missing teeth, emotional problems,
persistent anxiety, sleep disorders, cancers, joint and back pain, diabetes, and
high cholesterol. This link between meaning and their bodies was confirmed
for recruits in the commemorative ritual of telling and retelling their stories. A
banner that demanded access to PRAIS and was regularly unfurled at meetings
in Chile's southern regions toward the end of the first decade of the twenty-
first century read: "WE COMPLIED WITH THE COMPULSORY MILITARY SERVICE
LAW. WE ENTERED HEALTHY AND LEFT PHYSICALLY AND PSYCHOLOGICALLY
DAMAGED."[58] This same refrain resounded throughout the lobby's written
documents and videos, as well as groups' civil suits and the criminal case.[59] It
explicitly shaped testimony collected by groups, with individuals employing
variations on the phrase "I entered healthy and left damaged,"[60] and it both
captured and encouraged a dynamic that played out in less formal gatherings
and in private conversations. For example, former conscripts in the ninth region
regularly visited the Temuco office, dropping in to pay their monthly dues,
check the progress of the group's lobbying, or simply chat. While there, they
exchanged experiences with each other and the small staff who run the office,
and they often told or retold their stories with tactile reference to their own
bodies—pointing out marks, scars, and old injuries—or citing their emotional
or psychological issues.

The sharing of memories and the collective organization of the ex-conscript
narrative around scars, disorders, and ailments also allowed former recruits to
make connections between their stories. They drew on the examples of others'
complaints and injuries—usually those who had fared worse—to corroborate
their own recollections and contextualize their feelings of vulnerability. Individual ex-conscripts began, too, to speak in a collective voice of the damage
that had been done to "us." In this context, the ultimate expression of the ex-
conscript narrative of damage and conscript fears of harm or death and sense
of physical vulnerability were deaths or suicides inside the barracks. The video
prepared by REPACH Talcahuano includes footage of the sister of a former
recruit. The woman and her family were told that her brother (1988, Coyhaique)
had committed suicide, but they were not allowed to see the body. They refuse
to believe that the recruit took his own life and cannot reconcile his apparent
suicide with the tone of his letters and phone calls. "It cannot be," explained
the recruit's sister, "that a healthy person can go and die in the army."[61] This
sentiment was echoed in a 2011 text produced by the ex-conscript lobby, and
includes cases of conscripts who had died during their service. The document

calls for a one-off payment of 10 million pesos and a 350,000 peso lifelong pension for the families of conscripts killed during service. The state had failed, they argued, to live up to its responsibility to return sons to their families "safe and sound," just as they had been when they entered.[62]

The sense of physical danger that many ex-conscripts recall through their bodies, their scars, and the deaths of their compañeros is reflected in the mortality rates for recruits completing their military service. The army's presentation to the Rettig Commission listed thirty-four dead conscripts,[63] and the Rettig Report included seventeen conscripts among the dead or disappeared.[64] However, more recent sets of army figures cite around 650 conscript deaths between 1973 and 1990 (see table 2, sources). For the period 1964–99, general mortality for young Chilean males fell steadily, but for a reversal in 1972 and a sharp peak in 1973. By 1974 it had returned to the long-term trend. The conscript mortality rate for the period 1973–90 also peaks in 1973 at a rate approaching the rate for twenty- to twenty-four-year-old males, and above the rates for fifteen- to twenty-four-year-old nonconscript males and fifteen- to nineteen-year-old males.[65] Like the general rates, conscript mortality falls sharply in the years following the coup; however, it shows a secondary spike in the late 1970s, when it peaks above general rates for Chilean boys and young men. By the late 1980s, the death rate among recruits trends well below general rates, a pattern more in line with the medical screening of prospective recruits, and access to food, shelter, and medical services inside the barracks.[66] Comparisons between the rates are not perfect, given discrepancies in army figures (see table 1) and potential overlap between the general and army populations (see figure 1, sources). Nevertheless, the different rates do suggest that, at times during the military regime, it was more dangerous to be a conscript in the army than a boy or young man not recruited into the army. The fluctuations also suggest that the risk of death for recruits completing their military service under Pinochet rose and fell to the rhythm of Chile's wars inside the barracks, with mortality peaking with the coup and again when the perceived aggregate threats within the armed forces were at their highest.[67]

The embodiment of ex-conscript memory also established a parallel commemorative ritual. This more personal rhythm to embodied memory was not set by a calendar of events and anniversaries, nor by group meetings, conversations with other members, or by providing testimony, but by individual daily routines, seasonal aches and pains and bodily functions. While embodied memory meant former recruits remembered their service through their bodies in public moments and when communicating their stories, the shared and collectively built narrative also in turn informed the private experience of their ailing health. Daniel Gómez (1978–80, Punta Arenas) spoke in 2012 of his pain when he ate. It was the result, he explained, of exercises that involved him lying on the ground with his hands behind his head while instructors jumped on his chest. The exercises were to prepare them for what the Argentines would do to them. Also, when it was cold—which it often is Chile's ninth region—the side of his face hurts, he said, a result of blows he took to the head.[68] Gilberto A.* (1973–74) wrote of repeated blows to his left ear in the barracks and, decades later, being unable to carry out simple errands due to his hearing loss, while Pablo F.* (1982–84) left the barracks with a facial tic that he insisted in 2012 was the result of being forced to stand with a truck tire around his neck for almost a day.[69] Carlos Droguett (1973–74, San Bernardo) spoke of the beatings and blows he received as a "contemptuous Communist sympathizer": "They hit me in the stomach every day, I even had to spend a month in the infirmary as a result of the blows. Now I suffer the consequences, on repeated occasions I go to the toilet and I pass blood."[70] The intimate consequences of old reminders of service and emerging ailments subsequently attributed to service, such as those experienced by Daniel, Gilberto, Pablo, and Carlos, were experienced within a communal narrative. They activated a meaning that was networked, shared, and collectively constructed. As a result, these quiet routines could also be commemorative, as they nurtured the link between shared ex-conscript memory and individuals' bodies.[71]

The will to remember did not neatly replace the desire to forget. A tension between the two runs through many former conscripts' recollections, and it came to a head dramatically the day Guillermo L.* arrived at the office of the Agrupación de Reservistas in Temuco. Accompanied by his mother, he had come to give his testimony about his service, but at a certain point he panicked and fled the office. He was missing for a number of days before being found in the local hospital. Back at the office, Guillermo's identification card that he had left behind was pinned to the notice board waiting to be collected.[72] Similarly, commemorative embodied memory did not supplant the lonely contest of bodily memory. They coexisted, moving to different schedules. They intersected, however, in the sudden pauses and tears, and the moments when former conscripts were momentarily overwhelmed while telling their stories. Even a well-practiced narrative could activate unwanted or troubling memories.[73]

In 2012 Rodolfo R.* (1976, Punta Arenas) spoke of the cold, the isolation of the barracks, the suicides in his unit, and the accidental death of a compañero. He had witnessed his fellow conscript killed during a training exercise that used live ammunition. The enunciation of the "pah" of the shot stopped Rodolfo midsentence. He went quiet, lost eye contact with the others in the room, and tears began to fill his eyes. After a pause, he physically shook off the unbidden recollections and explained: "It's difficult to forget these things. [. . .] It's painful. I still remember, and it's a shame. That is, it moves me, knowing things. I don't know, I'm a little weak of heart, you see." Rodolfo was telling his story in a small office in the presence of two other former recruits, and after a glass of water and a moment to gather himself, his description of his service fell into the collective ritual of embodied memory. The three former recruits discussed housing difficulties and work troubles that had meant Rodolfo went to live in Argentina. A resolution to the movement's demands would perhaps allow him to return permanently to Chile, he said. They also began to compare the lingering effects of service, which tied into employment difficulties. Rodolfo explained that he could not walk quickly due to an old injury sustained when a conscript. The pain in his bones affected his back and leg, particularly when it was cold. The others agreed. They, too, suffered when the temperature dropped, and aches and pains that provided a link to their service worsened. "Well, this is what I have," Rodolfo said. "I've carried it with me ever since."[74]

Rodolfo's recollections are indicative of the ways ex-recruits remember their service "in the flesh." The contest of bodily memory overcame him, and the discourse of memory as an inability to forget what he carried within him framed the way he talked about remembering. He also grounded his broader sense of victimhood in his aging and aching body. He participated in the communal ex-conscript ritual that recast "reminders," unbidden thoughts, nightmares, the "blossoming" physical and psychological effects of service, the assumed physical and psychological effects of service, and the mounting health issues resulting from age, lifestyle, and poverty, as proof or expressions of physical and socioeconomic victimhood. This commemorative practice converted bodies divided against themselves by the contest of bodily memory into, also, sites of embodied, shared memory.

Conclusion

The Apolitics of Memory and the Limits of Human Rights

The ground floor of Santiago's Museum of Memory and Human Rights places Chile's truth and reconciliation commissions in a global context. The display highlights the universality of human rights by locating the Rettig and Valech reports among more than thirty other truth commissions in societies transitioning from civil war or dictatorial regimes. The exhibition on military rule in Chile begins on the second floor, running chronologically from 6:00 a.m. on the morning of September 11, 1973, until Chile's return to democracy. The staircase between the floors concretizes the necessary and paradoxical tension between the universal claims of human rights and the specificity of the violations under Pinochet, but it also became emblematic of the contentious memory of military rule.[1] The two images that flank the ascent—one of wealthy women calling for military intervention and a second showing Víctor Jara marching alongside protesting workers—are the only acknowledgement of the tension under Popular Unity.[2] The debate about when and how to start the story told by the museum is an example writ small of a broader preoccupation of Chilean memory and historiography. Amid genuine concerns about the museum's lack of historical background, calls for "context" from the political right reflected a strategic emphasis on the violence of the pre-coup years that had emerged, in particular, around the time of Pinochet's arrest in London. In response to this narrative that anchored memory of the regime in the 1960s and early 1970s, a group of historians countered with a 1999 manifesto. The Historians' Manifesto argued that a focus on the decade preceding the coup not only implicitly shifted the blame for subsequent human rights abuses to the dictatorship's victims; it also missed the larger picture. The document's signatories insisted that the appropriate context for understanding the political conflict of the early 1970s were long-term tensions between oligarchic rule and political and social movements that stretched back to the beginning of the century.[3] The museum and its controversies are emblematic of the particularly Chilean articulation of human rights and its intrinsic relationship with the memory and history of military rule. Ex-conscript memory lays bare the limitations of this composite and shifting paradigm. It reveals the potential silencing effect of the human rights framework and the inadequacy of the memory contest to make sense of the memory of military service.

From the early years of military rule, the universal claims of human rights were vital to uniting opposition to the regime and its political repression. Local human rights activism underpinned, and continues to underpin, efforts to establish truth and achieve justice. It established a moral responsibility to remember, anchoring one pole of Chile's memory struggle, and since the transition, in particular, the human rights framework has definitively shaped the Chilean "politics of memory." In Chile, as in postdictatorship societies throughout Latin America, the memory of military rule and political violence has been framed as a rolling contest between competing interpretations.[4] This "politics of memory" framework captures the most defining dynamic of Chilean memory, describing its central and fluid tension between opposing and mutually exclusive narratives of the past.[5] However, while the truth, institutions, and language of this contest in part provided the catalyst for the ex-conscript movement, they also excluded the memory narratives that bound that movement. The history of the memory of military service under Pinochet requires not only the type of long-term perspective advocated by the historians of the manifesto but one that also looks beyond the historiography of political conflict and the binary memory contest.

The ex-conscript movement emerged amid a convergence of social, cultural, economic, and corporeal factors: lifetimes of unemployment or poorly paid work, physically demanding work, mounting health complaints, high-profile corruption scandals, broader disenchantment with democracy and the "Chilean economic miracle," but also Chile's truth and reconciliation process. In the first decade of the twenty-first century, the state's reparations programs and the Valech Report provided former recruits with emblematic cases as well as the unifying languages of rights and torture, through which many ex-conscripts began to understand their experiences of service as part of a larger and shared narrative of victimhood. Reparations programs for victims, and the form that benefits took, resonated with ex-conscripts, linking recollections of their conscription with their daily lives decades later, as well as their hopes and concerns for the future. The reconciliation process also provided ex-conscript groups with a model for their evolving demands and legal strategies. Some groups held on to the idea of human rights as a universal framework that took precedence over national courts, planning to eventually have recourse to the Inter-American Court of Human Rights or evoking human rights to locate their claims outside local statutes of limitations. Legal and lobby arguments employed within the movement often drifted away from human rights, while the rights paradigm continued to help many members identify with a dictatorship-era sense of victimhood. Ex-conscript memory had an ambivalent relationship with human rights, which gave shape and voice to the nascent movement of former recruits but also imposed limits on ex-conscript narratives and reinforced their silences.

Ex-conscript silence was built most immediately on a desire not to remember and on fear. While these attempts to forget were often unsuccessful, they nonetheless ensured that ex-conscript stories remained private. Former recruits were also afraid of retribution from the armed forces if they talked, recalling specific threats or having internalized the surveillance of the intelligence service and the omnipresence of the armed forces. Many, too, were anxious about the potential reactions of their families, colleagues, and neighbors, and, more broadly, society's potential reception of their recollections. They felt preemptively condemned for having worn a uniform, and their sense of generalized rejection solidified during the state-led truth and reconciliation processes and in the context of the advancing of transitional justice. Their sense of victimhood was confronted with a memory contest shaped by a stark concept of responsibility that equated wearing the uniform as a conscript, and subsequently silence as an ex-conscript, with complicity with human rights abuses. The notion of silence as complicity rested in large part on the central and necessary moral imperative to remember the disappeared, the murdered, and the tortured. This morality also established the provision of information relevant to the broader memory question as a prerequisite to ex-conscript participation. There was, as a result, a dampening effect on their memories of their service, which tended to be personal accounts of suffering or an individual sense of injustice that was not centered on the fate of political detainees, and did not feed easily or consistently into either side of the memory debate. The shared memory narratives that emerged with the ex-conscript movement were, in part, defined by this exclusion.

Despite the universal claims of human rights, and the effort of the Rettig and Valech reports to legitimize the suffering on both sides of the ideological divide notwithstanding, victim statuses in Chile were politicized categories. As a result, ex-conscript victimhood fell outside the dominant patterns of remembering. Individuals often silenced—either as strategy or by instinct—political aspects of their stories, and ex-conscript groups at times tailored narratives that sidelined the "politics of memory." Perhaps more important than exclusion and the related incentive to depoliticize their stories, however, was the lack of a political consensus among ex-conscripts. Former recruits' opinions of Pinochet, military rule, and its legacy differed greatly, and individuals found meaning in different elements of the broader societal struggle about how to remember the coup and the dictatorship. Remembering within the movement, therefore, lacked a basis on which to participate in the memory contest. The otherwise highly relational narratives of salvation from chaos, economic triumphalism, violent rupture, and awakening to human rights abuses, as well as a deep indifference, were all compatible with the former recruits' shared sense of victimhood. In this sense, ex-conscript memory sat alongside the memory contest, with no necessary or consistent link to it. It was not based in a common political identity or project—beyond the narrow cause of gaining recognition and reparations—and did not necessarily represent an individual window to a national story. Beyond the limitations of the human rights paradigm and the exclusion from the memory contest, the shared narratives that bound former recruits must therefore be understood within an "apolitics of memory": a recognition that ex-conscript memory moves outside, and to a different rhythm than, the "politics of memory," and that the ruptures that shape it are grounded in long-term continuities, shared identities, and economic realities that provided a stable, slowly moving baseline to twentieth-century history, isolated from the fluctuations of social movements and political struggles.[6]

Many ex-conscripts remember their service as ruptured patriotism, as their love of the patria clashed with the military's mission to forge it. Throughout the century, officers identified themselves as the best of the nation, its moral reserve, and its disciplinarians. Defending the patria meant securing the borders but also making citizens of the masses. In this context, military service would provide a reserve capable of being mobilized, as well as educate and instill values in civilians. This nation-building project evolved throughout the century, responding to economic crises, world wars, and postwar ideas of counterinsurgency. Its evolution, however, took it away from the patria suspended in cyclical commemorations, and which formed the basis of boys' desire to defend it. Prospective recruits' love of their country was often rooted in a fondness for parades, uniforms, toy soldiers, and tales of heroism from the previous century. This clash of patrias lay at the heart of many ex-conscripts' sense of betrayal and disillusionment, and their memories of the front lines of Chile's wars.

The battlefront of the "internal war" was made clear to recruits: anyone beyond the edge of the barracks was the enemy. Many recalled this front line by contrasting the military's exclusive and politicized patria with their own inclusive and apolitical understanding of the nation. They confronted the demand that they be prepared to kill family members with an insistence that all civilians were their Chilean brothers and sisters. The consolidation of this dynamic among former recruits was staggered and uneven. For some, it resulted from an instant recognition that the prisoner or civilian in front of them was not their enemy. For others, it was a slower process, which was influenced in large part by the revelations and shifts in the broader "memory struggle." During service, however, the front line did not remain fixed at the regimental walls. It also cut through the barracks. The twentieth-century military project to define and defend the patria had, from the beginning, equated poverty with radical politics. This link was later reinforced by Cold War thinking on economic development and counterinsurgency. With the stakes rising in the wake of the Cuban Revolution, and amid increasing social conflict, conscription remained an important means by which to instill patriotic values, contribute to economic development, and combat communism. However, conscripts, typically drawn from the poorest parts of Chile, also increasingly represented a threat to the nation. While this dynamic was shaping military service in the late 1960s and early 1970s, the swift and massive radicalization of Latin America's urban and rural poor feared by the region's militaries did not materialize. The processes of politicization proved to be much more complex on the ground, and political activity often reflected immediate and concrete economic concerns instead of revolutionary ideals. Despite this complexity, ex-conscript testimony reveals a conflation inside the barracks of recruits with "terrorists" and "communists," as well as politically motivated, or ostensibly politically motivated, persecution and abuse that maintained a constant level of fear. A related front line also cut through the trenches on the border with Argentina.

Ex-conscript memories of the "almost-wars" are shaped by both patriotic pride and disillusionment. Many who served on the border took great satisfaction in their role in seeing off a foreign threat, but they also felt abandoned by their own army and their nation. Moreover, the stress of the long wait for war, the cold and hunger of their time spent dug into the hills, and the brutal punishments of training fortified a second front line between the recruits and their superiors. A similar division pitted recruits building the carretera austral against those giving the orders. The construction project was part of the same defense strategy as the troop buildup on the border, and it also belonged to a long geopolitical nation-building effort to integrate the far south. Here, too, the cold, hunger, forced labor, punishments, and danger convinced many recruits that their own officers were in fact the enemy. Recollections of time on the carretera contrast recruits' own boyhood aspirations of heroically defending the patria and the regime's celebration of the benefits of the "glorious" project with the memory of the long and dangerous days spent working in extreme conditions.

Many ex-conscripts also remember their service through a ruptured masculinity. They set their treatment in the barracks and their difficulties in the years since their discharge against the hopes and ambitions they had invested in the idea of conscription. From the beginning of the century and the inception of the draft, military service had emerged as a pathway to manhood for boys from those sectors of society where boyhood was shaped by poverty, subsistence, little and poor education, work, and familial responsibility. The education, training, discipline, employment opportunities, and career prospects offered by conscription often matched the aspirations and needs of prospective recruits and their families. This nexus of military service, work, and masculinity emerged from, and survived on, an experience of boyhood, a set of family dynamics, and an ideal of civilian masculinity that persisted throughout the century. Inside the barracks, however, conscripts were confronted with the military project to make them "hard men," which was based on brutal physical training and psychological degradation. The mistreatments described in ex-conscript testimonies reflect contemporaneous Western military thinking on resistance and the practices of repression and torture throughout the region. They are also, however, part of a longer local tradition of harsh military discipline and abuse that, while seeming to peak under military rule, both predated and survived the dictatorship.

The recruits' civilian masculinity was further undermined in the decades after leaving the barracks by the physical and mental effects attributed to their service. Ex-conscripts speak of persistent nightmares and unwanted thoughts, physical wounds and scars, infertility and domestic violence, as well as underemployment and unemployment that prevented them from living up to the roles of husband, father, and breadwinner. Moreover, many fear "infecting" their loved ones with their burden, passing on the damage from their conscription to the next generation. This "crisis of masculinity" among former recruits sits within a broader crisis throughout Chile, as the deep structural changes to the economy introduced by the junta definitively undermined the viability of the masculine and familial ideals that had been forged during the industrialization and modernization of the early decades of the twentieth century, and which only began to be seriously challenged in the early decades of the twenty-first.

The ruptures of ex-conscript memory were lived in former recruits' bodies. The men's silence was often shaped by an understanding of memory as a lonely and often debilitating contest between the desire to forget and unbidden thoughts, feelings, emotions, and physical reminders. They felt haunted by "ghosts": changes in their personalities, recollections of atrocities committed against detainees or fellow conscripts, the constant fear on the streets and in the barracks, the shame or guilt of participating in the abuse of civilians or their fellow conscripts, or the powerlessness to respond to their own mistreatment or that of others. They described living for decades with nightmares and insomnia, and the exhaustion of being permanently on edge. Everyday objects, situations, or sensations, as well as their own scars or ailments, triggered responses, which many fought with alcohol, drugs, physical distance, or emotional isolation. Parallel to this private and ongoing effort to forget, a collective will to remember emerged with the ex-conscript movement. In this context, former recruits' illnesses, aches, scars, and unwanted thoughts and emotions were recast as evidence. The process of giving testimony both reflected and reinforced the tendency among group members to corroborate their experiences by referencing their damaged bodies. A deeply felt burden of proof and the advocacy strategies of ex-conscript groups produced a medicalization of truth and evidence. At times, the links between illness and service were implausible or impossible, with some individuals establishing connections between their present and past using a very personal logic. Often, however, direct causality was not claimed, or even necessary. In the context of economic precariousness, physically demanding work, and failing bodies, health concerns became emblematic of a wider narrative of damage, victimization, and ruined prospects. This process of grounding a shared ex-conscript memory in members' own disorders, injuries, and sicknesses shadowed the construction in Chile of a "geography of remembrance." As sites of memory were claimed, reclaimed, or built throughout the country, ex-conscripts transformed their daily routines, seasonal aches, and regular meetings into commemorative rituals and their bodies into monuments to shared narratives of victimhood.

The history of the memory of military service under Pinochet spans the nineteenth through the twenty-first centuries. Ex-conscripts' shared memory narratives are rooted in long-term continuities, enduring identities, and generational cycles that are largely independent of the trajectory of political conflict and social struggle. These histories give shape to a way of remembering the Chilean dictatorship that sits alongside the "politics of memory" and beyond the limits of the human rights framework. They run through meetings, testimonies, conversations, and daily routines, and in Arica in 2012, they also wove through Mario's recollections of his time in the barracks and the decades since his discharge. Mario remembered his service through a sense of national pride built on nineteenth-century wars and twentieth-century parades, which was augmented by his experience of the "internal war" and the expectation of the "war that wasn't" with Peru. He recalled his conscription as an interruption of his youth and an unmet promise. His two years of service had betrayed his father's expectation it would make Mario a man, and the interruption lingered as he suffered nightmares and took refuge in drugs. The decades since his discharge were marked, too, by his mother's persistent—and unfounded, insisted Mario—suspicion that her son knew something about her other son's death. Decades later, this open wound was underscored when the case of his brother's 1974 murder was reopened, and the new investigation paralleled Mario's search for a sense of justice for himself and his fellow ex-conscripts. Mario lived, in many ways, at the front line of two of Chile's wars and at the center of the nation's memory struggles, but it is the apolitical narratives of masculinity, national identity, family, work, and health that give meaning to his experiences. It is these histories and their ruptures that in 2012 connected Mario to the boy on his reservist identification.

Appendix

Table 1. Annual draft intake by branch of the armed forces
(1964–2000)

Year	Army	Navy	Air Force	Armed Forces[c]
1964	—	352	499	—
1965	8,186	405	500	9,091
1966	8,916[a]	804	600	10,320
1967	7,561	867	678	9,106
1968	7,034	896	1,270	9,200
1969	11,730	892	1,384	14,006
1970	14,051	836	1,173	16,060
1971	16,421[a]	876	871	18,168
1972	17,373	960	1,190	19,523
1973	18,497[b]	1,990	1,472	21,959
1974	12,702	1,948	1,313	15,963
1975	12,702[b]	2,110	1,386	16,198
1976	16,796	2,222	1,294	20,312
1977	12,281	2,450	876	15,607
1978	12,059	2,176	219	14,454
1979	18,387	2,512	581	21,480
1980	16,780	1,766	321	18,867
1981	21,621	1,891	659	24,171
1982	19,856	2,512	853	23,221
1983	22,688	1,754	1,435	25,877
1984	17,267	1,290	1,343	19,900
1985	18,124	995	463	19,582

Continued on next page.

Table 1—*continued*.

Year	Army	Navy	Air Force	Armed Forces[c]
1986	21,160	2,049	1,013	24,222
1987	22,829	1,796	1,206	25,831
1988	31,340	2,517	1,366	35,223
1989	27,035	2,134	596	29,765
1973–1989	**322,124**	**34,112**	**16,396**	**372,632**
1990	22,151	1,432	885	24,468
1991	19,550	1,496	892	21,938
1992	12,985	1,509	990	15,484
1993	29,639	1,325	1,560	32,524
1994	26,637	1,096	1,109	28,842
1995	26,641	1,304	590	28,535
1996	25,046	1,300	1,242	27,588
1997	27,296	1,430	724	29,450
1998	25,277	1,375	763	27,415
1999	25,488	1,305	1,312	28,105
2000	26,992	1,012	1,124	29,128

Sources: The Estado Mayor (army) provided conscript figures for the army for the years 1965–2000 ("Response to Request AD006C-0000314," June 6, 2014). Navy figures for the periods 1964–72 and 1990–2000 were provided by the Estado Mayor (navy) ("Response to Request AD007C-0000346," June 19, 2014), while numbers for the years 1973–89 were provided by the Director General de Movilización Nacional (DGMN) ("Response to Request AD013W-0002354," December 5, 2013; and "Response to Request AD013W-0002368," December 30, 2013). Figures for the air force for the periods 1964–72 and 1990–2000 were provided by the Estado Mayor (air force) ("Response to Request AD008C-0000224," June 19, 2014), while information on the period 1973–89 was provided by the DGMN.

Notes:

[a] The listed figures for the army include two small, likely typographical discrepancies with figures it had previously provided for the years 1965–72 and 1990–2000 (Estado Mayor [army], "Response to Request AD006C-0000317," June 16, 2014): 8,919 (1966) and 16,241 (1971).

[b] The listed figures for the army include significant discrepancies with army figures for the period 1973–89 provided by the DGMN: 13,896 (1973) and 13,998 (1975).

[c] The totals listed are the aggregates of the listed figures for the individual branches. Totals in the DGMN figures differ given the discrepancies noted above. A 2013 report by the Ministry of the Interior and Public Safety cites different DGMN figures for the armed forces: 1973 (17,524); 1974 (16,138); 1975 (17,645); 1976 (20,431); 1977 (15,710); 1978 (14,571); 1979 (21,574); 1980 (18,934); 1981 (24,425); 1982 (23,649); 1983 (26,505); 1984 (20,544); 1985 (10,005); 1986 (24,867); 1987 (26,147); 1988 (36,207); 1989 (29,758); 1990 (25,427) (*Informe*).

Table 2. Conscript deaths during service by year and branch
of the armed forces (1965–2000)

Year	Army	Navy	Air Force	Armed Forces
1965	—	2	—	—
1966	—	—	—	—
1967	—	1	—	—
1968	—	—	—	—
1969	—	—	—	—
1970	—	—	2	—
1971	—	1	1	—
1972	—	3	4	—
1973	58	2	1	61
1974	46	3	3	52
1975	36	1	3	40
1976	36	0	9	45
1977	33	1	2	36
1978	55	1	2	58
1979	57	5	2	64
1980	32	7	0	39
1981	41	1	0	42
1982	37	2	0	39
1983	25	3	2	30
1984	25	5	2	32
1985	12	1	0	13
1986	21	2	1	24
1987	18	0	1	19
1988	16	1	0	17
1989	21	1	0	22
1990	28	1	0	29
1973–1990	**597**	**37**	**28**	**662**
1991	—	0	3	—
1992	—	2	0	—
1993	—	2	0	—
1994	—	0	1	—
1995	—	8	0	—
1996	—	0	0	—

Continued on next page.

Table 2—*continued.*

Year	Army	Navy	Air Force	Armed Forces
1997	—	3	0	—
1998	—	0	0	—
1999	—	4	0	—
2000	—	1	0	—

Sources: The Estado Mayor General (air force) provided details of cases of death including name of the recruit, year of death, cause of death, and age of the recruit from 1970 to 2000 ("Response to Request AD008C-0000220," June 11, 2014). The Estado Mayor General (navy) provided the listed figures for 1965–2000 ("Response to Request AD007C-0000371," September 5, 2014), which included some minor discrepancies with information it had earlier provided for the years 1984 to 2000 ("Response to Request AD007C-0000350," June 26, 2014). The Estado Mayor General (army) replied to request for information AD006C-0000314 (June 6, 2014) that it did not have such figures. Numbers for the army are instead taken from a 2008 report prepared by the Dirección del Personal of Estado Mayor (army) and produced in the context of the army's interaction with ex-conscript groups (the author was shown a copy of the report in the moments before a group meeting in Buin [field notes, November 10, 2013]). In response to request AD006C-0000332 (September 1, 2014) to confirm the above report, the Estado Mayor General (army) again noted that it did not have information. It did, however, provide information on disability benefits, which also appears unchanged in the 2008 report cited above. The formatting and headers of the report and the document provided by the Estado Mayor General (army) are also identical.

A 2013 report prepared for the Ministry of Defense and the Ministry of the Interior and Public Safety cites 649 conscript deaths in the army between 1973 and 1990 (402 in the "act of service"). This figure, however, was not broken down by year. The sources cited in the report were administrative summaries of internal investigations held in the general archive of the army (*Informe*).

The 2008 report (see above) indicated that 455 ex-conscripts had suffered a disability during conscription between 1973 and 1990. It broke the total down by year and provided the degree of the disability. First-degree disabilities (144) prevent recruits from continuing their service; second-class disabilities (304) leave them "physiologically" less able to earn a living in the private sector; and third-class disabilities (7) leave recruits permanently and irreversibly unable to care for themselves. The 2013 report (see above) lists 495 ex-conscripts (1973–90) who, according to information provided by the subsecretary for the armed forces, had had their disabilities accredited and were receiving benefits. For a disability to be accredited, claims had to be made within two years of the incident that produced the disability. Therefore, the total does not capture disabilities that emerged later or were not reported within the two-year period.

Figure 1. Mortality rates for young males (1964–99) and army conscripts (1973–90)

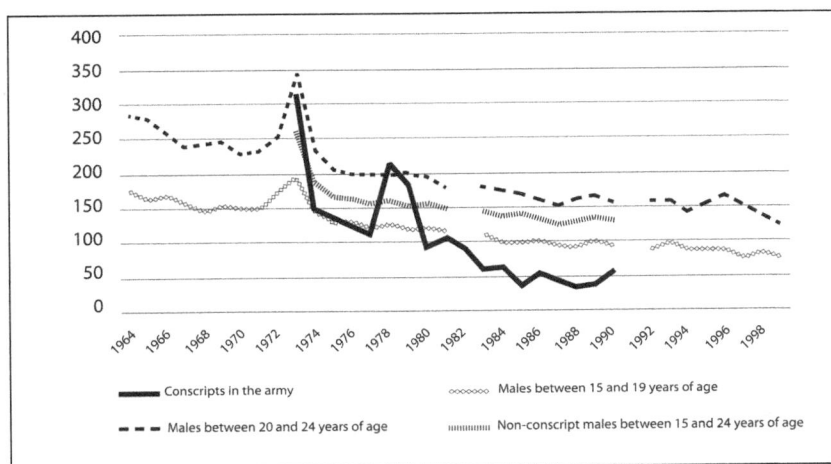

Legend:
- ▬▬ Conscripts in the army
- ∘∘∘∘∘∘ Males between 15 and 19 years of age
- – – – Males between 20 and 24 years of age
- ⅲⅲⅲⅲⅲ Non-conscript males between 15 and 24 years of age

Sources: Mortality rates (deaths per 100,000) for 15- to 19-year-old males, for 20- to 24-year-old males, and for 15- to 24-year-old nonconscript males were calculated using population estimates for each age group and the number of deaths of males published in annual demographic statistics compiled by the Dirección de Estadística y Censos (1964–67, 1971) and the Instituto Nacional de Estadísticas (1968–70, 1972–81, 1983–90, 1993–99). Population figures for 1992 were published in the 1992 census (Instituto Nacional de Estadísticas, *Chile: Ciudades, pueblos y aldeas, censo 1992* [Santiago: INE, 1995]), and figures on deaths of males by age group for 1992 were provided by the Chilean Institute of Statistics (Instituto Nacional de Estadísticas, "Response to Request AH007W-0010323," May 29, 2014). For the period 1973–90, these figures were supplemented with cases, as listed in the Rettig Report, of disappearance or murder of young males that were in some way concealed by the authorities (Comisión Nacional de Verdad y Reconciliación, *Informe*). In cases of disappearance, the victims are assumed to have died the year they were disappeared.

Army recruits who died were likely to have been 17, 18, 19, or 20 years of age at the time, but the specific ages are not known. For this reason, these deaths cannot be separated from the figures for the age brackets 15–19 and 20–24 years of age. Therefore, conscript mortality is compared to the mortality rate for 15- to 24-year-old nonconscript males.

Conscript mortality was calculated using information on annual cohorts in table 1 and numbers of army conscript deaths in table 2, which represent the most conservative of the figures discussed. To approximate the population of conscripts inside the barracks in a given year, the figures on the annual intakes were adjusted in line with information included in the report on ex-conscript demands prepared by the Ministry of the Interior and Public Safety in 2013 (*Informe*). The report outlined how the "class of '54" had their service extended from one to two years, and how from 1974 service was a standard "up to two years." In addition, some conscripts had their service extended beyond the mandated period. Given the lack of a searchable database at the army's General Archive, the report's authors sampled two hundred files and found that in 7.6 percent of the cases, conscripts served for a period longer than the mandated period, and that the average extension beyond the mandated period was 10.6 months. In 1974, therefore, the barracks population is taken to be that year's intake plus the 1973 cohort. From 1975, the annual population was taken to be the intake for the year in question plus the previous year's cohort plus 7.6 percent of the cohort from two year's prior.

Notes

Preface

1. Christian Democrat Eduardo Frei had been elected in 1964 on the back of support of local conservatives as well as US support (and CIA money), as the lesser of two evils. By 1970, the extent of Frei's reforms, most notably his agrarian reforms, had cost him the support of the political right. This loss of support contributed to Allende's narrow victory, despite a CIA-funded scare campaign. For an overview of Chile's presidential politics and elections from the 1940s to 1970, see Steve J. Stern, *Remembering Pinochet's Chile: On the Eve of London, 1998* (Durham, NC: Duke University Press, 2006), 8–19.

2. For detail on Allende's government (1970–73), the challenges it faced, and its successes and internal conflicts, see Peter Winn, *La revolución chilena* (Santiago: LOM, 2013).

3. For an overview of the deepening polarization in Chilean politics in the year prior to Allende's election, see Mark Ensalaco, *Chile under Pinochet: Recovering the Truth* (Philadelphia: University of Pennsylvania Press, 2000), 1–21.

4. The historiographical preoccupation with when to begin telling the story of the dictatorship—on September 11; amid the shortages, strikes, and unrest of the pre-coup decade; or at the turn of the twentieth century—is discussed in this book's conclusion.

5. On references to cancer and disease, see Pamela Constable and Arturo Valenzuela, *A Nation of Enemies: Chile under Pinochet* (New York: Norton, 1993), 47; and Carlos Huneeus, *El régimen de Pinochet* (Santiago: Editorial Sudamericana Chilena, 2002), 99. For details on the transnational aspects of the Cold War in Latin America, see John Dinges, *The Condor Years: How Pinochet and His Allies Brought Terrorism to Three Continents* (New York: New Press, 2004); Peter Kornbluh, *The Pinochet File: A Declassified Dossier on Atrocity and Accountability* (New York: New Press, 2004); J. Patrice McSherry, *Predatory States: Operation Condor and Covert War in Latin America* (Lanham, MD: Rowman & Littlefield, 2005); Hal Brands, *Latin America's Cold War* (Cambridge, MA: Harvard University Press, 2010); and Tanya Harmer,

Allende's Chile and the Inter-American Cold War (Chapel Hill: University of North Carolina Press, 2011).

6. For more detail, see Comisión Nacional sobre Prisión Política y Tortura, *Informe de la comisión nacional sobre prisión política y tortura* (Santiago: La Nación, 2004). For accounts of the initial phase of political repression (from the coup until the end of 1974), see Mary Helen Spooner, *Soldiers in a Narrow Land: The Pinochet Regime in Chile* (Berkeley: University of California Press, 1999), 49–82; and Ensalaco, *Chile under Pinochet*, 22–46. For Chile as a case study in Cold War torture in a transnational context, see Wolfgang S. Heinz, "The Military, Torture, and Human Rights: Experiences from Argentina, Brazil, Chile, and Uruguay," in *The Politics of Pain: Torturers and Their Masters*, ed. Ronald D. Crelinsten and Alex P. Schmid (Boulder, CO: Westview Press, 1995), 65–97; Gregory Weeks, "Fighting the Enemy Within: Terrorism, the School of the Americas, and the Military in Latin America," *Human Rights Review* 5, no. 1 (October–December 2003): 12–27; Alfred W. McCoy, *A Question of Torture: CIA Interrogation, from the Cold War to the War on Terror* (New York: Holt, 2007); and Michael Otterman, *American Torture: From the Cold War to Abu Ghraib and Beyond* (London: Pluto Press, 2007).

7. See the introduction for the effects of international attention on the junta's policies. For the Chilean case as part of a comparative, transnational perspective, see Luis Roniger and Mario Sznajder, *The Legacy of Human Rights Violations in the Southern Cone: Argentina, Chile, and Uruguay* (Oxford: Oxford University Press, 1999).

8. Constable and Valenzuela, *Nation of Enemies*, 160.

9. For more on the "Chicago boys," the "Chilean miracle," the neoliberal reorganization of the economy, and the deep and long-term social and cultural changes that resulted from the restructuring, see Constable and Valenzuela, *Nation of Enemies*, 166–98; Genero Arriagada, *Por la razón o la fuerza: Chile bajo Pinochet* (Santiago: Sudamericana Chilena, 1998), 51–58, 68–72, 75–87, and 99–100; Tomás Moulian, *Chile actual: Anatomía de un mito* (Santiago: LOM, 2002); Huneeus, *El régimen de Pinochet*, 389–436; and Peter Winn's edited collection *Victims of the Chilean Miracle: Workers and Neoliberalism in the Pinochet Era, 1973–2002* (Durham, NC: Duke University Press, 2004).

10. For detail on the economic crisis and protests of the early to mid-1980s, and the regime's crackdown against the protest, see Arriagada, *Por la razón*, 151–65 and 169–97; Spooner, *Soldiers*, 163–203; Ensalaco, *Chile under Pinochet*, 135–55; and Huneeus, *El régimen de Pinochet*, 499–549.

11. Quoted in Constable and Valenzuela, *Nation of Enemies*, 71.

12. Arriagada, *Por la razón*, 103–16. The constitution was subject to amendments under the *concertación* governments of the 1990s and early 2000s. The Concertación de Partidos por la Democracia (or Concertación) was a coalition of center-left political parties that put forward the successful candidate in every presidential election between 1990 and 2006. In 2013 Michelle Bachelet ran for a second presidential term on a platform that included rewriting the constitution.

13. For details on the lead-up to the 1988 plebiscite, see Arriagada, *Por la razón*, 219–64; and Huneeus, *El régimen de Pinochet*, 569–97. For Chile as a case study of

postconflict transition to democracy, see, for example, Gerardo L. Munck and Carol Skalnik Leff, "Modes of Transition and Democratization: South America and Eastern Europe in Comparative Perspective," *Comparative Politics* 29, no. 3 (1997): 343–62; and Jon Elster, ed., *Retribution and Reparation in the Transition to Democracy* (Cambridge: Cambridge University Press, 2006).

14. For an account of the formation and the work of the Rettig Commission and its report, see Ensalaco, *Chile under Pinochet*, 181–211.

15. Comisión Nacional sobre Prisión Política y Tortura, *Informe*.

16. For a regional perspective on the lingering influence of military regimes after the return to democracy, see Brian Loveman, "Protected Democracies: Antipolitics and Political Transitions in Latin America, 1978–1994," in *The Politics of Anti-Politics: The Military in Latin America*, ed. Thomas M. Davies Jr. and Brian Loveman (Lanham, MD: SR Books, 1997), 366–97.

17. For detail on Pinochet's role in posttransition Chile, including his arrest in London and the subsequent debates, see Roger Burbach, *The Pinochet Affair: State Terrorism and Global Justice* (London: Zed Books, 2003), particularly 56–145; and Mary Helen Spooner, *The General's Slow Retreat: Chile after Pinochet* (Berkeley: University of California Press, 2011).

18. For overviews of legal developments in posttransition Chile in relation to crimes of repression, see Cath Collins, "Human Rights Trials in Chile during and after the 'Pinochet Years,'" *International Journal of Transitional Justice* 4, no. 1 (2010): 67–86; Marny A. Requa, "A Human Rights Triumph? Dictatorship-Era Crimes and the Chilean Supreme Court," *Human Rights Law Review* 12, no. 1 (2012): 79–106; and Cath Collins, "The Politics of Justice: Chile beyond the Pinochet Case," in *The Politics of Memory in Chile: From Pinochet to Bachelet*, ed. Cath Collins, Katherine Hite, and Alfredo Joignant (Boulder, CO: First Forum Press, 2013), 61–89. For the Chilean case in regional and transnational perspective, see, for example, Cath Collins, *Posttransitional Justice: Human Rights Trials in Chile and El Salvador* (University Park: Pennsylvania State University Press, 2011); Alexander Laban Hinton, ed., *Transitional Justice: Global Mechanisms and Local Realities after Genocide and Mass Violence* (New Brunswick, NJ: Rutgers University Press, 2011); and Jessica Almqvist and Carlos Espósito, eds., *The Role of Courts in Transitional Justice: Voices from Latin America and Spain* (New York: Routledge, 2012).

19. See, for example, notes 5, 6, 7, 13, 16, and 18.

Introduction

1. Oral history with Mario Navarro (1973–75, Arica), September 3, 2012, Arica.

2. For detail on the historical makeup of the draft, see chap. 3, note 16. For figures for the years 1973–90, see table 1 in the appendix.

3. In addition to Mario's group, this book is based on information and documentation relating, in particular, to the following groups and coalitions: the Agrupación SMO in Santiago; the Agrupación Ex Soldados Conscriptos (Ex-Conscript Soldier Association) (later the Corporación para la Integración de los Derechos Humanos de

los Ex Conscriptos del período 1973–1990 [Corporation for the Inclusion of the Human Rights of Ex-Conscripts from the period 1973–1990] in Santiago); the Agrupación de Reservistas de la Defensa Nacional IX Region (Association of National Defense Reservists, Ninth Region) in Temuco (Agrupación de Reservistas); REPACH in Chillán; REPACH Talcahuano; the Coordinadora Nacional de Ex Soldados Conscriptos del SMO 1973–1990 (National Ex-Conscript Organization) based in Buin (Coordinadora); the Agrupación del Bío Bío de Ex Soldados Conscriptos de 1973–1990 (Bio Bio Association of Ex-Conscripts from the Period 1973–1990) based in Nacimiento; the Agrupación de Ex Conscriptos del período 1973 a 1990 (Association of Ex-Conscripts from the Period 1973–1990) in Iquique; the Agrupación ex conscriptos 1973–1990 Puente Alto (Association of Ex-Conscripts 1973–1990 Puente Alto) in Puente Alto (Agrupación Puente Alto); and the Comisión Nacional D.D.H.H. ex Soldados Conscriptos 1973–1990 (National Commission for the Human Rights of Ex-Conscripts, 1973–1990).

4. While the "movement" represents a significant number of members, many ex-conscripts—perhaps most—do not feel victimized by their service and do not find meaning in the movement's narratives. For an analysis of the movement and its emergence, see chapter 2.

5. The ex-conscript lobby was dominated by five national-level coalitions, which gathered together local and regional associations: the Agrupación de Reservistas de la Defensa Nacional (Association of National Defense Reservists), CENAEXSO (Centro Nacional de Ex Soldados Conscriptos [National Center for Ex-Conscript Soldiers]), the Coordinadora, the Asociación Nacional de Ex-Conscriptos (National Association for Ex-Conscripts), and the Agrupación V Región Centro Norte Sur (Association of the Fifth Region Center North South).

6. This network of groups (representing only recruits who served in 1973) launched three civil cases for damages: *Causa C-25.272, Pereira y otros / Fisco de Chile* (29° Juzgado Civil de Santiago, 2009); *Causa C-21.002, Aliste / Fisco de Chile* (23° Juzgado Civil de Santiago, 2010); and *Causa C-21.313, Allende / Fisco de Chile* (25° Juzgado Civil de Santiago, 2010). Also in 2009, the Agrupación de ex Conscriptos 73–90 de Maipú (Maipú Association for Ex-Conscripts 73–90) (later the Asociación Nacional de Ex-Conscriptos) launched its own civil cases for damages: *Causa C-14.431, Avello y otros / Fisco de Chile* (25° Juzgado Civil de Santiago, 2010); and *Causa C-15.448, Valenzuela y otros / Consejo de defensa del estado* (30° Juzgado Civil de Santiago, 2010), before shifting its focus back to the lobby effort.

7. The Agrupación Puente Alto launched a criminal case against members' former superiors (Hernán Montealgre Klenner, *Querella criminal: Rol 3356-2009*).

8. This book examines both the memory and the history of military service. It analyzes how ex-conscripts remember their service under Pinochet within the context of the twenty-first-century movement. However, it is also interested in understanding the experience of being a conscript during the dictatorship. The sources are predominantly testimonies produced many years after conscription, and the book examines them from the methodological perspective of memory. However, via the analysis,

historicization, and contextualization of ex-conscript memory, the book also draws careful conclusions about life inside the barracks between 1973 and 1990. As a result, the book advances the discussion of both the history of the memory of conscription (particularly 2005–15) and the history of conscription (1973–90). For an enlightening discussion of the line between "memory" and "history" when historicizing memory processes, see Stern, *Remembering Pinochet's Chile*, xxvi–xxix.

9. The approach to memory adopted here sits within a literature that typically takes as its starting point the work of sociologist Maurice Halbwachs. Writing in the early twentieth century, Halbwachs posited that memories, even the most personal memories, are made within social frameworks (*On Collective Memory*, trans. and ed. Lewis A. Coser [Chicago: University of Chicago Press, 1992]). For valuable contributions to the field that also provide useful overviews of the development of ideas of "collective memory," as well as debates and controversies within the literature, see Jan Assman, "Collective Memory and Cultural Identity," *New German Critique* 65 (1995): 125–33; Jeffrey K. Olick and Joyce Robbins, "Social Memory Studies: From 'Collective Memory' to the Historical Sociology of Mnemonic Practices," *Annual Review of Sociology* 24, no. 1 (1998): 105–40; Jeffrey K. Olick, "Collective Memory: The Two Cultures," *Sociological Theory* 17, no. 3 (1999): 333–48; Wulf Kansteiner, "Finding Meaning in Memory: A Methodological Critique of Collective Memory Studies," *History and Memory* 41, no. 2 (2002): 179–97; Jeffrey K. Olick, "'Collective Memory': A Memoir and Prospect," *Memory Studies* 1, no. 1 (2008): 19–25; and Wulf Kansteiner, *In Pursuit of German Memory: History, Television, and Politics after Auschwitz* (Athens: Ohio University Press, 2006), 11–27. In particular, this book's approach is especially indebted to Elizabeth Jelin's work on memory and military dictatorships in the Southern Cone (*Los trabajos de la memoria* [Madrid: Siglo XXI de España Editores, 2002]) and Stern's work on the memory of Pinochet's Chile (*Remembering Pinochet's Chile*, particularly xxvi–xxix and 104–33). The same introductory section on memory (xxvi–xxix) is also included in the second and third books of his trilogy (*Battling for Hearts and Minds: Memory Struggles in Pinochet's Chile, 1973–1988* [Durham, NC: Duke University Press, 2006] and *Reckoning with Pinochet: The Memory Question in Democratic Chile, 1989–2006* [Durham, NC: Duke University Press, 2010]). It also owes a debt to Clara Han's extension of the idea of memory beyond "narration and public acts" and into the detail and routine of everyday life (*Life in Debt: Times of Care and Violence in Neoliberal Chile* [Berkeley: University of California Press, 2012], in particular 96–97). Other aspects of memory, such as commemorative ritual, sites of memory, and the intergenerational transmission of myth, are discussed in later chapters as they arise.

10. Several ex-conscript blogs exist (see chapter 2), but information is most widely disseminated at group meetings.

11. For studies that understand the memory of military rule in Latin America as a set of competing memory frameworks, see Elizabeth Jelin, "The Politics of Memory: The Human Rights Movement and the Construction of Democracy in Argentina," *Latin American Perspectives* 21, no. 2 (1994): 38–58; Jelin, *Los trabajos*; João Roberto Martins Filho and Timothy Thompson, "The War of Memory: The Brazilian Military

Dictatorship according to Militants and Military Men," *Latin American Perspectives* 36, no. 5 (2009): 89–107; Paulo Drinot, "For Whom the Eye Cries: Memory, Monumentality, and the Ontologies of Violence in Peru," *Latin American Cultural Studies* 18, no. 1 (2009): 15–32; Emilio Crenzel, "Present Pasts: Memory(ies) of State Terrorism in the Southern Cone of Latin America," in *The Memory of State Terrorism in the Southern Cone: Argentina, Chile, and Uruguay*, ed. Francesca Lessa and Vincent Druliolle (New York: Palgrave Macmillan, 2011), 1–13; Vicki Bell, "The Politics of 'Memory' in the Long Present of the Southern Cone," in Lessa and Druliolle, *The Memory of State Terrorism*, 209–21; Ana Ros, *The Post-Dictatorship Generation in Argentina, Chile, and Uruguay: Collective Memory and Cultural Production* (New York: Palgrave Macmillan, 2012); Francesca Lessa, *Memory and Transitional Justice in Argentina and Uruguay: Against Impunity* (New York: Palgrave Macmillan, 2013); Peter Winn, ed., *No hay mañana sin ayer: Batallas por la memoria histórica en el cono sur* (Santiago: LOM, 2014); and Eugenia Allier-Montaño and Emilio Crenzel, eds., *The Struggle for Memory in Latin America: Recent History and Political Violence* (New York: Palgrave Macmillan, 2015).

12. In addition to Stern's seminal trilogy cited in note 9, see Alexander Wilde, "Irruptions of Memory: Expressive Politics in Chile's Transition to Democracy," *Journal of Latin American Studies* 31, no. 2 (1999): 473–500; Michael J. Lazzara, *Chile in Transition: The Poetics and Politics of Memory* (Gainesville: University Press of Florida, 2006); Elizabeth Lira, "Chile: Dilemmas of Memory," in Lessa and Druliolle, *The Memory of State Terrorism*, 107–32; and the following important collections of essays: Mario Garcés et al., eds., *Memoria para un nuevo siglo: Chile, miradas a la segunda mitad del siglo XX* (Santiago: LOM, 2000); Nelly Richard, ed., *Políticas y estéticas de la memoria* (Santiago: Editorial Cuarto Propio, 2006); and Collins et al., *The Politics of Memory* (in particular, these chapters: Katherine Hite, Cath Collins, and Alfredo Joignant, "The Politics of Memory in Chile from Pinochet to Bachelet," 1–29; and Alexander Wilde, "A Season of Memory: Human Rights in Chile's Long Transition," 31–60); and Steve J. Stern and Peter Winn, "El tortuoso camino chileno a la memorialización," in Winn, *No hay mañana*, 205–326.

13. Stern, *Battling for Hearts and Minds*; Stern, *Remembering Pinochet's Chile*; Stern, *Reckoning with Pinochet*.

14. Stern, *Battling for Hearts and Minds*, 11–136. For an overview of the emergence of organizations defending human rights, see Ensalaco, *Chile under Pinochet*, 58–68.

15. Stern, *Battling for Hearts and Minds*, 179–245; Wilde, "A Season of Memory," 35–36. For overviews of the period, see Spooner, *Soldiers*, 140–59; and Ensalaco, *Chile under Pinochet*, 125–35.

16. Stern, *Battling for Hearts and Minds*, 249–388; Wilde, "A Season of Memory," 35–36. For descriptions of protests, see Spooner, *Soldiers*, 183–203; and Ensalaco, *Chile under Pinochet*, 135–55.

17. Wilde, "Irruptions of Memory," 473–500; Wilde, "A Season of Memory," 36–38.

18. Stern, *Reckoning with Pinochet*, 65–210.

19. Stern, *Reckoning with Pinochet*, 211–64; Wilde, "A Season of Memory," 41–47. For an extended study of Pinochet's role in the "long transition," see Spooner, *The General's Slow Retreat*. For a global perspective on the "Pinochet effect," see Roger Burbach, *The Pinochet Affair: State Terrorism and Global Justice* (London: Zed Books, 2003). For detail on the legal debates and shifts, see Collins, "Human Rights Trials," 67–86; Requa, "A Human Rights Triumph?," 79–106; and Collins, "The Politics of Justice," 61–89.

20. Stern, *Reckoning with Pinochet*, 238–46; Wilde, "A Season of Memory," 41–44.

21. Michael J. Lazzara, "El fenómeno mocito (Las puestas en escena de un sujeto cómplice)," *A Contracorriente* 12, no. 1 (2014): 104.

22. Stern, *Reckoning with Pinochet*, 279–90; Wilde, "A Season of Memory," 44–47.

23. Stern, *Reckoning with Pinochet*, 298; Elizabeth Lira and Brian Loveman, "Torture as Public Policy: Chile 1810–2010," in Collins et al., *The Politics of Memory*, 117. Already in January of 2003, Cheyre had recognized the reality of, and lack of justification for, human rights violations, and stepped back from Pinochet's institutional legacy, declaring: "We are not the inheritors of any particular regime" (Collins, "Human Rights Trials," 80–83; Stern, *Reckoning with Pinochet*, 277).

24. Stern, *Reckoning with Pinochet*, 348–56; Alfredo Joignant, "Pinochet's Funeral: Memory, History, and Immortality," trans. Cath Collins, in Collins et al., *The Politics of Memory*, 165–95.

25. From around 2006, hard-liner communities mobilized—mainly online, but also by attending events and writing books—in support of officers convicted of crimes of repression and beginning to serve prison sentences. They described convicted officers as "political prisoners," spoke of Christian sacrifice in place of salvation, and framed convicted officers, and increasingly themselves, as human rights victims. They retained the existing idea of "human rights" as a political plot and legal fiction but also expressed their sense of victimhood via a discourse of rights, citing human rights treaties, international law, and the Chilean constitution (Leith Passmore, "Perpetrators as Victims: The Evolution of Pinochetista Memory in Chile and the Languages of Martyrdom, Political Imprisonment, and Human Rights" [unpublished manuscript]).

26. Wilde, "A Season of Memory," 35.

27. Cath Collins and Katherine Hite, "Memorial Fragments, Monumental Silences, and Reawakenings in Twenty-First-Century Chile," in Collins et al., *The Politics of Memory*, 151–52; Hite, Collins, and Joignant, "The Politics of Memory," 14–15; Stern and Winn, "El tortuoso camino chileno," 307–13.

28. Francisco Torrealba and Guillermo Turner, "Presidente Sebastián Piñera y su juicio a 40 años del golpe: 'Hubo muchos que fueron cómplices pasivos; Que sabían y no hicieron nada o no quisieron saber,'" *La Tercera*, August 31, 2013.

29. Michelle Bachelet, "Programa de Gobierno: Michelle Bachelet, 2014–2018," 2013, 16–21, 30–35, 164–65.

30. In the context of his interview of former recruit Cristián (1973), Stern writes of there being no room in Chile's "memory box" in the 1990s for conscript voices: "Voices of military memory were controlled from the top," and "too many socially

determining factors suffocated the possibility of conscript memory as one legitimate cultural expression of military memory" (*Remembering Pinochet's Chile*, 141).

Beyond the "voice from the top" and the evolving institutional narrative, other military voices include a narrative of—usually "constitutionalist"—dissent (see, for example, Jorge Magasich Airola, *Los que dijeron "no": Historia del movimiento de los marinos antigolpistas de 1973*, 2 vols. [Santiago: LOM, 2008]), and an unrepentant military voice, which shares many similarities with "perpetrator memory" throughout the region, including persistent denials of abuses; a reiteration of the narrative of a justified war; arguments for contextualization (as justification); assigning blame to the victims of human rights abuses; assigning responsibility for "excesses" to "rotten apples"; citing the idea of the chain of command; insisting on a model of amnesty rooted in forgetfulness; strategic individual amnesia concerning the details of the repression; a sense of victimization at the hands of "one-sided" or "biased" transitional justice; rarely, remorse; confessions in exchange for benefits or immunity; and sadistic confessions. See Martha K. Huggins, "Legacies of Authoritarianism: Brazilian Torturers' and Murderers' Reformulation of Memory," *Latin American Perspectives* 27, no. 2 (2000): 57–78; Marcia Esparza, "Casi la verdad: Silencios y secretos en la posdictadura del general Augusto Pinochet en Chile," *Antípoda* 5 (2007): 121–41; Leigh A. Payne, *Unsettling Accounts: Neither Truth nor Reconciliation in Confessions of State Violence* (Durham, NC: Duke University Press, 2008); Mariana Achugar, *What We Remember: The Construction of Memory in Military Discourse* (Philadelphia, PA: John Benjamins Publishing House, 2008); Martins Filho and Thompson, "The War of Memory," 89–107; and Farid Samir Benavides Vanegas, "Memoria y verdad judicial en Colombia: Los procesos de justicia y paz," *Revista de Derecho Público* 31 (2013): 2–23.

Ex-conscript memory is not military memory, dissenting or otherwise. Former recruits do not feel a uniform loyalty to the institution, and few consider themselves soldiers. Nor is it perpetrator memory. Ex-conscript memory is, instead, a unique shared memory of victimhood that does not sit within any of the existing memory frameworks of military rule and does not compete in the "memory contest."

While there are important differences between the military regimes in Chile and Argentina, the way they ended, and the wars they fought, Federico Lorenz's work on the Malvinas/Falklands war includes insightful analysis of the Argentine veterans' movement in the 1980s, in which former recruits identify as soldiers but differentiate themselves from the army that perpetrated the internal dirty war ("Testigos de la derrota: Malvinas; Los soldados y la guerra durante la transición democrática argentina, 1982–1987," in *Historizar el pasado vivido*, ed. Anne Pérotin-Dumon [2007], 1–63; and *Las guerras por Malvinas, 1982–2012* [Buenos Aires: Edhasa, 2012], 211–40). Also in the Argentine context, Valentina Salvi and Santiago Garaño examine the recollections of ex-conscripts as well as retired officers who participated in an extended antiguerilla operation in the Tucumán Province—Operation Independence—between 1975 and 1977. With regard to former recruits, they analyze the role of rumor and fear within the armed forces, and the construction of the figure of the enemy in ex-conscript memory as omnipresent, mobile and dangerous ("Las fotos y el helicóptero: Memorias de oficiales retirados y ex soldados conscriptos que participaron del Operativo Independencia [Tucumán, 1975–1977]," *Estudios Sociales* 24, no. 47 [2014]: 163–89).

Other studies on twentieth-century conscription in other Latin American countries have examined the cultural construction of military service, but not in the specific context of military rule, for example, Lesley Gill, "Creating Citizens, Making Men: The Military and Masculinity in Bolivia," *Cultural Anthropology* 12, no. 4 (1997): 527–50; Rolando J. Silla, "Ahora todo va a cambiar: El servicio militar obligatorio como rito de pasaje a la adultez masculina," in *Mosaico: Trabajos en Antropología Social y Arqueología*, ed. Mariana Carballido Calatayud (Buenos Aires: Fundación de Historia Natural "Félix de Azara," 2004), 213–21; and Elizabeth Shesko, "Constructing Roads, Washing Feet, and Cutting Cane for the Patria: Building Bolivia with Military Labor," *International Labor and Working-Class History* 80, no. 1 (2011): 6–28.

31. The Commissions did not exclude people performing military service from being considered victims. The Rettig Report, for example, includes seventeen cases of conscript deaths. However, the focus on politically motivated crimes did exclude abuses denounced by former recruits that had no discernable political motivation (see chapter 2).

32. Testimony on file in the office of the Agrupación de Reservistas in Temuco (on file in Temuco). It was common practice to bring recruits in from the provinces to patrol the capital's streets (see Spooner, *Soldiers*, 57).

33. For examples of ex-conscript accounts of being unsure who the enemy was when told on September 11, 1973, they were at war, see testimonies in Luis Seguel Mora, ed., *Al otro lado de las metralletas: Testimonios inéditos del servicio militar en Chile periodo 1973–1990* (Temuco: Out Sourcing Chile, 2007), by L.R.V.R. (1973) (page 270); and S.E.C.P. (1973–75, Angol) (285–86). For examples of punishment or death as a consequence of disobedience, see Stern, *Remembering Pinochet's Chile*, 136–37; the case of Michel Nash (1973) (chapter 2); and the broader discussion of violence against conscripts (chapter 4).

34. Comisión Nacional de Verdad y Reconciliación, *Informe de la comisión de verdad y reconciliación* (1991), 1:30–32; Constable and Valenzuela, *A Nation of Enemies*, 18 and 36; Comisión Nacional sobre Prisión Política y Tortura, *Informe*, 163–65; Stern, *Battling for Hearts and Minds*, 11–28.

35. Ensalaco, *Chile under Pinochet*, 22–30 and 35–36.

36. For a detailed and nuanced examination of Plan Z, see Stern, *Battling for Hearts and Minds*, 41–56. See also Spooner, *Soldiers*, 88–89; Ensalaco, *Chile under Pinochet*, 45; and Huneeus, *El régimen de Pinochet*, 85–87.

37. Patricia Verdugo, *Los zarpazos del puma: La caravana de la muerte* (Santiago: Ediciones Chile-América CESOC, 2001). See also Spooner, *Soldiers*, 67–75; Ensalaco, *Chile under Pinochet*, 39–44; Huneeus, *El régimen de Pinochet*, 101–3; and Stern, *Battling for Hearts and Minds*, 50–52.

38. For a broader perspective of the first days of the "war," see Arriagada, *Por la razón*, 21–40.

39. For detail, see chapter 1.

40. For detail on the DINA, see Arriagada, *Por la razón*, 47–51; and Huneeus, *El régimen de Pinochet*, 103–8.

41. Stern, *Battling for Hearts and Minds*, 366.

42. Stern, *Reckoning with Pinochet*, 85, 91–93, 109, 256.

43. Military leaders were concerned that conflict with the "internal enemy" would inhibit their ability to defend against attacks from Chile's neighbors and embolden those countries to launch attacks. Preparations for an expected conflict were carried out under the rubric *Hipótesis Vecinal 1* (Neighbor Hypothesis 1) or HV1, and the expectation was that HV1 would quickly lead to HV2 and, inevitably, to HV3, and war with all three neighboring countries. Chile would have been at a severe disadvantage with regard to men and equipment, in the event of HV3 (Dauno Tótoro Taulis, *La cofradía blindada: Chile civil y Chile militar; Trauma y conflicto* [Santiago: Planeta Chilena, 1998)], 179–84; Ascanio Cavallo, Manuel Salazar, and Oscar Sepúlveda, *La historia oculta del régimen militar: Memoria de una época 1973–1988* [Santiago: Uqbar, 2008], 89–91).

44. Conversation with Hugo M.* (1975–77, Arica) in the Temuco office of the Agrupación de Reservistas (notes, April 25, 2012).

45. Dennis R. Gordon, "The Question of the Pacific: Current Perspectives on a Long-Standing Dispute," *World Affairs* 141, no. 4 (1979): 321–24.

46. Tótoro Taulis, *La cofradía blindada*, 179–80; Cavallo et al., *La historia oculta*, 89.

47. Tótoro Taulis, *La cofradía blindada*, 181–82, 184; Augusto Varas, *Los militares en el poder: Régimen y gobierno militar en Chile, 1973–1986* (Santiago: Pehuén, 1987), 113–16.

48. Gordon, "The Question of the Pacific," 324.

49. Tótoro Taulis, *La cofradía blindada*, 181.

50. Cavallo et al., *La historia oculta*, 91.

51. Gordon, "The Question of the Pacific," 325–27; Tótoro Taulis, *La cofradía blindada*, 184; Cavallo et al., *La historia oculta*, 237, 241–43.

52. Testimony from 2006 on file in Temuco. Similarly, J.P.P., R.D.C.U., and S.A.V.F. testify to being sent north by ship and over land to the border in 1975 for the "war with Bolivia that never was" (Seguel Mora, *Al otro lado*, 175).

53. James L. Garrett, "The Beagle Channel Dispute: Confrontation and Negotiation in the Southern Cone," *Journal of Interamerican Studies and World Affairs* 27, no. 3 (1985): 82–85, 88–93; Tótoro Taulis, *La cofradía blindada*, 182; Cavallo et al., *La historia oculta*, 284–87.

54. Garrett, "The Beagle Channel Dispute," 93–97; Tótoro Taulis, *La cofradía blindada*, 183–84; Cavallo et al., *La historia oculta*, 289–93.

55. Garrett, "The Beagle Channel Dispute," 85 and 98–101.

56. Paolo Tripodi, "General Matthei's Revelation and Chile's Role during the Falklands War: A New Perspective on the Conflict in the South Atlantic," *Journal of Strategic Studies* 26, no. 4 (2003): 112–19.

57. Conversation with Javier R.* (1981–83, Tierra del Fuego) in the Temuco office of the Agrupación de Reservistas (notes, April 23, 2012).

58. The ex-conscript movement includes a range of experiences and senses of victimhood. The overall sense of rupture that organizes the three shared narratives analyzed in this book is flexible, and individuals give meaning to their experiences in different ways within that overarching structure.

Chapter 1. The Contours of Silence

1. Oral history with Patricio Farías (1973–75, Punta Arenas and Santiago) (July 19, 2013, Ñuñoa, Santiago).

2. Sergio Munizaga (1973–75, Iquique), who served at the same time as Patricio, similarly recalled being on constant alert for Russian submarines while a guard at the Pisagua prisoner camp in Chile's north (oral history [November 1, 2012, Pozo Almonte]).

3. The description of memory as "obstinate" is from Patricio Guzmán's 1997 documentary *Chile: La memoria obstinada*, which revisits Guzmán's three-part documentary *La batalla de Chile* (1975, 1976, and 1979) and its reception in posttransition Chile.

4. Steve Stern identifies two significant notions of forgetting: memory as struggle against oblivion, and the willful blind spots used to bolster the memories of Chilean elites. He also notes the impact of the "dialectic of memory versus forgetting" on the literature (*Remembering Pinochet's Chile*, xxvi–xxvii and 162n9).

5. The ex-conscript contest between forgetting and unwanted memories is examined in chapter 5.

6. Steve Stern notes how the Valech process, in particular, revealed a similarly intimate dimension to silence among former political prisoners (*Reckoning with Pinochet*, 293–95).

7. Conversation with Diego C.* (1983–85, Tierra del Fuego) in the Temuco office of the Agrupación de Reservistas Defensa Nacional IX Región (Agrupación de Reservistas) (notes, April 24, 2012).

8. Psychological report, on file in Temuco.

9. Testimony from 2010 on file in Temuco. A similar conflation of a sense of loyalty and a desire to forget physical mistreatment shaped the 2006 testimony given by Cristián M.* (1986–87, Temuco) (on file in Temuco).

10. Esparza, "Casi la verdad"; Marcia Esparza, "Courageous Soldiers (*valientes soldados*): Politics of Concealment in the Aftermath of State Violence in Chile," in *State Violence and Genocide in Latin America: The Cold War Years*, ed. Marcia Esparza, Henry R. Huttenbach, and Daniel Feierstein (New York: Routledge, 2010), 196–208. For military silence from a regional perspective, see Payne, *Unsettling Accounts*, 173–95.

11. Similar to the example of Pedro Cáceres cited below, Federico Lorenz writes of recruits in the Argentine military who served under military rule and fought in the Malvinas/Falklands war being forced to sign documents promising to remain silent about their experiences before leaving the barracks (*Las guerras por Malvinas*, 217).

12. Esteban Proboste (1978) explained that ex-conscripts had maintained their silence about the mistreatment they suffered because they thought it was "manly" to do so. In 2012, he said, he now understood that it was also "manly" to bring it out into the open (oral history [April 27, Temuco]).

With respect to ambivalence toward superiors and the institution, Miguel Saavedra (1978) writes in his 2012 memoir of recruits' patriotism associated with the traditional prestige of the armed forces, and he includes a 1979 letter of gratitude from his company to its captain, which stands in contrast to the descriptions of brutal mistreatment at the hands of other instructors (*Mi propia guerra* [San Bernardo: Imp. Roberto Vidal, 2012], in particular 139–41).

In terms of the indoctrination of recruits, many ex-conscripts left the barracks identifying strongly with the armed forces, and their sense of victimization only emerged years later. Similarly, and in the context of their work with conscripts who served in the early 1990s, psychologists Rosella Baronti and Sachiko Alfaro noted that while many finished their service with a strong identification with the military, the effects of service could manifest later ("Mecanismos y efectos psicológicos en la formación militar y la objeción de conciencia como una repuesta posible," in *Derechos de los jóvenes frente al servicio militar obligatorio: Sistematización de una experiencia de trabajo*, ed. Rosella Baronti and Álvaro Toro [Santiago: CODEPU, 1999], 52).

13. Montealegre, *Querella criminal*. Montealegre also frames former recruits' silence as the result of the late formation of groups advocating on behalf of families of the disappeared, political prisoners, and torture victims, as well as exhaustion and disinterest among human rights lawyers in taking on the case.

14. Joaquin G.* (1973–74, Iquique) wrote about threats to "leave them forever silent under the dunes" (2011 testimony on file in the office of the Agrupación de Ex Conscriptos del Período 1973 a 1990 in Iquique [on file in Iquique]). Accounts that include specific threats of retribution against conscripts or their families if they talked are included, for example, in the testimonies in Seguel Mora, *Al otro lado*, by J.A.H.S. (1973–76) (261), L.E.B. (1973–76, Calama) (212–13), J.A.M.R. (1974, Calama) (203–5), and R.J.M.M. (1977–79, Temuco) (242); and the 2010 testimony on file in Temuco by Arsenio O.* (1978, Punta Arenas). Similar warnings to remain silent were reported in the posttransition years. See the cases of Jorge Antonio Concha Meza (1991, Peldehue) and Alejandro Albano Lopez Aragon (1996, Arica) ("Casos atendidos por el programa de protección y asistencia de la corporación de promoción y defensa de los derechos del pueblo," CEDOC del Museo de la Memoria y los Derechos Humanos, Fondo CODEPU, Caja 32); and the 1998 cases of deserters in Arica and alleged abuse in Puerto Varas (Vicaría de la Solidaridad, *Situación de los derechos humanos durante el primer semestre de 1998* [Santiago: Fundación Documentación y Archivo de la Vicaría de la Solidaridad, 1998], 14).

15. Seguel Mora, *Al otro lado*, 278–79.

16. Comisión Nacional D.D.H.H. de ex Soldados Conscriptos 1973–1990, *Informe: Violación de derechos humanos y hechos de violencia vinculados con el servicio militar obligatorio en Chile entre los años 1973 a 1990* (2012), 89.

17. Diamela Eltit, *Los vigilantes* (Santiago: Editorial Planeta, 2011). The English title is from Elizabeth Quay Hutchison et al., eds., *The Chile Reader: History, Culture, Politics* (Durham, NC: Duke University Press, 2014), 534–37.

18. For examples of reprisal and fear of reprisal for breaking their silence, see, for example, the cases of Andrés Antonio Valenzuela Morales, an air force intelligence service member; Juan René Alcarón, a collaborator inside the National Stadium; and Eugenio Berrios, a biochemist and DINA agent (Payne, *Unsettling Accounts*, 188–90). Such cases add weight to the idea that ex-conscript fear of reprisal was plausible, but former recruits describe instead the atmosphere and their experiences inside the barracks, explicit threats, and the reach of the intelligence service in society as underpinning their silence.

19. Conversation with Eduardo F.* (1976–78) in the Temuco office of the Agrupación de Reservistas (recording and notes, April 26, 2012).

20. Interview with Carlos Palma (1973–75, Iquique) in his Ñuñoa *almacén* (suburban grocery shop) (notes, November 23, 2011).

21. Interview with Hernán Montealegre in his Santiago office (recording and notes, December 18, 2013).

22. Stern, *Remembering Pinochet's Chile*, 134.

23. For comparative statistics on public opinion, see CERC MORI, "Barómetro de la política: La imagen del Pinochetismo" (2015).

24. Interviews with Carlos Palma (1973–75, Iquique) in his Ñuñoa almacén (notes, November 23, 2011; and notes, April 9, 2012).

25. Interview with Fernando Mellado (1973, Santiago) in a café near the Los Leones metro station in Santiago (notes, December 21, 2011).

26. A group conversation with representatives of REPACH Chillán, REPACH Talcahuano, and the Agrupación de Reservistas in the Temuco office of the Agrupación de Reservistas (field notes, April 27, 2012).

27. Personal acts of vengeance were carried out, for example, in Salamanca, Isla de Maipo, Paine, Mulchén, Santa Bárbara, Quilaco, Laja, and Entre Lagos (Arriagada, *Por la razón*, 25–26). For details on the Lonquén case, perhaps the most prominent example of political repression masking local and personal grievances, see Ensalaco, *Chile under Pinochet*, 25; and Stern, *Battling for Hearts and Minds*, 156–67.

28. Constable and Valenzuela, *Nation of Enemies*, 35.

29. The approximate population cited falls between the figures listed in the 1970 and 1982 censuses (Instituto Nacional de Estadísticas, *Censos 1970–1982: Cifras comparativas* [Santiago: Instituto Nacional de Estadísticas, 1993], 3:156).

30. Carlos Véjar, "Reservista revela que se le ordenó ocultar cuerpos en la Isla Cautín," *El Austral de La Araucanía*, November 3, 2013. Additional details from this description of Arías's 1975 arrest were provided by the Temuco office of the Agrupación de Reservistas.

31. Carlos Véjar, "Ex conscripto que dice saber dónde hay detenidos desaparecidos en Temuco fue amenazado," *Soychile.cl*, November 7, 2013. Similarly, Jorgelino Vergara, the subject of the 2010 documentary *El mocito* by Marcela Said and Jean de Certeau

and the 2012 book *La danza de los cuervos: El destino final de los detenidos desaparecidos* by Javier Rebolledo, described living in fear and confirmed receiving death threats ("Reportaje a fondo: 'El mocito' asegura estar amenazado de muerte," online video, 9:07, posted by Chilevisión, May 13, 2014).

32. For detail on the group's criminal case, see chapter 2.

33. The approximate population cited falls between the figures listed in the 1970 and 1982 censuses (Instituto Nacional de Estadísticas, *Censos 1970–1982*, 2:182).

34. "El testimonio de dos ex conscriptos que hicieron su servicio militar en 1973," online video from the show *Una Nueva Mañana*, posted by Cooperativa TV, September 11, 2013.

35. Interview with Pedro Cáceres (1973–76, Puente Alto) and Manuel Ureta (1973, Puente Alto) as representatives of the Agrupación Puente Alto in Manuel's home in Puente Alto (recording and notes, January 7, 2014).

36. A regular meeting of the Agrupación SMO in Estación Central, Santiago (field notes, April 27, 2013). Mario had previously told the same story during an oral history (September 3, 2012, Arica). Constable and Valenzuela describe a similar dynamic—rumor, suspicion, and denial that produced a sense of isolation that cut through close relationships—among political prisoners who emerged from detention into life under military rule (*Nation of Enemies*, 148).

37. Patricia Politzer, *Fear in Chile: Lives under Pinochet* (New York: New Press, 2001), xiii, xiv. For psychological and sociological analyses of the "culture of fear" under military regimes in Chile and the region, see Eugenio Tironi, "Un rito de integración," in *La campaña del no: Vista por sus creadores* (Santiago: Ediciones Melquíades, 1989), 11–14; Elizabeth Lira, *Psicología de la amenaza política y del miedo* (Santiago: ILAS, 1991); and Juan E. Corradi, Patricia Weiss Fagen, and Manuel Antonio Garretón, eds., *Fear at the Edge: State Terror and Resistance in Latin America* (Berkeley: University of California Press, 1992); see also Stern, *Battling for Hearts and Minds*, 386–87, 483n3; and Freddy Timmermann's 2015 analysis of fear and its political instrumentalization in Chile (*El gran terror: Miedo, emoción y discurso Chile, 1973–1980* [Santiago: Ediciones Copygraph, 2015]).

38. In 1999 psychologist Rosella Baronti and lawyer Álvaro Toro with the Corporation for the Promotion and Defense of the Rights of the People (Corporación de Promoción y Defensa de los Derechos del Pueblo) (CODEPU) framed conscript fears within the broader fears that shaped life under military rule. Throughout the 1990s, CODEPU provided assistance to conscripts and deserters called up in the immediate posttransition years. Baronti and Toro asserted that the abuses testified to by posttransition conscripts were similar to those experienced by recruits under military rule, and they attributed their silence to a learned submissiveness and general sense of insecurity when confronting the regime. The professionals concluded that ex-conscript fear, in the context of the immense fear that defined the dictatorship, had most likely prevented recruits under Pinochet from coming forward (*Derechos de los jóvenes*, 9–10).

39. "Habla ex conscripto del 73," *Mqh2*, October 23, 2012; interview with Claudio

de la Hoz (1973–75) in the Temuco office of the Agrupación de Reservistas Defensa Nacional IX Región (Agrupación de Reservistas) (recording and notes, April 27, 2012).

40. Accounts of ex-conscripts not talking to their families are included, for example, in an interview with Carlos Palma (1973–75, Iquique) in his Ñuñoa almacén (notes, November 23, 2011); a conversation with Enrique P.* (1982–84, Tierra del Fuego) in the Temuco office of the Agrupación de Reservistas (notes, April 24, 2012); and the 2011 testimony by Juan S.* (1974–76, 1978) (on file in Temuco). Daniel Gómez (1978–80, Punta Arenas), who worked in the Temuco office receiving ex-recruits and their testimonies, spoke in 2012 of the strength of the animosity: one group member was regularly accompanied by his wife when he came to the office, but she always waited outside. The army had killed her father, Daniel explained, and she wanted nothing to do with *milicos* (soldiers) (interview with Daniel Gómez in the Temuco office of the Agrupación de Reservistas [notes, April 26]).

41. Between 2011 and 2014, ex-conscripts regularly and consistently reported to me that such taunts had followed them throughout the years.

42. Interview with Hernán Montealegre in his Santiago office (recording and notes, December 18, 2013).

43. Pedro Cáceres spoke in 2014 of the comments' sections on the internet as a recent expression of persistent accusations leveled at ex-conscripts (interview with Pedro Cáceres [1973–76, Puente Alto] and Manuel Ureta [1973, Puente Alto] as representatives of the Agrupación Puente Alto in Manuel's home in Puente Alto [recording and notes, January 7]). For a representative example, see comments by Raúl G. González Malpú, who insists ex-conscripts are not victims, that they had been old enough to stand up to their superiors, and that they are only after the money ("Diputados piden reparaciones para ex conscriptos de la era Pinochet," *La Nación*, October 2, 2013).

44. For René Rivera (1973), founding president of the Agrupación SMO, conscripts drafted after the coup should have known what was going on in the country and avoided the draft (interview with René Rivera in the cafeteria of the Universidad de Artes, Ciencias y Comunicaciones in Providencia, Santiago [notes, November 8, 2011]). However, it is difficult to imagine a young man refusing the call-up. Moreover, Rivera's assertion simplifies a complex set of motivations that saw teenage boys welcome service, the uneven and incremental awakening to human rights abuses, and the success of the official salvation narrative.

45. Several ex-conscripts did testify anonymously and as witnesses before the Rettig Commission (Stern, *Reckoning with Pinochet*, 75), and the Rettig Report does include conscript victims, but only those recruits who were "victims of political violence" either from civil society or from within the armed forces. Similarly, the Valech Commission's mandate excluded ex-conscript allegations of imprisonment or torture where a political motivation for the alleged act could not be determined (see chapter 2), meaning the commission did not consider abuses that were framed as part of recruits' training (see chapter 4).

46. Washington Lizana Ormazábal, *Gabriel Alejandro Avello Astete y otros / Fisco de Chile: C-14431* (2010).

47. See note 45.

48. Wally Kunstman Torres and Victoria Torres Ávila, eds., *Cien voces rompen el silencio: Testimonios de ex presos políticos de la dictadura militar en Chile (1973–1990)* (Santiago: Ediciones de la Dibam, 2008), 113 and 185.

49. For a description of the events surrounding Jara's death, see Comisión Nacional de Verdad y Reconciliación, *Informe*, 1:104 and 130.

50. Rafael Sarmiento, "Habla ex conscripto acusado de matar a Víctor Jara: 'Tienen que investigar a los altos mandos,'" *El Líder de San Antonio*, July 15, 2009.

51. The description of the reopening of the Jara case is based on a revision of the press coverage. In additional to the articles directly cited, see "Joan Jara: 'Tenía algo más de esperanza sobre la verdad por la muerte de Víctor,'" *El Mercurio*, May 16, 2008; "Confirman procesamiento de ex conscripto por crimen de Víctor Jara," *La Nación*, May 29, 2009; "Juez realiza recreación de muerte de Víctor Jara junto a conscripto," *La Nación*, May 29, 2009; Ximena Pérez, "Juez reabre investigación por muerte de Víctor Jara," *El Mercurio*, June 3, 2008; Jacmel Cuevas, "Los estremecedores testimonios de cómo y quiénes asesinaron a Víctor Jara," *Centro de Investigación Periodística*, May 26, 2009; "Ex conscriptos revelan identidad del 'príncipe,'" *La Nación*, May 27, 2009; "Habla pareja de ex soldado procesado por crimen de Víctor Jara: 'Él es un hombre bueno,'" *El Líder de San Antonio*, May 28, 2009; Ximena Pérez, "Corte confirma procesamiento de ex conscripto en caso Víctor Jara," *El Mercurio*, May 29, 2009; Alexis Paredes, "Con mi compañero jamás vimos a Víctor Jara," *El Líder de San Antonio*, May 30, 2009; "Abogado dijo que es 'completamente imposible' que ex conscripto haya matado a Víctor Jara," *Cooperativa.cl*, June 3, 2009; Cinthya Carvajal, "Procesado por crimen de Víctor Jara es imputable," *El Mercurio*, July 1, 2009; "Ministro de caso Víctor Jara otorga libertad a ex conscripto procesado," *El Líder de San Antonio*, July 10, 2009; Pedro Robledo, "Ex conscripto afirma ahora que no mató a Víctor Jara," *La Cuarta*, July 14, 2009; and "El supuesto asesino de Víctor Jara negó haber estado en el ex estadio Chile tras el golpe militar," *La Segunda*, May 17, 2012.

52. In 2006, before Paredes confessed and named Barrientos as the killer, Edwin Dimter Bianchi was outed (*funado*) as Jara's murderer at his workplace. Dimter—an army lieutenant in 1973—is thought to be the El Príncipe (The Prince) figure described in prisoner accounts of their time in the Chile Stadium.

53. "Víctor Jara: Procesado emplazó a ex oficiales," *La Nación*, June 5, 2009. Testimonies from former conscripts were in turn central to the 2016 case against Barrientos argued before a civil court in Florida, where the former soldier had lived since leaving Chile, and where a jury found him liable for Jara's torture and death ("Victory! Former Pinochet Lieutenant Found Liable for Murder and Torture of Chilean Folksinger," *The Center for Justice and Accountability*, June 27, 2016).

54. Interview with Pedro Cáceres (1973–76, Puente Alto) and Manuel Ureta (1973, Puente Alto) as representatives of the Agrupación Puente Alto in Manuel's home in Puente Alto (recording and notes, January 7, 2014).

55. Interview with representatives of the Agrupación SMO, Carlos Palma (1973–75, Iquique) and Paola García, in Paola's office in downtown Santiago (notes, April 15, 2013).

56. For examples of interest in the case, see the blog *Agrupación ex conscriptos 1973–1990 Puente Alto* ("Estimados socios," July 13, 2009; "Libertad de José Paredes," July 14, 2009). Despite Paredes not being a member, the group and its lawyer Hernán Montealegre aided the former recruit in his defense. On his release, the group's leadership linked Paredes's successful struggle for justice to their own continuing battle (Agrupación ex conscriptos 1973–1990 Puente Alto, "La justicia tarda pero llega," July 10, 2009). Similarly, the blog *Para que nunca más en Chile* followed the case ("Ex soldado de 1973 acusado del asesinato de Víctor Jara," May 20, 2009; "José Adolfo Paredes Márquez, soldado procesado," June 3, 2009; "Noticia del chilevisión," June 17, 2009; "Ex soldado José Paredes Márquez," July 20, 2009), framed Paredes's case as a test case for the movement ("Defensa de ex soldado detenido," June 4, 2009), and saw his release as confirmation that ex-conscripts bore no responsibility for crimes of repression and were themselves victims ("José Adolfo Paredes Márquez en libertad," July 14, 2009).

57. Spooner, *Soldiers*, 209–17; Ensalaco, *Chile under Pinochet*, 144; Kornbluh, *The Pinochet File*, 428–30; Stern, *Battling for Hearts and Minds*, 267–69, 300–301.

58. Fernando Tomás Guzmán Espíndola, "Statement Given in the "Quemados" Case (Rol 143-2013) (2014). See also "Ex conscripto en caso quemados vivos: 'Julio Castañer, ése es el nombre del asesino,'" *Cooperativa.cl*, July 23, 2015.

59. Héctor Salazar, lawyer on the case, confirmed in 2015 that Quintana had named Castañer as the man who set them alight in her 1987 statement to Amnesty International ("Querellante en 'caso quemados vivos': Julio Castañer fue protegido por la justicia militar," *Cooperativa.cl*, July 28, 2015).

60. "Caso quemados: Otro conscripto rompe el silencio y revela cómo se encubrió la verdad," *Cooperativa.cl*, July 26, 2015. The measures described by the former recruits to keep them quiet are in line with the sparse media coverage and the military disinformation campaign in the wake of the incident (Stern, *Battling for Hearts and Minds*, 300–302), as well as the burying of a compromising police report and the intimidation of witnesses, judges, and lawyers (Peter Kornbluh, "Los Quemados: Chile's Pinochet Covered Up Human Rights Atrocity," in *National Security Archive Electronic Briefing Book No. 523*, ed. Peter Kornbluh [2015]).

61. See the change on the blog *Para que nunca más en Chile* that took place between December 2014 and January 2015.

62. A rally in the Plaza de los Héroes in downtown Santiago organized by the Corporación para la Integración de los Derechos Humanos de los Ex Conscriptos del período 1973–1990 and attended by Santiago group members and groups members from regional centers (field notes, August 5, 2015).

63. For example, the 2015 reopening of the quemados case emboldened the president of the Agrupación SMO, Carlos Palma (1973–75, Iquique), as he felt it represented a new openness to ex-conscript stories. However, he also fielded worried phone calls, even though the Agrupación SMO only represented the "class of '54" (interview with Carlos Palma in his Ñuñoa almacén [notes, July 31, 2015]).

64. "Viuda de Víctor Jara: 'No tengo ninguna sensación de venganza en contra de ellos,'" *El Mercurio*, May 26, 2009.

65. Ximena Pérez, "Abogado pide datos a ex conscriptos en caso de Víctor Jara," *El Mercurio*, May 28, 2009.

66. "Abogado querellante pidió apuntar a 'los jefes' que ordenaron matar a Víctor Jara," *Cooperativa.cl*, May 26, 2009.

67. "Ministro de defensa pide colaboración a las FF.AA. para esclarecer caso Víctor Jara," online video, posted by Chilevisión, May 19, 2012.

68. Carlos Palma insisted that some conscripts who had acted against civilians had done so out of fear. He emphasized the point by forming a gun with his fingers and putting it to my temple (interview with Carlos Palma in his Ñuñoa almacén [notes, November 23, 2011]). He later spoke of how victims' groups labeled ex-conscripts murderers because they misunderstood the pressures on those who were involved in crimes against humanity (interview with Carlos Palma in his Ñuñoa almacén [notes, April 9, 2012]). In 2012 Carlos showed me his copy of the report that included Paz Rojas's statement on conscript complicity (interview with Carlos Palma in his Ñuñoa almacén [notes, October 19]).

69. The Rettig Report included 2,279 victims of death or disappearance (2,115 victims of human rights violations and 164 victims of "political violence"): 1,261 (1973); 309 (1974); 119 (1975); 139 (1976); 25 (1977); 9 (1978); 13 (1979); 15 (1980); 36 (1981); 8 (1982); 82 (1983); 74 (1984); 50 (1985); 50 (1986); 34 (1987); 27 (1988); 26 (1989); 2 (1990) (Comisión Nacional de Verdad y Reconciliación, *Informe*, 2:1311, 1317, and vol. 3). For the 1996 revision—from 2,279 to 3,197—see Stern, *Reckoning with Pinochet*, 108.

The figures for detentions by period are: 22,824 detentions between the coup and the end of 1973; 6,089 detentions between January 1974 and August 1977 (26.16 percent of which were carried out by the army, navy, and air force); and 4,308 detentions from August 1977 to March 1990 (7.18 percent of which were carried out by the army, navy, or air force) (Comisión Nacional sobre Prisión Política y Tortura, *Informe*, 203–21). Revisions to these figures were made as the result of Valech II (Comisión Asesora para la Calificación de Detenidos Desaparecidos, Ejecutados Políticos y Víctimas de Prisión Política y Tortura, *Informe de la comisión asesora para la calificación de detenidos desaparecidos, ejecutados políticos y víctimas de prisión política y tortura* [2011]).

Stern outlines the nonofficial estimates for death and political imprisonment (*Remembering Pinochet's Chile*, 158n3).

70. There are cases of conscripts serving with and as intelligence personnel, for example: Samuel Fuenzalida (1973–75) ("Samuel Enrique Fuenzalida Devia," *Memoriaviva.com*); Pedro Cáceres (1973–76, Puente Alto and Villa Grimaldi) ("El testimonio de dos ex conscriptos"); and Raúl Lara (Clarisa Muñoz, "Soldados de Pinochet," *En la mira*, Chilevisión, July 2, 2014).

71. The age of majority was reduced to eighteen in 1993. The emphasis on powerlessness expressed as youth and being underage was codified, for example, in Resolution 606 (Fuad Chahín et al., *Proyecto de acuerdo 606* [2012]).

In the case of Argentine veterans of the Malvinas conflict, Lorenz writes of former recruits rejecting the infantilization of the figure of the conscript soldier as a victim during the transition to democracy in that country ("Testigos de la derrota," 42–44; *Las guerras por Malvinas*, 235–38).

72. "Abogado dijo."

73. "El testimonio de dos ex conscriptos."

74. Montealegre, *Querella criminal*, emphasis in the original. The English translation is from the English version of the statute.

75. Both Article 214 and 211 require that an illegal order is protested, and that the subordinate did not participate in the decision to commit the crime.

76. The description of the 1973 killings and the 2008 reemergence of the case is based on a review of the press. In addition to those directly cited below, see "Crucial diligencia en caso Santelices realizó Montiglio," *La Nación*, May 8, 2008; "El general que entregó los presos a la caravana," *La Nación*, January 28, 2008; "Practicarán interrogatorio y careos a Santelices," *La Nación*, March 4, 2008; "Vidal habla de responsabilidad política," *La Nación*, February 6, 2008; "Abogado de Santelices argumentó que él era estudiante durante la caravana de la muerte," *Cooperativa.cl*, April 20, 2009; "Juez selló destino del general (R) Santelices," *La Nación*, April 16, 2009; "La caída de Santelices," *La Nación*, April 26, 2009; and "Rechazan exculpar al general (R) Santelices por crímenes de caravana," *La Nación*, May 5, 2009.

77. "Debate en Chile sobre la 'obediencia debida' tras la renuncia de un general," *El País*, February 8, 2008.

78. The courts had, however, applied Article 211 of the Military Code of Justice that outlines the concept of "undue obedience," which mitigates—but does not expunge—the responsibility of the person committing a crime if it is committed under orders. "Undue obedience" was established by Chilean courts as an extenuating circumstance that—usually in combination other extenuating circumstances—led to significant reductions in sentences (Observatorio de Derechos Humanos, "Secciones de códigos, leyes, decretos y la constitución chilena relevantes en causas de ddhh: Citas textuales y notas explicativas" [Santiago: ICSO Universidad Diego Portales, 2010], 24–26). In neighboring Argentina, "due obedience" was used to stifle transitional justice. For more on the 1986 Full Stop Law and the 1987 Law of Due Obedience (repealed in 2003) in Argentina, see Lessa, *Memory and Transitional Justice*, 113–18. In the Chilean context, supporters of officers charged or convicted of crimes of repression did not press for the application of due obedience but for upholding the 1978 amnesty law.

79. "Renuncia general acusado violación DDHH abre debate sobre 'obediencia debida,'" *Soitu.es*, February 7, 2008.

80. "Debate en Chile."

81. Human rights lawyer Hugo Gutiérrez argued that while criminal responsibility was to be determined by the judge, "ethically and morally" Santelices could not remain in the army ("Piden procesamiento y baja de general Gonzalo Santelices," *La Nación*, January 29, 2008).

82. Michael Lazzara draws on Primo Levi's notion of the "grey zone" in his analysis of representations of Jorgelino Vergara—*El mocito*—that appeared between 2010 and 2012. In his discussion of Marcela Said and Jean de Certeau's 2010 film *El mocito*, in particular, Lazzara sees a humanization of the figure of the accomplice that highlights the complexity of Vergara's situation ("El fenómeno mocito").

83. Quoted in Kyle G. Brown, "Chile's Dictatorship: Were Soldiers Victims, Too?," *Global Newsbeat.com*, January 15, 2014. See similar comments by Pizarro in Rodrigo Gutiérrez and Alejandro Meneses, "El pasado los condena," *24 horas*, TVN.

84. See comments made by Pizarro as well as Alicia Lira, president of the Agrupación de Familiares de Ejecutados Políticos (Association of Relatives of the Executed), in the television report by Muñoz, "Soldados de Pinochet."

85. Amparo Montoya and Constanza Reyes, "Cámara de diputados aprueba reparación de daño previsional a ex conscriptos," *Biobiochile.cl*, July 2, 2014.

86. "El testimonio de dos ex conscriptos."

87. Interview with Fernando Mellado in a café in Providencia, Santiago (notes, December 11, 2011).

88. Muñoz, "Soldados de Pinochet." In the wake of Mellado's 2014 claim, Lorena Pizarro was part of group that sought to compel the ex-conscript to reveal information he said he had ("Citarán a declarar a ex conscripto que sabría paradero de DDDD," *Nuevo Mundo*, July 9, 2014).

89. A rally in Plaza de los Héroes in downtown Santiago organized by the Corporación para la Integración de los Derechos Humanos de los Ex Conscriptos del período 1973–1990 and attended by Santiago group members and group members from regional centers (field notes, August 5, 2015).

90. The conviction that only fellow former recruits can understand, and that one "had to be there," was expressed, for example, in the following conversations at the Temuco office of the Agrupación de Reservistas: Hugo M.* (1975–77, Arica) (notes, April 25, 2012); Vicente A.* (1977–78, Temuco) (notes, April 25, 2012); Diego C.* (1983–85, Tierra del Fuego) (notes, April 24, 2012); and Alfonso J.* (1989–90) (notes, April 26, 2012).

91. A dinner event in Talcahuano put on by REPACH Talcahuano for its leadership, selected members, and visiting representatives, held after the celebration of the group's sixth anniversary (field notes, May 12, 2012).

92. In 2013 I attended three of the regular meetings of the Agrupación SMO in Estación Central, Santiago, at the invitation of the president, Carlos Palma (1973–75, Iquique) (field notes, April 27, May 25, and October 10).

93. The shift in dynamic when group meetings were recorded was noted by representatives of the Agrupación SMO (interview with Carlos Palma [1973–75, Iquique] and Paola García, in Paola's office in central Santiago [notes, April 15, 2013]).

94. Julio Torres (1973–76, Concepción) spoke of finding only "subversive propaganda" during searches, and how regimental weapons had been used in photos that appeared in the papers (oral history [July 8, 2012, Nacimiento]). Similarly, at a 2014 meeting, in which members watched a YouTube clip of an interview with Hermógenes Pérez de Arce and group leaders Félix Pinares and Carlos Palma (see chapter 3), a former recruit (1973) labeled Pérez de Arce's insistence on the existence of an armed enemy in Chile a "great lie." He had been assigned to the arsenal in 1973, and he spoke of guns being removed and sent around Chile to exhibit as proof that the country was full of armed extremists (field notes, June 14). René Rivera, founding president of the

Agrupación SMO, spoke of the identity of El Príncipe circulating among ex-conscripts well before it was publicly known (interview [notes, November 27, 2013]). Similarly, Pedro Cáceres spoke of information on the Víctor Jara case circulating within the Agrupación Puente Alto before the case reemerged, including a version of events that described Jara being killed outside the stadium, contradicting the Rettig Report and Paredes's confession (interview with Pedro Cáceres [1973–76, Puente Alto] and Manuel Ureta [1973, Puente Alto] as representatives of the Agrupación Puente Alto in Manuel's home in Puente Alto [recording and notes, January 7, 2014]).

95. Interview with Carlos Palma in his Ñuñoa almacén (notes, April 27, 2013).

96. For example, one member would tell the story of how his father arrived as a prisoner at his regiment but was quietly pulled from among the detainees after the recruit told his superior who he was. The remaining prisoners died. The ex-conscript in question would tell his story but would not commit it to paper (interview with representatives of the Agrupación SMO, Carlos Palma [1973–75, Iquique] and Paola García, in Paola's office in downtown Santiago [notes, April 15, 2013]).

97. Interview with René Rivera (1973), founding president of the Agrupación SMO in the cafeteria of the Universidad de Artes, Ciencias y Comunicaciones in Providencia, Santiago (notes, November 27, 2013).

98. Interview with representatives of the Agrupación SMO, Carlos Palma (1973–75, Iquique) and Paola García, in Paola's office in downtown Santiago (notes, April 15, 2013).

99. Oral history with Patricio Farías (1973–75, Punta Arenas and Santiago) (July 19, 2013, Ñuñoa, Santiago). Brackets around ellipses are used in this book to indicate the omission of text or spoken words from quotations of the source material. Ellipses without brackets indicate pauses in oral source material or ellipses included in the original written source material.

100. Conversation with Héctor L.* (1973) in the Temuco office of the Agrupación de Reservistas (recording and notes, April 26, 2012).

101. Gathering of Santiago and regional group leaders outside the Moneda (field notes, April 19, 2013).

102. Interview with René Rivera (1973), founding president of the Agrupación SMO, in the cafeteria of the Universidad de Artes, Ciencias y Comunicaciones in Providencia, Santiago (notes, November 27, 2013).

103. Julio Gutiérrez Delgado and Mario Navarro Cáceres to President Michelle Bachelet, November 2008, in possession of the author.

104. The Arica cohort would later join other groups representing only the "class of '54" in launching a civil case for damages, and not the ex-conscript lobby.

Chapter 2. A Movement

1. Oral history with Daniel Pizarro (1973–75, Los Andes and Santiago) (May 11, 2012, La Pincoya, Santiago).

2. Daniel was drafted into the Guardia Vieja Regiment in Los Andes in January 1973. His timeline of the unit's movements and his description of detainees being held

at the Parque Cerrillos in Maipú are consistent with details in the Rettig and Valech Reports (Comisión Nacional de Verdad y Reconciliación, *Informe*, 1:117; Comisión Nacional sobre Prisión Política y Tortura, *Informe*, 455).

3. Conversation with Jovino S.* (1971–72, 1973, San Bernardo) outside an ex-conscript meeting in a local hall in Buin (notes, December 8, 2013).

4. A letter from the Military History Department of the Army to the Secretary of the General Staff of the Army (Secretario del Estado Mayor General del Ejército) from July 19, 2006, notes the "rumor" about reparations as well as the existence of a leaflet outlining the process for obtaining the certificate of service. The Chief of the General Staff of the Army (Jefe del Estado Mayor General del Ejército) requested the investigation into the "rumor in relation to a supposed payment of retroactive pension contributions or compensation to persons who completed their Military Service after 1973." The report prepared by the Dirección de Inteligencia del Ejército (DINE) and sent to the Jefe del Estado Mayor General del Ejército on August 30, 2006, identified the Agrupación Nacional de Ex-Soldados Conscriptos del Ejército de Chile (National Association of Ex-Conscript Soldiers of the Chilean Army) (ANESCEC) and the Asociación Gremial de ex Conscriptos (AGEXSCO), which in July 2006 joined to form REPACH (Reservistas Patrióticas de Chile) with groups in Arica, Cabildo, La Ligua, Valparaíso, Quillota, Santiago, Cauquenes, San Carlos, Chillán, Nacimiento, Arauco, Valdivia, Osorno, Punta Arenas, and Talcahuano; Amigos Adultos General Carlos Prats (Adult Friends of General Carlos Prats) with members from Chillán, San Carlos, Concepción, and Talcahuano; and the Agrupación de Reservistas de la Comuna de Galvarino (Reservists' Association of the Commune of Galvarino). It also identified the Agrupación de Ex-SSLLCC de los años 1970 a 1985 (Association of Ex-Conscript Soldiers from the Years 1970 to 1985) with groups in Cañete, Lebu, and Penco, describing payments made at the end of the meeting of the group in Penco; and it quoted directly statements made during a meeting of reservists in the commune of Los Sauces in early August 2006. The documents were shown to me in the General Archive of the Army (field notes, December 2, 2013).

5. In addition to examples cited below relating to the Agrupación Social de Ex Soldados Conscriptos 1973—Clase 54 in Arica, the Santiago-based Agrupación SMO and the Agrupación Puente Alto, and the congressional resolutions, see also the 2006 letter from the Agrupación de Reservistas in Temuco to the president of the Human Rights Commission ("Carta enviada a Tucapel Jiménez," *Reservistas novena región* [blog], June 9, 2007); the 2009 document outlining the legal case of the Agrupación de Reservistas in Temuco—based on laws 11.133, 18.423, and 10.383—for pension payments to be made to former recruits (Luis Seguel Mora, *Ley de justicia previsional para reservistas de la defensa nacional* [April 2009]); the 2006 founding document of ANESCEC ("Carta fundamental de ANESCEC," *La historia tiene tres aristas falta la nuestra* [blog], January 19, 2006); and the 2009 statement by president of AGEXSCO, Máximo Núñez ("Denuncia llegada a AGEXSCOCHILE," *Federacion de ex SMO 1973 al 1990 de Chile* [blog], August 28, 2009).

6. For example, the Agrupación Social de Ex Soldados Conscriptos 1973—Clase 54 in Arica (see introduction), as well as the Organización social de reservistas de Lonquimay (Lonquimay Reservists' Social Organization), Agrupación social de reservistas Santiago (Santiago Reservists' Social Association), Agrupación social reservistas de las Fuerzas Armadas de Puerto Montt (Puerto Montt Social Association of Armed Forces' Reservists), and the Agrupación social de reservistas de la defensa nacional Pudeto de Ancud (Pudeto, Ancud Social Association for National Defense Reservists) ("Directiva nacional," *Reservistas novena región* [blog], November 11, 2008).

7. For example, ex-conscripts in Temuco began sharing stories at informal gatherings around 2004, before officially forming the Agrupación de Reservistas in 2006. The group registered 3,583 members in its first year, with annual totals of new members decreasing in the following years. As of the end of 2013, the group had almost 5,000 members (figures provided during a meeting with staff in the Temuco office, field notes, December 16, 2013). The Agrupación SMO in Santiago also began out of a sense of solidarity before switching to advocacy (see chapter 1). Steve Stern describes a similar evolution—from support to advocacy—among former political prisoners (*Reckoning with Pinochet*, 77).

8. Statistics kept for internal reporting purposes (2005–9) reveal that between 2005 and 2007 the archive received 10,170 requests via ex-conscript groups throughout Chile, and an additional 13,022 individual requests (that is, requests from any class and for any reason, the majority of which, however—around 80 percent, archive staff guessed on the spot—likely involved ex-conscripts in the movement). In 2008 requests via groups jumped to 19,709 and individual requests rose to 20,923. The following year to September 16, group requests tallied 4,487 and individual requests reached 5,707. Numbers for 2010 were not available. The database returned a total 19,482 certificates issued from March 2011 to December 2013. This figure includes certificates from all classes and for all reasons and it does not include pending applications (meeting with archive staff responsible for processing applications in the General Archive of the Army, field notes, December 2, 2013).

9. For examples, see the blog *Reservistas novena región* ("Carta petitoria tarjeta PRAIS," June 6, 2007; "Carta al ministro del interior," June 10, 2007; "Carta al intendente regional," June 10, 2007; "Carta petitoria presidenta de Chile," June 11, 2007; "Audiencias," October 5, 2007; "Audiencia," November 19, 2007; "Audiencia," January 8, 2008; "Ministra de salud," February 4, 2008; "Buscando respaldo," June 23, 2008; "Carta a la presidenta," June 27, 2008; "Ministro del interior," July 4, 2008; "Visita de la presidenta a cherquenco," July 19, 2008; "Reunión en el ministerio del trabajo y previsión social," July 19, 2008; "Audiencia con el diputado Eugenio Tuma Zedan," July 19, 2008; "Ministerio del trabajo y subsecretaria de guerra," September 15, 2008; "En esta reunión . . . ," November 8, 2008; "Viaje a Punta Arenas," January 10, 2009; "Comisión de defensa de la cámara del senado," January 10, 2009).

10. For examples, see the blog *Reservistas novena región* ("Ejército," October 8, 2007; "Reunión con el ejército," October 2, 2008).

11. For examples (2007–9), see the blogs *Reservistas novena región* ("Monseñor Cristian Contreras," August 7, 2007; "Respuesta de la iglesia," June 23, 2008) and *Para que nunca más en Chile* ("Carta al señor arzobispo de Santiago," January 30, 2008; "Carta enviada al señor cardenal," February 12, 2008; "Reunión con Monseñor Errazuriz," May 19, 2008; "Reunión con cardenal arzobispo," October 9, 2009).

12. For examples (2007–9), see the blogs *Reservistas novena región* ("Conferencia prensa 19 de julio de 2007," July 21, 2007) and *Para que nunca más en Chile* ("Comunicado de prensa," May 16, 2008; "Entrevista en telecanal," December 26, 2008; "Comunicado de prensa," June 15, 2009).

13. For example, see the blog *Reservistas novena región*, "Audiencias," October 5, 2007. See also the legal strategies pursued by the Agrupación SMO (Santiago) and the Agrupación Puente Alto (cited below).

14. For examples (2007–9), see the blogs *Reservistas novena región* ("Reunión 20/05/2007," June 17, 2007; "Reunión 29/07/07," July 17, 2007; "Reunión nacional," November 5, 2007; "Reunión," January 10, 2008) and *Para que nunca más en Chile* ("Reunión en Arica," July 8, 2008; "Reunión en Nacimiento," July 28, 2008; "Reunión en Talca," August 26, 2008; "Reunión en Santiago," August 26, 2008; "Reunión en Iquique," April 13, 2009; "Reunión en Iquique," September 21, 2009; "Reunión en ciudad de Los Ángeles," September 21, 2009; "Reunión en la ciudad de Quilpué," September 23, 2009; "Reunión en ciudad de Nacimiento," September 30, 2009).

15. For examples, see the blogs *Para que nunca más en Chile* ("Inscripciones en la IX región," January 30, 2008; "Información a través radio colo colo," March 6, 2009) and *Agrupación ex conscriptos 1973–1990 Puente Alto* ("Entrevista en el diario local *Puente Alto al día*," April 1, 2008).

16. For example: *La historia tiene tres aristas falta la nuestra* (from January 2006), *Reservistas novena región* (from April 2007), *Para que nunca más en Chile* (from January 2008), *Agrupación ex conscriptos 1973–1990 Puente Alto* (from March 2008) and *Agrupación ex conscriptos de Maipú* (from August 2008).

17. For examples (2007–9), see the blogs *Reservistas novena región* ("Marcha en Temuco," June 9, 2007; "Marcha en Santiago," July 12, 2007; "Sinopsis viaje a Santiago," August 18, 2007; "Marcha en Temuco," September 24, 2008) and *Para que nunca más en Chile* ("Inédita marcha de ex conscriptos por reconocimiento previsional," September 15, 2008; "Ex soldados en marcha por reivindicaciones laborales," September 15, 2008; "Ex conscriptos protestaron por daño previsional," September 15, 2008; "Movimiento en plaza Bulnes," May 20, 2009).

18. Offices were set up, for example, in Puente Alto in 2008 ("Agrupación Puente Alto Informa," *Agrupación Ex Conscriptos 1973–1990 Puente Alto* [blog], April 1, 2008) and Santiago in 2008 ("Inscripciones en Santiago," *Para que nunca más en Chile* [blog], March 17, 2008).

19. For 2008 examples, see the blog *Para que nunca más en Chile* ("Inscripciones en la IX región," January 30; "Reunión en Buin," January 30; "Reunión en Melipilla," January 30; "Reunión en Puente Alto," January 30; "Reunión en Santa Cruz," March 17; "Reuniones en Longaví, Santa Cruz, San Fernando," March 28; "Reunión en Santa

Bárbara," April 11; "Reunión en la comuna de Buin," April 11; "Reunión en Talcahuano," April 11; "Reunión en la ciudad de Calama," April 11; "Reunión en la ciudad de Osorno," April 11; "Reunión en Talca," July 21; "Reunión en Iquique," July 29; "Reunión San Francisco de Mostazal," September 25; "Reunión en San Fernando," November 20).

20. For examples (2006–9), see the blogs *Reservistas novena región* ("Reunión de agrupaciones," November 19, 2007; "Reunión," January 10, 2008) and *Para que nunca más en Chile* ("Directiva nacional con nuevas directivas," April 9, 2008; "Asamblea nacional," June 19, 2008; "Reuniones de la directiva nacional," July 9, 2008; "Reunión de directivas nacionales," August 7, 2008; "Reunión directivas nacionales," September 15, 2008; "Ampliado nacional," September 28, 2008; "Reunión en San Fernando," December 26, 2008; "Reunión de directivas nacionales," February 3, 2009).

21. Interview with Juan Díaz and Víctor Calderón in an apartment in Providencia, Santiago (notes, April 26, 2016).

22. "Directiva nacional," *Reservistas novena región* (blog), November 11, 2008.

23. "Directiva nacional," *Para que nunca más en Chile* (blog), January 28, 2008.

24. For example, Juan Díaz participated in the coalition representing the Agrupación del Bío Bío de Ex Soldados conscriptos de 1973–1990, which was based in Nacimiento, had resulted from meetings with other groups in Chillán, San Carlos, and Talcahuano, and had emerged initially to campaign on the issue of unpaid pensions (interview with Juan Díaz and Víctor Calderón in an apartment in Providencia, Santiago [notes, April 26, 2016]).

25. The forty groups were based in Arica, Iquique, Salamanca, Quilpué, San Antonio, Casablanca, Cabildo, Curacaví, San Felipe, Santiago Centro, Santiago Poniente, Buin, San Francisco de Mostazal, Codegua, San Vicente de Tagua Tagua, Rengo, San Fernando, Nancagua, Santa Cruz, Chimbarongo, Chillán, San Carlos, Coelemu, Talcahuano, Lebu, Coronel, Talca, Longaví, Parral, Linares, Curicó, Constitución, Nacimiento, Cunco, Cauquenes, Osorno, Puyehue, Panguipulli, Paillaco, and Coyhaique ("Nómina de Agrupaciones a Nivel Nacional," *Para que nunca más en Chile* [blog], December 31, 2008).

26. AGEXSCO parted ways with the coordinadora and later cooperated with the coalition led by the Temuco-based Agrupación de Reservistas (see "Expulsión de Máximo Núñez de la directiva nacional," *Para que nunca más en Chile* [blog], January 28, 2008; and "A todos los ex soldados del país," *Para que nunca más en Chile* [blog], March 15, 2012). For details on the remaining groups and the reach of their representation in 2012, see note 84.

27. Francisco Chahuán et al., *Proyecto de acuerdo 287* (2007).

28. Germán Becker et al., *Proyecto de acuerdo 842* (2009).

29. See chapter 1.

30. In terms of the lobbyist coalitions, distinctions between cohorts at the local level tended to dissolve as part of the consolidation of national alliances representing all years between 1973 and 1990. For example, the Agrupación reservistas de los años 70 de Galvarino (Galvarino Association of Reservists from the 1970s) and the Agrupación de reservistas los veteranos del 78 Villarrica (Villarica Association of Reservists,

Veterans of 1978) were represented at the national level by the coalition based in Temuco that advocated for former recruits of all classes (1973–90) ("Directiva nacional," *Reservistas novena región* [blog], November 11, 2008).

31. See below for detail. Gutiérrez's personal involvement ended with his election to the lower house of congress.

32. See below for detail. The case is also cited in chapter 1.

33. See below for detail. The Agrupación Puente Alto ended its involvement with the coordinadora in April 2008 ("Puente Alto se retira de la agrupación nacional," *Para que nunca más en Chile* [blog], April 23, 2008).

34. "Entrevista en el diario local *Puente Alto al Día*," *Agrupación ex conscriptos 1973–1990 Puente Alto* (blog), April 1, 2008.

35. The blog *Agrupación ex conscriptos 1973–1990 Puente Alto*.

36. For example, see comments by Lorena Pizarro, president of the AFDD (Muñoz, "Soldados de Pinochet"); the subsecretary of the interior, Rodrigo Ubilla ("Ubilla rechaza protestas de ex conscriptos de la dictadura," *Noticias Terra Chile*, September 25, 2012); former members of the armed forces in the 2010 documentary *El soldado que no fue* (directed by Leopoldo Gutiérrez [Polo Communications]); and members of the Confederación de las Fuerzas Armadas en Retiro (field notes, September 5, 2013).

37. Luis Burgos spoke of "macho exaggeration" (interview in the Temuco office of the Agrupación de Reservistas [notes, April 23, 2012]); in a representative exchange at a group meeting in Buin, President Víctor Calderón addressed murmurs of profiteering from within the group and projected them outward at other organizations (field notes, June 8, 2014); in an interview in a Providencia café, group leader Fernando Mellado spoke in broad terms of abuses, training, and relationships with prisoners, while acknowledging that many ex-conscripts still would not talk, and a small number would lie (December 21, 2011).

38. References to benefits awarded to others are included, for example, in published testimonies (Seguel Mora, *Al otro lado*, 128–30, 261–62); and in oral histories with Daniel Pizarro (May 11, 2012, La Pincoya, Santiago), Mario Navarro (September 2, 2012, Arica), and Guillermo Raillard (September 3, 2012, Arica). In 2012 interviews in the Temuco office of the Agrupación de Reservistas, group leaders Luis Burgos (notes, April 23) and Claudio de la Hoz (recording and notes, April 27) spoke specifically of the role of others' benefits in the formation of the movement. For an example of the benefits awarded to the exonerados, those returning from exile, and victims of torture providing a model for lobby demands, see Chahuán et al., *Proyecto de acuerdo 287*.

39. In Pozo Almonte in 2012, Tomas P.* spoke of ex-conscript demands in the context of benefits awarded to the exonerados, "fake" political prisoners, and the exiled, who had—by his interpretation—escaped suffering while "humble people" had paid the price (notes, November 1, 2012). Ex-conscripts in different parts of the country made similar comments (interview with Carlos Palma [1973–75, Iquique] in his Ñuñoa almacén [notes, January 18, 2012]); comments made during a lunch attended by group leaders after a regional meeting held in Nacimiento (field notes, July 8, 2012).

40. See, for example, Francisco Chahuán et al., *Proyecto de acuerdo 287* (2007); the 2006 founding document of the group ANESCEC ("Carta fundamental de ANESCEC," *La historia tiene tres aristas falta la nuestra* [blog], January 19, 2006); and the example cited above of the blog maintained by the Agrupación Puente Alto.

41. Elizabeth Lira and Brian Loveman, *Políticas de reparación: Chile 1990–2004* (Santiago: LOM, 2005), 327. The controversy surrounding the exonerados also included accusations of fraud, which again resurfaced in 2013 ("Contraloría cuestionó pensiones de 3.000 exonerados políticos," *Cooperativa.cl*, May 28, 2013).

42. Accounts of service organized around a rupture in former recruits' working lives are included, for example, in a conversation with Patricio M.* (1973) on the edge of a public meeting in Paseo Bulnes led by Fernando Mellado (notes, October 14, 2012); the 2007 testimony by Alonso G.* (1973–75, Angol) (on file in Temuco); the 2006 testimony by Oscar C.* (1974–76, 1976–78) (on file in Temuco); an oral history with Gustavo Martínez (1977–79) (November 1, 2012, Pica); the 2010 testimony by Gustavo D.* (1981, Arica) (on file in Temuco); and testimonies in Seguel Mora, *Al otro lado*, by M.E.B.A. (1975–78, Temuco) (on page 98), T.E.M.A. (1977–79, Porvenir) (100), A.E.G.C. (1987–88, San Bernardo) (138), and E.W.M.F. (60).

43. Interview with Pedro Cáceres (1973–76, Puente Alto) and Manuel Ureta (1973, Puente Alto) as representatives of the Agrupación Puente Alto in Manuel's home in Puente Alto (recording and notes, January 7, 2014).

44. Comisión Nacional D.D.H.H., *Informe*, 98–113.

45. For 1980s pension reform in the context of broader changes to health and education, and a second wave of privatization, see Arriagada, *Por la razón*, 201–16.

46. Stern, *Reckoning with Pinochet*, 336–37.

47. For example, 2007 testimony by Franco C.* (1973–74) (on file in Temuco); 2007 testimony by René B.* (1983–84, Chillán) (on file in the office of REPACH Chillán [on file in Chillán]); and testimony by J.G.J.P., N.D.B.CH., and J.A.H.F. (1987, Santiago) (Seguel Mora, *Al otro lado*, 258).

48. Testimony from 2007 on file in Temuco.

49. For a detailed account of the PRAIS (up to 2004), see Lira and Loveman, *Políticas de reparación*, 373–405.

50. Testimony on file in Temuco.

51. Andrés Solimano, *Chile and the Neoliberal Trap: The Post-Pinochet Era* (Cambridge: Cambridge University Press, 2012), 107.

52. Stern, *Reckoning with Pinochet*, 336–37.

53. Conversation with Manuel T.* (1972–73, 1973–76, Valdivia) in the Temuco office of the Agrupación de Reservistas (recording and notes, April 25, 2012).

54. Stern, *Reckoning with Pinochet*, 182–89; Han, *Life in Debt*, 56–60.

55. For more on the Pinocheques case, the boinazo, the Riggs case, and their resonance, see Wilde, "Irruptions of Memory," 485–86; Stern, *Reckoning with Pinochet*, 54–60, 119–25, 298–300; and Han, *Life in Debt*, 114–17.

56. Han, *Life in Debt*, 103–17.

57. See testimonies in Seguel Mora, *Al otro lado*, by J.G.S. (1975, Angol) (23);

E.V.V.R. (1979, Temuco) (38); L.H.R.S. (Coyhaique) (45); J.J.R.P. (1985, Temuco) (56); R.L.C. (Temuco) (58); W.O.R.H. (Temuco) (90); P.S.H.M. (1976–78, Temuco) (94); F.D.G.B. (Punta Arenas) (106); L.D.T.L.R. (1986–87) (129); J.B.L.I. (1976–78, Temuco and Puerto Montt) (131); C.E.C.S. (1976–79) (149); J.F.F.S. (Porvenir) (167); G.H.A.M. (1975–77, Temuco) (244); T.J.B.LL. (246); and F.J.P.J. (1973, Temuco) (272).

58. Ministry of Defense and Ministry of the Interior and Public Safety, *Informe: Ex soldados conscriptos* (2013).

59. Complaints about missing savings are included, for example, in the 2006 testimony by Camilo L.* (1973) on file in Temuco; testimony by Renato S.* (1974–77, Antofagasta) on file in Chillán; interview with Claudio de la Hoz (1973–75), April 27, 2012; and testimony by J.R.M.M. (1973) (Seguel Mora, *Al otro lado*, 267).

60. Seguel Mora, *Al otro lado*, 244–45.

61. Interview with Carlos Palma (1973–75, Iquique) in his Ñuñoa almacén (notes, October 24, 2012).

62. CH.F.H.M. (1983–85) wrote of the deductions to his pay for "a supposed savings book" and the "unscrupulous pockets" the money presumably ended up in (Seguel Mora, *Al otro lado*, 140). Similarly, a preoccupation with the destination of their savings runs through other testimonies in Seguel Mora, *Al otro lado*, for example, F.L.LL.C. (1979–81, Punta Arenas) (125); C.D.C.A. (1982) (31); J.C.M.G. (1979–81, Coyhaique) (112); and J.G.S. (1975–77, Calama) (23).

63. A gathering of leaders in a domestic residence after a regional meeting held in Nacimiento (field notes, July 8, 2012).

64. A public meeting organized by Fernando Mellado in the municipal stadium in San Bernardo (field notes, December 11, 2011).

65. The names of the individual groups were: Agrupación Social de Reservistas de la Provincia de Osorno (Social Association for Reservists from the Osorno Province); Agrupación Social Libertador Bernardo O'Higgins Riquelme de Chillán (Social Association Bernardo O'Higgins, Liberator of Chile, in Chillán); Agrupación Social de ex soldados conscriptos de Lebu (Social Association of Ex-Conscript Soldiers in Lebu); Centro Social-Cultural AGEXSOLCON, Río Claro de Talca (Social and Cultural Center AGEXSOLCON in Río Claro, Talca Province); Agrupación de Reservistas "Alas Azules" de Puerto Montt, Provincia de Llanquihue ("Blue Wings" Reservists' Association in Puerto Montt, Llanquihue Province); and Agrupación Social de ex soldados conscriptos de Puerto Octay, Provincia de Osorno (Social Association of Ex-Conscript Soldiers in Puerto Octay, Osorno Province) (Comisión Nacional D.D.H.H., *Informe*, 9).

66. The stated objectives of the Ex-conscript Commission's report were to document violations of human rights committed in the context of compulsory military service; compile the details of individual cases; recommend measures to help the victims; and make recommendations regarding reparations (Comisión Nacional D.D.H.H., *Informe*, 8).

67. A small protest by representatives of the National Commission for the Human Rights of Ex-conscripts 1973–1990 in Constitution Square behind the Moneda (field notes, January 29, 2014).

68. Luis Roniger and Mario Sznajder write of a lack of a "rights consciousness" as an obstacle to the human rights movements in the region, and they give Chile as an example of a context where a rights-based consciousness needed to be created in response to the abuses under military rule (*Legacy of Human Rights Violations*, 39–42).

69. Rosella Baronti Barella, "Servicio militar obligatorio: Una mirada psicológica," in *Opinión y Perspectivas 2* (Santiago: CODEPU, 1997), 25; Baronti and Toro, *Derechos de los jóvenes*, 9–10.

70. Montealegre also noted a lack of human rights lawyers willing to help, due, in part, he asserted, to exhaustion at establishing new categories of victim (Montealegre, *Querella criminal*).

71. For an insightful analysis of how the language of torture resonated with former political prisoners as a metaphor for twenty-first-century economic suffering, see Han, *Life in Debt*, 92–128.

72. Conversation with Andrés V.* (1975–77) in the Temuco office of the Agrupación de Reservistas (recording and notes, April 23, 2012).

73. Melissa Gutiérrez, "La eterna batalla legal de los conscriptos de la dictadura," *The Clinic*, June 17, 2015.

74. The legal argument cites the code of military justice, the criminal code, the constitution, and international treaties (Montealegre, *Querella criminal*). For a discussion of conscript responsibility, see chapter 1.

75. Gutiérrez, "La eterna batalla legal."

76. Ibid.

77. *Causa C-25.272, Pereira y otros / Fisco de Chile* (29° Juzgado Civil de Santiago, 2009); *Causa C-21.002, Aliste / Fisco de Chile* (23° Juzgado Civil de Santiago, 2010); and *Causa C-21.313, Allende / Fisco de Chile* (25° Juzgado Civil de Santiago, 2010). The legal argument cited Article 2329 of the civil code for the concept of damage, and the constitution to establish the state's responsibility to compensate for damage (Fernando Monsalve, *Causa C-25272* [2009]).

78. The case histories can be accessed using case codes, year, and court (civil court) or name (court of appeal) on the following sites: http://civil.poderjudicial.cl/CIVILPORWEB/ (civil court) or http://corte.poderjudicial.cl/SITCORTEPORWEB/ (court of appeal).

79. *Causa C-14.431, Avello y otros / Fisco de Chile* (25° Juzgado Civil de Santiago, 2010); and *Causa C-15.448, Valenzuela y otros / Consejo de defensa del estado* (30° Juzgado Civil de Santiago, 2010). The legal argument cited Articles 6, 7, and 38 of the constitution to establish state responsibility, Articles 2314 and 2329 of the civil code to establish the obligation to compensate for damage due to malice or negligence, and international treaties to argue for imprescriptibility (Washington Lizana Ormazábal, *Gabriel Alejandro Avello Astete y otros / Fisco de Chile: C-14431* [2010]).

80. The status of the cases was checked on May 3, 2016. The case histories can be accessed using case codes, year, and court on the following site: http://civil.poderjudicial.cl/CIVILPORWEB/.

81. Patricio Rosende Lynch, subsecretary of the interior, to coordinadora de ex SLC del SMO, April 27, 2009.

82. I am grateful to Patricio Rosende for a conversation in 2014 (July 3), and to the staff of the Human Rights Program of the Interior Ministry for email correspondence in 2014, which provided insights into the program's activities.

83. Rodrigo Hinzpeter, coordinador general of the comando presidencial Sebastián Piñera to the coordinadora nacional de ex soldados conscriptos, 2009.

84. In early 2012, the blog *Para que nunca más*, administered by Fernando Mellado—at this point, cooperating with the coordinadora coalition—provided an overview of the groups represented by the five organizations invited to participate: the Agrupación de Reservistas (president: Luis Burgos) represented groups in Ancud, Talcahuano, Linares, Panguipulli, Galvarino, Temuco, Puerto Montt, Puerto Octay, Chillán (two groups), Parral, Osorno, Coronel, Coelemu, Tomé, San Antonio, Longaví, Santiago, Curacautín, San Fernando, San Francisco de Mostazal, Coyhaique, Iquique, Arica, Calama, Limache, Olmue, Quillota, Quilpué, Queilén, Quellón, Chiloé, Cunco, and Quinteros, as well as the AGEXCO Chile (Asociación Gremial de ex Conscriptos) group; CENAEXSO (Centro Nacional de Ex Soldados Conscriptos) (president: Juan Suárez) represented ex-conscripts in San Vicente de Tagua Tagua, Rengo, Santiago, Chimbarongo, Constitución, Rancagua, Cabildo, Santa Cruz, and Codegua; the Coordinadora Nacional de Ex Conscriptos (president: Víctor Calderón) represented ex-conscripts in Curacaví, Puyehue, Nacimiento, San Carlos, Salamanca, San Antonio, Punta Arenas, Santiago, and Buin; the Asociación Nacional de Ex-Conscriptos (president: Rubén Cornejo) represented ex-conscripts in Antofagasta, Copiapó, Chillán, Curepto, Lontue, Maipú, and Colina; and the Agrupación V Región Centro Norte Sur (president: José Castillo) represented ex-conscripts in Tocopilla, La Ligua, Quilpué, Casablanca, and San Antonio ("A todos los ex soldados del país," *Para que nunca más en Chile* [blog], March 15, 2012).

85. Interview with Juan Díaz and Víctor Calderón in an apartment in Providencia, Santiago (notes, April 26, 2016).

86. Víctor Calderón et al., *Conceptos reparatorios por derechos humanos vulnerados a personal servicio militar obligatorio período 1973–1990: Antecedentes y fundamentos* (2011 or 2012). The groups involved were the Asociación Nacional de Ex-conscriptos, CENAEXO Chile, Agrupación V Región Centro Norte Sur, and Agrupación Nacional de Reservistas. In December 2013 the Ministry of Defense and the Ministry of the Interior and Public Safety prepared a response to the legal arguments made by the ex-conscript lobby (see note 108).

87. Ministry of Defense and Ministry of the Interior and Public Safety, *Informe*, 1.

88. Founding president of the Agrupación SMO, René Rivera, for example, had hoped that the group would become a stakeholder in the reconciliation process but quickly discovered that it would not be possible given the lack of political consensus among members (interview in the cafeteria of the Universidad de Artes, Ciencias y Comunicaciones in Providencia, Santiago [notes, November 27, 2013]).

In 2013 Hernán Montealegre noted the intransigence of victims' groups in recognizing conscript victims and a societal preference to tend to other categories of victims as reasons behind the late emergence of ex-conscript groups and demands (interview in his Santiago office [recording and notes, December 18, 2013]).

In the context of the Malvinas veterans' movement in Argentina, Federico Lorenz writes of the movement's difficult relationship with the human rights movement given the complex mix of political elements and symbolism and the clash of meanings it entailed (*Las guerras por Malvinas*, 224–25). See also Lorenz's analysis of the shifting narratives of the movement and its interaction with postdictatorship memory in Argentina ("Testigos de la derrota," 1–63).

89. Katrien Klep, "Tracing Collective Memory: Chilean Truth Commissions and Memorial Sites," *Memory Studies* 5, no. 3 (2012): 261; Wilde, "A Season of Memory," 46.

90. Comisión Nacional sobre Prisión Política y Tortura, *Informe*, 543.

91. Lira, "Chile," 124.

92. Comisión Nacional de Verdad y Reconciliación, *Informe*, 1:233; Comisión Nacional de Verdad y Reconciliación, *Informe*, 3:253.

93. A regular meeting of the Agrupación SMO in Estación Central, Santiago (field notes, April 27, 2013).

94. Oral history with Carlos Droguett (1973–74, San Bernardo) (June 17, 2013, La Pintana, Santiago).

95. In September 2014 the comuna of Recoleta renamed a street to honor Michel Nash, with Lorena Pizarro, president of the AFDD, attending the inauguration ("Homenaje a Michel Nash en Recoleta 2014," YouTube video, 2:14, posted by "Defendamos Recoleta," October 1, 2014).

96. Baronti Barella, "Servicio militar obligatorio," 26–27; Baronti and Toro, *Derechos de los jóvenes*, 35–45.

97. Daniela Cori Zürrer, "Análisis de caso: Tragedia de Antuco; Crisis en las filas del ejército," in *Gestión de crisis: Teoría y práctica de un modelo comunicacional*, ed. Daniel Halpern (Santiago: RIL Editores, 2010), 30–31.

98. A regional meeting held in a school hall in Nacimiento (field notes, July 8, 2012).

99. Seguel Mora, *Al otro lado*, 210. The exaggeration stems from the extrapolation of a small sample of self-selected testimonies. For a discussion of conscript mortality, see table 2 in the appendix.

100. Untitled film, produced by the Agrupación de Reservistas Defensa Nacional IX Región (MG Producciones, undated). For examples of the use of the Antuco tragedy to contextualize dictatorship-era experiences, see testimony by T.E.S.S. (1973–75) (Seguel Mora, *Al otro lado*, 43–44); the memoir by César Rivas Vergara (1984–86, Manantiales) (*Las Baguales de Manantiales: Mi servicio militar en los ochenta* [Santiago: Dhiyo, 2011], 7 and 49); and José Pérez et al., *Proyecto de acuerdo 851* (2009).

101. Resolution 287, for example, had called for ex-conscript demands to be processed and investigated by existing organisms, including the Commission for Human Rights, Nationality, and Citizenship (Chahuán et al., *Proyecto de acuerdo 287*).

102. Chahín et al., *Proyecto de acuerdo 606*.

103. Fuad Chahín et al., *Proyecto de acuerdo 965* (2013). In 2014, and in the context of the incoming Bachelet government's focus on human rights, Resolution 967 called for reparations, pensions, and damages, and returned to the previous call for access to PRAIS (Amparo Montoya and Constanza Reyes, "Cámara de diputados aprueba

reparación de daño previsional a ex conscriptos," *Biobiochile.cl*, July 2, 2014). Also, the Agrupación Nacional de Ex Soldados Conscriptos del Servicio Militar Obligatorio (SMO) período 1973–1990 changed its name to Corporación para la Integración de los Derechos Humanos de los Ex Conscriptos del período 1973–1990 in early 2015. During a large gathering in August 2015, the coalition's leaders nevertheless continued to frame ex-conscript victimhood in terms of "illegal and arbitrary acts" and not human rights violations (field notes, August 5, 2015).

104. This diversity was evident when, during a gathering after a regional meeting in Nacimiento, the conversation between leaders of local groups and representatives from Santiago drifted toward the legacy of military rule. Those leaders touting the triumph of the Chilean economy met resistance from others highlighting human rights violations, before the discussion was steered back to a common sense of victimhood (field notes, July 8, 2012).

105. For example, Resolution 965 was approved during a hotly debated special session of the Chamber of Deputies on October 1, 2013, that briefly made the ex-conscript cause an example of a broken campaign promise and a chance to score political points during the presidential campaign.

106. See chap. 2, note 1, for examples of interest. In a quirk of judicial timing, members of the Agrupación SMO (1973) were due to give evidence in one of their civil cases about events forty years prior on the day after the 2013 anniversary (interview with Carlos Palma [1973–75, Iquique] in his Ñuñoa almacén [notes, September 6, 2013]). The group's president, Carlos Palma, was also enthused by the apology made by the Chilean Judges' Association in early September for the failures of the courts to protect basic human rights under the military regime ("Jueces piden perdón por sus 'acciones y omisiones' durante la dictadura militar," *El Mercurio*, September 4, 2013).

107. The protest in Santiago was at the end of a three-day march from Rancagua to the capital (field notes, November 13, 2013). Preparations for the march were discussed at a meeting in a local hall in Buin (field notes, November 10, 2013).

108. The report prepared for the Ministries of Defense (Ministerio de Defensa) and the Interior and Public Safety (Ministerio del Interior y Seguridad Pública) opens by citing opinions issued by the comptroller general—8.818 (1986), 55.828 (2006), 43.127 (2008), 22.516 (2010), and 68.029 (2010)—that ex-conscript demands had no basis as they fell outside of the statute of limitations (*Informe*).

With respect to extended service, the report dramatically reduced the scope of the ex-conscript claim. Ex-conscript groups cited Law 11.170 (1953) that set the period of service at one year to argue that service beyond this period was unlawful. The report countered that Article 29 of the law allowed for conscription to be extended by three months in time of peace. Moreover, Law 17.970 (1973) extended service to up to two years, and Decree Law 2.306 (1978), which replaced Law 11.170, established service as up to two years in Article 35. Decree Law 2.306 also specified that in cases of "emergency," "external or internal war," "internal commotion," "latent subversion," or "public calamity," the cohort in the barracks would remain on active duty for as long as "national security" required it. In addition, the subsecretary of war enacted specific extensions that: extended service of the "class of '54" to two years, bringing it in line with Law 17.970 (Supreme Decree 969, 1973); and extended service by a further ninety days for the cohorts that entered on April 1, 1976 (Supreme Decree 609 [1978]), October 1, 1976 (Supreme Decree 1.458 [1978]), and January 2, 1977 (Supreme Decree 1.902 [1978]). As a result, only two limited groups could have had their service unlawfully extended: members of the "class of '54" who had served beyond a year (as the 1973 law was applied retrospectively); and members of subsequent classes who served beyond two years. After studying a sample of two hundred files from the General Archive of the Army, the report's authors concluded that this population represented 7.6 percent of recruits between 1973 and 1990.

With regard to unpaid wages, the report included the ex-conscript argument — citing Articles 3 and 106 of Decree Law 234 (1974) — that conscripts completing their service in the month of September 1973 would receive, from that month, a monthly wage equivalent to 75 percent of a professional soldier's wage for the first year and 100 percent from the second year. It also included the response from the National Directorate of the Army (Dirección Nacional del Ejército) that those payments had been made (less deductions made for services and food) and signed for by conscripts. Records, the army maintained, had been destroyed. The report also included opinions from the comptroller general — 8.818 (1986), 33.416 (1988), and 43.127 (2008) — that military service is a public duty, not a provision of a service nor an employment situation, and therefore recruits are not employees of the state.

The report also addressed the issue of recruits' pensions under the old system (1973–82) and the new system (1983–90). Between 1973 and 1982, in general, no contributions were made for conscripts. Instead, and in line with Law 11.133, time in the barracks was recognized for the purposes of social security. Conscripts who were working formally at the time of their call-up had the right to have contributions made on their behalf in line with Article 8 of Law 10.383; however, this applied to very few recruits, as the majority had not been working formally. Recruits who after their service entered the old system had a period of two years to have their time in the barracks recognized, in which case contributions had to be paid from their own pocket. Between 1983 and 1990, Law 18.423 established that contributions for recruits who were affiliated with a pension fund when called up were the responsibility of the armed forces for the duration of the recruits' service.

The report reviewed 333,865 cases and found that for 159,035 former recruits, military service did not affect their pension (127,155 were not part of the old system when called up [two-thirds went on to affiliate themselves with a private pension fund after 1980], 18,324 recruits drafted after 1983 were part of neither system when conscripted, 13,484 had had payments made, and 72 qualified as exonerados and received compensation); service could have affected the pensions of 119,074 ex-conscripts who served between 1973 and 1982 and were part of the old system (66,322 have no recognition bond [*bono de reconocimiento*] acknowledging their time served [but it is unknown how many would have had a right to one and it is probable, argues the report, that they did not request one because they were not eligible], 13,489 have a bono de reconocimiento that recognizes entirely or partially their years served, and 39,263 have a bono de recono-cimiento that does not recognize time in the barracks, and this group could have a case for demanding recognition and mechanisms have always been open to them); and service could have affected the pensions of 55,756 recruits who served between 1983 and 1990 and were incorporated in a private pension fund at the time of service, and this group only has recourse to legal proceedings.

The report also rejected the complaint that service had disrupted recruits' plans and ambitions for their lives (*proyectos de vida*), claims regarding guard duty at nuclear facilities, and claims relating to deaths or physical and psychological damage. It also rejected claims relating to human rights violations, arguing erroneously—see this chapter—that nothing had prevented ex-conscripts from presenting their cases to the truth and reconciliation commissions and qualifying as victims.

Regarding demands for reparations for those sent to Chile's borders for the poten-tial conflicts with Bolivia, Peru, and Argentina, as well as for those who worked on the carretera austral, the report cited the constitutional obligation to comply with military service and the activities it entailed, provided those activities were legal. The activities described in group's demands were, the report's authors argued, legal.

109. While not having legislation passed under Piñera dealt a significant blow to lobby unity, cracks had already appeared in the years prior. In early 2014, for example, disgruntled ex-conscripts from groups in Punta Arenas, San Ramón, and Maipú met in a mall in San Bernardo with representatives from Buin. They described the process of internal splintering in their respective groups, the loss of faith in the groups' respective leaders, reductions in attendance at meetings, and allegations of profiteering (field notes, February 12).

110. In the context of the Malvinas veterans' movement in Argentina, Lorenz notes that the movement was not homogeneous in terms of politics, but that it had common core demands: recognition, economic, medical, and psychological support, and work and education, as well as a clarification of what happened in the war. He also notes the gap between the public and political face of the veterans' movement in Argentina and veterans' individual and private opinions (*Las guerras por Malvinas*, 226).

Chapter 3. Defending *la Patria*

1. For examples of media interest, see Jorge Rojas, "La pirámide del dictador," *The Clinic*, September 5, 2013; Eleazar Garviso, "Relato de un conscripto," *El Día*, September 8, 2013; Víctor Gómez Lizama, "Así vivieron el 11 los conscriptos en 73," online video posted by Chilevisión, September 10, 2013; "El testimonio de dos ex con-scriptos"; "Las torturas que sufrieron los conscriptos en dictadura," online video, 22:07, of interview on *Radio cooperativa*, posted by "cooperativa.cl," September 11, 2013; and the documentary series *Chile: Las imágenes prohibidas* (Chilevisión, 2013) that aired in the lead-up to the anniversary and included the story of ex-conscript Rafael Silva who grew up in Santiago and after the coup found himself guarding prisoners from his población of La Legua, including his brother, inside the National Stadium.

Rafael had previously told his story as part of the documentaries *Estadio Nacional* (directed by Carmen Luz Parot [CreateSpace, 2003]) and *El soldado que no fue* (directed by Leopoldo Gutiérrez [Polo Communications, 2010]).

2. "Debate junto a Hermógenes Pérez de Arce y ex conscriptos del '73 sobre el 11 de septiembre (Parte 1)," YouTube video, 11:06, from the television show *Mañaneros*, August 28, 2013, posted by "Hola Chile La Red," August 28, 2013; "Debate junto a Hermógenes Pérez de Arce y ex conscriptos del '73 sobre el 11 de septiembre (Parte 2)," YouTube video, 9:25, from the television show *Mañaneros*, August 28, 2013, posted by "Hola Chile La Red," August 28, 2013.

3. Oral history with Félix Pinares (1973-76, Iquique) (June 19, 2013, Recoleta, Santiago).

4. "Debate junto a Hermógenes Pérez de Arce (Parte 2)."

5. J.L.M.V. (1981-83, Punta Arenas), for example, recalled reporting for service alongside other young men with their hearts full of euphoria (Seguel Mora, *Al otro lado*, 222).

6. Brian Loveman, *For la Patria: Politics and the Armed Forces in Latin America* (Wilmington, DE: Scholarly Resources, 1999), 27-31; Gabriel Cid and Alejandro San Francisco, "Introducción: Nación y nacionalismo en Chile, siglo XIX: Balances y problemas historiográficos," in Cid and San Francisco, *Nación y nacionalismo*, 1:xiii-xv; Gabriel Cid and Isabel Torres Dujisin, "Conceptualizar la identidad: Patria y nación en el vocabulario chileno del siglo XIX," in Cid and San Francisco, *Nación y nacionalismo*, 1:23-51; Ricardo Krebs, "Orígenes de la conciencia nacional chilena," in Cid and San Francisco, *Nación y nacionalismo*, 1:3-13; Rafael Pedemonte, "'Cantemos la gloria': Himnos patrióticas e identidad nacional en Chile (1810-1840)," in Cid and San Francisco, *Nación y nacionalismo*, 2:3-38; Trinidad Zaldívar and Macarena Sánchez, "Símbolos, emblemas y ritos en la construcción da la nación: La fiesta cívica republicana; Chile 1810-1830," in Cid and San Francisco, *Nación y nacionalismo*, 2:73-115.

7. Frederick M. Nunn, "Emil Körner and the Prussianization of the Chilean Army: Origins, Process, and Consequences, 1885-1920," *Hispanic American Historical Review* 50, no. 2 (1970): 302; Cid and Torres Dujisin, "Conceptualizar la identidad," 40-44; Krebs, "Orígenes de la conciencia," 20; Pedemonte, "'Cantemos la gloria,'" 24-29; Gabriel Cid Rodríguez, "Memorias, mitos y ritos de guerra: El imaginario de la batalla de Yungay durante la guerra del pacífico," *Universum* 26, no. 2 (2011): 101-20.

8. Jorge Larraín, *Identidad chilena* (Santiago: LOM, 2001), 148-49; Erika Beckman, "The Creolization of Imperial Reason: Chilean State Racism in the War of the Pacific," *Journal of Latin American Cultural Studies* 18, no. 1 (2009): 74-86; Gabriel Cid, "Un icono funcional: La invención del roto como símbolo nacional," in Cid and San Francisco, *Nación y nacionalismo*, 1:221-54.

9. Cid and Torres Dujisin, "Conceptualizar la identidad," 45-46.

10. Luis Barros Lezaeta, "La profesionalización del ejército y su conversión en un sector innovador hacia comienzos del siglo xx," in *La guerra civil de 1891: 100 años hoy*, ed. Luis Ortega (Santiago de Chile: Universidad de Santiago de Chile, 1991), 56.

11. For the makeup of the Chilean forces during the War of the Pacific, the moment of self-reflection, the reform process, and the institutional understanding of la patria and the self-assigned patriotic mission that emerged from that process, see Nunn, "Emil Körner; Frederick M. Nunn, *Yesterday's Soldiers: European Military Professionalism in South America, 1890–1940* (Lincoln: University of Nebraska Press, 1983), 34–37, 49–52, 100–112; Patricio Quiroga and Carlos Maldonado, *El prusianismo el las fuerzas armadas chilenas: Un estudio histórico 1885–1945* (Santiago: Ediciones Documentas, 1988); Enrique Brahm García, "Del soldado romántico al soldado profesional: Revolución en el pensamiento militar chileno, 1885–1940," *Historia* 25 (1990): 5–37; Barros Lezaeta, "La profesionalización del ejército," 49–63; Tótoro Taulis, *La cofradía blindada*; William F. Sater and Holger H. Herwig, *The Grand Illusion: The Prussianization of the Chilean Army* (Lincoln: University of Nebraska Press, 1999); Verónica Valdivia Ortiz de Zárate, "Las fuerzas armadas e integración social: Una mirada histórica," *Mapocho* 48 (2000): 298–99; Enrique Brahm García, *Preparados para la guerra: Pensamiento militar chileno bajo influencia alemana 1885–1930* (Santiago: Ediciones Universidad Católica de Chile, 2003); Carlos Donoso and Juan Ricardo Couyoumdjian, "De soldado orgulloso a veterano indigente: La guerra del pacífico," in Sagredo and Gazmuri, *Historia de la vida privada*, 2:239; and Verónica Valdivia, "La vida en el cuartel," in Sagredo and Gazmuri, *Historia de la vida privada*, 3:204. For a historical overview of military "anti-politics" in Latin America—an institutional disdain for politics and politicians—see Brian Loveman and Thomas M. Davies Jr., "The Politics of Antipolitics," in Davies and Loveman, *The Politics of Anti-Politics*, 3–14. For regional reviews of the modernization process of Latin American militaries, see Nunn, *Yesterday's Soldiers*; and Frederick M. Nunn, "An Overview of the European Military Missions in Latin America," in Davies and Loveman, *The Politics of Anti-Politics*, 32–40.

12. Quiroga and Maldonado, *El prusianismo*, 47–48, 101–5; Brahm García, "Del soldado romántico," 30–32; Sater and Herwig, *The Grand Illusion*, 83; Brahm García, *Preparados para la guerra*, 44; Sergio Grez Toso, *Los anarquistas y el movimiento obrero: La alborada de "la idea" en Chile, 1893–1915* (Santiago: LOM, 2007), 141–44; Valdivia, "La vida en el cuartel," 218–19. Conscription was introduced in Argentina in 1904, shortly after Chile implemented the draft, and for similar reasons: to undergird national unity and instill in young men national values (Lorenz, *Las guerras por Malvinas*, 32).

13. Tobías Barros Ortiz, *Vigilia de armas: Charlas sobre la vida militar destinadas a un joven teniente* (Santiago: Fuerzas Armadas de Chile, 1988), 46–47.

14. Lieutenant Colonel Guillermo Caparro described laborers in the cities and the countryside as contaminated with socialist ideas (Quiroga and Maldonado, *El prusianismo*, 98).

15. As Valdivia notes, soldiers understood democracy as equality within a hierarchy, and not as debate, pluralism, and participation ("La vida en el cuartel," 208).

16. Sater and Herwig, *The Grand Illusion*, 102–8. For the census years 1970, 1982, and 1992, annual cohorts (see table 1), while not being limited to eighteen-year-olds, represent around 18 percent, 18 percent, and 14 percent respectively of the eighteen-year-old male population. See also Spooner, *Soldiers*, 13.

17. Oral history with Félix Pinares (1973–76, Iquique) (June 19, 2013, Recoleta, Santiago).

18. For a regional perspective, see Loveman and Davies, "The Politics of Antipolitics," 8–9.

19. Barros Lezaeta, "La profesionalización del ejército"; Felipe Agüero, "Militares, estado y sociedad en Chile: Mirando el futuro desde la comparación histórica," *Revista de Ciencia Política* 22, no. 1 (2002): 44; Brahm García, *Preparados para la guerra*, 35–49.

20. Frederick M. Nunn, *Chilean Politics 1920–1931: The Honorable Mission of the Armed Forces* (Albuquerque: University of New Mexico Press, 1970); Nunn, "The Military in Chilean Politics, 1924–32," in Davies and Loveman, *The Politics of Anti-Politics*, 83–91; Valdivia Ortiz de Zárate, "Las fuerzas armadas," 297–304; Verónica Valdivia Ortiz de Zárate, *El golpe después del golpe: Leigh vs. Pinochet; Chile 1960–1980* (Santiago: LOM, 2003), 12–20; Valdivia Ortiz de Zárate, "Del 'Ibañismo' al 'Pinochetismo': Las fuerzas armadas chilenas entre 1932–1973," in *Frágiles suturas: Chile a treinta años del gobierno de Salvador Allende*, ed. Francisco Zapata (Mexico City: Colegio de México, 2006), 159–68.

21. Quiroga and Maldonado, *El prusianismo*, 97–101.

22. Valdivia Ortiz de Zárate, "Del 'Ibañismo' al 'Pinochetismo,'" 162–68, 173; Valdivia, "La vida en el cuartel," 217–21.

23. In the literature on the Chilean armed forces, there are two main positions regarding the relationship between local traditions and the influence of postwar counterinsurgency: first, that the military, lacking direction from the civilian government after the return to the barracks, existed in an ideological "vacuum" that was filled by the doctrine of national security, which stressed the threat posed by the internal, communist enemy; and second, that the armed forces' ideological foundation provided a basis for the local implementation of the doctrine of national security (Agüero, "Militares, estado y sociedad," 46; Valdivia Ortiz de Zárate, *El golpe después del golpe*, 12–20; Macarena Muñoz, "Legitimación de las fuerzas armadas en el marco de la doctrina de seguridad nacional: El servicio militar obligatorio como contenedor de la subversión, 1955–1973" [Undergraduate thesis, Universidad de Santiago de Chile, 2005], 6–10; Valdivia Ortiz de Zárate, "Del 'Ibañismo' al 'Pinochetismo,'" 157–59). This chapter follows the second position. For a regional perspective, see Frederick M. Nunn, *The Time of the Generals: Latin American Professional Militarism in World Perspective* (Lincoln: University of Nebraska Press, 1992); Loveman and Davies, "The Politics of Antipolitics," 7–14; and J. Patrice McSherry, *Predatory States: Operation Condor and Covert War in Latin America* (Lanham, MD: Rowman & Littlefield, 2005), 51.

24. Gregory Weeks, "Fighting the Enemy Within: Terrorism, the School of the Americas, and the Military in Latin America," *Human Rights Review* 5, no. 1 (October–December 2003): 16–17; Valdivia Ortiz de Zárate, "Las fuerzas armadas," 295–311; Valdivia Ortiz de Zárate, *El golpe después del golpe*, 21–62; Valdivia Ortiz de Zárate, "Del 'Ibañismo' al 'Pinochetismo,'" 168–80; Valdivia, "La vida en el cuartel," 211, 221–23. For a regional perspective, see Shesko, "Constructing Roads," 22; and McSherry, *Predatory States*, 47.

25. Valdivia Ortiz de Zárate, *El golpe después del golpe*, 63–95; Muñoz, "Legitimación de las fuerzas armadas"; Magasich, *Los que dijeron "no,"* 1:251–431.

26. Valdivia, "La vida en el cuartel," 217, 221–22.

27. Verónica Valdivia Ortiz de Zárate, "'¡Estamos en guerra, señores!': El régimen militar de Pinochet y el 'pueblo,' 1973–1980," *Historia* 43, no. 1 (2010): 163–201.

28. Interview with Claudio de la Hoz (1973–75) in the Temuco office of the Agrupación de Reservistas Defensa Nacional IX Región (Agrupación de Reservistas) (recording and notes, April 27, 2012).

29. Constable and Valenzuela, *Nation of Enemies*, 40; Valdivia, "La vida en el cuartel," 199–201.

30. Descriptions from conversations in the Temuco office of the Agrupación de Reservistas with Hugo M.* (1975–77, Arica) (notes, April 25, 2012); Vicente A.* (1977–78, Temuco) (notes April 25, 2012); Sergio H.* (1987–89) (recording and notes, April 24, 2012); and Alfonso J.* (1989–90) (notes, April 26, 2012); and testimony by J.A.R.F. (1981–83) (Seguel Mora, *Al otro lado*, 78).

31. The meanings of sites of memory are not fixed. They shift and in some cases fade away. Nevertheless, the top-down narratives that monuments typically embody are stories of "timeless" and essential collective identities, a common past, and a shared destiny. This type of commemoration differs from grassroots sites of memory that emerged from civil societies in the wake of military regimes of the late twentieth century. However, both are relevant to ex-conscript memory. Monuments and the cycle of anniversaries discussed here cemented Chile's nineteenth century as the foundation of twentieth-century national identity. The grassroots transformation of former recruits' bodies into sites of ex-conscript memory is discussed in chapter 5.

32. Barros Ortiz, *Vigilia de armas*, 47.

33. Gonzalo Drago, *El Purgatorio* (Santiago: LOM, 1996), 25, 106–8, 132.

34. Candelaria Pérez, or Sargento Candelaria, served in the War of the Confederation, first serving food and drink to the men, but later taking up arms as well.

35. Oral history with Mario Navarro (1973–75, Arica) (September 3, 2012, Arica). Despite the requirement that recruits during the War of the Pacific be at least sixteen years old, boys as young as ten went to war as musicians, and the excitement of going to war drove boys to sign up despite the restriction (Donoso and Couyoumdjian, "De soldado orgulloso," 237–38).

36. Bernardo Guerrero Jiménez, "Bandas de guerra: Jóvenes y nacionalismo en Iquique," *Última Década* 32 (2010): 129–30.

37. Interview with Ricardo Flores (1973, Iquique) and Freddy Valdivia (1973, Iquique) in the Iquique office of the Agrupación de Ex Conscriptos del periodo 1973 a 1990 (notes, October 31, 2012).

38. Armand Mattelart and Michèle Mattelart, *Juventud chilena: Rebeldía y conformismo* (Santiago: Editorial Universitaria, 1970), 213–14.

39. Azun Candina Polomer, "El día interminable: Memoria e instalación del 11 de septiembre de 1973 en Chile (1974–1999)," in *Las conmemoraciones: Las disputas en las fechas "in-felices,"* ed. Elizabeth Jelin (Madrid: Siglo Veintiuno, 2002), 9–48; Bernardo

Guerrero Jiménez, "Bailar, jugar y desfilar: La identidad cultural de los nortinos," *Revistas de Ciencias Sociales* 14 (2004): 79; Stern, *Battling for Hearts and Minds*, 67–76, 412n61; Luis Hernán Errázuriz, "Dictadura militar en Chile: Antecedentes del golpe estético-cultural," *Latin American Research Review* 44, no. 2 (2009): 136–57; Guerrero Jiménez, "Bandas de guerra."

40. For example, testimonies in Seguel Mora, *Al otro lado* by L.F.C.F. (1974) (256); J.P.P., R.D.C.U., and S.A.V.F. (1975) (175); V.E.C.C. (1975) (46); J.C.N. (1978) (86); M.A.M.B. (1978) (91); M.E.D.D. (1979) (159); R.A.S.V. (163); J.L.M.V. (1981) (222); M.D.C.S. (1986) (61–62); and R.A.S.C. (1986) (76).

41. Nelson Castillo Pasten, *Hacé patria, matá un chileno* (2011), 15.

42. Conversation with Enrique P.* (1982–84, Tierra del Fuego) in the Temuco office of the Agrupación de Reservistas (notes, April 24, 2012).

43. Seguel Mora, *Al otro lado*, 110.

44. Seguel Mora, *Al otro lado*, 113.

45. For examples of recollections of service organized around a rupture in patriotism, see testimonies in Seguel Mora, *Al otro lado*, by J.E.P.V. (1973) (45–46); L.F.C.F. (1974–75, Temuco) (256); V.E.C.C. (1975, Temuco) (46); A.D.C.F. (1978, Temuco) (153–54); M.A.M.B. (1978) (91); J.C.N. (1978–80, Punta Arenas) (86); E.V.V.R. (1979, Temuco) (37); M.E.D.D. (1979) (159); J.L.L.F. (1981) (197–98); J.L.M.V. (1981–83, Punta Arenas) (222); M.D.C.S. (1986–87) (61–62); and R.A.S.C. (1986–88, Temuco) (76); testimonies in Washington Lizana Ormazábal, *Complementa demanda de autos: Rol No 14431-2010* (June 19, 2012), by Patricio Hernán Lastarria Cáceres (6) and Alejandro Florín Henríquez Moreno (San Bernardo) (12); and testimonies by Matías C.* (1974, Lautaro) (2007, on file in Temuco), Abraham L.* (1974–75) (on file in Iquique), Tránsito R.* (1974–76, Iquique) (2011, on file in Iquique), Maximiliano F.* (1983, Temuco) (2006, on file in Temuco), and Iván C.* (1983–84, Valdivia) (on file in Chillán).

46. Some former conscripts understood patriotic rupture instead as an aberration, and the metaphor they employ is a "stain" on the uniform, or their "crazy" instructors as hiding "behind" the uniform, while the uniform itself remains a proud symbol of the "timeless" patria. See testimonies in Seguel Mora, *Al otro lado*, by E.V.V.R. (1979, Temuco) (37–38); L.E.B. (1973–76, Calama) (212–13); H.T.L.B. (1976–79, Coyhaique) (219); and N.R.M.P (Punta Arenas) (221–22).

47. For example, 2007 testimony by Roberto H.* (1973–75) (on file in Temuco); conversation with Nicolas P.* (1973–74, Temuco and Antofagasta) in the Temuco office of the Agrupación de Reservistas (recording and notes, April 25, 2012); television interview with Carlos Palma ("Debate junto a Hermógenes Pérez de Arce [Parte 1]"); and 2006 testimony by Miguel M.* (1973, Santiago) (on file in Temuco).

48. Interview with Ricardo Flores (1973, Iquique) and Freddy Valdivia (1973, Iquique) in the Iquique office of the Agrupación de Ex Conscriptos del periodo 1973 a 1990 (notes, October 31, 2012); oral history with Daniel Gómez (1978–80, Punta Arenas) (April 24, 2012, Temuco).

49. Seguel Mora, *Al otro lado*, 128.

50. Testimony on file in Chillán. Similar testimony about hatred for civilians and the need to be able to kill one's own father was given by L.H.D.C. (1973–74) (Seguel Mora, *Al otro lado*, 249–50).

51. "1992 Statement by Former Conscript Jorge Antonio Concha Meza (1991–1992, Peldehue)," CEDOC del Museo de la Memoria y los Derechos Humanos, Fondo CODEPU, Caja 32.

52. Comisión Nacional sobre Prisión Política y Tortura, *Informe*, 165.

53. A regular meeting of the Agrupación SMO in Estación Central, Santiago (field notes, October 19, 2013). Similarly, Ricardo Flores (1973) spoke of conscripts who took advantage of the situation, and, in particular, of rape (interview with Ricardo Flores [1973, Iquique] and Freddy Valdivia [1973, Iquique] in the Iquique office of the Agrupación de Ex Conscriptos del periodo 1973 a 1990 [notes, October 31, 2012]).

54. *El soldado que no fue*. Mary Helen Spooner also writes of recruits' enjoyment of firing their weapons (*Soldiers*, 57).

55. Stern, *Battling for Hearts and Minds*, 336–52.

56. Interview with Carlos Palma (1973–75, Iquique) and Paola García, representatives of the Agrupación SMO, in Paola's office in downtown Santiago (notes, April 15, 2013).

57. Interview with Hernán Montealegre in his Santiago office (recording and notes, December 18, 2013).

58. Oral history with Félix Pinares (1973–76, Iquique) (June 19, 2013, Recoleta, Santiago).

59. Comisión Nacional de Verdad y Reconciliación, *Informe*, 1:240.

60. "El testimonio de dos ex conscriptos"; interview with Pedro Cáceres (1973–76, Puente Alto) and Manuel Ureta (1973, Puente Alto) as representatives of the Agrupación Puente Alto in Manuel's home in Puente Alto (recording and notes, January 7, 2014).

61. For detail on the Lonquén case, see Stern, *Battling for Hearts and Minds*, 156–67.

62. For the impact of Verdugo's *Los zarpazos del puma*, see Stern, *Reckoning with Pinochet*, 14–16.

63. Muñoz, "Soldados de Pinochet."

64. Oral history with Sergio Munizaga (1973–75, Iquique) (November 1, 2012, Pozo Almonte).

65. Interview with Carlos Palma ("Debate junto a Hermógenes Pérez de Arce [Parte 1]," August 28, 2013); oral history with Julio Torres (1973–76, Concepción) (July 8, 2012); testimony by Luis Humberto Castro Valderrama (1973–74, Santiago) (Lizana Ormazábal, *Complementa demanda de autos*, 18).

66. Testimony on file in Iquique. Similarly, Gerardo P.* (1986, Arica) writes of being sent out onto the streets of Arica during protests to beat "innocent" people and shoot at pobladores (2011 testimony on file in Iquique).

67. Lorenz similarly writes of young men in Argentina being seen by the military regime there as both a possible threat and the future of the nation (*Las guerras por*

Malvinas, 41). Also in the Argentine context, Santiago Garaño examines the Argentine military construction of conscription, as well as the institution's fear of infiltration and suspicion of recruits during the 1970s. He argues that the army understood the role of the conscript within a moral code based on ideas of heroism/treason, purity, and danger ("Entre héroes y traidores: Sentidos militares y militantes acerca del rol de los conscriptos en los años 70," *Cuadernos de antropología social*, no. 33 [2011]: 93–110; and "Soldados sospechosos: Militancia, conscripción y fuerzas armadas durante los años setenta," *Contenciosa* 1, no. 1 [2013]: 1–16).

68.   Comisión Nacional de Verdad y Reconciliación, *Informe*, 1:34.

69.   For example, the group Quilapayún revived the history of the 1907 Santa Maria School Massacre of striking miners with its "Cantata de Santa María de Iquique" (1970) and called on soldiers to abandon the barracks and not shoot their "brothers" in "El soldado" (1970) and in their interpretation of the Spanish Civil War song "Dicen que la patria es" (1970). A decade later, the 1980 poem "Dime soldado" by René Tapia recalled the appeals made to young soldiers by the Nueva Canción to remember their roots among the pueblo and not pull the trigger (Corporación José Domingo Cañas, *Tortura en poblaciones del Gran Santiago, 1973–1990: Colectivo de memoria histórica* [Santiago: Corporación José Domingo Cañas, 2005], 169). The patria of the Nueva Canción, leftist appeals, and the 1980 poem to recruits place the figure of the conscript in a revolutionary narrative and a broader political and ideological struggle. The patriotic rupture of ex-conscript memory, however, is different: while compatible with any partisan interpretation of the coup and military rule, it sits outside the ideological struggle between revolution and counterrevolution.

70.   Stern, *Battling for Hearts and Minds*, 23–24; Brian Loveman, "Antipolitics in Chile, 1973–94," in Davies and Loveman, *The Politics of Anti-Politics*, 292–93.

71.   Elisabeth Reimann Weigert and Fernando Rivas Sánchez, *La fuerzas armadas de Chile: Un caso de penetración imperialista* (Havana: Editorial de Ciencias Sociales, 1976), 207.

72.   Ibid., 120–21.

73.   See the following works on Chile in the 1960s, 1970s, and 1980s that confront the "myth" of the radical poor and question the assumption that urbanization led to politicization, the link between poverty and ideological extremism, and the homogeneous political image of workers and pobladores; view the process of politicization as messy, uneven, and dependent on more than socioeconomic factors; and understand immediate and concrete concerns as more relevant to ostensibly political activity than abstract ideological concepts or class antagonism: Alejandro Portes, "The Urban Slum in Chile: Types and Correlates," *Land Economics* 47, no. 3 (1971): 235–48; Howard Handelman, "The Political Mobilization of Urban Squatter Settlements: Santiago's Recent Experience and Its Implications for Urban Research," *Latin American Research Review* 10, no. 2 (1975): 35–72; Peter Winn, "Loosing the Chains: Labor and the Chilean Revolutionary Process, 1970–1973," *Latin American Perspectives* 3, no. 1 (1976): 70–84; Eugenio Tironi, "Pobladores e integración social," *Proposiciones* 14 (1987): 64–84; Ton Salman, "The Diffident Movement: Generation and Gender in the Vicissitudes of the

Chilean Shantytown Organizations, 1973-1990," *Latin American Perspectives* 21, no. 3 (1994): 8-31; and Cathy Lisa Schneider, *Shantytown Protest in Pinochet's Chile* (Philadelphia, PA: Temple University Press, 1995). See also Hal Brands, *Latin America's Cold War* (Cambridge, MA: Harvard University Press, 2010), 53-54, 82, 164-65; and Stern, *Battling for Hearts and Minds*, 395n5. For works that note the complexities of politicization in the pre-coup decade, as well as resignation and fatalism, and a lack of solidarity in the countryside in the 1970s, see Heidi Tinsman, *Partners in Conflict: The Politics of Gender, Sexuality, and Labor in the Chilean Agrarian Reform, 1950-1973* (Durham, NC: Duke University Press, 2002), 255-60; and Conferencia Episcopal de Chile, "Carta pastoral para los campesinos (August 1979)," Fundación de Documentación y Archivo de la Vicaría de la Solidaridad, file Campesinos, Pobladores, A.T.N. 65, 5-7.

74. Tina Rosenberg, *Children of Cain: Violence and the Violent in Latin America* (New York: Penguin Books, 1991), 373-75.

75. Ibid., 380.

76. An observation made, for example, by Carlos Palma (1973-75, Iquique) (interview in his Ñuñoa almacén [notes, November 23, 2011]) and Mario Navarro (1973-75, Arica) prior to a regular meeting of the Agrupación SMO in Estación Central, Santiago (field notes, April 27, 2013). For examples of reservists recalled to the barracks after the coup, see Jovino S.* (see chapter 2); Pedro S.* (1971, 1973) (2006 testimony on file in Temuco); Ignacio C.* (1972, Iquique; 1973, Santiago) (2012 testimony on file in Iquique); and testimonies in Seguel Mora, *Al otro lado*, by H.O.QU.F. (1972-73, 1973-74, 1978) (192) and N.R.U. (1972-73, 1973, 1978) (266-67).

77. Seguel Mora, *Al otro lado*, 163. The period of R.A.S.V.'s service is not listed. The approximate years of his service listed here were deduced from the year of his birth (1962).

78. Rivas Vergara, *Las Baguales de Manantiales*, 18.

79. The risks were outlined, for example, in accounts by Miguel M.* (1973, Santiago) (2006 testimony on file in Temuco); Claudio de la Hoz (1973-75) (interview in the Temuco office of the Agrupación de Reservistas [recording and notes, April 27, 2012]); L.D.T.L.R. (1986-87) (Seguel Mora, *Al otro lado*, 129); and Alberto D.* (1986-88) in the Temuco office of the Agrupación de Reservistas (recording and notes, 26 April 2012). See also note 86.

80. For example, 2011 testimony by Joaquin G.* (1973-74, Iquique) (on file in Iquique).

81. Comisión Nacional de Verdad y Reconciliación, *Informe*, 1:229-30, and vol. 3. See also the similar 1974 case of murdered conscripts Juan Peña and Sergio Pantoja (Observatorio de Justicia Transicional Universidad Diego Portales, *Boletín informativo* 30 [May and June, 2015], 11).

82. See chapter 4.

83. Seguel Mora, *Al otro lado*, 270-71.

84. The commander in chief of the army, Juan Emilio Cheyre, released a statement in 2004 assuming institutional responsibility for crimes of repression under military rule and announcing the end of the Cold War "vision" (*Ejército de Chile: El fin de una visión*). See also chapter 4.

85. Rosella Baronti Barella, "Servicio militar obligatorio," 33. With regard to the alleged mistreatment, Baronti and Álvaro Toro list thirty-three cases of what they term torture, including strikes with fists and feet, extended hours of exercises, beatings, being hung, asphyxia, threats of death or disappearance, threats of being shot, incarceration, humiliation, and, in some cases, sexual abuse (*Derechos de los jóvenes*).

86. See the cases of Hugo Riquelme (1990), Benjamin Ernesto Rodriguez Salazar (1990–91), Juan Jose Iturriaga Rumay (1990), José Cristian Arriagada Melo (1991, Santiago), and Antonio Lenin Sanchez Pardo (1990, Peldehue) ("Casos atendidos por el programa de protección y asistencia de la corporación de promoción y defensa de los derechos del pueblo," CEDOC del Museo de la Memoria y los Derechos Humanos, Fondo CODEPU, Caja 32: 1, 2 and 5–6).

87. Baronti and Toro, *Derechos de los jóvenes*, 22–23, 48.

88. Oral history with Raúl Acuña (1976–78) (April 24, 2012, Temuco).

89. Seguel Mora, *Al otro lado*, 222. Similar accounts of conscript deaths were given by Rodolfo R.* (1976, Punta Arenas) (conversation in the Temuco office of the Agrupación de Reservistas [recording and notes, April 27, 2012]) and Carlos Droguett (1973) (Gutiérrez and Meneses, "El pasado los condena"). For detail on realism in training, see chapter 4.

90. Seguel Mora, *Al otro lado*, 179.

91. "Debate junto a Hermógenes Pérez de Arce (Parte 2)."

92. Comisión Nacional de Verdad y Reconciliación, *Informe*, 1:233–34 and 430–31, and vol. 3.

93. "Familiares de ejecutados funaron homenaje oficial a Soldado Pedro Prado, abatido tras el golpe militar," *Edición Cero*, March 26, 2014.

94. The following account of the echo of Prado's death in Iquique, the 2014 inauguration of a memorial to him, and efforts to confirm the fates of the disappeared detainees Marín and Millar is based a review of local press. See Camilo Aravena Arraigada, "La historia desconocida de Pedro Prado," *Estrella de Iquique*, February 10, 2005; Anyelina Rojas, "El falso enfrentamiento de Marín y Millar contra soldado Pedro Prado: Tres víctimas de la misma dictadura," *Edición Cero*, August 11, 2013; "En medio de manifestaciones inauguraron monumento del soldado Pedro Prado," *El Longino de Iquique*, March 26, 2014; and "Familiares de ejecutados."

95. Aravena Arraigada, "La historia desconocida."

96. "Familiares de ejecutados."

97. "En medio de manifestaciones."

98. "Familiares de ejecutados."

99. Ejército de Chile, *Presentación del ejército de Chile a la comisión nacional de verdad y reconciliación* (Santiago: Ejército de Chile, 1990), 2:59.

100. The Rettig Report lists seventeen conscripts as either disappeared (7), killed by civilians or as the result of "political violence" (7), killed by armed forces personnel (2), or accidentally shot during an anti-guerrilla operation (1) (Comisión Nacional de Verdad y Reconciliación, *Informe*, vol. 3).

101. For more representative figures on conscript mortality, see table 2 and figure 1, both in the appendix.

102. Ejército de Chile, *Presentación del ejército*, vol. 2. For a more detailed discussion on the army's presentation, see Stern, *Reckoning with Pinochet*, 91–93.

103. Saavedra, *Mi propia guerra*, 2–3, 10, 23–25, 31–33, 110–11, 139–41.

104. Seguel Mora, *Al otro lado*, 106. Similar accounts of letter writing are included in testimonies by V.E.G.R. (1978, Punta Arenas) (149) and A.D.C.F. (1978, Temuco) (154).

105. Saavedra, *Mi propia guerra*, 50–51, 128.

106. Descriptions that emphasize the cold, hunger, lack of appropriate clothing and adequate food, illness, and supplementing food by hunting or scavenging are included, for example, in Seguel Mora, *Al otro lado*: S.D.R.S.M. (153); F.D.G.B. (Punta Arenas) (106); L.H.R.S. (Coyhaique) (44–45); G.E.V.R. (1977–79, Lonquimay) (122); P.F.V.R. (1977–80, Punta Arenas) (157–58); J.D.P.D. (1978, Lonquimay) (152); C.L.M.H. (1978–80, Punta Arenas) (150); and E.V.V.R. (1979, Temuco) (37–38); and the 2008 testimony by Luis U.* (on file in Temuco).

107. Saavedra, *Mi propia guerra*, 44, 55, 47, 60, 63, 90, 93.

108. Seguel Mora, *Al otro lado*, 155.

109. Ibid., 122. See also testimonies by C.L.M.H. (1978–80, Punta Arenas) (150) and M.E.D.D. (1979, Punta Arenas) (159–60). In Argentina, and in contrast to Chilean ex-conscript memory, veterans' memory of the Malvinas/Falklands conflict emerged almost immediately after the conflict, in part due to the swift demise of the military regime after the defeat. Federico Lorenz writes of the image of conscripts in the first postwar months as having been victimized more by their superiors and the armed forces than the British, given the terrible conditions and mistreatment they suffered ("Testigos de la derrota," 23–24).

110. Seguel Mora, *Al otro lado*, 146. L.A.J.F. (Punta Arenas) described the same suicide (148), and L.H.R.S. (Coyhaique) wrote of his constant fear during training and the "psychological tension" of waiting for war (44–45).

111. Some former recruits also explain the lust for war or sense of invincibility on the front line as the result of the *chupilca del diablo* (a mixture of gunpowder and red wine or, less commonly, *chicha* [a fermented alcoholic beverage made from apples or grapes]), for example, C.E.C.S. (1976–79) (Seguel Mora, *Al otro lado*, 148–49) and Daniel Gómez (1978–80, Punta Arenas) (oral history [April 24, 2012, Temuco]). According to legend, this concoction was used to fuel bloodlust during the War of the Pacific. Similar rumors about drugging also emerged among recruits who participated in the coup as way to understand their state of mind (Stern, *Remembering Pinochet's Chile*, 140 and 212n6).

112. Seguel Mora, *Al otro lado*, 154. Similarly, J.A.F.M. (1978, Punta Arenas) testified to wanting the war to start to alleviate the anxiety and loneliness of endlessly waiting for it (79).

113. Seguel Mora, *Al otro lado*, 147.

114. Saavedra, *Mi propia guerra*, 54, 118, 119, 128–29 and 132.

115. Photos of meetings featuring the banners on the wall of the Temuco office of the Agrupación de Reservistas (field notes, April 25, 2012). Donoso and Couyoumdjian describe a similar sense of abandonment among veterans of the War of the Pacific ("De soldado orgulloso," 265–66). In the case of Argentine veterans of the Malvinas/Falklands

conflict, Lorenz notes a similar dichotomy: nationalistic pride and the sense that, for many, their prospects had been ruined (*Las guerras por Malvinas*, 220).

116. Valdivia Ortiz de Zárate writes of the SMT adding the shovel to the rifle as part of the military project ("Del 'Ibañismo' al 'Pinochetismo,'" 173). Around the time Valdivia was writing, M.E.E.U. (1987–88) testified that they had not used guns on the CLA; instead, they were supposedly defending la patria with construction tools (Seguel Mora, *Al otro lado*, 247).

117. "Otra provocación Argentina en aguas australes de Chile," *El Mercurio*, February 25–March 3, 1982.

118. "Inaugurados 420 kilómetros de la carretera austral," *El Mercurio*, February 25–March 3, 1982.

119. "'En puerto porvenir se hace soberanía,'" *El Mercurio*, February 25–March 3, 1982.

120. The caption noted by me during a visit to the Military School in Las Condes, Santiago (field notes, May 27, 2012).

121. Another indication of the centrality of the CLA to the Pinochet legacy is the 2013 trip by loyalists from the pro-Pinochet groups Corporación 11 de septiembre and Avanzada nacional to unveil a monument to the "Carretera Presidente Augusto Pinochet Ugarte" on the fortieth anniversary of the coup. While Santiago was the focal point for levels of commemorative activity not seen for a decade, these supporters shifted their commemoration to the far south (Jorge Rojas, "2.000 kilómetros con la barra brava de Pinochet," *The Clinic*, September 27, 2013, 8–12).

122. The term *frontera interior* (internal frontier) is used by Pinochet, for example, in a 1994 speech (Augusto Pinochet Urgarte, *Discursos principales 1990–1994* [Santiago: Geriart, 1995], 91–97). In his geopolitical texts that predated the beginning of the construction of the CLA, Pinochet wrote instead of *fajas fronterizas* (border belts). Military historians credit Pinochet's geopolitics for the realization of the CLA (Ignacio Bascuñán Pacheco, *Breve historia de Aisén y la carretera austral* [Santiago: Estado Mayor General del Ejército, 1984], 99; Germán García Arraigada, "Visión geopolítica de la carretera longitudinal austral," in *Antología geopolítica de autores militares chilenos*, ed. Carlos Meirelles Müller [Santiago: Centro de Estudios e Investigaciones Militares, 2000], 279). For Chilean postwar geopolitics in a regional context, see Nunn, *The Time of the Generals*, 32–33.

123. For the geopolitical significance of the CLA, see Antonio Horvath Kiss, "Aisén y su integración física," *Seguridad Nacional* 21 (1981): 129–36; Bascuñan Pacheco, *Breve historia*; Sergio Castillo Aranguiz, "Chile y su territorio," *Memorial del Ejército* 427 (1987): 104–15; ODEPLAN (Oficina de Planificación Nacional), *La carretera austral y su impacto regional* (Santiago: ODEPLAN, 1988); Germán García Arraigada, "Carretera longitudinal austral: La respuesta a un desafío," *Memorial del Ejército* 433 (1989): 90–122; and García Arraigada, "Visión geopolítica."

124. In the late 1980s, government and military authors placed the construction of the CLA in a tradition of colonization efforts stretching back over a century (Bascuñan Pacheco, *Breve historia*, 39–43; ODEPLAN, *La carretera austral*; García Arraigada, "Carretera longitudinal austral," 97–99).

125. Bascuñan Pacheco, *Breve historia*, 81–83 and 95.

126. Rojas, "La pirámide del dictador," 40.

127. Response from the Estado Mayor General of the army to request for information AD022W-000607 (September 29, 2014).

128. Simon Collier and William F. Sater, *A History of Chile, 1808–2002* (Cambridge: Cambridge University Press, 2004), 366, 370–71.

129. García Arraigada, "Visión geopolítica," 273; García Arraigada, "Carretera longitudinal austral," 91; Horvath Kiss, "Aisén y su integración física," 131–34.

130. The first section—420 km between Chaitén and Coyhaique—was inaugurated in 1982. In 1988 the 242 km section between Puerto Montt and Chaitén and the 337 km section between Coyhaique and Cochrane were opened (ODEPLAN, *La carretera austral*, 1). García Arraigada lists 452.7 km of roads built by the CMT between 1976 and 1989: 106.6 km transversal, and 346.1 km longitudinal ("Carretera longitudinal austral," 103).

131. Bascuñán Pacheco, *Breve historia*, 116.

132. ODEPLAN, *La carretera austral*, 2.

133. Accounts of the cold, lack of clothing, and begging or stealing from local settlers are included, for example, in testimonies in Seguel Mora, *Al otro lado*, by P.R.D.G. (60) and H.H.R.F. (1986) (59).

134. For descriptions that include physical mistreatment, see, for example, testimonies in Seguel Mora, *Al otro lado*, by H.I.P.A. (1982–84) (56); E.R.G.F. (1987) (64); F.J.Z.O. (1990) (58–59); and testimony by Alex Rodríguez (1985, Osorno) (Rojas, "La pirámide del dictador," 44). Quotas and punishments for not meeting them are mentioned, for example, by Braulio S.* (1996–97, Osorno) (2007 testimony on file in Temuco) and Eleodoro Muñoz (1984, Osorno) (Rojas, "La pirámide del dictador," 41). In his 2013 interview, Abad acknowledged the work was tough but professed to know nothing of the mistreatment of conscripts (Rojas, "La pirámide del dictador," 40). Like in the case of abusive training techniques discussed in chapter 4, there seems to have been some room for mistreatment on the CLA resulting in part from the extreme isolation. While abuse took place within a permissive institutional structure, some former recruits report being hidden from visiting dignitaries, including Pinochet (for example, testimony by H.H.R.F. [1986] [Seguel Mora, *Al otro lado*, 59]).

135. Testimony from 2008 on file in Temuco.

136. Rojas, "La pirámide del dictador," 44.

137. R.L.C. wrote of routine rope failures resulting in injuries while drilling through rock on the side of hills (Seguel Mora, *Al otro lado*, 58). Accounts of physical punishments and the use of explosives without training are included, for example, in testimony by M.J.A.R. (1984) (34–35) and statements by Alex Rodríguez (1985, Osorno) (Rojas, "La pirámide del dictador," 44).

138. Seguel Mora, *Al otro lado*, 229.

139. R.F.G.M., for example, who spent six months on the project, describes deaths from accidents as regular, and writes of the CLA as a slaughterhouse (Seguel Mora, *Al otro lado*, 229–30). For Chaitén locals' descriptions of the dead under the

asphalt, see Pía Barros, "Cuando el sur es realmente el sur," in *Autorretrato de Chile*, ed. Alfonso Calderón, Guillermo Blanco, and Pablo Azócar (Santiago: LOM, 2004), 48.

140. Pérez et al., *Proyecto de acuerdo 851* (2009).

141. The figures include one conscript death in 1983, one in 1984, three on the same day in 1985, and two on the same day in 1987 (Estado Mayor General [army], "Response to Request AD022W-000607," September 29, 2014).

142. Seguel Mora, *Al otro lado*, 53. Similarly, M.A.L.A. (1976) volunteered in Osorno to go to Yelcho to work on the CLA, and describes it as six months of physical abuse and punishment (55).

143. Seguel Mora, *Al otro lado*, 52–54.

144. Accounts of time spent on the CLA that refer to the construction site as a "concentration camp," a "Nazi concentration camp," a "forced labor camp," or a "prisoner of war camp" are included, for example, in testimonies in Seguel Mora, *Al otro lado*, by R.H.A.H. (93); D.R.M. (1988, Lautaro) (19–20); J.R.Ñ.C. (1982–83) (120); M.J.A.R. (1984) (34–35); and R.M.B.M. (1987) (112).

145. The use of "glorious" in inverted commas is included, for example, in testimonies in Seguel Mora, *Al otro lado*, by M.R.C.P. (1987) (63) and S.Q.U.O. (1988–89, Temuco) (42). Examples of descriptions of recruits as "slaves" are included in testimonies by R.F.G.M. (Seguel Mora, *Al otro lado*, 229–30); L.D.T.L.R. (1986–87) (Seguel Mora, *Al otro lado*, 128–29); and Esteban W.* (1986–87) (2007, on file in Temuco).

146. Seguel Mora, *Al otro lado*, 64–65.

147. Bascuñán Pacheco, *Breve historia*, 107.

148. Testimony on file in Chillán. See also testimony by M.D.C.S. (1986–87) (Seguel Mora, *Al otro lado*, 61–62).

149. Bascuñán Pacheco, *Breve historia*, 80.

150. "El cuerpo militar del trabajo," *Memorial del Ejército de Chile* 333 (1966): 120–21.

151. Horvath Kiss, "Aisén y su integración física," 132. See also Bascuñán Pacheco, *Breve historia*, 103.

Chapter 4. Making Men

1. Conversation with Andrés V.* (1975–77) in the Temuco office of the Agrupación de Reservistas Defensa Nacional IX Región (Agrupación de Reservistas) (recording and notes, April 23, 2012).

2. Seguel Mora, *Al otro lado*, 33.

3. The descriptions listed are from testimonies in Seguel Mora, *Al otro lado*, 91, 146, and 280; the 2006 testimony by Miguel M.* (1973, Santiago) (on file in Temuco); a conversation with Cristóbal L.* (1982–84) in the Temuco office of the Agrupación de Reservistas (recording and notes, April 24, 2012); and an oral history with Guillermo Raillard (1973, Arica) (September 3, 2012, Arica).

4. Vicaría Pastoral Juvenil, "Documento de trabajo para asesores de pastoral juvenil zona rural costa, vicaría pastoral juvenil," Fundación de Documentación y Archivo de

la Vicaría de la Solidaridad, File Campesinos, Pobladores, A.T.N.: 65 B. The document is undated, but descriptions and references within it suggest it is from the late 1970s or early 1980s.

The sociological discussion during the dictatorship about whether Chile's poor and working-class enjoyed a youth—a period between childhood and adulthood—often conflated youth with time spent in the educational system and equated leaving school to work with becoming an adult (Juan Eduardo García-Huidobro and José Weinstein, eds, *Diez entrevistas sobre la juventud chilena actual* [Santiago: CIDE, 1983], 128; Oscar Corvalán and Ricardo Andreani, "La preparación para el trabajo de la juventud chilena," in Generaciones, *Los jóvenes*, 77–78).

5. For works that highlight the heterogeneity of Chile's youth and caution against identifying youth in general with the "myth" of the rebellious youth of the 1960s, or the politically active youth of the 1980s, see García-Huidobro and Weinstein, *Diez entrevistas*, particularly 13–14; Mario Marcel, "Juventud y empleo: Drama en tres actos y un epilogo," in *Juventud chilena: Razones y subversiones*, ed. Irene Agurto, Gonzalo de la Maza, and Manuel Canales (Santiago: ECO, 1985), particularly 23; Víctor Muñoz Tamayo, "Imágenes y estudios cuantitativos en la construcción social de 'la juventud' chilena: Un acercamiento histórico (2003-1967)," *Última Década* 20 (2004): 71–94; and Stern, *Battling for Hearts and Minds*, 261–70.

6. Oral history with Daniel Gómez (1978–80, Punta Arenas) (April 24, 2012, Temuco).

7. Interview with Daniel Gómez (1978–80, Punta Arenas) in the Temuco office of the Agrupación de Reservistas (notes, April 26, 2012).

8. See chapter 2.

9. Mattelart and Mattelart, *Juventud chilena*, 21, 28, 73–75, 191, 240–41.

10. Oral history with Luis Cortés (1973, Iquique) (November 1, 2012, Pozo Almonte).

11. Eugenio Gutiérrez and Paulina Osorio, "Modernización y transformaciones de las familias como procesos del condicionamiento social de dos generaciones," *Última Década* 29 (2008): 113–14. For descriptions of childhood work within a family unit in early-century Viña del Mar and 1940s Cadillal, see Luis Vildósola Basualto, "'A los 14 años mi papá se sentía que ya era un hombre': El sujeto popular en Viña del Mar durante la primera mitad del siglo XX," *Última Década* 3 (1995): 2; and Yanko González Cangas, "Óxidos de identidad: Memoria rural en el sur de Chile (1935-2003): Tomo II, anexos" (PhD diss., Universitat Autónoma de Barcelona, 2004), 70–71.

12. Mattelart and Mattelart, *Juventud chilena*, 84. Seven years prior to the Mattelart and Mattelart survey, the 1960 census found that 80 percent of rural males over five years of age did not attend any type of educational institution, and that 20.6 percent of rural males (12–14 years of age) and 79.7 percent of rural teenagers (15–19 years of age) were economically active (Dirección de Estadística y Censos, *Censo población 1960* [Santiago: La Dirección de Estadística y Censos, 1969], 76, 95, and 111).

13. Tinsman, *Partners in Conflict*, 135 and 141.

14. Mattelart and Mattelart, *Juventud chilena*, 226–29.

15. Ibid., 216–18.

16. Florencia E. Mallon, *"Barbudos,* Warriors, and Rotos: The MIR, Masculinity, and Power in the Chilean Agrarian Reform, 1965–74," in *Changing Men and Masculinities in Latin America*, ed. Matthew C. Gutmann (Durham, NC: Duke University Press, 2003), 179–89; Tinsman, *Partners in Conflict*, 235.

17. The recollections of Manuel Barrientos, a rural activist with the Revolutionary Left Movement (Movimiento de Izquierda Revolucionaria), reveal a similar city/country divide among activists. See Mallon, *"Barbudos,* Warriors, and Rotos," 188–202.

18. Oral history with Fernando Gálvez (1973–75, Calama) (November 11, 2012, Pica).

19. Oral history with Guillermo Navarrete (1974, Arica) (April 26, 2012, Temuco).

20. Oral history with Daniel Pizarro (1973–75, Los Andes and Santiago) (May 11, 2012, La Pincoya, Santiago).

21. Marcel, "Juventud y empleo," 16; Irene Agurto and Gonzalo de la Maza, "Ser joven poblador en Chile hoy," in Agurto et al., *Juventud chilena*, 66; José Weinstein, "Juventud urbano-popular y familia," in Agurto et al., *Juventud chilena*, 74; Oscar Corvalán Vasquez and Erika Santibañez, *Situación socio-laboral de la juventud chilena: Diagnóstico y perspectivas* (Santiago: CIDE, 1986), 14; José Weinstein, *Los jóvenes pobladores en las protestas nacionales (1983–1984): Una visión sociopolítica* (Santiago: CIDE, 1989), 9–11.

22. Weinstein, *Los jóvenes pobladores*, 18. Similarly, psychologist Domingo Asún noted spikes in school abandonment around the fourth and again around the seventh or eighth year of primary education in the población of José María Caro (García-Huidobro and Weinstein, *Diez entrevistas*, 28).

23. Oral history with Luis Zapata (1981–83, Punta Arenas) (May 25, 2012, Estación Central, Santiago).

24. Weinstein, "Juventud urbano-popular," 74–76; Weinstein, *Los jóvenes pobladores*, 17; Corvalán and Santibañez, *Situación socio-laboral*, 124. Similarly, psychologists working with young pobladores in Santiago found that they felt that their parents blamed them for being unemployed and not contributing to the household (Eugenia Weinstein, "Los del patio de atrás," in *La campaña del no: Vista por sus creadores* [Santiago: Ediciones Melquíades, 1989], 21).

25. Vicaría Pastoral Juvenil, "Documento de trabajo." See also Conferencia Episcopal de Chile, "Carta Pastoral," 5–7.

26. Similarly, a church report from 1978 on families that used soup kitchens in the south laments family breakdown, unemployment, absent fathers, a lack of parental control, child vagrancy, and children's feelings of responsibility leading them to abandon school and look for work they never end up finding ("Minuta exposición grupo ad hoc [July, 1978]," Fundación de Documentación y Archivo de la Vicaría de la Solidaridad, File Campesinos, Pobladores, A.T.N.: 65 B).

27. Alejandra Serrano and Gonzalo Vío, "Capacitación de los jóvenes rurales: Algo más que un problema de empleo," in Generaciones, *Los jóvenes*, 88–89.

28. Cecilia Díaz and Esteban Durán, *Los jóvenes del campo Chileno: Una identidad fragmentada* (Santiago: GIA, 1986), 16–20, 77; Serrano and Vío, "Capacitación de los jóvenes," 93–94.

29. In the early 1980s, agronomist Ximena Quezada identified the eighth year of school as the stage that young people in the countryside began abandoning school to work (García-Huidobro and Weinstein, *Diez entrevistas*, 128).

30. Conversation with Diego C.* (1983–85, Tierra del Fuego) in the Temuco office of the Agrupación de Reservistas (notes, April 24, 2012).

31. Loveman, "Antipolitics in Chile, 1973–94," 269–71.

32. García-Huidobro and Weinstein, *Diez entrevistas*, 130 (see also interviews with psychologist Domingo Asún [28–29] and sociologist Irene Agurto [80 and 91]). Similarly, in the late 1980s, Eugenia Weinstein observed an absence of historical memory and an inability to define or give an example of democracy ("Los del patio de atrás," 22).

33. Jorge Rojas and Gonzalo Rojas, "Auditores, lectores, televidentes y espectadores: Chile mediatizado, 1973–1990," in Sagredo and Gazmuri, *Historia de la vida privada*, 3:392. At around the time Diego entered the barracks, the Vicaría Pastoral Juvenil working document described TV in the countryside as the only permanent distraction ("Documento de trabajo").

34. Constable and Valenzuela, *Nation of Enemies*, 155–56; Rojas and Rojas, "Auditores, lectores," 399, 414–17.

35. Ruth Aedo-Richmond and Mark Richmond, "Recent Curriculum Change in Post-Pinochet Chile," *Compare: A Journal of Comparative and International Education* 26, no. 2 (1996): 201–2.

36. Descriptions taken from Paulo Hidalgo, "Los jóvenes y la política: Una relación conflictiva," in Generaciones, *Los jóvenes*, 233; and interviews with Priest Miguel Ortega and sociologist Irene Agurto in García-Huidobro and Weinstein, *Diez entrevistas*, 36–41 and 89–91. For a discussion of the heterogeneity of Chilean youth from the 1980s to the first decade of the twenty-first century, see Stern, *Reckoning with Pinochet*, 191–92 and 263–64.

37. García-Huidobro and Weinstein, *Diez entrevistas*, 24–26. See also Corvalán and Santibañez, *Situación socio-laboral*, 103–5.

38. Weinstein, "Los del patio de atrás," 21–23. Also cited by Stern (*Battling for Hearts and Minds*, 364–65).

39. Vicaría Pastoral Juvenil, "Documento de trabajo"; Agurto and de la Maza, "Ser joven poblador," 65; Weinstein, "Juventud urbano-popular," 83; Corvalán and Santibañez, *Situación socio-laboral*, 13 and 125; Díaz and Durán, *Los jóvenes del campo*, 16–17; Serrano and Vío, "Capacitación de los jóvenes," 93; José Olavarría, *¿Hombres a la deriva? Poder, trabajo y sexo* (Santiago: FLACSO, 2001), 15–17, 21–26; Olavarría, "Masculinidades, poderes y vulnerabilidades," in *Chile 2003–2004: Los nuevos escenarios (inter)nacionales*, ed. FLACSO (Santiago: FLACSO, 2004), 227–44; Heidi Tinsman, "More Than Victims: Women Agricultural Workers and Social Change in Rural Chile," in Winn, *Victims of the Chilean Miracle*, 276; Gutiérrez and Osorio, "Modernización y transformaciones," 110; Jaime Barrientos, "Sexual Initiation for Heterosexual

Individuals in Northern Chile," *Sexuality Research and Social Policy* 7, no. 1 (2010): 38–41.

40. For examples from the mid-twentieth century of the importance of military service as a familial and societal threshold to manhood, see Yanko González Cangas, "Servicio militar obligatorio y disciplinamiento cultural: Aproximaciones al caso Mapuche-Hilliche en el siglo XXI," *Alpha* 24 (2007): 111–37. For a similar dynamic in neighboring Argentina, see Lorenz, "Testigos de la derrota," 7; and Lorenz, *Las guerras por Malvinas*, 32.

41. Conversation with Álvaro B.* (1976–78) in the Temuco office of the Agrupación de Reservistas (recording and notes, April 27, 2012).

42. Conversation with Eduardo F.* (1976–78) in the Temuco office of the Agrupación de Reservistas (recording and notes, April 26, 2012). Eduardo did his military service with the air force.

43. Conversation with Alberto C.* (1976, Temuco) in the Temuco office of the Agrupación de Reservistas (recording and notes, April 26, 2012).

44. Oral history with Luis Cortés (1973, Iquique) (November 1, 2012, Pozo Almonte).

45. Testimony from 2011 on file in Iquique.

46. Testimony from 2011 on file in Temuco. Similar testimonies are given by J.A.H.S. (1973) (Seguel Mora, *Al otro lado*, 261) and by Angelo J.* (1973) (2009 testimony on file in Temuco).

47. Weinstein, *Los jóvenes pobladores*, 15; Leonor Cariola and Cristián Cox, "La educación de los jóvenes: Crisis de la relevancia y calidad de la enseñanza media," in Generaciones, *Los jóvenes*, 20.

48. Serrano and Vío, "Capacitación de los jóvenes," 92–93; Díaz and Durán, *Los jóvenes del campo*, 36–38.

49. Cariola and Cox, "La educación de los jóvenes," 19–38; Díaz and Durán, *Los jóvenes del campo*, 74; Weinstein, *Los jóvenes pobladores*, 15; Corvalán and Santibañez, *Situación socio-laboral*, 75–82.

50. García-Huidobro and Weinstein, *Diez entrevistas*, 27.

51. José Weinstein, "Víctimas y beneficiarios de la modernización: Inventario (incompleto) de cambios en la juventud pobladora (1965–1990)," *Proposiciones* 20 (1991): 261. Similarly, a survey conducted in Quinta Normal revealed that 10 percent of secondary students wanted to enter the armed forces, which was seen as the most secure and structured career path (Cariola and Cox, "La educación de los jóvenes," 27–28).

52. Díaz and Durán describe how many rural recruits in the mid-1980s spoke fondly of finding a sense of family and belonging in the barracks. Nevertheless, military service did not help them find work (*Los jóvenes del campo*, 75–76). See also Corvalán and Santibañez, *Situación socio-laboral*, 96.

53. Rivas Vergara, *Las Baguales de Manantiales*, 10–13.

54. Emilio Meneses, Patricio Valdivieso, and Carlos Martin, "El servicio militar obligatorio en Chile: Fundamentos y motivos de una controversia," *Estudios Públicos* 81 (2001): 129–75.

55. Baronti Barella, "Servicio militar obligatorio, 28; Baronti and Toro, *Derechos de los jóvenes*, 11.

56. Marcela Ramos Arellano and Juan Guzman de Luigi, *La extraña muerte de un soldado en tiempos de paz (El caso de Pedro Soto Tapia)* (Santiago: LOM, 1998), 32. See also Daniela Cori Zürrer, "Análisis de caso: Tragedia de Antuco; Crisis en las filas del ejército," in *Gestión de crisis: Teoría y práctica de un modelo comunicacional,* ed. Daniel Halpern (Santiago: RIL Editores, 2010), 30; and Claudio Fuentes, "Comentario: ¿Quieren los jóvenes un servicio militar obligatorio?" *Revista Fuerzas Armadas y Sociedad* 9, no. 1 (1994): 31. In the case of Argentina and recruits who fought in the Malvinas/ Falklands war, Lorenz writes of prospective recruits being vaguely aware of physical and psychological mistreatment inside the barracks, but that many still wanted to do their service (*Las guerras por Malvinas*, 36–38).

57. Meneses et al., "El servicio militar obligatorio," 153–55. For the role of the high-profile death of a recruit in 1994 in sparking reform of military service in Argentina, see Silla, "Ahora todo va a cambiar," 214–15; and Santiago Garaño, "The Opposition Front against Compulsory Military Service: The Conscription Debate and Human-Rights Activism in Post-dictatorship Argentina," *Genocide Studies and Prevention* 5, no. 2 (2010): 174–190.

58. Discussion in the Temuco office of the Agrupación de Reservistas (field notes, April 23, 2012).

59. Poblete, "Servicio militar."

60. Ibid.

61. Around the transition, Cariola and Cox noted how mothers in low socio-economic areas attached the same expectations (discipline, good habits, and values) to secondary school that they once attached to military service ("La educación de los jóvenes," 29). See also Fuentes, "Comentario," 31; and Claudio Fuentes, "Los jóvenes y el servicio militar obligatorio: Estudio de encuestas de opinión pública," *Fuerzas Armadas y Sociedad* 8, no. 2 (1993): 27–36.

62. Meneses et al., "El servicio militar obligatorio," 147n52.

63. "El servicio militar: Tu oportunidad de crecer" (Meneses et al., "El servicio militar obligatorio," 154). In 2013 the slogan was "Tu futuro empieza ahora" (Your future starts now).

64. Conversation with Vicente* A. (1977–78, Temuco) in the Temuco office of the Agrupación de Reservistas (notes, April 25, 2012).

65. Former conscripts testified to the existence of "valleys of tears" along the length of the country and across classes in, for example, testimonies in Seguel Mora, *Al otro lado* (35, 39, 63, 88, 106, 126, 145, 151, 147, 177, 186, 202); testimonies on file in Temuco by Oscar C.* (1974–75, 1976–78, Calama) (2006), Arturo L* (1979) (2006), Cristóbal L.* (1982–84) (2006), Isaac G.* (1983) (2006), Esteban W.* (1986, La Unión) (2007), Felipe Q.* (1975–77, Calama) (2008), Franco G.* (1988, Valdivia) (2008), Gustavo D.* (1981, Arica) (2010); 2007 testimony on file in Chillán by René B.* (1983–84, Coyhaique); 2012 testimony on file in Iquique by Hernán F.* (1976–78, Iquique); and a conversation with Pablo F.* (1982–84) in the Temuco office of the Agrupación

de Reservistas (notes, April 27, 2012). Punishments in the "valley of tears" are also described in testimonies in Lizana Ormazábal, *Complementa demanda de autos*, by Fernando Gaete (4–5), Luis Muñoz (1973) (7), Darwin Canales (1979–81, Iquique and Arica) (9), and Fernando Reyes (Arica) (22–23).

66. Conversation with Cristóbal L.* (1982–84) in the Temuco office of the Agrupación de Reservistas (recording and notes, April 24, 2012). Similarly, J.H.B. (1982, Tierra del Fuego) wrote of instructors beating recruits to "make them men" (Seguel Mora, *Al otro lado*, 110).

67. Testimony by F.D.G.B. (Punta Arenas) (Seguel Mora, *Al otro lado*, 106).

68. Seguel Mora, *Al otro lado*, 83.

69. Exercises are described, for example, in Comisión Nacional D.D.H.H., *Informe*, 80–81; and throughout Seguel Mora, *Al otro lado*.

70. R. Wayne Eisenhart, "You Can't Hack It Little Girl: A Discussion of the Covert Psychological Agenda of Modern Combat Training," *Journal of Social Issues* 31, no. 4 (1975): 14–15; William Arkin and Lynne R. Dobrofsky, "Military Socialization and Masculinity," *Journal of Social Issues* 34, no. 1 (1978): 158–64; Richard Holmes, *Acts of War: The Behavior of Men in Battle* (New York: Free Press, 1989), 36 and 47; Ronald D. Crelinsten, "In Their Own Words: The World of the Torturer," in Crelinsten and Schmid, *The Politics of Pain*, 47; and Joanna Bourke, *An Intimate History of Killing: Face-to-Face Killing in Twentieth-Century Warfare* (New York: Basic Books, 1999), 67–70. In a regional context, see Gill, "Creating Citizens," 533; Silla, "Ahora todo va a cambiar," 216; and Valdivia, "La vida en el cuartel," 203.

71. Comisión Nacional D.D.H.H., *Informe*, 77.

72. Seguel Mora, *Al otro lado*, 151.

73. Conversation with Eugenio T.* (1977–79) in the Temuco office of the Agrupación de Reservistas (notes, April 25, 2012).

74. Accounts of humiliation, powerlessness, and anger are included, for example, in the 2007 testimony by Matías C.* (1974, Lautaro) (on file in Temuco) and the 2011 testimony by Patricio V.* (1973–76) (on file in Iquique).

75. Suicides, suicide attempts, suicidal thoughts, and self-mutilation are reported in conscript testimony as a response to physical mistreatment and psychological pressure. Accounts of one or multiple suicides were included, for example, in testimonies in Seguel Mora, *Al otro lado*, by D.A.M.E. (227), J.H.Z.C. (284), L.A.J.F. (148), J.J.S.S. (Santiago) (215), J.R.B.C. (Entrevientos) (228), L.G.S.V. (Punta Arenas) (240), P.A.V.R. (Puerto Montt) (212), R.N.O.F. (1974–75, Santiago) (191), L.A.H.P. (1975, Calama) (225), V.R.A.P. (1975–77, Arica) (235), P.P.C.L. (1975–77) (264), P.J.F.G. (1975–77, Melipeuco and Arica) (234), H.T.L.B. (1976–79, Coyhaique) (218–19), H.M.N.C. (1978–79, Punta Arenas) (146), M.P.Q.H. (1978–80, Punta Arenas) (224), J.G.A.G. (1979–82, Punta Arenas) (228), L.A.P.E. (1981–83, Lautaro) (227), D.A.B.T. (1981–83, Tierra del Fuego) (148), C.D.C.A. (1982, Tierra del Fuego) (31), S.Q.S. (1982, Porvenir) (235), L.B.Y.A. (1983, Santiago) (27), L.O.C.O. (1983–85, Punta Arenas) (228), J.A.V.S. (1985, Valdivia) (231), and J.H.R.P. (1988–89, Coyhaique) (221); in conversations in the Temuco office of the Agrupación de Reservistas with Javier R.*

(1981–83, Tierra del Fuego) (notes, April 23, 2012), Cristóbal L.* (1982–84) (recording and notes, April 24, 2012), and Diego C.* (1983–85, Tierra del Fuego) (notes, April 24, 2012); and the memoir by Saavedra (*Mi propia guerra*, 33).

Unsuccessful suicide attempts made by recruits' compañeros are described in Seguel Mora, *Al otro lado*, by C.G.A.T. (188), J.E.V.S. (1975–76) (220), O.A.P.M. (1975–77, Lautaro) (82), and F.L.LL.C. (1979–81, Punta Arenas) (126), also by Isidoro G.* (1987–89, Punta Arenas) (testimony on file in Chillán). Recruits' own suicide attempts and suicidal thoughts are also described in testimonies in Seguel Mora, *Al otro lado*, by M.A.H.S. (Iquique) (87), H.F.P.C. (1987) (141), and CH.F.H.M. (1983–85, Punta Arenas) (140); and by Osvaldo F.* (1977–78, Santiago) (conversation on the edge of a public meeting in Paseo Bulnes in downtown Santiago led by Fernando Mellado [notes, October 14, 2012]).

Former recruits give accounts of fellow recruits' acts of self-mutilation in testimonies in Seguel Mora, *Al otro lado*, by R.A.J.C. (Temuco) (71), M.A.G. (1973) (190), M.A.F.G. (1976, Coyhaique) (102), J.C.P.A. (1985–87, Temuco) (183), and J.R.B.C. (Entrevientos) (228); and the 2012 testimony by Hernán F.* (1976–78, Iquique) (on file in Iquique). Gregorio Arriaza (1978–79, San Antonio, Tejas Verdes) spoke of his own self-mutilation in a press interview (Carlos Rodríguez, "Veteranos de una guerra que no fue . . . ," *La Estrella*, October 24, 2012). For a case of self-mutilation from the early posttransition years, see "Casos atendidos por el programa de protección y asistencia de la corporación de promoción y defensa de los derechos del pueblo," CEDOC del Museo de la Memoria y los Derechos Humanos, Fondo CODEPU, Caja 32: 3.

76. Seguel Mora, *Al otro lado*, 190.

77. Interview with Claudio de la Hoz (1973–75) in the Temuco office of the Agrupación de Reservistas (recording and notes, April 27, 2012).

78. From two separate conversations with Pedro M.* (1976–78): outside the Moneda as group leaders met with government representatives inside (notes, January 19, 2012); and on the edge of a public meeting in Paseo Bulnes led by Fernando Mellado (notes, October 14, 2012). For accounts of the use of the white blouse in combination with other punishments, see, for example, testimonies in Seguel Mora, *Al otro lado*, by E.V.V.R. (1979) (38) and M.A.H.S. (87).

79. Descriptions cited are from 2009 testimony by Angelo J.* (1973–74) (on file in Temuco); testimony by F.R.Q.R. (Seguel Mora, *Al otro lado*, 230); and 2008 testimony by Víctor L.* (1978–80, Temuco) (on file in Temuco).

80. Seguel Mora, *Al otro lado*, 196. Similar accounts of rage, frustration, and a sense of powerless in the face of the denigration of their mothers and sisters are included, for example, in testimony by J.P.G.Y. (1973–75, Temuco) (Seguel Mora, *Al otro lado*, 284) and a conversation with Alfonso J.* (1989–90) in the Temuco office of the Agrupación de Reservistas (notes, April 26, 2012). The 2012 report by the Exconscript Commission also describes, in general terms, the humiliation of having to say or sing denigrating things about loved ones (Comisión Nacional D.D.H.H., *Informe*, 86).

81. "Pelao [pelado]" is a term for conscript soldier, and "culiao [culiado]" is a highly offensive term (literally "fucked in the ass"). For examples of gendered insults,

see the 2006 testimony by Maximiliano F.* (1983, Temuco) and the 2010 testimony by Gustavo D.* (1981, Arica), both on file in Temuco. For similar accounts from the 1990s, see Baronti and Toro, *Derechos de los jóvenes*, 47. For similar examples in the Bolivian context, see Gill, "Creating Citizens," 534-36. For gendered insults and the language of family as part of basic training, see Holmes, *Acts of War*, 46.

82. Seguel Mora, *Al otro lado*, 186. Similar accounts of sexual humiliation and forced sexual activity are included in testimonies by E.E.V.M. (1977-79, Lautaro) (170); J.P.P, R.D.C.U., and S.A.V.F. (1974, Lautaro) (175); Maximiliano F.* (1983, Temuco) (2006 testimony on file in Temuco); and René B.* (1983-84, Chillán and Coyhaique) (2007 testimony on file in Chillán).

83. Seguel Mora, *Al otro lado*, 160.

84. Seguel Mora, *Al otro lado*, 116-17.

85. Oral history with Raúl Acuña (1976) (April 24, 2012, Temuco). Similar descriptions about naked exercises or punishments in the extreme cold of the south are made by N.R.M.P. (Punta Arenas) (Seguel Mora, *Al otro lado*, 222); Claudio de la Hoz (1973-75) (interview in the Temuco office of the Agrupación de Reservistas [recording and notes, April 27, 2012]); Arturo L.* (1979, Punta Arenas) (2006 testimony on file in Temuco); Javier R.* (1981-83, Tierra del Fuego) (conversation in the Temuco office of the Agrupación de Reservistas [notes, April 23, 2012]); and Ricardo H.* (1988) (testimony on file in Chillán).

86. Oral history with Sergio Munizaga (1973-75, Iquique) (November 1, 2012, Pozo Almonte).

87. Interview with Samuel Fuenzalida in the humanities faculty of the University of Chile (recording and notes, October 11, 2012).

88. Miguel Tejeda Lawrence, *El Servicio Militar Obligatorio* (Santiago: Soc. Imp. i Lit. Universo, 1920), 29.

89. Food was also used as a mechanism of control and humiliation, with recruits being set the impossible task of consuming meals or hot liquids while jogging or in only seconds. Miguel Saavedra writes of being served his food from a height in Chile's south, where most was carried away by the wind (*Mi propia guerra*, 65). In other instances, instructors made recruits eat off the floor like animals, or consume excrement or their own vomit (for example, testimonies by J.C.M.G. [1979-81, Coyhaique] [Seguel Mora, *Al otro lado*, 112] and Iván C.* [1983-84, Valdivia] [testimony on file in Chillán]).

90. Seguel Mora, *Al otro lado*, 275.

91. Comisión Nacional de Verdad y Reconciliación, *Informe*, 1:38.

92. Seguel Mora, *Al otro lado*, 26, 32, 246, 294-96, and 2006 testimony by Bernardo D.* (1982, Tierra del Fuego) on file in Temuco.

93. Testimony by L.A.J.F. (1978-79) (Seguel Mora, *Al otro lado*, 147). Similar accounts of stealing (crabs, sheep, eggs, pets) or begging in order to eat were given in an interview with Raúl Acuña (1976-78) (April 24, 2012) and testimony by T.J.B.LL. (Seguel Mora, *Al otro lado*, 246). Federico Lorenz writes of Argentine veterans of the Malvinas conflict recalling having to steal or hunt in order to eat ("Testigos de la derrota," 23).

94. Seguel Mora, *Al otro lado*, 182-83.

95. Oral history with Daniel Gómez (1978–80, Punta Arenas) (April 24, 2012, Temuco).

96. Individual descriptions of the "prisoner camp" and "prisoner" exercises are made by, for example, Jaime R.* (1973) (2006 testimony on file in Temuco); Matías C.* (1974, Lautaro) (2007 testimony on file in Temuco); Maximiliano F.* (1983, Temuco) (2006 testimony on file in Temuco); and Alfredo C.* (1984, Punta Arenas) (2007 testimony on file in Temuco); in testimonies in Seguel Mora, *Al otro lado* by B.L.F.R. (1975, Temuco) (168), M.A.G.L. (1975, Temuco) (201), L.H.V.E. (1975–77, San Pedro de Atacama) (226), P.J.F.G. (1975–77) (234), F.F.G.J. (1975–77, San Pedro de Atacama) (241), P.R.J.V. (1979–81, Punta Arenas) (200), F.L.LL.C. (1979–81, Punta Arenas) (126), D.I.M.B. (1980–82, Valdivia) (203), A.M.M.C. (1983, sector "Ojo Bueno") (186), and D.A.G.V. (1983–85, Punta Arenas) (132); in testimony by Pedro Andrés Naigual (1988) (Comisión Nacional D.D.H.H., *Informe*, 88); and in testimonies in Lizana Ormazábal, *Complementa demanda de autos* by Jaime Luis Salinas Santibáñez (1976, Santiago) (3), José Alfonso Gamboa Ibacache (1985, Arica) (7), Luis Alberto Rodríguez Leviman (1973, Antofagasta) (8–9), Darwin Iván Canales Cartes (1979–81, Iquique and Arica) (9), Ricardo Rolando Gajardo Correa (10), Juan Eduardo Gálvez Ortiz (19), Luis Javier Cifuentes Arrey (20), and Mauricio Fredy Rosales Nietzschmann (1984, Santiago) (21).

A 2012 psychologist's report on ex-conscripts in Osorno described "prisoner camp" exercises as involving stripping and tying up the "prisoners" in front of the battalion, trying to extract "confessions" by applying electrical current to different parts of the their bodies — including the testicles and nipples — or submerging their heads or entire bodies in barrels of water (Comisión Nacional D.D.H.H., *Informe*, 141). In his 2011 memoir, César Rivas Vergara (1984–86, Manantiales) described his cohort being woken up in the night and interrogated one by one. Rivas was pressed for his superiors' names and at the same time told not to give them. After refusing to give names, he was secured to a metal frame and subjected to "the guitar." After the exercise, instructors explained that the exercise was called campo de prisioneros and that the enemy would be one hundred times worse (*Las Baguales de Manantiales*, 25–28).

97. Comisión Nacional D.D.H.H., *Informe*, 54, 58, 62, 67, 74. The remaining drawings labeled "CP" show beatings, the use of tear gas, and the application of electricity (54 and 67). The report also includes sketches, dated from the late 1970s to 1990, of methods not explicitly marked as "CP" exercises that depict beatings, often while naked; stress positions, including exposure to extreme climatic conditions; the guitar and beatings with a stick while suspended by the wrists (51–55, 57–60, 63–64, 68–70, 73–74). The document also includes four black-and-white photos that reportedly depict "prisoner training" in the northern desert (82–84). Copies of the same photos were handed to me in April 2012 by Fernando Mellado, and they appear in Gutiérrez's 2010 documentary *El soldado que no fue*. I was unable to locate the photographer or otherwise verify the photos.

98. Comisión Nacional D.D.H.H., *Informe*, 87; Rivas Vergara, *Las Baguales de Manantiales*, 26–27.

99. Seguel Mora, *Al otro lado*, 37–38.

100. Saavedra, *Mi propia guerra*, 23–25.

101. Ibid., 160. Alvarado's use of the term "improvisations" recalls the characterization of human rights abuses against political prisoners in the 1990s as "excesses."

102. César Rivas Vergara (1984–86, Manantiales) describes how when beating recruits with sticks was prohibited, instructors used pipes instead (*Las Baguales de Manantiales*, 33). There is some evidence, particularly in the case of the carretera austral, of conscripts and the conditions conscripts faced being hidden from visiting superiors (Seguel Mora, *Al otro lado*, 59 and 64).

103. Conversation with Tomas P.* (1977) in Pozo Almonte (notes, November 1, 2012); the unpublished memoir by Guillermo Raillard (1973–75, Iquique) ("Clase 54" [2011]); and testimonies in Seguel Mora, *Al otro lado*, by L.O.D.S. (Puerto Montt) (51), P.R.J.V. (1979–81, Punta Arenas) (200), and J.D.U.G. (1980) (179).

104. Elizabeth Lira and Brian Loveman understand Pinochet's repressive apparatus within a history of torture and abuse in Chile that spans the nineteenth to the twenty-first centuries ("Torture as Public Policy," 95–106).

105. For the evolution and propagation of the theory and techniques of anti-"subversive" torture, including the CIA research programs "Bluebird" (1950), "Artichoke" (1951), and MKUltra (1953–63), US military training and survival courses, the role of the School of the Americas, and US training manuals including the "Kubark Counterintelligence Interrogation" handbook, see McSherry, *Predatory States*, 35–58; Alfred W. McCoy, *A Question of Torture: CIA Interrogation, from the Cold War to the War on Terror* (New York: Holt, 2007); Ruth Blakeley, "Still Training to Torture? US Training of Military Forces from Latin America," *Third World Quarterly* 27, no. 8 (2006): 1439–61; and Michael Otterman, *American Torture: From the Cold War to Abu Ghraib and Beyond* (London: Pluto Press, 2007).

106. McSherry, *Predatory States*, 16–17, 49, 53, 57–58, and 71; Wolfgang S. Heinz, "The Military, Torture, and Human Rights: Experiences from Argentina, Brazil, Chile, and Uruguay," in Crelinsten and Schmid, *The Politics of Pain*, 69–71; John Dinges, *The Condor Years: How Pinochet and His Allies Brought Terrorism to Three Continents* (New York: New Press, 2004), 107; Blakeley, "Still Training to Torture?," 1441–44; Jose Quiroga and James M. Jaranson, "Politically-Motivated Torture and Its Survivors: A Desk Study Review of the Literature," *Torture* 16, nos. 2–3 (2005): 10; Gabriel Salazar, *Las letras del horror*, vol. 1, *La DINA* (Santiago: LOM, 2011), 7–46.

107. For "stress inoculation" and SERE training, its evolution as a response to Chinese and Soviet methods, the Korean War as a catalyst for SERE programs, and the techniques practiced by US personnel, see Anthony P. Doran, Gary Hoyt, and Charles A. Morgan III, "Survival, Evasion, Resistance, and Escape (SERE) Training: Preparing Military Members for the Demands of Captivity," in *Military Psychology: Clinical and Operational Applications*, ed. Carrie H. Kennedy and Eric A. Zillmer (New York: Guilford Press, 2006), 241–61; Otterman, *American Torture*, 28–41; and Stephen Soldz, "Healers or Interrogators: Psychology and the United States Torture Regime," *Psychoanalytic Dialogues* 18, no. 5 (2008): 592–613.

108. Heinz, "The Military," 85. The written "code" for how Chilean soldiers should behave as prisoners of war was still based on a respect for international law and prisoner rights (Ejército de Chile, Comandancia en Jefe, *Reglamento de instrucción individual de combate (para todas las armas)* [Santiago de Chile: Ministerio de Defensa Nacional, 1976], 325–26).

109. The ideas of "hardness" also shaped the notion of loyalty within the DINA, which purged or killed officers it deemed "soft" (Comisión Nacional de Verdad y Reconciliación, *Informe*, 2:744).

110. Descriptions by former conscript and former boina negra "González" as well as reservist lieutenant "Pérez" in Reimann Weigert and Rivas Sánchez, *La fuerzas armadas*, 48–49, 184 and 188, 193–96.

111. Comisión para el Esclarecimiento Histórico, *Guatemala: Memoria del silencio* (1999), 2:59–60.

112. The report by the Ex-conscript Commission describes prisoner exercises as an opportunity for professional soldiers to practice on conscripts (Comisión Nacional D.D.H.H., *Informe*, 87). For examples of this type of practical torturer training in a regional context, see Archdiocese of São Paulo, Brazil, *Torture in Brazil: A Shocking Report on the Pervasive Use of Torture by Brazilian Military Governments, 1964–1979*, trans. Jaime Wright, ed. Joan Dassin (Austin: University of Texas Press, 1998), 13–15; and Crelinsten, "In Their Own Words," 49–50.

113. Interview with Claudio de la Hoz (1973–75) in the Temuco office of the Agrupación de Reservistas (recording and notes, April 27, 2012).

114. Seguel Mora, *Al otro lado*, 222.

115. Oral history with Daniel Gómez (1978–80, Punta Arenas) (April 24, 2012, Temuco). Similar ratios are reported from the late 1960s (Reimann Weigert and Rivas Sánchez, *La fuerzas armadas*, 188 and 192); the mid-1970s (interview with Ricardo Flores [1973, Iquique] and Freddy Valdivia [1973, Iquique] in the Iquique office of the Agrupación de Ex Conscriptos del periodo 1973 a 1990 [notes, October 31, 2012]); the late 1970s (Saavedra, *Mi propia guerra*, 94); 1984 (Rivas Vergara, *Las Baguales de Manantiales*, 52–53); and 2011 (Tania Horta Valles, "Servicio militar voluntario: Puertas para una movilidad social ascendente" [Undergraduate thesis, Universidad Academia de Humano Cristiano, 2011], 72–73).

116. Testimony from 2008 on file in Temuco.

117. Descriptions of eating dog or cat meat or drinking animal blood during "survival exercises" are included in testimonies by F.D.G.B., M.A.M.B., and E.A.F.C. (Seguel Mora, *Al otro lado*, 106, 90–91, 168); Jaime R.* (1973) (2006 testimony on file in Temuco); and Darwin Canales (1979–81, Iquique and Arica) (Lizana Ormazábal, *Complementa demanda de autos*, 9).

118. Seguel Mora, *Al otro lado*, 178. Similar accounts of ritualistic killings of animals (most often dogs), forced contact with the carcasses, consuming the flesh, consuming the blood, or painting recruits' faces with the blood are included, for example, in testimonies by M.P.Q.H. (1978–80, Punta Arenas), P.E.V.R. (1977–80, Punta Arenas), and G.V.A. (1985, La Unión) (Seguel Mora, *Al otro lado*, 224, 157–58, 62); testimony

by an unnamed former conscript (1981) (Comisión Nacional D.D.H.H., *Informe*, 154); the 2011 memoir by César Rivas Vergara (1984–86, Manantiales) (*Las Baguales de Manantiales*, 25–28); testimonies in Lizana Ormazábal, *Complementa demanda de autos* by José León (1975, Santiago and Pisagua) (5), Roy del Carmen Sepúlveda Arias (1979, Iquique) (12), and Leopoldo del Carmen Marin Vargas (1974) (19); and the memoir by Miguel A. Saavedra (1977–79, San Bernardo) (*Mi propia guerra*, 20–21).

119. Seguel Mora, *Al otro lado*, 177.

120. Seguel Mora, *Al otro lado*, 146.

121. Oral history with Raúl Acuña (1976) (April 24, 2012, Temuco).

122. For example, testimonies in Seguel Mora, *Al otro lado*, by R.H.A.H. (Chaitén) (93) and P.E.G.M. (1983–84, Punta Arenas) (207).

123. For the intersection of military training and psychology, as well as the development of "realism" in training and "battle inoculation," see Holmes, *Acts of War*, 53; Bourke, *An Intimate History*, 60–76, 83–90; Edgar Jones, "The Psychology of Killing: The Combat Experience of British Soldiers during the First World War," *Journal of Contemporary History* 41, no. 2 (2006): 230; and Dave Grossman, *On Killing: The Psychological Cost of Learning to Kill in War and Society* (New York: Back Bay Books, 2009), 30–37, 251–54.

124. Holmes, *Acts of War*, 53–54; Bourke, *An Intimate History*, 140–43 and 150.

125. Heinz, "The Military," 67.

126. For pre-coup examples: Raúl Valenzuela, "La guerra psicológica," *Memorial del Ejército de Chile* 42, no. 225 (1948): 33–46; S. Haraldsen, "La guerra psicológica," *Memorial del Ejército de Chile* 45, no. 243 (1951): 105–10; Baillif, "Psicología y las fuerzas armadas," *Memorial del Ejército de Chile* 57, no. 315 (1963): 30–38; and Jorge Court Moock, "La psicología y el ejército," *Memorial del Ejército de Chile* 59, no. 327 (1965): 71–88. For detail on the *White Book of the Change of Government in Chile* (*Libro blanco del cambio de gobierno en Chile*), known as the *White Book*, see Stern, *Battling for Hearts and Minds*, 46–50.

127. For examples of army publications on the psychology of instincts theory, combat, obedience, habits, and the need for realism in training, see Gustave Le Bon, "Factores psicológicos de las luchas guerreras," *Memorial del Ejército de Chile* 8 (1913): 813–25; Taboureau, "Elementos de psicología militar," *Memorial del Ejército de Chile* 19, no. 2 (1924): 548–64; Rafael Poblete, "Psicología militar," *Memorial del Ejército de Chile* 20, no. 2 (1925): 50–56; Leon Lavín, "Plan para un curso de capacitación psicológica," *Memorial del Ejército de Chile* 23, no. 169 (1940): 529–31; and "La psicología de las tropas en la defensa," trans. Eduardo Gutiérrez, *Memorial del Ejército de Chile* 25, no. 176 (1942): 785–90.

128. Ejército de Chile, Comandancia en Jefe, *Reglamento de instrucción*, 11–12.

129. Comisión para el Esclarecimiento Histórico, *Guatemala*, 55–56. See also the report of the truth commission in Ecuador: La Comisión de la Verdad, *Sin verdad no hay justicia: Informe de la comisión de la verdad*, vol. 1, *Violaciones de los derechos humanos en Ecuador 1984–2008* (Quito: Ediecuatorial, 2010), 105–6.

130. Comisión para el Esclarecimiento Histórico, *Guatemala*, 58.

131. Ibid., 60.

132. D.R. Oficina de Derechos Humanos del Arzobispado de Guatemala, *Guatemala: Nunca más*, vol. 2, *Los mecanismos del horror* (1998).

133. Seguel Mora, *Al otro lado*, 242.

134. Seguel Mora, *Al otro lado*, 203. Similar accounts of killing animals (most often dogs) as well as eating their flesh or drinking their blood are included in, for example, testimonies by M.L.L. (Calama) and L.A.R.H. (1975–77, Temuco) (Seguel Mora, *Al otro lado*, 87 and 282); and Vicente* A. (1977–78, Temuco) (conversation in the Temuco office of the Agrupación de Reservistas [notes, April 25, 2012]).

135. Drago, *El purgatorio*, 97–100.

136. Testimony from 2008 on file in Temuco.

137. Seguel Mora, *Al otro lado*, 194. Accounts of whippings as punishment, often with wires, and usually in front the group, are included, for example, in testimonies in Seguel Mora, *Al otro lado*, by J.F.F.S. (Porvenir) (166), S.E.C.P. (Angol, 1973–75) (285), H.O.QU.F. (1972–73, 1973–74, 1978) (192–93), J.I.M.J. (1974–76, Temuco and Calama) (199), P.F.V.R. (1977–80, Punta Arenas) (158); and testimonies on file in Temuco by Roberto H.* (1973–75) (2007), Marco D.* (1973) (2007), and Alejandro S.* (1973–75) (2006). Lashings had been a staple of military discipline throughout the region since the nineteenth century (Loveman, *For* la Patria, 42; Sater and Herwig, *The Grand Illusion*, 30 and 104).

138. Seguel Mora, *Al otro lado*, 193.

139. Muñoz, "Soldados de Pinochet."

140. A former Chilean torturer described how desensitization of conscripts to suffering worked in tandem with the dehumanization of prisoners (Crelinsten, "In Their Own Words," 48).

141. Testimony from 2009 on file in Temuco.

142. Gutiérrez and Meneses, "El pasado los condena."

143. Holmes, *Acts of War*, 53–54; Bourke, *An Intimate History*, 76, 140–50; McCoy, *A Question of Torture*, 52–53.

144. Seguel Mora, *Al otro lado*, 132–33.

145. Conversation with Osvaldo F.* (1977–78, Santiago) on the edge of a public meeting in Paseo Bulnes in downtown Santiago led by Fernando Mellado (notes, October 14, 2012). Similar accounts of ongoing feelings of powerlessness, shame, bitterness, and sadness at watching fellow conscripts being punished are included, for example, in testimonies by O.A.S.S., J.I.M.J. (1974–76, Temuco and Calama), and L.E.B. (1973–76, Calama) (Seguel Mora, *Al otro lado*, 165, 199–200 and 212); and the 2008 testimony by Franco G.* (1988, Valdivia) on file in Temuco. See also Comisión Nacional D.D.H.H., *Informe*, 86. Similarly, the Valech Report describes feelings of culpability, humiliation, and defenselessness produced in political prisoners who were forced to watch torture (Comisión Nacional sobre Prisión Política y Tortura, *Informe*, 503–4).

146. In practice, the tradition of penal and police abuse that had provided a basis for systematic torture under the regime continued into the twenty-first century (Brian Loveman and Elizabeth Lira, "Marco histórico: Terrorismo de estado y tortura en

Chile," in *De la tortura no se habla: Agüero versus Meneses*, ed. Patricia Verdugo [Santiago: Catalonia, 2004], 181–211; Lira and Loveman, "Torture as Public Policy").

147. Baronti and Toro, *Derechos de los jóvenes*, 22–23; Baronti and Alfaro, "Mecanismos y efectos psicológicos," 49–51.

148. Baronti and Toro, *Derechos de los jóvenes*, 9–10.

149. Jan Hopman, "El machismo: Su relación con los excesos al interior de las fuerzas armadas," in *Hombres: Identidades y Violencia*, ed. José Olavarría (Santiago: FLACSO, 2001), 141–42.

150. "Casos atendidos," 9.

151. Oral history with Luis Zapata (1981–83, Punta Arenas) (May 25, 2012, Estación Central, Santiago).

152. In its 2012 report, the Ex-conscript Commission acknowledges the importance of piedra alumbre as an anaphrodisiac in ex-conscript "collective memory" but argues it was instead used to cover up the effects of mistreatment by "dissolving" bruises. Nevertheless, the commission also ascribes to piedra alumbre long-term and terminal health effects (Comisión Nacional D.D.H.H., *Informe*, 91–92).

153. Descriptions taken from an interview with Claudio de la Hoz (1973–75) in the Temuco office of the Agrupación de Reservistas (recording and notes, April 27, 2012); an oral history with Julio Torres (1973–76, Concepción) (July 8, 2012, Nacimiento); an interview with Víctor Calderón in a café in downtown Santiago (recording and notes, June 26, 2012); and a press interview with Ricardo Flores (1973, Iquique) ("Ex conscriptos ariqueños pedirán indemnización por las consecuencias de haber usado piedra alumbre," *Soyarica*, May 22, 2013).

154. The use of piedra alumbre as an anaphrodisiac is also mentioned by former conscripts who are not involved with the movement and do not make a connection to health complaints (interview with Samuel Fuenzalida [1973–75] in the humanities faculty of the University of Chile [recording and notes, October 11, 2012]; statement by Manuel Carrillo Vallejos [Santiago, 1973] in Diego Rivera, "A 30 años del golpe: Combatientes del golpe frente a frente," *El periodista* 2, no. 43 [2003]; former political prisoners [Kunstman Torres and Torres Ávila, *Cien voces*, 44–45]; and Hernán Valdés, *Diary of a Chilean Concentration Camp* [London: Victor Gollancz, 1975], 90).

155. Lorenz notes how in Argentina, like in Chile, military service marked an important threshold to manhood. However, unlike Chilean ex-conscripts who argued that service had hindered their passage to manhood, groups representing Malvinas veterans insisted that war had made them men. The Argentine narrative was part of a rejection of the infantilization of the figure of the conscript in postdictatorship Argentina ("Testigos de la derrota," 7 and 42–44).

156. The realities of male unemployment, the impossibility (for most Chileans) of the gendered division of labor, globalization and cultural exchange, demographic changes, and the HIV/AIDS pandemic and increased visibility of the homosexual community opened up space for different conceptions of family, manhood, and sexuality (Olavarría, "Masculinidades," 233–34; Sergio Bernales Matta, "Las relaciones familiares en el Chile de los 90," *Proposiciones Sur* 26 [1995]: 15–21).

157. For work on masculinities in nineteenth-century Chile, see Gabriel Salazar and Julio Pinto, *Historia contemporánea de Chile*, vol. 4, *Hombría y feminidad* (Santiago: LOM, 2010), 16–53. For the evolution and shape of twentieth-century, working-class, and poor masculinity, see Thomas Miller Klubock, "Working-Class Masculinity, Middle-Class Morality, and Labor Politics in the Chilean Copper Mines," *Journal of Social History* 30, no. 2 (1996): 436–40; Karin Rosemblatt, "Masculinidad y trabajo: El salario familiar y el estado de compromiso, 1930–1950," *Proposiciones* 26 (1995): 70–75; Rosemblatt, *Gendered Compromises: Political Cultures and the State in Chile, 1920–1950* (Chapel Hill: University of North Carolina Press, 2000), 59–71 and 150; Heidi Tinsman, "Wife-Beating and Sexual Control in Rural Chile, 1964–1988," in *The Gendered Worlds of Latin American Women Workers*, ed. John D. French and Daniel James (Durham, NC: Duke University Press, 1997), 273–82; Tinsman, *Partners in Conflict*, 132–46; and Tinsman, "More Than Victims," 267–76.

For more on the construction of masculinity in Chilean society and its relationship to family in the twentieth century, see José Olavarría, "Ser padre en Santiago de Chile," in *Paternidades en América Latina*, ed. Norma Fuller (San Miguel: Fondo Editorial, 2000), 130–31; Olavarría, *¿Hombres a la deriva?*, 15–17; José Olavarría, "Men at Home? Child Rearing and Housekeeping among Chilean Working-Class Fathers," in Gutmann, *Changing Men and Masculinities*, 334; Olavarría, "Masculinidades," 227–44; Ximena Valdés, "El lugar que habita el padre en Chile contemporáneo: Estudio de las representaciones sobre la paternidad en distintos grupos sociales," *Polis* 8, no. 23 (2009): 389–90; and Gutiérrez and Osorio, "Modernización y transformaciones," 106–9.

158. Seguel Mora, *Al otro lado*, 195.

159. Ibid., 124.

160. Ibid., 289–90. D.D.T.O. (1975, Lautaro) provides a similar testimony (118).

161. Ibid., 200.

162. Comisión Nacional D.D.H.H., *Informe*, 100.

163. Testimony on file in Temuco.

164. The Ex-conscript Commission, for example, describes how the physical and psychological effects of service transcend the individual to affect the family (Comisión Nacional D.D.H.H., *Informe*, 91).

165. Conversation with Andrés V.* (1975–77) in the Temuco office of the Agrupación de Reservistas (recording and notes, April 23, 2012).

166. For ex-conscript claims for damages and the 2011 reemergence of the case, see "Familias de ex soldados afectados por radiación demandarán al estado," *Cooperativa .cl*, October 1, 2009; "Comisión chilena de energía nuclear desestimó que ex conscriptos fallecieran por radiaciones," *Cooperativa.cl*, October 2, 2009; "Ex conscriptos afectados con radiación demandaron el estado," *La Nación*, October 20, 2009; "Muere ex conscripto que vigiló reactores nucleares en Santiago," *El Mostrador*, January 22, 2010; Claudia Uriqueta, "Las secuelas de los ex conscriptos que vigilaron dos centros nucleares en Chile," *La Tercera*, March 20, 2011; and "Diputado Ojeda no descarta que se vuelva a investigar denuncias de contaminación en centros nucleares chilenos," *Cámara de Diputados de Chile*, March 22, 2011.

167. Victor Calderón et al., *Conceptos reparatorios*. Luis Burgos, a coauthor of the document, also spoke of the effects of radiation on conscripts in the context of outlining the damage done to conscripts under Pinochet (interview in the Temuco office of the Agrupación de Reservistas [notes, April 23, 2012]).

168. Interview with Daniel Gómez (1978–80, Punta Arenas) in the Temuco office of the Agrupación de Reservistas (notes, April 23, 2012).

169. Claudio de la Hoz (1973–75) in the Temuco office of the Agrupación de Reservistas (recording and notes, April 27, 2012).

170. Domestic violence as a problem among ex-conscripts and as a result of military service was discussed by group leaders, for example, in Santiago (gathering of group leaders outside the Moneda after meeting with government representatives inside [field notes, January 19, 2012]) and Nacimiento (gathering in a domestic residence after a regional meeting held in Nacimiento [field notes, July 8, 2012]). Also, a 2010 report by a social worker in Osorno highlighted familial conflict among ex-conscripts fueled by domestic violence, authoritarian parenting, and alcoholism (Comisión Nacional D.D.H.H., *Informe*, 110).

171. Conversation with Pedro M.* (1976–78) outside the Moneda as group leaders met with government representatives inside (notes, January 19, 2012). A similar account was given by Sergio H.* (1987–89) (conversation in the Temuco office of the Agrupación de Reservistas [recording and notes, April 24, 2012]).

172. Comisión Nacional D.D.H.H., *Informe*, 94.

173. Testimony from 2006 on file in Temuco. Similarly, Luis Burgos, president of the group in Temuco, described how in addition to reservists' short tempers, emotional instability, flashbacks, fears, and paranoias, disagreements over money and former conscripts' inability to provide for their families also fueled domestic violence (interview in the Temuco office of the Agrupación de Reservistas [notes, April 23, 2012]).

174. Comisión Nacional D.D.H.H., *Informe*, 141.

175. Ibid., 93. This same rupture between educational expectations and difficult working lives is articulated, too, in Lizana Ormazábal, *Gabriel Alejandro Avello*.

176. Testimony from 2010 on file in Temuco.

177. Conversation with Diego C.* (1983–85, Tierra del Fuego) in the Temuco office of the Agrupación de Reservistas (notes, April 24, 2012). Similar accounts about the physical effects of service being passed on via the ex-conscript's reduced ability or inability to work, support a family, or educate their children, or all three, are included, for example, in testimonies by J.H.H. (1983–85, Punta Arenas) (Seguel Mora, *Al otro lado*, 104) and Matías C.* (1974, Lautaro) (2007 testimony on file in Temuco).

178. Testimony from 2006 on file in Temuco.

179. Interview with David Wiederhold (1977–79) beside a rural road outside Temuco (recording and notes, April 27, 2012).

180. As cited in Rodríguez, "Veteranos de una guerra que no fue . . ." Similar descriptions of service denying recruits the ability to perform the role of provider they had already assumed are in testimonies by M.A.L.A. (1976) and L.D.T.L.R. (1986–87) (Seguel Mora, *Al otro lado*, 55 and 128); and Martín P.* (1984–86) (on file in Iquique).

See also Drago's fictional account based on his own service in Valparaíso in the 1920s (*El purgatorio*, 67).

181. Chahín et al., *Proyecto de acuerdo 606*, 1–2. See also Becker et al., *Proyecto de acuerdo 842*; and Chahín et al., *Proyecto de acuerdo 965*.

182. Calderón et al., *Conceptos reparatorios*.

183. Han, *Life in Debt*, 111. Han also relates a similar link between political imprisonment and a perceived failure to provide in Héctor's case (100).

184. Comisión Nacional sobre Prisión Política y Tortura, *Informe*, 495–512. See also Sofia Salimovich, Elizabeth Lira, and Eugenia Weinstein, "Victims of Fear: The Social Psychology of Repression," in Corradi et al., *Fear at the Edge*, 79–87; Elizabeth Lira, "El testimonio de experiencias políticas traumáticas: Terapia y denuncia en Chile (1973–1985)," in *Historizar el pasado vivo en América Latina*, ed. Anne Pérotin-Domun (2007), 12; Elizabeth Lira, "La vida como sobreviviente: Las secuelas de la dictadura en sus víctimas," in Sagredo and Gazmuri, *Historia de la vida privada*, 3:370–72; Stern, *Reckoning with Pinochet*, 293; and Arturo Roizblatt, Niels Biederman, and Jac Brown, "Extreme Traumatization in Chile: The Experience and Treatment of Families," *Journal of Family Therapy* 36 (2014): 28.

185. Mara Viveros Vigoya writes of a "crisis of masculinity" across Latin America in the last decades of the twentieth century ("Contemporary Latin American Perspectives on Masculinity," in Gutmann, *Changing Men and Masculinities*, 28). In Chile, Corvalán and Santibañez described the same dynamics as a crisis of the family (*Situación socio-laboral*, 124), and Agurto and de la Maza write of a "crisis de la familia popular" (crisis of the low-income, urban family) ("Ser joven poblador," 65–66).

186. Tinsman, "Wife-Beating," 282; Tinsman, "More Than Victims," 275–76; Olavarría, "Ser padre," 130–31; Constable and Valenzuela, *Nation of Enemies*, 223–25; Max Koch, "Changes in Chilean Social Structure: Class Structure and Income Distribution between 1972 and 1994," *European Review of Latin American and Caribbean Studies* 66 (June 1999): 7.

187. Agurto and de la Maza, "Ser joven poblador," 63; Marcel, "Juventud y empleo," 14–19, 24; Weinstein, "Juventud urbano-popular," 73–77; Weinstein, *Los jóvenes pobladores*, 12; Corvalán and Santibañez, *Situación socio-laboral*, 45–46, 60, 124–27; Weinstein, "Víctimas y beneficiarios," 252–53.

188. For the effects of military regime economic policies in specific sectors of the economy and their impact on social, familial, and gender relations, see the following contributions to Winn, *Victims of the Chilean Miracle*: Thomas Miller Klubock, "Class, Community, and Neoliberalism in Chile: Copper Workers and the Labor Movement during the Military Dictatorship and the Restoration of Democracy," 209–60; Thomas Miller Klubock, "Labor, Land, and Environmental Change in the Forestry Sector in Chile, 1973–1998," 337–87; Rachel Schurman, "Shuckers, Sorters, Headers, and Gutters: Labor in the Fisheries Sector," 298–36; Joel Stillerman, "Disciplined Workers and Avid Consumers: Neoliberal Policy and the Transformation of Work and Identity among Chilean Metalworkers," 164–208; and Peter Winn, "'No Miracle for Us': The Textile Industry in the Pinochet Era, 1973–1998," 125–63.

189. Constable and Valenzuela, *Nation of Enemies*, 225–26.

Chapter 5. In the Flesh

1. Conversation with Hugo M.* (1975–77, Arica) in the Temuco office of the Agrupación de Reservistas Defensa Nacional IX Región (Agrupación de Reservistas) (notes, April 25, 2012).

2. For example, Andrés V.* (1975–77) (conversation in the Temuco office of the Agrupación de Reservistas [recording and notes, April 23, 2012]); Sergio H.* (1987–89) (conversation in the Temuco office of the Agrupación de Reservistas [recording and notes, April 24, 2012]); L.H.D.C. (1973–74) (Seguel Mora, *Al otro lado*, 249); and Juan (1973–75, Santiago) (Garviso, "Relato de un conscripto").

3. Seguel Mora, *Al otro lado*, 279.

4. The description of memories as "alive and latent" is from testimony by H.M.N.C. (1977–79, Punta Arenas) (Seguel Mora, *Al otro lado*, 147). Similarly, H.O.QU.F. (1972–73, 1973–74, 1978) describes as "alive and latent" the image and scent of human hair and fresh blood in a truck he was ordered to clean (Seguel Mora, *Al otro lado*, 192–93).

5. The phrase was used, for example, by Vicente A.* (1977–78, Temuco) (conversation in the Temuco office of the Agrupación de Reservistas [notes, April 25, 2012]); and Andrés V.* (1975–77, Temuco) (conversation in the Temuco office of the Agrupación de Reservistas [recording and notes, April 23, 2012]).

6. Undated testimony on file in Chillán.

7. Testimony from 2006 on file in Temuco.

8. Testimony from 2006 on file in Temuco.

9. Seguel Mora, *Al otro lado*, 283–84. The date and location of J.H.Z.C.'s service are not part of the published testimony but were confirmed with the office in Temuco. For similar accounts of the effects of fellow recruits' suicides, see, for example, testimonies by P.J.F.G. (1975–77, Melipeuco and Arica) and P.P.C.L. (1975–77) (Seguel Mora, *Al otro lado*, 234 and 264); and José Gamboa (1985, Arica) (Lizana Ormazábal, *Complementa demanda de autos*, 7).

10. Testimony from 2007 on file in Temuco.

11. Seguel Mora, *Al otro lado*, 79.

12. Ibid., 102.

13. Muñoz, "Soldados de Pinochet."

14. Conversation with Andrés V.* (1975–77) in the Temuco office of the Agrupación de Reservistas (recording and notes, April 23, 2012).

15. Conversation with Alberto C.* (1976, Temuco) in the Temuco office of the Agrupación de Reservistas (recording and notes, April 26, 2012).

16. Seguel Mora, *Al otro lado*, 203–5.

17. Ibid., 274–75. Similar testimony (on file in Chillán) about the sight of soldiers triggering memories is provided by Iván C.* (1983–84, Valdivia).

18. Conversation with Enrique P.* (1982–84, Tierra del Fuego) in the Temuco office of the Agrupación de Reservistas (notes, April 24, 2012).

19. Oral history with Patricio Farías (1973–75, Punta Arenas) (July 19, 2013, Ñuñoa, Santiago).

20. Conversation with Jorge P.* (1983–85, Temuco) in the Temuco office of the Agrupación de Reservistas (notes, April 25, 2012).

21. Testimony from 2011 on file in Iquique.

22. Seguel Mora, *Al otro lado*, 194–95.

23. Oral history with Mario Navarro (1973–75, Arica) (September 3, 2012, Arica).

24. Testimony from 2011 on file in Iquique.

25. For example, testimonies by R.A.P.G. (1976–78, Temuco), J.A.F.M. (1978, Punta Arenas), R.G.S.CH. (Tierra del Fuego), C.J.C.S. (1976–79, Coyhaique), A.J.P.M. (1983) (Seguel Mora, *Al otro lado*, 37, 79–80, 97, 118–19, 120), and Ricardo H.* (1988) (testimony on file at Chillán). In the context of political prisoners, Jorge Montealegre writes of "recuerdos" of imprisonment and torture in and on the body—scars, tattoos, disabilities, tics, stammers—and in responses to smells, sounds, images, and tastes (*Las memorias eclipsadas: Duelo y resiliencia comunitaria en la prisión política* [Santiago: Ediciones Asterión, 2013], 141–42).

26. Seguel Mora, *Al otro lado*, 113.

27. C.D.C.A. (1982) testified to trying to "kill" his memories and nightmares with drugs and alcohol (Seguel Mora, *Al otro lado*, 33).

28. For similar symptoms, behaviors, and adaptive responses observed in victims of human rights under Pinochet, see Sofia Salimovich et al., "Victims of Fear," 74–79; and Comisión Nacional sobre Prisión Política y Tortura, *Informe*, 496–504. For the psychology of traumatic memory, more generally, see Daniel Schacter, *Searching for Memory: The Brain, the Mind, and the Past* (New York: Basic Books, 1996); and Richard J. McNally, *Remembering Trauma* (Cambridge, MA: Belknap Press of Harvard University Press, 2005), 30–35.

29. See, for example, testimonies in Seguel Mora, *Al otro lado*, by J.R.N.H. (1975–76, Valdivia) (107–8); R.M.B.M. (1987, Temuco) (112); J.H.R.M. (1978, Lonquimay) (116); and 2006 testimonies on file in Temuco by Oscar C.* (1974–76, 1976–78) and Cristián M.* (1986–87, Temuco).

30. REPACH Talcahuano, Untitled film (undated).

31. The website of the Human Rights Program (http://www.ddhh.gov.cl/mapa/) contains information on the memorials the program supported.

32. For more on the emergence of memory sites in Chile from the end of the 1990s, the increase in memory sites during the first decade of the twenty-first century, the shift in government policy on memorialization, as well as analyses of individual sites of memory, see Wilde, "Irruptions of Memory," 473–500; Katherine Hite, "El monumento a Salvador Allende en el debate político chileno," in *Monumentos, memoriales y marcas territoriales*, ed. Elizabeth Jelin and Victoria Langland (Madrid: Siglo Veintiuno, 2003), 19–55; Michael J. Lazzara, "Tres recorridos de Villa Grimaldi," in Jelin and Langland, *Monumentos*, 127–47; Katherine Hite, "Estadio nacional: Monumento y lugar de conmemoración," in Verdugo, *De la tortura*, 213–27; Lazzara, *Chile in Transition*, 129–53; Alexander Wilde, "Avenues of Memory: Santiago's General Cemetery and Chile's Recent Political History," *A Contracorriente: A Journal on Social History and Literature in Latin America* 5, no. 3 (2008): 134–69; Stern, *Reckoning with*

Pinochet, 169–76, 265–72 and 314–23; Katherine Hite, *Politics and the Art of Commemoration: Memorials to Struggle in Latin America and Spain* (New York: Routledge, 2012); Klep, "Tracing Collective Memory," 259–69; Wilde, "A Season of Memory," 31–60; Collins and Hite, "Memorial Fragments," 133–63; and Stern and Winn, "El tortuoso camino chileno," 205–326.

33. "Sites of memory" are understood as physical spaces or objects that are invested with meaning by groups of people. The meaning is not inherent in the space or object, but constructed, and it is maintained via commemorative rituals. The meaning can evolve or be reinterpreted, and the link between meaning and the site can be lost if not maintained. For more on "sites of memory" in postconflict societies in Latin America beyond the Chilean context, see Elizabeth Jelin, Introduction to Jelin, *Las conmemoraciones,* 1–8; Hugo Achugar, "El lugar de la memoria, a propósito de monumentos (motivos y paréntesis)," in Jelin and Langland, *Monumentos,* 191–216; Elizabeth Jelin and Victoria Langland, "Introducción: Las marcas territoriales como nexo entre pasado y presente," in Jelin and Langland, *Monumentos,* 1–18; and Elizabeth Jelin, "Public Memorialization in Perspective: Truth, Justice, and Memory of Past Repression in the Southern Cone of South America," *International Journal of Transitional Justice* 1, no. 1 (2007): 138–56.

Beyond the Latin American context, Pierre Nora's conceptualization of "sites of memory" has been influential in the literature ("Between Memory and History: Les Lieux de Mémoire," *Representations* 26 [1989]: 7–24). See also James E. Young, *The Texture of Memory: Holocaust Memorials and Meaning* (New Haven, CT: Yale University Press, 1993), 1–7; Timothy G. Ashplant, Graham Dawson, and Michael Roper, "The Politics of War Memory and Commemoration: Contexts, Structures, and Dynamics," in *Commemorating War: The Politics of Memory,* ed. Timothy G. Ashplant, Graham Dawson, and Michael Roper (New Brunswick, NJ: Transaction, 2004), 3–85; and Jay Winter, "Sites of Memory," in *Memory: Histories, Theories, Debates,* ed. Susannah Radstone and Bill Schwarz (New York: Fordham University Press, 2010), 312–24. Nora argues that rather than concretizing "memory," sites of memory instead concretize historical interpretations, usually national myths, especially as living memory of the events memorialized is lost. However, as Stern notes, postconflict societies in Latin America have not—yet—reached that point (*Remembering Pinochet's Chile,* 199n2). While the dynamic Nora describes is important to the history of the ex-conscript narrative of ruptured patriotism (see chapter 3), the type of distance it requires does not exist in the specific case of the memory of military service. Isolated examples of memorials to individual conscripts—see Michel Nash (see chapter 2) and Pedro Prado (see chapter 3)—do not "concretize" ex-conscript narratives.

34. Stern writes of a "new memorialization" that produced "an enlarged civic geography of remembrance" (*Reckoning with Pinochet,* 316).

35. Reception of a former recruit in the Temuco office of the Agrupación de Reservistas (field notes, April 26, 2012).

36. In her analysis of sites of trauma transformed into memorials or museums—including Villa Grimaldi in Chile—Patrizia Violi writes of the fundamental "indexical"

character of such sites: "They are the very places where the traumatic events in question have occurred, and the demonstration of such a continuity is an essential part of their inherent and constructed meaning." This meaning is not "embedded" in the site; instead, the "physical space is developed into a narrative, and its indexical nature is transformed from purely causal contiguity into a meaningful element" ("Trauma Site Museums and Politics of Memory: Tuol Sleng, Villa Grimaldi, and the Bologna Ustica Museum," *Theory, Culture & Society* 29, no. 1 [2012]: 39). For ex-conscripts, too, the indexical, or presumed indexical, link to past mistreatment is important to how they have grounded shared memory narratives in their own bodies.

37. Comisión Nacional D.D.H.H., Informe, 124–26. The report includes the 2010 Puerto Montt report, which summarized the findings in 38 cases (155–58); the 2012 Osorno report, which involved 123 participants (136–47); the 2012 Puerto Octay document, which reported on 12 cases (148–54); the 2009 medical report compiled in Osorno, which summarized the findings of consultations with 110 ex-conscripts (127–30); and the 2010 social work report in Osorno (114–23).

Federico Lorenz writes of the incorporation of the Argentine ex-conscripts' experiences of the Malvinas conflict into the narrative of the transition via veterans' illnesses and ailments, which, like the damage done to political prisoners, were the responsibility of the armed forces ("Testigos de la derrota," 27–28). This incorporation was possible because the conflict was a popular war fought against a foreign power and because defeat precipitated the end of Argentine military rule. In contrast, throughout the negotiated Chilean transition and into the twenty-first century, Chilean ex-conscripts were typically seen as part of the armed forces and not their victims.

38. Comisión Nacional de Verdad y Reconciliación, *Informe*, 2:1317.

39. Comisión Nacional D.D.H.H., *Informe*, 130.

40. Comisión Nacional sobre Prisión Política y Tortura, *Informe*, 41–42 and 74. While it relied on the link between mistreatment and health complaints, the Ex-conscript Commission also acknowledged that in many cases the damage had healed (Comisión Nacional D.D.H.H., *Informe*, 42).

For the shifting role of political prisoner testimony from therapeutic tool to evidence (where truth was based in the victims' firsthand accounts, and not in victims ailments as identified by health professionals), see Elizabeth Lira, "El testimonio de experiencias políticas traumáticas: Terapia y denuncia en Chile (1973–1985)," in *Historizar el pasado vivo en América Latina*, ed. Anne Pérotin-Domun (2007), 1–40; and Elizabeth Lira, "Trauma, duelo, reparación y memoria," *Revista de Estudios Sociales* 36 (2010): 14–28.

41. For more on the evolving role of the SML and its expert testimony in torture cases, see the annual *Informe anual sobre derechos humanos en Chile* from the Centro de Derechos Humanos of the Facultad de Derecho at the Universidad Diego Portales (Santiago: Ediciones Universidad Diego Portales) for 2012 (36–37), 2013 (58–59), and 2014 (53–54).

42. Lira, "El testimonio," 1–40; Lira, "Trauma, duelo, reparación," 14–28.

43. Baronti and Toro, *Derechos de los jóvenes*, 23; Baronti and Alfaro, "Mecanismos y efectos psicológicos," 48.

44. Baronti and Alfaro, "Mecanismos y efectos psicológicos," 47–48.

45. Testimony from 2009 on file in Temuco.

46. Examples taken from 2006 testimony on file in Temuco by Camilo L.* (1973, Santiago); testimonies in Seguel Mora, *Al otro lado*, by R.M.M. (1979–81) (123) and S.A.B. (127); 2008 testimony on file in Temuco by Olga F.* about her late husband Sebastian A.* (1972–75, Lautaro); testimony by Luis Humberto Castro Valderrama (1973–74, Santiago) (Lizana Ormazábal, *Complementa demanda de autos*, 18); and a meeting in a San Bernardo mall with representatives from Buin, Maipú, Punta Arenas, and San Ramón (field notes, February 12, 2014).

47. Public meeting organized by Fernando Mellado in the municipal stadium in San Bernardo (field notes, December 11, 2011); regional meeting held in a school hall in Nacimiento (field notes, and July 8, 2012). See also the following note 48.

48. Descriptions used by group leaders Luis Burgos (interview [notes, April 23, 2012]), Claudio de la Hoz (interview [notes, April 27, 2012]), Víctor Calderón (interview [notes, June 26, 2012]), and Claudio González (meeting in a San Bernardo mall with leaders from Buin, Maipú, Punta Arenas, and San Ramón [field notes, February 12, 2014]); an oral history with Julio Torres (1973–76, Concepción) (July 8, 2012, Nacimiento); and 2012 testimony by Martín S.* (1974–75, Iquique) (on file in Iquique).

49. Testimony on file in Iquique.

50. Luis Burgos used the word *florecer* (to blossom) to describe the emergence physical and psychological symptoms (interview [notes, April 23, 2012]).

51. Saavedra, *Mi propia guerra*, 128–29. In the context of former political prisoners, the Valech Report describes a similar potential delay (Comisión Nacional sobre Prisión Política y Tortura, *Informe*, 498).

52. Interview with Carlos Palma in his Ñuñoa almacén (notes, May 30, 2014). Similarly, in the video prepared by REPACH Talcahuano, the sister of a recruit (1988, Coyhaique) who died during his service linked the memory of her brother's death to her mother's blindness and leg problems. For examples of this link between the memory of trauma and current physical ailments as expressed by relatives of victims of political repression, see Stern, *Reckoning with Pinochet*, 73; and Han, *Life in Debt*, 126.

53. For example, Maximiliano F.* (1983, Temuco) writes of having electrical current applied to him during prisoner training, and connects his employment difficulties with his lack of teeth and kidney pain, which he attributes to his service (2006 testimony on file in Temuco). Sergio H.* (1987–89) spoke of his poor emotional control that he attributes to having electrical current applied to his body, his advancing osteoarthritis that affected his ability to work, as well as his concerns about being able to pay for his children's education (conversation in the Temuco office of the Agrupación de Reservistas [recording and notes, April 24, 2012]). Sergi Oliva (1985–86) described on television having electrical current applied to his face, testicles, and ribs during training, and he and his wife spoke of his neurological damage. A doctor's letter that suggests he likely contracted his disease from eating raw dog meat during his service was shown prominently on screen, and Sergi spoke of his shame and anger at not being able to work to feed his family (Muñoz, "Soldados de Pinochet"). Miguel Moraga (1975–77,

Iquique) insists the northern sun damaged his vision during his service and that as a result, he cannot use a computer and has difficulty finding and keeping a job (Lizana Ormazábal, *Complementa demanda de autos*, 1).

54. A regular meeting of the Agrupación SMO in Estación Central, Santiago (field notes, May 25, 2013).

55. Testimony from 2011 on file in Iquique.

56. Testimony from 2011 on file in Iquique.

57. A video produced by the Agrupación de Reservistas Defensa Nacional IX Región features footage and still shots of scars, as well as former conscripts describing their broken ribs, perforated lungs, testicular tumors, back pain, or showing their missing teeth, cysts, scarred limbs and torsos, immobile limbs, or, in one case, an open leg wound that has never healed. These scenes are presented without context and left to speak for themselves (Untitled film [MG Producciones, undated]).

In some cases, weighting testimonies toward current health issues or demands was a way to avoid narrating the events that caused the issues in question (testimonies in Seguel Mora, *Al otro lado*: R.H.A.H. [93], J.J.R.C. [242], and J.G.D. [1974–76, Calama] [247]).

58. Photos of events seen in the Temuco office of the Agrupación de Reservistas (field notes, April 25, 2012).

59. The 2009 civil case for damages by the Agrupación SMO notes the physical and psychological damage done to former recruits. Nevertheless, the subjective nature of *daño moral* (moral damage) in Chilean law does not require the kind of objective proof the Ex-conscript Commission sought to collate (Fernando Monsalve, *Causa C-25272* [2009]). Similarly, the 2010 Maipú civil case was also built around the idea of psychological damage (Lizana Ormazábal, *Gabriel Alejandro Avello*). Moreover, the *Complementa demanda de autos* relating to the case includes 135 short testimonies structured around psychical and psychological rupture, and is prefaced with a brief introduction that explicitly highlights the before-and-after narrative structure of the testimonies (Lizana Ormazábal, *Complementa demanda de autos*). The 2009 criminal case prepared by Hernán Montealegre also notes the lingering psychological damage done to ex-conscripts, while nevertheless focusing on the acts of torture and abuse and the individuals responsible for them, not their consequences (*Querella criminal*, 32).

60. For examples, see testimonies in Seguel Mora, *Al otro lado*, by R.H.M. (1974, Valdivia) (100–101); R.A.P.G. (1976, Coyhaique) (37); M.A.F.G. (1976–78, Coyhaique) (103); J.R.F.P. (1978, Temuco) (94); R.M.M. (1979–81, Temuco) (123); M.E.S.O. (1979–81) (139); H.F.J.F. (1982, Lonquimay) (142); F.D.A.L. (1982) (172); M.A.LL.CH. (1983–84) (114); A.A.E.V. (1986, Punta Arenas) (86); and W.O.R.H. (Temuco) (90).

61. REPACH Talcahuano, Untitled. Similarly, in her 2011 testimony on file in Iquique, Estefanía L.* wrote of delivering her son to the army in early 1989 "healthy" and receiving his body in August in a coffin.

62. Calderon et al., *Conceptos reparatorios*.

63. Ejército de Chile, *Presentación*, vol. 2. For a more detailed discussion of the army's presentation, see Stern, *Reckoning with Pinochet*, 91–93. For a more representative set of figures for conscript deaths and mortality, see table 2 and figure 1.

64. Comisión Nacional de Verdad y Reconciliación, *Informe*, vol. 3.

65. For the methodology behind the rates, see figure 1, sources. Using the number of army conscripts provided by the General Directorate for National Mobilization (Dirección General de Movilización Nacional, or DGMN) for the year 1973 instead of the figure from the Estado Mayor General of the army (see table 1), conscript mortality would have peaked well above the general rates.

66. For US figures during a comparable period, see Stephanie L. Scoville, John W. Gardner, and Robert N. Potter, "Traumatic Deaths during U.S. Armed Forces Basic Training, 1977–2001," *American Journal of Preventive Medicine* 26, no. 3 (2004): 195. There is anecdotal evidence from former recruits in Chile that medical screening of recruits was not always carried out or that when it was, young men were at times recruited despite not being fit for service.

67. While the numbers suffer from a reporting bias in addition to the caveats that frame the figures on deaths (see table 2, sources), the annual rate of recruits who left the barracks with a disability, calculated using the same methodology as figure 1, follows the same pattern as conscript mortality: it peaks in 1973 and again between 1977 and 1981.

68. Interview with Daniel Gómez (1978–80, Punta Arenas) in the Temuco office of the Agrupación de Reservistas (notes, April 23, 2012).

69. Testimony of Gilberto A.* on file in Chillán; conversation with Pablo F.* in the Temuco office of the Agrupación de Reservistas (notes, April 27, 2012).

70. Written testimony by Carlos Droguett (1973–74, San Bernardo), volunteered as part of an oral history (June 17, 2013, La Pintana, Santiago).

71. Tess Burton argues that the corporeal experience of chronic pain is the opposite of commemoration and "marked by an almost complete absence of communal performance or formal significance within the life of a community" ("Painful Memories: Chronic Pain as a Form of Re-membering," *Memory Studies* 4, no. 1 [2011]: 29). However, the meaning of former recruits' corporeal experiences of their health complaints, which can include chronic pain, is not simply limited to the individual; it is shared, collectively constructed, and interconnected with others.

72. Interviews with the staff in the Temuco office of the Agrupación de Reservistas (notes, April 23, 2012; and notes, December 16, 2013).

73. For example, testimony by Alesandri González during a 2014 television report on the movement (Muñoz, "Soldados de Pinochet").

74. Conversation with Rodolfo R.* (1976, Punta Arenas) in the Temuco office of the Agrupación de Reservistas (recording and notes, April 27, 2012).

Conclusion

1. For the inherent paradox of human rights, see Steve J. Stern and Scott Straus, "Embracing Paradox: Human Rights in the Global Age," in *The Human Rights Paradox: Universality and Its Discontents*, ed. Steve J. Stern and Scott Straus (Madison: University of Wisconsin Press, 2014), 3–28.

2. Michael J. Lazzara, "Dos propuestas de conmemoración pública: Londres 38 y el museo de la memoria y los derechos humanos (Santiago de Chile)," *A Contracorriente:*

A Journal on Social History and Literature in Latin America 8, no. 3 (2011): 69. For a review of the museum's conception, construction, and reception, see Stern and Winn, "El tortuoso camino chileno," 273–84.

3. The Historians' Manifesto was a response to Pinochet's 1998 "Letter to Chileans," written while he was detained in London, and newspaper supplements by historian Gonzalo Vial, published shortly after the letter. Both the letter and the supplements reduced the events of 1973 to an isolated period of economic, institutional, and political crisis, initiated by the Left in the preceding decade. This partially foreshadowed the 2000 statement that emerged from the dialog table, which while not a defensive extension of the war narrative, coming as it did out of a collaborative, nonpartisan process to establish common ground, nevertheless also began the story of the coup amid the spiraling violence of the 1960s. For the manifesto, commentaries, and responses, see Sergio Grez and Gabriel Salazar, eds., *Manifiesto de historiadores* (LOM: Santiago, 1999).

4. See examples from across the region: Jelin, "The Politics of Memory," 38–58; Jelin, *Los trabajos*; Martins Filho and Thompson, "The War of Memory," 89–107; Paulo Drinot, "For Whom the Eye Cries," 15–32; Crenzel, "Present Pasts," 1–13; Vicki Bell, "The Politics of 'Memory,'" 209–21; Ros, *The Post-Dictatorship Generation*, 6–10; Lessa, *Memory and Transitional Justice*, 19–23; Winn, *No hay mañana*; and Allier-Montaño and Crenzel, *The Struggle for Memory*.

5. See, for example, Wilde, "Irruptions of Memory," 473–500; Lazzara, *Chile in Transition*; Stern, *Remembering Pinochet's Chile*; Stern, *Battling for Hearts and Minds*; Stern, *Reckoning with Pinochet*; Lira, "Chile," 107–32; Stern and Winn, "El tortuoso camino chileno," 205–326; and these important collections of essays: Mario Garcés et al, *Memoria*; Richard, *Políticas y estéticas*; and Collins et al., *The Politics of Memory* (in particular the chapters by Hite et al., "The Politics of Memory," 1–29; and Wilde, "A Season of Memory," 31–60).

6. Parts of the case for an "apolitics of memory" have been advanced in Leith Passmore, "The Apolitics of Memory: Remembering Military Service under Pinochet through and alongside Transitional Justice, Truth, and Reconciliation," *Memory Studies* 9, no. 2 (2016): 173–86.

Works Cited

For details on oral histories, conversations, interviews, field notes, and unpublished written testimonies, see the note on sources (pp. xxv–xxvii).

Ex-conscript Testimonies (Published and Unpublished Audiovisual) and Memoirs (Published and Unpublished)

Castillo Pasten, Nelson. *Hacé patria, matá un chileno.* 2011.

Guzmán Espíndola, Fernando Tomás. "Statement Given in the 'Quemados' Case (Rol 143-2013)." 2014. http://www.cooperativa.cl/noticias/site/artic/20150722 /asocfile/20150722113110/declaracion.pdf.

Raillard, Guillermo. "Clase 54." Unpublished manuscript. 2011. In possession of the author.

Rivas Vergara, César. *Las Baguales de Manantiales: Mi servicio militar en los ochenta.* Santiago: Dhiyo, 2011.

Saavedra, Miguel A. *Mi propia guerra.* San Bernardo: Imp. Roberto Vidal, 2012.

Seguel Mora, Luis, ed. *Al otro lado de las metralletas: Testimonios inéditos del servicio militar en Chile periodo 1973–1990.* Temuco: Out Sourcing Chile, 2007.

Untitled film. Produced by REPACH Talcahuano. Undated. In possession of the author.

Untitled film. Produced by the Agrupación de Reservistas Defensa Nacional IX Región. MG Producciones, undated. In possession of the author.

Documents Produced in the Context of Ex-conscript Groups' Legal and Lobby Activities

Becker, Germán, Sergio Ojeda, Osvaldo Palma, Manuel Monsalve, Carolina Goic, René Manuel García, Rodrigo González, and Alfonso de Urresti. *Proyecto de acuerdo 842.* 2009. https://www.camara.cl/pdf.aspx?prmID=2579&prmTipo=PACUERDO.

Calderón, Víctor, Rubén Cornejo, Juan Suárez, José Castillo, and Luis Burgos. *Conceptos reparatorios por derechos humanos vulnerados a personal servicio militar obligatorio período 1973–1990: Antecedentes y fundamentos*. 2011 or 2012. In possession of the author.

Chahín, Fuad, Carolina Goic, Adriana Muñoz, Osvaldo Andrade, Miodrag Marinovic, Enrique Accorsi, René Saffirio, Sergio Ojeda, Marcelo Schilling, and Hugo Gutiérrez. *Proyecto de acuerdo 606*. 2012. https://www.camara.cl/pdf.aspx?prmID=3277&prmTipo=PACUERDO.

Chahín, Fuad, Ricardo Rincón, Mario Venegas, Matías Walker, Jorge Sabag, Gabriel Silber, Roberto León, Víctor Torres, Alfonso de Urresti, and Marcos Espinosa. *Proyecto de acuerdo 965*. 2013. https://www.camara.cl/pdf.aspx?prmid=3945&prmtipo=SOBRETABLA.

Chahuán, Francisco, Roberto Sepúlveda, Alejandro García-Huidobro, Pablo Galilea, and Amelia Herrera. *Proyecto de acuerdo 287*. 2007. https://www.camara.cl/pdf.aspx?prmid=375&prmtipo=PACUERDO.

Comisión Nacional D.D.H.H. de ex Soldados Conscriptos 1973–1990. *Informe: Violación de derechos humanos y hechos de violencia vinculados con el servicio militar obligatorio en Chile entre los años 1973 a 1990*. 2012. In possession of the author.

Gutiérrez, Julio, and Mario Navarro to Michelle Bachelet. November 2008. In possession of the author.

Hinzpeter, Rodrigo. Letter from the coordinador general of the comando presidencial Sebastián Piñera to the coordinadora nacional de ex soldados conscriptos. 2009. In possession of the author.

Lizana Ormazábal, Washington. *Complementa demanda de autos: Rol 14431-2010*. June 19, 2012. http://civil.poderjudicial.cl/CIVILPORWEB/DownloadFile.do?TIP_Documento=2&TIP_Archivo=3&COD_Opcion=1&COD_Tribunal=283&CRR_IdEscrito=21566394&CRR_IdDocEscrito=12721018.

———. *Gabriel Alejandro Avello Astete y otros / Fisco de Chile: C-14431*. 2010. In possession of the author.

Marinovic, Miodrag, Jorge Ulloa, Sergio Bobadilla, Gastón Von Mühlenbrock, Leopoldo Pérez, Ramón Barros, Iván Norambuena, Alejandro Santana, Gaspar Rivas, and Romilio Gutiérrez. *Proyecto de acuerdo 967*. 2013. https://www.camara.cl/pdf.aspx?prmid=3947&prmtipo=SOBRETABLA.

Ministerio de Defensa and Ministerio del Interior y Seguridad Pública. *Informe: Ex soldados conscriptos*. 2013. https://www.camara.cl/sala/verComunicacion.aspx?comuid=10673.

Monsalve, Fernando. *Causa C-25272*. 2009. In possession of the author.

Montealegre Klenner, Hernán. *Querella criminal: Rol 3356-2009*. 2009. In possession of the author.

Núñez, Marco Antonio, René Alinco, José Pérez, Cristián Campos, Pepe Auth, Orlando Vargas, Marcos Espinoza, Mario Venegas, Patricio Hales, and Miodrag Marinovic. *Proyecto de acuerdo 966*. 2013. https://www.camara.cl/pdf.aspx?prmid=3946&prmtipo=SOBRETABLA.

Pérez, José, Fernando Meza, Alberto Robles, Marcos Espinosa, and Alejandro Sule. *Proyecto de acuerdo 851.* 2009. https://www.camara.cl/pdf.aspx?prmid=2590 &prmtipo=PACUERDO.

Rosende Lynch, Patricio, subsecretary of the interior, to coordinadora de ex SLC del SMO. April 27, 2009. In possession of the author.

Seguel Mora, Luis. *Ley de justicia previsional para reservistas de la defensa nacional.* April 2009. In possession of the author.

Ex-conscript Group Blogs

Agrupación ex conscriptos de Maipú. http://agrupacionexconscriptosmaipu.blogspot.cl.

Agrupación ex conscriptos 1973–1990 Puente Alto. http://puentealtoexconscriptos73al90 .blogspot.com.

Dignificación para los ex soldados 73–90. http://dignificacionparalosexsoldados73-90 .blogspot.cl.

Federación de ex SMO 1973 al 1990 de Chile. http://federacionreservistasdelestado .blogspot.cl.

La historia tiene tres aristas falta la nuestra. http://anescec.blogspot.cl.

Para que nunca más en Chile. http://agrupacionexconscriptos.blogspot.com.

Reservistas novena región. http://reservistasnovenaregion.blogspot.com.

Testimonios de tortura aplicada a ex soldados en época de dictadura . . . aquello que los medios y el gobierno esconden. http://laverguenzadechile.blogspot.com.

Responses to Requests for Information Made via Chile's Transparency Law

Director General de Movilización Nacional. "Response to Request AD013W-0002354." December 5, 2013.

———. "Response to Request AD013W-0002368." December 30, 2013.

Estado Mayor (air force). "Response to Request AD008C-0000224." June 19, 2014.

Estado Mayor (army). "Response to Request AD006C-0000314." June 6, 2014.

———. "Response to Request AD006C-0000317." June 16, 2014.

Estado Mayor (navy). "Response to Request AD007C-0000346." June 19, 2014.

Estado Mayor General (air force). "Response to Request AD008C-0000220." June 11, 2014.

Estado Mayor General (army). "Response to Request AD006C-0000314." June 6, 2014.

———. "Response to Request AD006C-0000332." September 1, 2014.

———. "Response to Request AD022W-000607." September 29, 2014.

Estado Mayor General (navy). "Response to Request AD007C-0000350." June 26, 2014.

———. "Response to Request AD007C-0000371." September 5, 2014.

Instituto Nacional de Estadísticas. "Response to Request AH007W-0010323." May 29, 2014.

Archival Documents

"Casos atendidos por el programa de protección y asistencia de la corporación de promoción y defensa de los derechos del pueblo." CEDOC del Museo de la Memoria y los Derechos Humanos. Fondo CODEPU. Caja 32.

Conferencia Episcopal de Chile. "Carta pastoral para los campesinos (August 1979)." Fundación de Documentación y Archivo de la Vicaría de la Solidaridad. File Campesinos, Pobladores, A.T.N. 65.

"Minuta exposición grupo ad hoc (July 1978)." Fundación de Documentación y Archivo de la Vicaría de la Solidaridad. File Campesinos, Pobladores, A.T.N.: 65 B.

"1997 Medical Histories of Johnny Daniel Pérez Torres, Dagbarto Boris Contreras Yáñez, Mauricio Eugenio Saavedra Aguilera and Andrés Jorge Serrano Leiva." CEDOC del Museo de la Memoria y los Derechos Humanos. Fondo CODEPU. Caja 16, unnumbered leaves.

"1992 Statement by Former Conscript Jorge Antonio Concha Meza (1991–1992, Peldehue)." CEDOC del Museo de la Memoria y los Derechos Humanos. Fondo CODEPU. Caja 32, unnumbered leaves.

Vicaría Pastoral Juvenil. "Documento de trabajo para asesores de pastoral juvenil zona rural costa, vicaría pastoral juvenil." Fundación de Documentación y Archivo de la Vicaría de la Solidaridad. File Campesinos, Pobladores, A.T.N.: 65 B.

Demographic Publications

Dirección de Estadística y Censos. *Censo población 1960: Resumen país*. Santiago: La Dirección de Estadística y Censos, 1969.

———. *Demografía, año 1964*. Santiago: Dirección de Estadística y Censos. http://www.deis.cl/wp-content/uploads/2013/07/Demograf%C3%ADa-1964.pdf.

———. *Demografía, año 1965*. Santiago: Dirección de Estadística y Censos. http://www.deis.cl/wp-content/uploads/2013/07/Demograf%C3%ADa-1965.pdf.

———. *Demografía, año 1966*. Santiago: Dirección de Estadística y Censos. http://www.deis.cl/wp-content/uploads/2013/07/Demograf%C3%ADa-1966.pdf.

———. *Demografía, año 1967*. Santiago: Dirección de Estadística y Censos. http://www.deis.cl/wp-content/uploads/2013/07/Demograf%C3%ADa-1967.pdf.

———. *Demografía, año 1971*. Santiago: Dirección de Estadística y Censos. http://www.deis.cl/wp-content/uploads/2013/07/Demograf%C3%ADa-1971.pdf.

Dirección General de Estadística. *Censo de población de la república de Chile levantado el 15 de diciembre de 1920*. Santiago: Soc. imp. y litografía Universo, 1925.

———. *Resultados del X censo de la población efectuado el 27 de noviembre de 1930 y estadísticas comparativas con censos anteriores*. Santiago: Impr. Universo, 1931.

Instituto Nacional de Estadísticas. *Anuario de demografía, año 1974*. Santiago: INE. http://www.deis.cl/wp-content/uploads/2013/07/Demograf%C3%ADa-1974.pdf.

———. *Anuario de demografía, 1983*. Santiago: INE. http://www.deis.cl/wp-content/uploads/2013/07/Demograf%C3%ADa-1983.pdf.

———. *Anuario de demografía, 1984.* Santiago: INE. http://www.deis.cl/wp-content
/uploads/2013/07/Demograf%C3%ADa-1984.pdf.

———. *Anuario de demografía, 1985.* Santiago: INE. http://www.deis.cl/wp-content
/uploads/2013/07/Demograf%C3%ADa-1985.pdf.

———. *Anuario de demografía, 1986.* Santiago: INE. http://www.deis.cl/wp-content
/uploads/2013/07/Demograf%C3%ADa-1986.pdf.

———. *Anuario de demografía, 1987.* Santiago: INE. http://www.deis.cl/wp-content
/uploads/2013/07/Demograf%C3%ADa-1987.pdf.

———. *Anuario de demografía, año 1988.* Santiago: INE. http://www.deis.cl/wp-content
/uploads/2013/07/Demograf%C3%ADa-1988.pdf.

———. *Anuario de demografía, 1989.* Santiago: INE. http://www.deis.cl/wp-content
/uploads/2013/07/Demograf%C3%ADa-1989.pdf.

———. *Anuario de demografía, 1990.* Santiago: INE. http://www.deis.cl/wp-content
/uploads/2013/07/Demograf%C3%ADa-1990.pdf.

———. *Anuario de demografía, 1993.* Santiago: INE, 1995. http://www.deis.cl/wp-con
tent/uploads/2013/07/Demograf%C3%ADa-1993.pdf.

———. *Anuario de demografía, 1994.* Santiago: INE, 1996. http://www.deis.cl/wp-con
tent/uploads/2013/07/Demograf%C3%ADa-1994.pdf.

———. *Anuario de demografía, 1995.* Santiago: INE, 1996. http://www.deis.cl/wp-con
tent/uploads/2013/07/Demograf%C3%ADa-1995.pdf.

———. *Anuario de demografía, 1996.* Santiago: INE, 1998. http://www.deis.cl/wp-con
tent/uploads/2013/07/Demograf%C3%ADa-1996.pdf.

———. *Anuario de demografía, 1997.* Santiago: INE, 1999. http://www.deis.cl/wp-con
tent/uploads/2013/07/Demograf%C3%ADa-1997.pdf.

———. *Anuario de demografía, 1998.* Santiago: INE, 1999. http://www.deis.cl/wp-con
tent/uploads/2013/07/Demograf%C3%ADa-1998.pdf.

———. *Anuario de demografía, 1999.* Santiago: INE, 2001. http://www.deis.cl/wp-con
tent/uploads/2013/07/Demograf%C3%ADa-1999.pdf.

———. *Censos 1970–1982: Cifras comparativas.* Vols. 2–3. Santiago: Instituto Nacional
de Estadísticas, 1993.

———. *Chile: Ciudades, pueblos y aldeas, censo 1992.* Santiago: INE, 1995.

———. *Demografía, año 1968.* Santiago: INE. http://www.deis.cl/wp-content/uploads
/2013/07/Demograf%C3%ADa-1968.pdf.

———. *Demografía, año 1969.* Santiago: INE. http://www.deis.cl/wp-content/uploads
/2013/07/Demograf%C3%ADa-1969.pdf.

———. *Demografía, año 1970.* Santiago: INE. http://www.deis.cl/wp-content/uploads
/2013/07/Demograf%C3%ADa-1970.pdf.

———. *Demografía, años 1972–1973.* Santiago: INE. http://www.deis.cl/wp-content
/uploads/2013/07/Demograf%C3%ADa-1972-1973.pdf.

———. *Demografía, año 1975.* Santiago: INE. http://www.deis.cl/wp-content/uploads
/2013/07/Demograf%C3%ADa-1975.pdf.

———. *Demografía, año 1976–1977.* Santiago: INE. http://www.deis.cl/wp-content
/uploads/2013/07/Demograf%C3%ADa-1976-1977.pdf.

———. *Demografía, año 1978*. Santiago: INE. http://www.deis.cl/w-content/uploads
/2013/07/Demograf%C3%AD-1978.pdf.

———. *Demografía, año 1979*. Santiago: INE, 1981. http://www.deis.cl/wp-content
/uploads/2013/07/Demograf%C3%ADa-1979.pdf.

———. *Demografía, año 1980*. Santiago: INE. http://www.deis.cl/wp-content/uploads
/2013/07/Demograf%C3%ADa-1980.pdf.

———. *Demografía, año 1981*. Santiago: INE. http://www.deis.cl/wp-content/uploads
/2013/07/Demograf%C3%ADa-1981.pdf.

———. *XIV Censo de población y III de vivienda*. Santiago: INE, 1970.

———. *XV Censo nacional de población y IV de vivienda*. Vol. 2. Santiago: INE, 1986–87.

Servicio Nacional de Estadística y Censos. *XII Censo general de población y I de vivienda:
levantado el 24 de abril de 1952*. Santiago: Dirección General de Estadistica, Secretaria
General del Censo, 1953.

Published Sources

Achugar, Hugo. "El lugar de la memoria, a propósito de monumentos (motivos y
paréntesis)." In Jelin and Langland, *Monumentos*, 191–216.

Achugar, Mariana. *What We Remember: The Construction of Memory in Military Discourse*. Philadelphia, PA: John Benjamins, 2008.

Aedo-Richmond, Ruth, and Mark Richmond. "Recent Curriculum Change in Post-
Pinochet Chile." *Compare: A Journal of Comparative and International Education*
26, no. 2 (1996): 197–215.

Agüero, Felipe. "Militares, estado y sociedad en Chile: Mirando el futuro desde la
comparación histórica." *Revista de Ciencia Política* 22, no. 1 (2002): 39–65.

Agurto, Irene, and Gonzalo de la Maza. "Ser joven poblador en Chile hoy." In Agurto
et al., *Juventud chilena*, 57–71.

Agurto, Irene, Gonzalo de la Maza, and Manuel Canales, *Juventud chilena: Razones y
subversiones*. Santiago: ECO, 1985.

Allier-Montaño, Eugenia, and Emilio Crenzel, eds. *The Struggle for Memory in Latin
America: Recent History and Political Violence*. New York: Palgrave Macmillan, 2015.

Almqvist, Jessica, and Carlos Espósito, eds. *The Role of Courts in Transitional Justice:
Voices from Latin America and Spain*. New York: Routledge, 2012.

Archdiocese of São Paulo, Brazil. *Torture in Brazil: A Shocking Report on the Pervasive
Use of Torture by Brazilian Military Governments, 1964–1979*. Translated by Jaime
Wright and edited by Joan Dassin. Austin: University of Texas Press, 1998.

Arkin, William, and Lynne R. Dobrofsky. "Military Socialization and Masculinity."
Journal of Social Issues 34, no. 1 (1978): 151–68.

Arriagada, Genaro. *Por la razón o la fuerza: Chile bajo Pinochet*. Santiago: Sudamericana
Chilena, 1998.

Ashplant, Timothy G., Graham Dawson, and Michael Roper. "The Politics of War
Memory and Commemoration: Contexts, Structures and Dynamics." In *Com-
memorating War: The Politics of Memory*, edited by Timothy G. Ashplant, Graham
Dawson, and Michael Roper, 3–85. New Brunswick, NJ: Transaction, 2004.

Assman, Jan. "Collective Memory and Cultural Identity." *New German Critique* 65 (1995): 125–33.

Bachelet, Michelle. "Programa de Gobierno: Michelle Bachelet, 2014–2018." 2013. http://michellebachelet.cl/programa/.

Baillif. "Psicología y las fuerzas armadas." *Memorial del Ejército de Chile* 57, no. 315 (1963): 30–38.

Baronti Barella, Rosella. "Servicio militar obligatorio: Una mirada psicológica." In *Opinión y Perspectivas* 2, 23–42. Santiago: CODEPU, 1997.

Baronti, Rosella, and Sachiko Alfaro. "Mecanismos y efectos psicológicos en la formación militar y la objeción de conciencia como una repuesta posible." In Baronti and Toro, *Derechos de los jóvenes*, 47–57.

Baronti, Rosella, and Álvaro Toro. *Derechos de los jóvenes frente al servicio militar obligatorio: Sistematización de una experiencia de trabajo.* Santiago: CODEPU, 1999.

Barrientos, Jaime. "Sexual Initiation for Heterosexual Individuals in Northern Chile." *Sexuality Research and Social Policy* 7, no. 1 (2010): 37–44.

Barros, Pía. "Cuando el sur es realmente el sur." In *Autorretrato de Chile*, edited by Alfonso Calderón, Guillermo Blanco, and Pablo Azócar, 44–49. Nosotros los chilenos 10. Santiago: LOM, 2004.

Barros Lezaeta, Luis. "La profesionalización del ejército y su conversión en un sector innovador hacia comienzos del siglo xx." In *La guerra civil de 1891: 100 años hoy*, edited by Luis Ortega, 49–63. Santiago de Chile: Universidad de Santiago de Chile, 1991.

Barros Ortiz, Tobías. *Vigilia de armas: Charlas sobre la vida militar destinadas a un joven teniente.* Santiago: Fuerzas Armadas de Chile, 1988. First published 1920.

Bascuñán Pacheco, Ignacio. *Breve historia de Aisén y la carretera austral.* Santiago: Estado Mayor General del Ejército, 1984.

Beckman, Erika. "The Creolization of Imperial Reason: Chilean State Racism in the War of the Pacific." *Journal of Latin American Cultural Studies* 18, no. 1 (2009): 73–90.

Bell, Vicki. "The Politics of 'Memory' in the Long Present of the Southern Cone." In Lessa and Druliolle, *The Memory of State Terrorism*, 209–21.

Benavides Vanegas, Farid Samir. "Memoria y verdad judicial en Colombia: Los procesos de justicia y paz." *Revista de Derecho Público* 31 (2013): 2–23.

Bernales Matta, Sergio. "Las relaciones familiares en el Chile de los 90." *Proposiciones Sur* 26 (1995): 14–33.

Blakeley, Ruth. "Still Training to Torture? US Training of Military Forces from Latin America." *Third World Quarterly* 27, no. 8 (2006): 1439–61.

Bourke, Joanna. *An Intimate History of Killing: Face-to-Face Killing in Twentieth-Century Warfare.* New York: Basic Books, 1999.

Brahm García, Enrique. "Del soldado romántico al soldado profesional: Revolución en el pensamiento militar chileno, 1885–1940." *Historia* 25 (1990): 5–37.

———. *Preparados para la guerra: Pensamiento militar chileno bajo influencia alemana 1885–1930.* Santiago: Ediciones Universidad Católica de Chile, 2003.

Brands, Hal. *Latin America's Cold War*. Cambridge, MA: Harvard University Press, 2010.

Burbach, Roger. *The Pinochet Affair: State Terrorism and Global Justice*. London: Zed Books, 2003.

Burton, Tess. "Painful Memories: Chronic Pain as a Form of Re-membering." *Memory Studies* 4, no. 1 (2011): 23–32.

Candina Polomer, Azun. "El día interminable: Memoria e instalación del 11 de septiembre de 1973 en Chile (1974–1999)." In *Las conmemoraciones: Las disputas en las fechas "in-felices,"* edited by Elizabeth Jelin, 9–48. Madrid: Siglo Veintiuno, 2002.

Cariola, Leonor, and Cristián Cox. "La educación de los jóvenes: Crisis de la relevancia y calidad de la enseñanza media." In *Los jóvenes en Chile hoy*, edited by Generaciones, 19–38. Santiago: CIDE/CIEPLAN/INCH/PSI PIRQUE/SUR, 1990.

Castillo Aranguiz, Sergio. "Chile y su territorio." *Memorial del Ejército* 427 (1987): 104–15.

Cavallo, Ascanio, Manuel Salazar, and Oscar Sepúlveda. *La historia oculta del régimen militar: Memoria de una época 1973–1988*. Santiago: Uqbar, 2008.

Centro de Derechos Humanos, Facultad de Derecho, Universidad Diego Portales. *Informe anual sobre derechos humanos en Chile 2012*. Santiago: Ediciones Universidad Diego Portales, 2012.

———. *Informe anual sobre derechos humanos en Chile 2013*. Santiago: Ediciones Universidad Diego Portales, 2013.

———. *Informe anual sobre derechos humanos en Chile 2014*. Santiago: Ediciones Universidad Diego Portales, 2014.

CERC MORI. "Barómetro de la política: La imagen del Pinochetismo." 2015. http://morichile.cl/wp-content/uploads/2015/08/Imagen-de-Pinochet-y-la-Dictadura-Bar%C3%B3metro-de-la-pol%C3%ADtica-Julio-2015I.pdf.

Cheyre, Juan Emilio. *Ejército de Chile: El fin de una visión*. 2004. http://www.revistas.uchile.cl/index.php/ADH/article/view/13361.

Cid, Gabriel. "Un icono funcional: La invención del roto como símbolo nacional." In Cid and San Francisco, *Nación y nacionalismo*, 1:221–54.

Cid, Gabriel, and Alejandro San Francisco. "Introducción: Nación y nacionalismo en Chile, siglo XIX; Balances y problemas historiográficos." In Cid and San Francisco, *Nación y nacionalismo*, 1:xi–xxviii.

———. *Nación y nacionalismo en Chile: Siglo XIX*. 2 vols. Santiago: Centro de Estudios Bicentenario, 2009.

Cid, Gabriel, and Isabel Torres Dujisin. "Conceptualizar la identidad: Patria y nación en el vocabulario chileno del siglo XIX." In Cid and San Francisco, *Nación y nacionalismo*, 1:23–51.

Cid Rodríguez, Gabriel. "Memorias, mitos y ritos de guerra: El imaginario de la batalla de yungay durante la guerra del pacífico." *Universum* 26, no. 2 (2011): 101–20.

Collier, Simon, and William F. Sater. *A History of Chile, 1808–2002*. Cambridge: Cambridge University Press, 2004.

Collins, Cath. "Human Rights Trials in Chile during and after the 'Pinochet Years.'" *International Journal of Transitional Justice* 4, no. 1 (2010): 67–86.

———. "The Politics of Justice: Chile beyond the Pinochet Case." In Collins et al., *The Politics of Memory*, 61–89.

———. *Post-transitional Justice: Human Rights Trials in Chile and El Salvador*. University Park: Pennsylvania State University Press, 2011.

Collins, Cath, and Katherine Hite. "Memorial Fragments, Monumental Silences, and Reawakenings in Twenty-First-Century Chile." In Collins et al., *The Politics of Memory*, 133–63.

Collins, Cath, Katherine Hite, and Alfredo Joignant, eds. *The Politics of Memory in Chile from Pinochet to Bachelet*. Boulder, CO: First Forum Press, 2013.

Comisión Asesora para la Calificación de Detenidos Desaparecidos, Ejecutados Políticos y Víctimas de Prisión Política y Tortura. *Informe de la comisión asesora para la calificación de detenidos desaparecidos, ejecutados políticos y víctimas de prisión política y tortura*. 2011. http://www.indh.cl/wp-content/uploads/2011/10/Informe2011.pdf.

Comisión Nacional de Verdad y Reconciliación. *Informe de la comisión de verdad y reconciliación*. Vols. 1–3. 1991. http://www.gob.cl/informe-rettig/.

Comisión Nacional sobre Prisión Política y Tortura. *Informe de la comisión nacional sobre prisión política y tortura*. Santiago: La Nación, 2004.

Comisión para el Esclarecimiento Histórico. *Guatemala: Memoria del silencio*. Vol. 2. 1999. http://www.centrodememoriahistorica.gov.co/descargas/guatemala-memoria-silencio/guatemala-memoria-del-silencio.pdf.

Constable, Pamela, and Arturo Valenzuela. *A Nation of Enemies: Chile under Pinochet*. New York: Norton, 1993.

Cori Zürrer, Daniela. "Análisis de caso: Tragedia de Antuco; Crisis en las filas del ejército." In *Gestión de crisis: Teoría y práctica de un modelo comunicacional*, edited by Daniel Halpern, 30–44. Santiago: RIL Editores, 2010.

Corporación José Domingo Cañas. *Tortura en poblaciones del Gran Santiago, 1973–1990: Colectivo de memoria histórica*. Santiago: Corporación José Domingo Cañas, 2005.

Corradi, Juan E., Patricia Weiss Fagen, and Manuel Antonio Garretón, eds. *Fear at the Edge: State Terror and Resistance in Latin America*. Berkeley: University of California Press, 1992.

Corvalán Vasquez, Oscar, and Erika Santibañez. *Situación socio-laboral de la juventud chilena: Diagnóstico y perspectivas*. Santiago: CIDE, 1986.

Corvalán, Oscar, and Ricardo Andreani. "La preparación para el trabajo de la juventud chilena." In Generaciones, *Los jóvenes*, 72–85.

Court Moock, Jorge. "La psicología y el ejército." *Memorial del Ejército de Chile* 59, no. 327 (1965): 71–88.

Crelinsten, Ronald D. "In Their Own Words: The World of the Torturer." In Crelinsten and Schmid, *The Politics of Pain*, 35–64.

Crelinsten, Ronald D., and Alex P. Schmid, eds. *The Politics of Pain: Torturers and Their Masters*. Boulder, CO: Westview Press, 1985.

Crenzel, Emilio. "Present Pasts: Memory(ies) of State Terrorism in the Southern Cone of Latin America." In Lessa and Druliolle, *The Memory of State Terrorism*, 1–13.

Davies, Thomas M. Jr., and Brian Loveman, eds. *The Politics of Anti-Politics: The Military in Latin America*. Lanham, MD: SR Books, 1997.

Díaz, Cecilia, and Esteban Durán. *Los jóvenes del campo chileno: Una identidad fragmentada*. Santiago: GIA, 1986.

Dinges, John. *The Condor Years: How Pinochet and His Allies Brought Terrorism to Three Continents*. New York: New Press, 2004.

Donoso, Carlos, and Juan Ricardo Couyoumdjian. "De soldado orgulloso a veterano indigente: La guerra del Pacífico." In *Historia de la vida privada en Chile*, vol. 2, *El Chile moderno, de 1840 a 1925*, edited by Rafael Sagredo and Cristián Gazmuri, 237–73. Santiago: Taurus, 2005.

Doran, Anthony P., Gary Hoyt, and Charles A. Morgan III. "Survival, Evasion, Resistance, and Escape (SERE) Training: Preparing Military Members for the Demands of Captivity." In *Military Psychology: Clinical and Operational Applications*, edited by Carrie H. Kennedy and Eric A. Zillmer, 241–61. New York: The Guilford Press, 2006.

Drago, Gonzalo. *El Purgatorio*. Santiago: LOM, 1996.

Drinot, Paulo. "For Whom the Eye Cries: Memory, Monumentality, and the Ontologies of Violence in Peru." *Latin American Cultural Studies* 18, no. 1 (2009): 15–32.

D. R. Oficina de Derechos Humanos del Arzobispado de Guatemala. *Guatemala: Nunca más*. Vol. 2, *Los mecanismos del horror*. 1998. http://www.odhag.org.gt/html/TOMO2C3.HTM.

Eisenhart, R. Wayne. "You Can't Hack It Little Girl: A Discussion of the Covert Psychological Agenda of Modern Combat Training." *Journal of Social Issues* 31, no. 4 (1975): 13–23.

Ejército de Chile. *Presentación del ejército de Chile a la comisión nacional de verdad y reconciliación*. Vol. 2. Santiago: Ejército de Chile, 1990.

Ejército de Chile, Comandancia en Jefe. *Reglamento de instrucción individual de combate (para todas las armas)*. Santiago: Ministerio de Defensa Nacional, 1976.

"El cuerpo militar del trabajo." *Memorial del Ejército de Chile* 333 (1966): 120–25.

Elster, Jon, ed. *Retribution and Reparation in the Transition to Democracy*. Cambridge: Cambridge University Press, 2006.

Eltit, Diamela. *Los vigilantes*. Santiago: Editorial Planeta, 2011.

Ensalaco, Mark. *Chile under Pinochet: Recovering the Truth*. Philadelphia: University of Pennsylvania Press, 2000.

Errázuriz, Luis Hernán. "Dictadura militar en Chile: Antecedentes del golpe estético-cultural." *Latin American Research Review* 44, no. 2 (2009): 136–57.

Esparza, Marcia. "Casi la verdad: Silencios y secretos en la posdictadura del general Augusto Pinochet en Chile." *Antípoda* 5 (2007): 121–41.

———. "Courageous Soldiers (*valientes soldados*): Politics of Concealment in the Aftermath of State Violence in Chile." In *State Violence and Genocide in Latin America: The Cold War Years*, edited by Marcia Esparza, Henry R. Huttenbach, and Daniel Feierstein, 196–208. New York: Routledge, 2010.

Fuentes, Claudio. "Comentario: ¿Quieren los jóvenes un servicio militar obligatorio?" *Revista Fuerzas Armadas y Sociedad* 9, no. 1 (1994): 30–32.

———. "Los jóvenes y el servicio militar obligatorio: Estudio de encuestas de opinión pública." *Fuerzas Armadas y Sociedad* 8, no. 2 (1993): 27–36.

Garaño, Santiago. "Entre héroes y traidores: Sentidos militares y militantes acerca del rol de los conscriptos en los años 70." *Cuadernos de Antropología Social*, no. 33 (2011): 93–110.

———. "Soldados sospechosos: Militancia, conscripción y fuerzas armadas durante los años setenta." *Contenciosa* 1, no. 1 (2013): 1–16.

———. "The Opposition Front against Compulsory Military Service: The Conscription Debate and Human-Rights Activism in Post-dictatorship Argentina." *Genocide Studies and Prevention* 5, no. 2 (2010): 174–190.

García Arraigada, Germán. "Carretera longitudinal austral: La respuesta a un desafío." *Memorial del Ejército* 433 (1989): 90–122.

———. "Visión geopolítica de la carretera longitudinal austral." In *Antología geopolítica de autores militares chilenos*, edited by Carlos Meirelles Müller, 272–91. Santiago: Centro de Estudios e Investigaciones Militares, 2000.

García-Huidobro, Juan Eduardo, and José Weinstein. *Diez entrevistas sobre la juventud chilena actual*. Santiago: CIDE, 1983.

Garcés, Mario, Pedro Milos, Myriam Olguín, Julio Pinto, Maria Teresa Rojas, and Miguel Urrutia, eds. *Memoria para un nuevo siglo: Chile, miradas a la segunda mitad del siglo XX*. Santiago: LOM, 2000.

Garrett, James L. "The Beagle Channel Dispute: Confrontation and Negotiation in the Southern Cone." *Journal of Interamerican Studies and World Affairs* 27, no. 3 (1985): 81–109.

Gill, Lesley. "Creating Citizens, Making Men: The Military and Masculinity in Bolivia." *Cultural Anthropology* 12, no. 4 (1997): 527–50.

González Cangas, Yanko. "Óxidos de identidad: Memoria rural en el sur de Chile (1935–2003): Tomo II, anexos." PhD diss., Universitat Autónoma de Barcelona, 2004.

———. "Servicio militar obligatorio y disciplinamiento cultural: Aproximaciones al caso Mapuche-Hilliche en el siglo XXI." *Alpha* 24 (2007): 111–37.

Gordon, Dennis R. "The Question of the Pacific: Current Perspectives on a Long-Standing Dispute." *World Affairs* 141, no. 4 (1979): 321–35.

Grez, Sergio, and Gabriel Salazar, eds. *Manifiesto de historiadores*. Santiago: LOM, 1999.

Grez Toso, Sergio. *Los anarquistas y el movimiento obrero: La alborada de "la idea" en Chile, 1893–1915*. Santiago: LOM, 2007.

Grossman, Dave. *On Killing: The Psychological Cost of Learning to Kill in War and Society*. New York: Back Bay Books, 2009.

Guerrero Jiménez, Bernardo. "Bailar, jugar y desfilar: La identidad cultural de los nortinos." *Revistas de Ciencias Sociales* 14 (2004): 71–83.

———. "Bandas de guerra: Jóvenes y nacionalismo en Iquique." *Última Década* 32 (2010): 121–36.

Gutiérrez, Eugenio, and Paulina Osorio. "Modernización y transformaciones de las familias como procesos del condicionamiento social de dos generaciones." *Última Década* 29 (2008): 103-35.

Gutmann, Matthew C. *Changing Men and Masculinities in Latin America.* Durham, NC: Duke University Press, 2003.

Halbwachs, Maurice. *On Collective Memory.* Translated and edited by Lewis A. Coser. Chicago: University of Chicago Press, 1992.

Han, Clara. *Life in Debt: Times of Care and Violence in Neoliberal Chile.* Berkeley: University of California Press, 2012.

Handelman, Howard. "The Political Mobilization of Urban Squatter Settlements: Santiago's Recent Experience and Its Implications for Urban Research." *Latin American Research Review* 10, no. 2 (1975): 35-72.

Haraldsen, S. "La guerra psicológica." *Memorial del Ejército de Chile* 45, no. 243 (1951): 105-10.

Harmer, Tanya. *Allende's Chile and the Inter-American Cold War.* Chapel Hill: University of North Carolina Press, 2011.

Heinz, Wolfgang S. "The Military, Torture, and Human Rights: Experiences from Argentina, Brazil, Chile, and Uruguay." In Crelinsten and Schmid, *The Politics of Pain,* 65-97.

Hidalgo, Paulo. "Los jóvenes y la política: Una relación conflictiva." In Generaciones, *Los jóvenes,* 230-41.

Hinton, Alexander Laban, ed. *Transitional Justice: Global Mechanisms and Local Realities after Genocide and Mass Violence.* New Brunswick, NJ: Rutgers University Press, 2011.

Hite, Katherine. "El monumento a Salvador Allende en el debate político chileno." In Jelin and Langland, *Monumentos,* 19-55.

———. "Estadio nacional: Monumento y lugar de conmemoración." In Verdugo, *De la tortura,* 213-27.

———. *Politics and the Art of Commemoration: Memorials to Struggle in Latin America and Spain.* New York: Routledge, 2012.

Hite, Katherine, Cath Collins, and Alfredo Joignant. "The Politics of Memory in Chile from Pinochet to Bachelet." In Collins et al., *The Politics of Memory,* 1-29.

Holmes, Richard. *Acts of War: The Behavior of Men in Battle.* New York: Free Press, 1989.

Hopman, Jan. "El machismo: Su relación con los excesos al interior de las fuerzas armadas." In *Hombres: Identidades y violencia,* edited by José Olavarría, 133-45. Santiago: FLACSO, 2001.

Horta Valles, Tania. "Servicio militar voluntario: Puertas para una movilidad social ascendente." Undergraduate thesis, Universidad Academia de Humano Cristiano, 2011.

Horvath Kiss, Antonio. "Aisén y su integración física." *Seguridad Nacional* 21 (1981): 129-36.

Huggins, Martha K. "Legacies of Authoritarianism: Brazilian Torturers' and Murderers' Reformulation of Memory." *Latin American Perspectives* 27, no. 2 (2000): 57-78.

Huneeus, Carlos. *El régimen de Pinochet*. Santiago: Editorial Sudamericana Chilena, 2002.

Jelin, Elizabeth. Introduction to *Las conmemoraciones: Las disputas en las fechas "in-felices,"* edited by Elizabeth Jelin, 1–8. Madrid: Siglo Veintiuno, 2002.

———. *Los trabajos de la memoria*. Madrid: Siglo XXI de España Editores, 2002.

———. "The Politics of Memory: The Human Rights Movement and the Construction of Democracy in Argentina." *Latin American Perspectives* 21, no. 2 (1994): 38–58.

———. "Public Memorialization in Perspective: Truth, Justice, and Memory of Past Repression in the Southern Cone of South America." *The International Journal of Transitional Justice* 1, no. 1 (2007): 138–56.

Jelin, Elizabeth, and Victoria Langland. "Introducción: Las marcas territoriales como nexo entre pasado y presente." In *Monumentos, memoriales y marcas territoriales*, edited by Elizabeth Jelin and Victoria Langland, 1–18. Madrid: Siglo Veintiuno, 2003.

Joignant, Alfredo. "Pinochet's Funeral: Memory, History, and Immortality." Translated by Cath Collins. In Collins et al., *The Politics of Memory*, 165–95.

Jones, Edgar. "The Psychology of Killing: The Combat Experience of British Soldiers during the First World War." *Journal of Contemporary History* 41, no. 2 (2006): 229–46.

Kansteiner, Wulf. "Finding Meaning in Memory: A Methodological Critique of Collective Memory Studies." *History and Memory* 41, no. 2 (2002): 179–97.

———. *In Pursuit of German Memory: History, Television, and Politics after Auschwitz*. Athens: Ohio University Press, 2006.

Klep, Katrien. "Tracing Collective Memory: Chilean Truth Commissions and Memorial Sites." *Memory Studies* 5, no. 3 (2012): 259–69.

Klubock, Thomas Miller. "Class, Community, and Neoliberalism in Chile: Copper Workers and the Labor Movement during the Military Dictatorship and the Restoration of Democracy." In Winn, *Victims of the Chilean Miracle*, 209–60.

———. "Labor, Land, and Environmental Change in the Forestry Sector in Chile, 1973–1998." In Winn, *Victims of the Chilean Miracle*, 337–87.

———. "Working-Class Masculinity, Middle-Class Morality, and Labor Politics in the Chilean Copper Mines." *Journal of Social History* 30, no. 2 (1996): 435–63.

Koch, Max. "Changes in Chilean Social Structure: Class Structure and Income Distribution between 1972 and 1994." *European Review of Latin American and Caribbean Studies* 66 (June 1999): 5–18.

Kornbluh, Peter. *The Pinochet File: A Declassified Dossier on Atrocity and Accountability*. New York: New Press, 2004.

Krebs, Ricardo. "Orígenes de la conciencia nacional chilena." In Cid and San Francisco, *Nación y nacionalismo*, 1:3–22.

Kunstman Torres, Wally, and Victoria Torres Ávila, eds. *Cien voces rompen el silencio: Testimonios de ex presos políticos de la dictadura militar en Chile (1973–1990)*. Santiago: Ediciones de la Dibam, 2008.

La Comisión de la Verdad. *Sin verdad no hay justicia: Informe de la comisión de la verdad.* Vol. 1, *Violaciones de los derechos humanos en Ecuador 1984–2008.* Quito: Ediecuatorial, 2010.

"La psicología de las tropas en la defensa." Translated by Eduardo Gutiérrez. *Memorial del Ejército de Chile* 25, no. 176 (1942): 785–90.

Larraín, Jorge. *Identidad chilena.* Santiago: LOM, 2001.

Lavín, Leon. "Plan para un curso de capacitación psicológica." *Memorial del Ejército de Chile* 23, no. 169 (1940): 529–31.

Lazzara, Michael J. *Chile in Transition: The Poetics and Politics of Memory.* Gainesville: University Press of Florida, 2006.

——. "Dos propuestas de conmemoración pública: Londres 38 y el museo de la memoria y los derechos humanos (Santiago de Chile)." *A Contracorriente: A Journal on Social History and Literature in Latin America* 8, no. 3 (2011): 55–90.

——. "El fenómeno mocito (Las puestas en escena de un sujeto cómplice)." *A Contracorriente* 12, no. 1 (2014): 89–106.

——. "Tres recorridos de Villa Grimaldi." In Jelin and Langland, *Monumentos,* 127–47.

Le Bon, Gustave. "Factores psicolójicos de las luchas guerreras." *Memorial del Ejército de Chile* 8 (1913): 813–25.

León, Leonardo. 2002. "Reclutas forzados y desertores de la patria: El bajo pueblo chileno en la guerra de la independencia, 1810–1814." *Historia* 35, http://www.scielo.cl/scielo.php?script=sci_arttext&pid=S0717-71942002003500010&lng=es&nrm=iso&tlng=es.

Lessa, Francesca. *Memory and Transitional Justice in Argentina and Uruguay: Against Impunity.* New York: Palgrave Macmillan, 2013.

Lessa, Francesca, and Vinent Druliolle, eds. *The Memory of State Terrorism in the Southern Cone: Argentina, Chile, and Uruguay.* New York: Palgrave Macmillan, 2011.

Lira, Elizabeth. "Chile: Dilemmas of Memory." In Lessa and Druliolle, *The Memory of State Terrorism,* 107–32.

——. "El testimonio de experiencias políticas traumáticas: Terapia y denuncia en Chile (1973–1985)." In *Historizar el pasado vivo en América Latina,* edited by Anne Pérotin-Domun, 1–40. Santiago: Universidad Alberto Hurtado, 2007.

——. "La vida como sobreviviente: Las secuelas de la dictadura en sus víctimas." In Sagredo and Gazmuri, *Historia de la vida privada,* 3:351–79.

——. *Psicología de la amenaza política y del miedo.* Santiago: ILAS, 1991.

——. "Trauma, duelo, reparación y memoria." *Revista de Estudios Sociales* 36 (2010): 14–28.

Lira, Elizabeth, and Brian Loveman. *Políticas de reparación: Chile 1990–2004.* Santiago: LOM, 2005.

——. "Torture as Public Policy: Chile 1810–2010." In Collins et al., *The Politics of Memory,* 91–132.

Lorenz, Federico. *Las guerras por Malvinas, 1982–2012.* Buenos Aires: Edhasa, 2012.

———. "Testigos de la derrota: Malvinas; Los soldados y la guerra durante la transición democrática argentina, 1982–1987." In *Historizar el pasado vivido en América Latina*, edited by Anne Pérotin-Dumon, 1–63. Santiago: Universidad Alberto Hurtado, 2007.

Loveman, Brian. "Antipolitics in Chile, 1973–94." In Davies and Loveman, *The Politics of Anti-Politics*, 268–99.

———. *For* la Patria: *Politics and the Armed Forces in Latin America*. Wilmington, DE: Scholarly Resources, 1999.

———. "Protected Democracies: Antipolitics and Political Transitions in Latin America, 1978–1994." In Davies and Loveman, *The Politics of Anti-Politics*, 366–97.

Loveman, Brian, and Thomas M. Davies Jr. "The Politics of Antipolitics." In Davies and Loveman, *The Politics of Anti-Politics*, 3–14.

Loveman, Brian, and Elizabeth Lira. "Marco histórico: Terrorismo de estado y tortura en Chile." In Verdugo, *De la tortura*, 181–211.

Magasich Airola, Jorge. *Los que dijeron "no": Historia del movimiento de los marinos antigolpistas de 1973*. 2 vols. Santiago: LOM, 2008.

Mallon, Florencia E. "*Barbudos*, Warriors, and Rotos: The MIR, Masculinity, and Power in the Chilean Agrarian Reform, 1965–74." In Gutmann, *Changing Men and Masculinities*, 179–202.

Marcel, Mario. "Juventud y empleo: Drama en tres actos y un epilogo." In Agurto et al., *Juventud chilena*, 13–26.

Martins Filho, João Roberto, and Timothy Thompson. "The War of Memory: The Brazilian Military Dictatorship according to Militants and Military Men." *Latin American Perspectives* 36, no. 5 (2009): 89–107.

Mattelart, Armand, and Michèle Mattelart. *Juventud chilena: Rebeldía y conformismo*. Santiago: Editorial Universitaria, 1970.

McCoy, Alfred W. *A Question of Torture: CIA Interrogation, from the Cold War to the War on Terror*. New York: Holt, 2007.

McNally, Richard J. *Remembering Trauma*. Cambridge, MA: Belknap Press of Harvard University Press, 2005.

McSherry, J. Patrice. *Predatory States: Operation Condor and Covert War in Latin America*. Lanham, MD: Rowman & Littlefield, 2005.

Meneses, Emilio, Patricio Valdivieso, and Carlos Martin. "El servicio militar obligatorio en Chile: Fundamentos y motivos de una controversia." *Estudios Públicos* 81 (2001): 129–75.

Montealegre Iturra, Jorge. *Las memorias eclipsadas: Duelo y resiliencia comunitaria en la prisión política*. Santiago: Ediciones Asterión, 2013.

Moulian, Tomás. *Chile actual: Anatomía de un mito*. Santiago: LOM, 2002.

Munck, Gerardo L., and Carol Skalnik Leff. "Modes of Transition and Democratization: South America and Eastern Europe in Comparative Perspective," *Comparative Politics* 29, no. 3 (1997): 343–62.

Muñoz, Macarena. "Legitimación de las fuerzas armadas en el marco de la doctrina de seguridad nacional: El servicio militar obligatorio como contenedor de la subversión, 1955–1973." Undergraduate thesis, Universidad de Santiago de Chile, 2005.

Muñoz Tamayo, Víctor. "Imágenes y estudios cuantitativos en la construcción social de 'la juventud' chilena: Un acercamiento histórico (2003–1967)." *Última Década* 20 (2004): 71–94.

Nora, Pierre. "Between Memory and History: Les Lieux de Mémoire," *Representations* 26 (1989): 7–24.

Nunn, Frederick M. *Chilean Politics 1920–1931: The Honorable Mission of the Armed Forces*. Albuquerque: University of New Mexico Press, 1970.

———. "Emil Körner and the Prussianization of the Chilean Army: Origins, Process, and Consequences, 1885–1920." *Hispanic American Historical Review* 50, no. 2 (1970): 300–322.

———. "The Military in Chilean Politics, 1924–32." In Davies and Loveman, *The Politics of Anti-Politics*, 83–91.

———. "An Overview of the European Military Missions in Latin America." In Davies and Loveman, *The Politics of Anti-Politics*, 32–40.

———. *The Time of the Generals: Latin American Professional Militarism in World Perspective*. Lincoln: University of Nebraska Press, 1992.

———. *Yesterday's Soldiers: European Military Professionalism in South America, 1890–1940*. Lincoln: University of Nebraska Press, 1983.

Observatorio de Derechos Humanos. "Secciones de códigos, leyes, decretos y la constitución chilena relevantes en causas de ddhh: Citas textuales y notas explicativas." Santiago: ICSO Universidad Diego Portales, 2010. http://www.icso.cl/images/leyes_relevantes.pdf.

Observatorio de Justicia Transicional Universidad Diego Portales. *Boletín informativo* 30 (May and June 2015).

ODEPLAN (Oficina de Planificación Nacional). *La carretera austral y su impacto regional*. Santiago: ODEPLAN, 1988.

Olavarría, José. *¿Hombres a la deriva? Poder, trabajo y sexo*. Santiago: FLACSO, 2001.

———. "Masculinidades, poderes y vulnerabilidades." In *Chile 2003–2004: Los nuevos escenarios (inter)nacionales*, edited by FLACSO, 227–44. Santiago: FLACSO, 2004.

———. "Men at Home? Child Rearing and Housekeeping among Chilean Working-Class Fathers." In Gutmann, *Changing Men and Masculinities*, 333–50.

———. "Ser padre en Santiago de Chile." In *Paternidades en América Latina*, edited by Norma Fuller, 129–72. San Miguel: Fondo Editorial, 2000.

Olick, Jeffrey K. "'Collective Memory': A Memoir and Prospect." *Memory Studies* 1, no. 1 (2008): 19–25.

———. "Collective Memory: The Two Cultures." *Sociological Theory* 17, no. 3 (1999): 333–48.

Olick, Jeffrey K., and Joyce Robbins. "Social Memory Studies: From 'Collective Memory' to the Historical Sociology of Mnemonic Practices." *Annual Review of Sociology* 24, no. 1 (1998): 105–40.

Otterman, Michael. *American Torture: From the Cold War to Abu Ghraib and Beyond.* London: Pluto Press, 2007.

Passmore, Leith. "The Apolitics of Memory: Remembering Military Service under Pinochet through and alongside Transitional Justice, Truth, and Reconciliation." *Memory Studies* 9, no. 2 (2016): 173–86.

Payne, Leigh A. *Unsettling Accounts: Neither Truth nor Reconciliation in Confessions of State Violence.* Durham, NC: Duke University Press, 2008.

Pedemonte, Rafael. "'Cantemos la gloria': Himnos patrióticas e identidad nacional en Chile (1810–1840)." In Cid and San Francisco, *Nación y nacionalismo*, 2:3–38.

Pinochet Urgarte, Augusto. *Discursos principales 1990–1994.* Santiago: Geriart, 1995.

Poblete, Rafael. "Psicología militar." *Memorial del Ejército de Chile* 20, no. 2 (1925): 50–56.

Politzer, Patricia. *Fear in Chile: Lives under Pinochet.* New York: New Press, 2001.

Portes, Alejandro. "The Urban Slum in Chile: Types and Correlates." *Land Economics* 47, no. 3 (1971): 235–48.

Quay Hutchison, Elizabeth, Thomas Miller Klubock, Nara B. Milanich, and Peter Winn, eds. *The Chile Reader: History, Culture, Politics.* Durham, NC: Duke University Press, 2014.

Quiroga, Jose, and James M. Jaranson. "Politically-Motivated Torture and Its Survivors: A Desk Study Review of the Literature." *Torture* 16, nos. 2–3 (2005): 1–111.

Quiroga, Patricio, and Carlos Maldonado. *El prusianismo el las fuerzas armadas chilenas: Un estudio histórico 1885–1945.* Santiago: Ediciones Documentas, 1988.

Ramos Arellano, Marcela, and Juan Guzmán de Luigi. *La extraña muerte de un soldado en tiempos de paz. (El caso de Pedro Soto Tapia).* Santiago: LOM, 1998.

Rebolledo, Javier. *La danza de los cuervos: El destino final de los detenidos desaparecidos.* Santiago: Ceibo Ediciones, 2012.

Reimann Weigert, Elisabeth, and Fernando Rivas Sánchez. *La fuerzas armadas de Chile: Un caso de penetración imperialista.* Havana: Editorial de Ciencias Sociales, 1976.

Requa, Marny A. "A Human Rights Triumph? Dictatorship-Era Crimes and the Chilean Supreme Court." *Human Rights Law Review* 12, no. 1 (2012): 79–106.

Richard, Nelly, ed. *Políticas y estéticas de la memoria.* Santiago: Editorial Cuarto Propio, 2006.

Roizblatt, Arturo, Niels Biederman, and Jac Brown. "Extreme Traumatization in Chile: The Experience and Treatment of Families." *Journal of Family Therapy* 36 (2014): 24–38.

Rojas, Jorge, and Gonzalo Rojas. "Auditores, lectores, televidentes y espectadores: Chile mediatizado, 1973–1990." In Sagredo and Gazmuri, *Historia de la vida privada*, 3:381–424.

Roniger, Luis, and Mario Sznajder. *The Legacy of Human Rights Violations in the Southern Cone: Argentina, Chile, and Uruguay.* Oxford: Oxford University Press, 1999.

Ros, Ana. *The Post-Dictatorship Generation in Argentina, Chile, and Uruguay: Collective Memory and Cultural Production.* New York: Palgrave Macmillan, 2012.

Rosemblatt, Karin Alejandra. *Gendered Compromises: Political Cultures and the State in Chile, 1920–1950*. Chapel Hill: University of North Carolina Press, 2000.

———. "Masculinidad y trabajo: El salario familiar y el estado de compromiso, 1930–1950." *Proposiciones* 26 (1995): 70–86.

Rosenberg, Tina. *Children of Cain: Violence and the Violent in Latin America*. New York: Penguin Books, 1991.

Sagredo, Rafael, and Cristián Gazmuri, eds. *Historia de la vida privada en Chile*. Vol. 3, *El Chile contemporáneo: De 1925 a nuestros días*. Santiago: Taurus, 2008.

Salazar, Gabriel. *Las letras del horror*. Vol. 1, *La DINA*. Santiago: LOM, 2011.

Salazar, Gabriel, and Julio Pinto. *Historia contemporánea de Chile*. Vol. 4, *Hombría y feminidad*. 4th ed. Santiago: LOM, 2010.

Salimovich, Sofia, Elizabeth Lira, and Eugenia Weinstein. "Victims of Fear: The Social Psychology of Repression." In Corradi et al., *Fear at the Edge*, 72–89.

Salman, Ton. "The Diffident Movement: Generation and Gender in the Vicissitudes of the Chilean Shantytown Organizations, 1973–1990." *Latin American Perspectives* 21, no. 3 (1994): 8–31.

Salvi, Valentina, and Santiago Garaño. "Las fotos y el helicóptero: Memorias de oficiales retirados y ex soldados conscriptos que participaron del Operativo Independencia (Tucumán, 1975–1977)." *Estudios Sociales* 24, no. 47 (2014): 163–189.

Sater, William F., and Holger H. Herwig. *The Grand Illusion: The Prussianization of the Chilean Army*. Lincoln: University of Nebraska Press, 1999.

Schacter, Daniel. *Searching for Memory: The Brain, the Mind, and the Past*. New York: Basic Books, 1996.

Schneider, Cathy Lisa. *Shantytown Protest in Pinochet's Chile*. Philadelphia, PA: Temple University Press, 1995.

Schurman, Rachel. "Shuckers, Sorters, Headers, and Gutters: Labor in the Fisheries Sector." In Winn, *Victims of the Chilean Miracle*, 298–336.

Scoville, Stephanie L., John W. Gardner, and Robert N. Potter. "Traumatic Deaths during U.S. Armed Forces Basic Training, 1977–2001." *American Journal of Preventive Medicine* 26, no. 3 (2004): 194–204.

Serrano, Alejandra, and Gonzalo Vío. "Capacitación de los jóvenes rurales: Algo más que un problema de empleo." In Generaciones, *Los jóvenes*, 86–99.

Shesko, Elizabeth. "Constructing Roads, Washing Feet, and Cutting Cane for the Patria: Building Bolivia with Military Labor." *International Labor and Working-Class History* 80, no. 1 (2011): 6–28.

Silla, Rolando J. "Ahora todo va a cambiar: El servicio militar obligatorio como rito de pasaje a la adultez masculina." In *Mosaico: Trabajos en antropología social y arqueología*, edited by Mariana Carballido Calatayud, 213–21. Buenos Aires: Fundación de Historia Natural "Félix de Azara," 2004.

Soldz, Stephen. "Healers or Interrogators: Psychology and the United States Torture Regime." *Psychoanalytic Dialogues* 18, no. 5 (2008): 592–613.

Solimano, Andrés. *Chile and the Neoliberal Trap: The Post-Pinochet Era*. Cambridge: Cambridge University Press, 2012.

Spooner, Mary Helen. *The General's Slow Retreat: Chile after Pinochet*. Berkeley: University of California Press, 2011.

———. *Soldiers in a Narrow Land: The Pinochet Regime in Chile*. Berkeley: University of California Press, 1999.

Stern, Steve J. *Battling for Hearts and Minds: Memory Struggles in Pinochet's Chile, 1973–1988*. Durham, NC: Duke University Press, 2006.

———. *Reckoning with Pinochet: The Memory Question in Democratic Chile, 1989–2006*. Durham, NC: Duke University Press, 2010.

———. *Remembering Pinochet's Chile: On the Eve of London, 1998*. Durham, NC: Duke University Press, 2006.

Stern, Steve J., and Scott Straus. "Embracing Paradox: Human Rights in the Global Age." In *The Human Rights Paradox: Universality and Its Discontents*, edited by Steve J. Stern and Scott Straus, 3–28. Madison: University of Wisconsin Press, 2014.

Stern, Steve J., and Peter Winn. "El tortuoso camino chileno a la memorialización." In *No hay mañana sin ayer: Batallas por la memoria histórica en el cono sur*, edited by Peter Winn, 205–326. Santiago: LOM, 2014.

Stillerman, Joel. "Disciplined Workers and Avid Consumers: Neoliberal Policy and the Transformation of Work and Identity among Chilean Metalworkers." In Winn, *Victims of the Chilean Miracle*, 164–208.

Taboureau. "Elementos de psicología militar." *Memorial del Ejército de Chile* 19, no. 2 (1924): 548–64.

Tejeda Lawrence, Miguel. *El Servicio Militar Obligatorio*. Santiago: Soc. Imp. i Lit. Universo, 1920.

Timmermann, Freddy. *El gran terror: Miedo, emoción y discurso, Chile 1973–1980*. Santiago: Ediciones Copygraph, 2015.

Tinsman, Heidi. "More Than Victims: Women Agricultural Workers and Social Change in Rural Chile." In Winn, *Victims of the Chilean Miracle*, 261–97.

———. *Partners in Conflict: The Politics of Gender, Sexuality, and Labor in the Chilean Agrarian Reform, 1950–1973*. Durham, NC: Duke University Press, 2002.

———. "Wife-Beating and Sexual Control in Rural Chile, 1964–1988." In *The Gendered Worlds of Latin American Women Workers*, edited by John D. French and Daniel James, 264–96. Durham, NC: Duke University Press, 1997.

Tironi, Eugenio. "Pobladores e integración social." *Proposiciones* 14 (1987): 64–84.

———. "Un rito de integración." In *La campaña del no: Vista por sus creadores*, 11–14. Santiago: Ediciones Melquíades, 1989.

Tótoro Taulis, Dauno. *La cofradía blindada: Chile civil y Chile militar; Trauma y conflicto*. Santiago: Planeta Chilena, 1998.

Tripodi, Paolo. "General Matthei's Revelation and Chile's Role during the Falklands War: A New Perspective on the Conflict in the South Atlantic." *Journal of Strategic Studies* 26, no. 4 (2003): 108–23.

Valdés, Hernán. *Diary of a Chilean Concentration Camp*. London: Victor Gollancz, 1975.

Valdés, Ximena. "El lugar que habita el padre en Chile contemporáneo: Estudio de las representaciones sobre la paternidad en distintos grupos sociales." *Polis* 8, no. 23 (2009): 385–410.

Valdivia, Verónica. "La vida en el cuartel." In Sagredo and Gazmuri, *Historia de la vida privada*, 3:199–227.

Valdivia Ortiz de Zárate, Verónica. "Del 'Ibañismo' al 'Pinochetismo': Las fuerzas armadas chilenas entre 1932–1973." In *Frágiles suturas: Chile a treinta años del gobierno de Salvador Allende*, edited by Francisco Zapata, 157–96. Mexico City: Colegio de México, 2006.

———. *El golpe después del golpe: Leigh vs. Pinochet; Chile 1960–1980*. Santiago: LOM, 2003.

———. "'¡Estamos en guerra, señores!': El régimen militar de Pinochet y el 'pueblo,' 1973–1980." *Historia* 43, no. 1 (2010): 163–201.

———. "Las fuerzas armadas e integración social: Una mirada histórica." *Mapocho* 48 (2000): 295–311.

Valenzuela, Raúl. "La guerra psicológica." *Memorial del Ejército de Chile* 42, no. 225 (1948): 33–46.

Varas, Augusto. *Los militares en el poder: Régimen y gobierno militar en Chile, 1973–1986*. Santiago: Pehuén, 1987.

Verdugo, Patricia. *De la tortura no se habla: Agüero versus Meneses*. Santiago: Catalonia, 2004.

———. *Los zarpazos del puma: La caravana de la muerte*. Santiago: Ediciones Chile-América CESOC, 2001.

Vicaría de la Solidaridad. *Situación de los derechos humanos durante el primer semestre de 1998*. Santiago: Fundación Documentación y Archivo de la Vicaría de la Solidaridad, 1998.

Vildósola Basualto, Luis. "'A los 14 años mi papá se sentía que ya era un hombre': El sujeto popular en Viña del Mar durante la primera mitad del siglo XX." *Última Década* 3 (1995): 1–21.

Violi, Patrizia. "Trauma Site Museums and Politics of Memory: Tuol Sleng, Villa Grimaldi, and the Bologna Ustica Museum." *Theory, Culture & Society* 29, no. 1 (2012): 36–75.

Viveros Vigoya, Mara. "Contemporary Latin American Perspectives on Masculinity." In Gutmann, *Changing Men and Masculinities*, 27–57.

Weeks, Gregory. "Fighting the Enemy Within: Terrorism, the School of the Americas, and the Military in Latin America." *Human Rights Review* 5, no. 1 (October–December 2003): 12–27.

Weinstein, Eugenia. "Los del patio de atrás." In *La campaña del no: Vista por sus creadores*, 19–25. Santiago: Ediciones Melquíades, 1989.

Weinstein, José. "Juventud urbano-popular y familia." In Agurto et al., *Juventud chilena*, 72–87.

———. *Los jóvenes pobladores en las protestas nacionales (1983–1984): Una visión socio-política*. Santiago: CIDE, 1989.

———. "Víctimas y beneficiarios de la modernización: Inventario (incompleto) de cambios en la juventud pobladora (1965–1990)." *Proposiciones* 20 (1991): 250–74.

Wilde, Alexander. "Avenues of Memory: Santiago's General Cemetery and Chile's Recent Political History." *A Contracorriente: A Journal on Social History and Literature in Latin America* 5, no. 3 (2008): 134–69.

———. "Irruptions of Memory: Expressive Politics in Chile's Transition to Democracy." *Journal of Latin American Studies* 31, no. 2 (1999): 473–500.

———. "A Season of Memory: Human Rights in Chile's Long Transition." In Collins et al., *The Politics of Memory*, 31–60.

Winn, Peter. *La revolución chilena*. Santiago: LOM, 2013.

———. "Loosing the Chains: Labor and the Chilean Revolutionary Process, 1970–1973," *Latin American Perspectives* 3, no. 1 (1976): 70–84.

———, ed. *No hay mañana sin ayer: Batallas por la memoria histórica en el cono sur*. Santiago: LOM, 2014.

———. "'No Miracle for Us': The Textile Industry in the Pinochet Era, 1973–1998." In Winn, *Victims of the Chilean Miracle*, 125–63.

———, ed. *Victims of the Chilean Miracle: Workers and Neoliberalism in the Pinochet Era, 1973–2002*. Durham, NC: Duke University Press, 2004.

Winter, Jay. "Historians and Sites of Memory." In *Memory in Mind and Culture*, edited by Pascal Boyer and James V. Wertsch, 252–71. Cambridge: Cambridge University Press, 2009.

———. "Sites of Memory." In *Memory: Histories, Theories, Debates*, edited by Susannah Radstone and Bill Schwarz, 312–24. New York: Fordham University Press, 2010.

Young, James E. *The Texture of Memory: Holocaust Memorials and Meaning*. New Haven, CT: Yale University Press, 1993.

Zaldívar, Trinidad, and Macarena Sánchez. "Símbolos, emblemas y ritos en la construcción da la nación: La fiesta cívica republicana; Chile 1810–1830." In Cid and San Francisco, *Nación y nacionalismo*, 2:73–115.

Newspaper Articles and Websites

"100 mil reservistas del ejército de Chile piden proyecto de ley pro indemnización." *El Ciudadano*, November 26, 2012. http://www.elciudadano.cl/2012/11/26/60723/100-mil-reservistas-del-ejercito-de-chile-piden-proyecto-de-ley-pro-indemnizacion/.

"Abogado de Santelices argumentó que él era estudiante durante la caravana de la muerte." *Cooperativa.cl*, April 20, 2009. http://www.cooperativa.cl/noticias/pais/dd-hh/judicial/abogado-de-santelices-argumento-que-el-era-estudiante-durante-la-caravana-de-la-muerte/2009-04-20/145056.html.

"Abogado dijo que es 'completamente imposible' que ex conscripto haya matado a Víctor Jara." *Cooperativa.cl*, June 3, 2009. http://www.cooperativa.cl/noticias/entretencion/musica/victor-jara/abogado-dijo-que-es-completamente-imposible-que-ex-conscripto-haya-matado-a-victor-jara/2009-06-03/142435.html.

"Abogado querellante pidió apuntar a 'los jefes' que ordenaron matar a Víctor Jara." *Cooperativa.cl*, May 26, 2009. http://www.cooperativa.cl/abogado-querellante-pi dio-apuntar-a-los-jefes-que-ordenaron-matar-a-victor-jara/prontus_nots /2009-05-26/134802.html.

"Abordan demandas pendientes de ex conscriptos del régimen militar." *Senado de la República de Chile*, June 17, 2014. http://www.senado.cl/abordan-demandas-pendien tes-de-ex-conscriptos-del-regimen-militar/prontus_senado/2014-06-17/135634 .html.

Aravena Arraigada, Camilo. "La historia desconocida de Pedro Prado." *Estrella de Iquique*, February 10, 2005. http://www.estrellaiquique.cl/prontus4_nots/site /artic/20050210/pags/20050210004535.html.

Blanche Goldsack, Carolina. "Ex conscriptos de la dictadura vuelven a la carga por indemnizaciones." *Radio.uchile.cl*, March 29, 2013. http://radio.uchile.cl/2013/03/29 /ex-conscriptos-de-la-dictadura-vuelven-a-la-carga-por-indemnizaciones-tam bien-somos-victimas/.

Brown, Kyle G. "Chile's Dictatorship: Were Soldiers Victims, Too?" *Global Newsbeat.com*, January 15, 2014. http://globalnewsbeat.com/2014/01/15/chiles-mili tary-dictatorship-were-soldiers-victims-too/.

Carvajal, Cinthya. "Procesado por crimen de Víctor Jara es imputable." *El Mercurio*, July 1, 2009. http://diario.elmercurio.com/detalle/index.asp?id=%7Bc285d880- 6ec2-4164-b73e-d19596fbd87c%7D.

"Caso quemados: Otro conscripto rompe el silencio y revela cómo se encubrió la verdad." *Cooperativa.cl*, July 26, 2015. http://www.cooperativa.cl/noticias/pais /dd-hh/judicial/caso-quemados-otro-conscripto-rompe-el-silencio-y-revela-co mo-se/2015-07=26/225829.html.

"Citarán a declarar a ex conscripto que sabría paradero de DDDD." *Nuevo Mundo*, July 9, 2014. http://www.radionuevomundo.cl/citaran-a-declarar-a-ex-conscrip to-que-sabria-paradero-de-dddd/.

"Comisión chilena de energía nuclear desestimó que ex conscriptos fallecieran por radiaciones." *Cooperativa.cl*, October 2, 2009. http://www.cooperativa.cl/noticias /pais/ff-aa-y-de-orden/ejercito/comision-chilena-de-energia-nuclear-de sestimo-que-ex-conscriptos-fallecieran-por-radiaciones/2009-10-02/095811.html.

"Confirman procesamiento de ex conscripto por crimen de Víctor Jara." *La Nación*, May 29, 2009. http://www.lanacion.cl/noticias/site/artic/20090529/pags /20090529104955.html.

"Contraloría cuestionó pensiones de 3.000 exonerados políticos." *Cooperativa.cl*, May 28, 2013. http://www.cooperativa.cl/noticias/pais/dd-hh/exonerados/contralo ria-cuestiono-pensiones-de-3-000-exonerados-politicos/2013-05-28/130330.html.

"Crucial diligencia en caso Santelices realizó Montiglio." *La Nación*, May 8, 2008. http://prontus2.lanacion.cl/crucial-diligencia-en-caso-santelices-realizo-mon tiglio/noticias/2008-05-07/213741.html.

Cuevas, Jacmel, "Los estremecedores testimonios de cómo y quiénes asesinaron a

Víctor Jara." *Centro de Investigación Periodística*, May 26, 2009. http://ciperchile
.cl/2009/05/26/los-estremecedores-testimonios-de-como-y-quienes-asesinaron-a-vic
tor-jara/.

"Debate en Chile sobre la 'obediencia debida' tras la renuncia de un general." *El País*,
February 8, 2008. http://internacional.elpais.com/internacional/2008/02/08/ac
tualidad/1202425205_850215.html.

Delgado, Bruno. "Puntaje nacional que prefirió el SM: 'De chico nunca jugué juegos
de guerra." *La Nación*, January 6, 2014. http://www.lanacion.cl/noticias/pais/na
cional/puntaje-nacional-que-prefirio-el-sm-de-chico-nunca-jugue-juegos-de-
guerra/2014-01-06/185031.html.

"Diputado Ojeda no descarta que se vuelva a investigar denuncias de contaminación
en centros nucleares chilenos." *Cámara de Diputados de Chile*, March 22, 2011.
https://www.camara.cl/prensa/noticias_detalle.aspx?prmid=42736.

"Diputados piden reparaciones para ex conscriptos de la era Pinochet." *La Nación*,
October 2, 2013. http://www.lanacion.cl/diputados-piden-reparaciones-para-ex-con
scriptos-de-la-era-pinochet/noticias/2013-10-02/095833.html.

"El general que entregó los presos a la caravana." *La Nación*, January 28, 2008. http://
lanacion.cl/prontus_noticias_v2/site/artic/20080126/pags/20080126225344.html.

"El supuesto asesino de Víctor Jara negó haber estado en el ex estadio Chile tras el
golpe militar." *La Segunda*, May 17, 2012. http://www.lasegunda.com/Noticias
/Nacional/2012/05/747078/Supuesto-asesino-de-Victor-Jara-nego-haber-esta
do-en-el-ex-Estadio-Chile-tras-el-golpe-militar.

"En medio de manifestaciones inauguraron monumento del soldado Pedro Prado." *El
Longino de Iquique*, March 26, 2014. http://diariolongino.cl/?p=1843.

"'En puerto porvenir se hace soberanía.'" *El Mercurio*, February 25–March 3, 1982.

"Ex conscripto en caso quemados vivos: 'Julio Castañer, ése es el nombre del asesino.'"
Cooperativa.cl, July 23, 2015. http://www.cooperativa.cl/noticias/pais/dd-hh/judi
cial/ex-conscripto-en-caso-quemados-vivos-julio-castaner-ese-es-el-nombre
/2015-07-23/075315.html.

"Ex conscriptos afectados con radiación demandaron el estado." *La Nación*, October
20, 2009. http://www.lanacion.cl/noticias/site/artic/20091019/pags/20091019214
537.html.

"Ex conscriptos ariqueños pedirán indemnización por las consecuencias de haber
usado piedra alumbre." *Soyarica*, May 22, 2013. http://www.soychile.cl/Arica/Socie
dad/2013/05/22/175584/Ex-militares-ariquenos-pediran-indemnizacion-por-las-con
secuencias-de-haber-usado-Piedra-Lumbre.aspx.

"Ex conscriptos revelan identidad del 'príncipe.'" *La Nación*, May 27, 2009. http://
www.lanacion.cl/ex-conscriptos-revelan-identidad-del-principe/noticias
/2009-05-27/010256.html.

"Familiares de ejecutados funaron homenaje oficial a soldado Pedro Prado, abatido
tras el golpe militar." *Edición Cero*, March 26, 2014. http://www.edicioncero.cl/?p
=46141.

"Familias de ex soldados afectados por radiación demandarán al estado." *Cooperativa .cl*, October 1, 2009. http://www.cooperativa.cl/familias-de-ex-soldados-afecta dos-por-radiacion-demandaran-al-estado/prontus_nots/2009-10-01/144336.html.

Garviso, Eleazar. "Relato de un conscripto." *El Día*, September 8, 2013. http://diarioeldia .cl/articulo/relato-un-conscripto.

Gutiérrez, Melissa. "La eterna batalla legal de los conscriptos de la dictadura." *The Clinic*, June 17, 2015. http://www.theclinic.cl/2015/06/17/la-eterna-batalla-legal-de-los-con scriptos-de-la-dictadura/.

"Habla ex conscripto del 73." *Mqh2*, October 23, 2012. http://mqh02.wordpress.com /2012/10/23/habla-ex-conscripto-del-73/.

"Habla pareja de ex soldado procesado por crimen de Víctor Jara: 'Él es un hombre bueno.'" *El Líder de San Antonio*, May 28, 2009. http://www.lidersanantonio.cl /prontus4_nots/site/artic/20090528/pags/20090528000835.html.

"Inaugurados 420 kilómetros de la carretera austral." *El Mercurio*, February 25–March 3, 1982.

"Joan Jara: 'Tenía algo más de esperanza sobre la verdad por la muerte de Víctor.'" *El Mercurio*, May 16, 2008. http://www.emol.com/noticias/nacional/2008/05/16 /304510/joan-jara-tenia-algo-mas-de-esperanza-sobre-la-verdad-por-la-muerte-de-victor.html.

"Jueces piden perdón por sus 'acciones y omisiones' durante la dictadura militar." *El Mercurio*, September 4, 2013. http://www.emol.com/noticias/nacional/2013/09/04 /618067/jueces-piden-perdon-por-el-rol-que-cumplieron-durante-el-regimen-mili tar.html.

"Juez realiza recreación de muerte de Víctor Jara junto a conscripto." *La Nación*, May 29, 2009. http://www.lanacion.cl/noticias/site/artic/20090528/pags/20090528 224458.html.

"Juez selló destino del general (R) Santelices." *La Nación*. April 16, 2009. http://www .lanacion.cl/noticias/site/artic/20090415/pags/20090415223121.html.

Kornbluh, Peter. "Los Quemados: Chile's Pinochet Covered Up Human Rights Atrocity." In *National Security Archive Electronic Briefing Book No. 523*, edited by Peter Kornbluh. 2015. http://nsarchive.gwu.edu/NSAEBB/NSAEBB523-Los-Que mados-Chiles-Pinochet-Covered-up-Human-Rights-Atrocity/.

"La caída de Santelices." *La Nación*, April 26, 2009. http://www.lanacion.cl/la-caida-de-santelices/noticias/2009-04-25/181412.html.

"Las torturas que sufrieron los conscriptos en dictadura." *Cooperativa.cl*, September 11, 2013, http://www.cooperativa.cl/noticias/pais/dd-hh/las-torturas-que-sufrie ron-los-conscriptos-en-dictadura/2013-09-11/133251.html.

"Ministro de caso Víctor Jara otorga libertad a ex conscripto procesado." *El Líder de San Antonio*, July 10, 2009. http://www.lidersanantonio.cl/prontus4_nots/site /artic/20090710/pags/20090710000835.html.

Montoya, Amparo, and Constanza Reyes. "Cámara de diputados aprueba reparación de daño previsional a ex conscriptos." *Biobiochile.cl*, July 2, 2014. http://www

.biobiochile.cl/2014/07/02/por-64-votos-a-favor-diputados-aprueban-repara
cion-de-dano-previsional-a-ex-conscriptos.shtml.

"Muere ex conscripto que vigiló reactores nucleares en Santiago." *El Mostrador*,
January 22, 2010. http://www.elmostrador.cl/pais/2010/01/22/muere-ex-con
scripto-que-vigilo-reactores-nucleares-en-santiago/.

"Otra provocación Argentina en aguas australes de Chile." *El Mercurio*, February 25–
March 3, 1982.

Paredes, Alexis. "Con mi compañero jamás vimos a Víctor Jara." *El Líder de San Antonio*, May 30, 2009. http://www.lidersanantonio.cl/prontus4_nots/site/artic/2009
0530/pags/20090530000808.html.

Pérez, Ximena. "Abogado pide datos a ex conscriptos en caso de Víctor Jara." *El Mercurio*, May 28, 2009. http://diario.elmercurio.com/detalle/index.asp?id=%7B981f3
3a2-4b63-439f-b8d1-66b81d9d6d3d%7D.

———. "Corte confirma procesamiento de ex conscripto en caso Víctor Jara." *El Mercurio*, May 29, 2009. http://www.emol.com/noticias/nacional/2009/05/29/360390
/corte-confirma-procesamiento-de-ex-conscripto-en-caso-victor-jara.html.

———. "Juez reabre investigación por muerte de Víctor Jara." *El Mercurio*, June 3,
2008. http://www.emol.com/noticias/nacional/2008/06/03/306958/juez-reabre-in
vestigacion-por-muerte-de-victor-jara.html.

"Piden procesamiento y baja de general Gonzalo Santelices." *La Nación*, January 29,
2008. http://www.lanacion.cl/prontus_noticias_v2/site/artic/20080129/pags
/20080129133058.html.

"Plantean mejorar incentivos para quienes se presenten a cumplir con el servicio militar
voluntario." *Senado de la República de Chile*, March 13, 2012. http://www.senado
.cl/plantean-mejorar-incentivos-para-quienes-se-presenten-a-cumplir-con-el-ser
vicio-militar-voluntario/prontus_senado/2012-03-13/172734.html.

Poblete, Jorge. "Servicio militar: Gobierno activa plan para evitar llamado obligatorio." *La Tercera*, March 11, 2012. http://diario.latercera.com/2012/03/11/01/con
tenido/pais/31-103452-9-servicio-militar-gobierno-activa-plan-para-evitar-lla
mado-obligatorio.shtml.

"Practicarán interrogatorio y careos a Santelices." *La Nación*, March 4, 2008. http://
www.lanacion.cl/noticias/site/artic/20080303/pags/20080303223211.html.

"Querellante en 'caso quemados vivos': Julio Castañer fue protegido por la justicia
militar." *Cooperativa.cl*, July 28, 2015. http://www.cooperativa.cl/noticias/pais
/dd-hh/judicial/querellante-en-caso-quemados-vivos-julio-castaner-fue-prote
gido-por/2015-07-28/171325.html.

"Rechazan exculpar al general (R) Santelices por crímenes de caravana." *La Nación*,
May 5, 2009. http://www.lanacion.cl/noticias/site/artic/20090504/pags/2009050
4213941.html.

"Renuncia general acusado violación DDHH abre debate sobre 'obediencia debida.'"
Soitu.es, February 7, 2008. http://www.soitu.es/soitu/2008/02/07/info/120240
8319_079699.html.

Rivera, Diego, "A 30 años del golpe: Combatientes del golpe frente a frente." *El periodista* 2, no. 43 (2003). http://www.elperiodista.cl/newtenberg/1449/article-37614|.html.

Robledo, Pedro. "Ex conscripto afirma ahora que no mató a Víctor Jara." *La Cuarta*, July 14, 2009. http://www.lacuarta.com/noticia/ex-conscripto-afirma-ahora-que-no-mato-a-victor-jara/.

Rodríguez, Carlos. "Veteranos de una guerra que no fue . . ." *La Estrella*, October 24, 2012.

Rojas, Anyelina. "El falso enfrentamiento de Marín y Millar contra soldado Pedro Prado: Tres víctimas de la misma dictadura." *Edición Cero*, August 11, 2013. http://www.edicioncero.cl/?p=38244.

Rojas, Jorge. "2.000 kilómetros con la barra brava de Pinochet." *The Clinic*, September 27, 2013. http://www.theclinic.cl/2013/09/27/2-000-kilometros-con-la-barra-brava-de-pinochet/.

———. "La pirámide del dictador." *The Clinic*, September 5, 2013.

"Samuel Enrique Fuenzalida Devia." *Memoriaviva.com*. http://www.memoriaviva.com/criminales/criminales_f/fuenzalida_devia_samuel.htm.

Sarmiento, Rafael. "Habla ex conscripto acusado de matar a Víctor Jara: 'Tienen que investigar a los altos mandos.'" *El Líder de San Antonio*, July 15, 2009. http://www.lidersanantonio.cl/prontus4_nots/site/artic/20090715/pags/20090715000821.html.

"Senadores piden al gobierno elevar indemnización a conscriptos de la dictadura." *La Nación*, March 25, 2013. http://www.lanacion.cl/respaldan-inquietud-de-conscriptos-de-la-dictadura-tras-cita-con-el-gobierno/noticias/2013-03-25/211640.html.

Torrealba, Francisco, and Guillermo Turner. "Presidente Sebastián Piñera y su juicio a 40 años del golpe: 'Hubo muchos que fueron cómplices pasivos; Que sabían y no hicieron nada o no quisieron saber.'" *La Tercera*, August 31, 2013. http://www.latercera.com/noticia/presidente-sebastian-pinera-y-su-juicio-a-40-anos-del-golpe-hubo-muchos-que-fueron-complices-pasivos-que-sabian-y-no-hicieron-nada-o-no-quisieron-saber/.

"Ubilla rechaza protestas de ex conscriptos de la dictadura." *Noticias Terra Chile*, September 25, 2012. http://noticias.terra.cl/nacional/ubilla-rechaza-protestas-de-ex-conscriptos-de-la-dictadura,c01819a24aff93101VgnVCM5000009ccceboaRCRD.html.

Uriqueta, Claudia. "Las secuelas de los ex conscriptos que vigilaron dos centros nucleares en Chile." *La Tercera*, March 20, 2011. http://diario.latercera.com/2011/03/20/01/contenido/pais/31-63073-9-las-secuelas-de-los-ex--conscriptos-que-vigilaron-dos-centros-nucleares-en-chile.shtml.

Véjar, Carlos. "Ex conscripto que dice saber donde hay detenidos desaparecidos en Temuco fue amenazado." *Soychile.cl*, November 7, 2013. http://www.soychile.cl/Temuco/Policial/2013/11/07/211425/Ex-conscripto-que-dice-saber-donde-hay-detenidos-desaparecidos-en-Temuco-fue-amenazado.aspx.

———. "Reservista revela que se le ordenó ocultar cuerpos en la Isla Cautín." *El Austral de La Araucanía*, November 3, 2013. http://www.australtemuco.cl/impresa/2013/11/03/full/2/.

"Víctor Jara: Procesado emplazó a ex oficiales." *La Nación*, June 5, 2009. http://www
.lanacion.cl/noticias/site/artic/20090605/pags/20090605084403.html.

"Victory! Former Pinochet Lieutenant Found Liable for Murder and Torture of
Chilean Folksinger." *The Center for Justice and Accountability*, June 27, 2016. http://
cja.org/jaravictory/.

"Vidal habla de responsabilidad política." *La Nación*, February 6, 2008. http://www
.lanacion.cl/noticias/site/artic/20080205/pags/20080205223703.html.

"Viuda de Víctor Jara: 'No tengo ninguna sensación de venganza en contra de ellos.'"
El Mercurio, May 26, 2009. http://www.emol.com/noticias/nacional/2009/05
/26/359960/viuda-de-victor-jara-no-tengo-ninguna-sensacion-de-venganza-en-con
tra-de-ellos.html.

Audiovisual Sources

Chile: Las imágenes prohibidas. Chilevisión, 2013.

"Debate junto a Hermógenes Pérez de Arce y ex conscriptos del '73 sobre el 11 de septiembre (Parte 1)." YouTube video, 11:06, from the television show *Mañaneros*,
August 28, 2013, posted by "Hola Chile La Red," August 28, 2013. http://www
.youtube.com/watch?v=X5hChZlSl_Y.

"Debate junto a Hermógenes Pérez de Arce y ex conscriptos del '73 sobre el 11 de
septiembre (Parte 2)." YouTube video, 9:25, from the television show *Mañaneros*, August 28, 2013, posted by "Hola Chile La Red," August 28, 2013. http://www
.youtube.com/watch?v=ezz9c2XDy2E.

"El testimonio de dos ex conscriptos que hicieron su servicio militar en 1973." Online
video from the show *Una Nueva Mañana*, posted by Cooperativa TV, September
11, 2013. http://www.cooperativa.cl/noticias/pais/el-testimonio-de-dos-ex-con
scriptos-que-hicieron-su-servicio-militar-en-1973/2013-09-11/130711.html.

Gómez Lizama, Víctor. "Así vivieron el 11: Los conscriptos en 1973." Online video
posted by Chilevisión, September 10, 2013. http://www.chvnoticias.cl/nacional
/asi-vivieron-el-11-los-conscriptos-en-1973/2013-09-10/221411.html.

Gutiérrez, Leopoldo. *El soldado que no fue*. Polo Communications, 2010.

Gutiérrez, Rodrigo, and Alejandro Meneses. "El pasado los condena." *24 horas*. TVN.
In possession of the author.

Guzmán, Patricio. *Chile: La memoria obstinada*. Les films d'Ici and L'office nqational
du film du Canada et la sept arte, 1997.

"Homenaje a Michel Nash en Recoleta 2014." YouTube video, 2:14, posted by "Defendamos Recoleta," October 1, 2014. https://www.youtube.com/watch?v=tLfns
IUmnbM.

"Las torturas que sufrieron los conscriptos en dictadura." Online video, 22:07, of interview on Radio cooperativa, posted by "coopertvia.cl," September 11, 2013.
http://www.cooperativa.cl/noticias/pais/dd-hh/las-torturas-que-sufrieron-los-con
scriptos-en-dictadura/2013-09-11/133251.html.

Luz Parot, Carmen. *Estadio Nacional*. CreateSpace, 2003.

"Ministro de defensa pide colaboración a las FF.AA. para esclarecer caso Víctor Jara."
Online video, posted by Chilevisión, May 19, 2012.

Muñoz, Clarisa. "Soldados de Pinochet." *En la mira*. Chilevisión, July 2, 2014.

"Reportaje a Fondo: 'El mocito' asegura estar amenazado de muerte." Online video,
9:07, posted by Chilevisión, May 13, 2014. http://www.chilevision.cl/noticias/chvno
ticias/reportaje-a-fondo/reportaje-a-fondo-el-mocito-asegura-estar-amena
zado-de-muerte/2014-05-13/215500.html.

Said, Marcela, and Jean de Certeau. *El mocito*. IcalmaFilms, 2010.

Index

Page numbers followed by t *refer to tables.*

over attending, 41, 58, 73, 108–11, 221n24, 221n26, 222n29. *See also* student movements

School of the Americas, 79

second war council, 86

silence as complicity, 43–44. *See also* conscripts

silence, pact of, 18, 26–27, 39

simulated warfare. *See* conscripts

Sinclair, Santiago, 38

sites of memory, 148, 239n33. *See also* memorials

SMT (Military Work Service), 79, 104, 217n116

social pension, 53, 59

social security rights, 55

Solar, Franklin, 44

Soto, Manuel, 137

Soto Tapia, Pedro, 115

Special Forces training, 123–24. *See also* conscripts

state of emergency, 17, 88

state of siege, 7, 13, 17

sterility, 132–33. *See also* health issues: physical

Stern, Steve, 6–8, 28, 183n4, 183n6

stress inoculation, 21, 123. *See also* conscripts

strikes, 14, 71, 94, 109, 116–18, 130

student movements, 23, 59–60, 83, 109, 116

Suárez, Juan, 54

suicide, 143, 155, 225n75, 237n9

Supreme Court, The, 43

Survival, Evasion, Resistance, Escape (SERE) training, 123. *See also* conscripts

survival training. *See* conscripts

Taberna, Freddy, 86

Tancazo, the, 85

the exonerated (*los exonerados*), 49, 56–57, 59, 198nn38–39, 199n41, 205n108

There Is No Tomorrow without Yesterday initiative (2003), 9

Tierra del Fuego, 17

Toro, Álvaro, 186n38, 215n85

Torres, Juan José, 15

Torres, Julio, 192n94

Torres, Patricio, 98

torture: of civilians, 9, 13, 27, 30, 32, 35, 40, 74, 87, 89, 154, 238n25; of conscripts, 21, 26, 49, 56, 64–66, 84, 91–92, 101, 121–35, 144–45, 150–52, 157, 215n85, 228n97,

229n102, 230n112, 232n137, 232n145, 241n53. *See also* conscripts

Treaty of Santiago (1929), 16

Tucapel Regiment, 29, 115

Turner, Joan, 39, 41

undue obedience, 191n78

Ureta, Manuel, 30–31, 36, 86, 187n43, 192n94

US torture research, 122–23

Valdivia, Freddy, 82, 212n53

Valech Commission, 9–10, 34, 40–41, 57, 62, 64–65, 68, 138, 150–51, 159, 181n31, 187n45

Valech II (2011), 10, 159, 190n69

Valech Report (2004), 9–10, 40, 68, 84–85, 150, 159–61, 232n145

valley of tears, 117–18, 224n65

Valparaíso strike, 77

Vargas, Alfonso, 115–16

Velasco, Juan Francisco, 14–16

Verdugo, Patricia, 87

Vergara, Jorgelino, 191n82

Vicaría Pastoral Juvenil, 107, 110

victim status, 19, 34, 43, 45, 62, 65, 68, 108, 162

Vietnam War, 123, 126

Vigilia de armas (Barros), 77

Villa Grimaldi, 148, 239n36

volunteers, military (posttransition), 115–16

war: dirty, 11, 13, 21, 122; "internal," 14–17, 20, 84–95, 104, 163; invented, 87; narrative, 13, 25, 74, 94–95, 244n3. *See also* almost wars

War of the Confederation, 75, 81

War of the Pacific, 14–16, 76, 81–82, 99, 120, 216n111

warriors, 75–76

wars-that-weren't. *See* almost wars

Weinstein, José, 110

White Book, The, 126

Wiederhold, David, 137, 147–48

Wilde, Alexander, 8

World War I, 78

World War II, 122–23, 126

Zapata, Luis, 110, 131

Critical Human Rights

www.ingramcontent.com/pod-product-compliance
Lightning Source LLC
Chambersburg PA
CBHW071015280326
41935CB00011B/1359